Bullying in the Workplace

Bullying in the workplace is a phenomenon that has recently intrigued researchers studying management and organizational issues, leading to such questions as why it occurs and what causes such harassment. This volume, written by experts in a wide range of fields including industrial and organizational psychology, counseling, management, law, education, and health, presents research on workplace bullying which can result in lost productivity, employee turnover, and costly lawsuits. Understanding this phenomenon is important to managers and employee morale.

John Lipinski is an Associate Professor of Management at Middle Tennessee State University, Murfreesboro. He earned his Ph.D. in Business Administration from the University of Pittsburgh in 2007, his M.B.A. from the University of Michigan in 1997, and his B.A. from the University of Pittsburgh in 1993. Prior to starting his academic career, Dr Lipinski held managerial positions with companies such as Procter & Gamble, Warner Lambert, and PNC Bank. He continues consulting with both large, established corporations and startups. His publication record includes 19 peer-reviewed journal articles and he regularly presents at regional and international management conferences. Dr Lipinski's work explores topics in management, technology commercialization, and corporate strategy.

Laura M. Crothers is a Professor of School Psychology at Duquesne University, Pittsburgh. She received her D.Ed. in School Psychology in 2001, her Ed.S. in School Psychology in 1997, and her M.Ed. in Educational Psychology in 1995 from Indiana University of Pennsylvania. She received her B.A. in Psychology from Grove City College, Pennsylvania, in 1994. Dr Crothers has been named a national expert in childhood bullying by the National Association of School Psychologists, and serves on several journal editorial boards. Dr Crothers is the author of over 50 peer-reviewed manuscripts, monographs, and book chapters, five books, and has conducted presentations regionally, nationally, and internationally. Dr Crothers has contributed to the source literature by studying bullying in children, adolescents, and adults.

SERIES IN APPLIED PSYCHOLOGY

Jeanette N. Cleveland, Colorado State University
Kevin R. Murphy, Landy Litigation and Colorado State University
Series Editors

Edwin A. Fleishman, Founding Series Editor (1987–2010)

Winfred Arthur, Jr., Eric Day, Winston Bennett, Jr., and Antoinette Portrey
Individual and Team Skill Decay: The Science and Implications for Practice

Gregory Bedny and David Meister
The Russian Theory of Activity: Current Applications to Design and Learning

Winston Bennett, David Woehr, and Charles Lance
Performance Measurement: Current Perspectives and Future Challenges

Michael T. Brannick, Eduardo Salas, and Carolyn Prince
Team Performance Assessment and Measurement: Theory, Research, and Applications

Neil D. Christiansen and Robert P. Tett
Handbook of Personality at Work

Jeanette N. Cleveland, Margaret Stockdale, and Kevin R. Murphy
Women and Men in Organizations: Sex and Gender Issues at Work

Aaron Cohen
Multiple Commitments in the Workplace: An Integrative Approach

Russell Cropanzano
Justice in the Workplace: Approaching Fairness in Human Resource Management, Volume 1

Russell Cropanzano
Justice in the Workplace: From Theory to Practice, Volume 2

David V. Day, Stephen Zaccaro, and Stanley M. Halpin
Leader Development for Transforming Organizations: Growing Leaders for Tomorrow's Teams and Organizations.

Stewart I. Donaldson, Mihaly Csikszentmihalyi, and Jeanne Nakamura
Applied Positive Psychology: Improving Everyday Life, Health, Schools, Work, and Safety

James E. Driskell and Eduardo Salas
Stress and Human Performance

Sidney A. Fine and Steven F. Cronshaw
Functional Job Analysis: A Foundation for Human Resources Management

Sidney A. Fine and Maury Getkate
Benchmark Tasks for Job Analysis: A Guide for Functional Job Analysis (FJA) Scales

J. Kevin Ford, Steve W. J. Kozlowski, Kurt Kraiger, Eduardo Salas, and Mark S. Teachout
Improving Training Effectiveness in Work Organizations

Jerald Greenberg
Insidious Workplace Behavior

Jerald Greenberg
Organizational Behavior: The State of the Science, Second Edition

Ann Hergatt Huffman and Stephanie R. Klein
Green Organizations: Driving Change with I-O Psychology

Edwin Hollander
Inclusive Leadership: The Essential Leader-Follower Relationship

Jack Kitaeff
Handbook of Police Psychology

Uwe E. Kleinbeck, Hans-Henning Quast, Henk Thierry, and Hartmut Häcker
Work Motivation

Laura L. Koppes
Historical Perspectives in Industrial and Organizational Psychology

Ellen Kossek and Susan Lambert
Work and Life Integration: Organizational, Cultural, and Individual Perspectives

Martin I. Kurke and Ellen M. Scrivner
Police Psychology into the 21st Century

Joel Lefkowitz
Ethics and Values in Industrial and Organizational Psychology

John Lipinski and Laura M. Crothers
Bullying in the Workplace: Causes, Symptoms, and Remedies

Manuel London
How People Evaluate Others in Organizations

Manuel London
Job Feedback: Giving, Seeking, and Using Feedback for Performance Improvement, Second Edition

Manuel London
Leadership Development: Paths to Self-Insight and Professional Growth

Robert F. Morrison and Jerome Adams
Contemporary Career Development Issues

Michael D. Mumford
Pathways to Outstanding Leadership: A Comparative Analysis of Charismatic, Ideological, and Pragmatic Leaders

Michael D. Mumford, Garnett Stokes, and William A. Owens
Patterns of Life History: The Ecology of Human Individuality

Kevin R. Murphy
Validity Generalization: A Critical Review

Kevin R. Murphy and Frank E. Saal
Psycology in Organizations: Integrating Science and Practice

Kevin Murphy
A Critique of Emotional Intelligence: What Are the Problems and How Can They Be Fixed?

Susan E. Murphy and Rebecca J. Reichard
Early Development and Leadership: Building the Next Generation of Leaders

Susan E. Murphy and Ronald E. Riggio
The Future of Leadership Development

Margaret A. Neal and Leslie Brett Hammer
Working Couples Caring for Children and Aging Parents: Effects on Work and Well-Being

Robert E. Ployhart, Benjamin Schneider, and Neal Schmitt
Staffing Organizations: Contemporary Practice and Theory, Third Edition

Steven A.Y. Poelmans
Work and Family: An International Research Perspective

Erich P. Prien, Jeffery S. Schippmann, and Kristin O. Prien
Individual Assessment: As Practiced in Industry and Consulting

Robert D. Pritchard, Sallie J. Weaver, and Elissa L. Ashwood
Evidence-Based Productivity Improvement: A Practical Guide to the Productivity Measurement and Enhancement System

Ned Rosen
Teamwork and the Bottom Line: Groups Make a Difference

Eduardo Salas, Stephen M. Fiore, and Michael P. Letsky
Theories of Team Cognition: Cross-Disciplinary Perspectives

Heinz Schuler, James L. Farr, and Mike Smith
Personnel Selection and Assessment: Individual and Organizational Perspectives

John W. Senders and Neville P. Moray
Human Error: Cause, Prediction, and Reduction

Lynn Shore, Jacqueline Coyle-Shapiro, and Lois E. Tetrick
The Employee–Organization Relationship: Applications for the 21st Century

Kenneth S. Shultz and Gary A. Adams
Aging and Work in the 21st Century

Frank J. Smith
Organizational Surveys: The Diagnosis and Betterment of Organizations Through Their Members

Dianna Stone and Eugene F. Stone-Romero
The Influence of Culture on Human Resource Processes and Practices

Kecia M. Thomas
Diversity Resistance in Organizations

George C. Thornton III and Rose Mueller-Hanson
Developing Organizational Simulations: A Guide for Practitioners and Students

George C. Thornton III and Deborah Rupp
Assessment Centers in Human Resource Management: Strategies for Prediction, Diagnosis, and Development

Yoav Vardi and Ely Weitz
Misbehavior in Organizations: Theory, Research, and Management

Patricia Voydanoff
Work, Family, and Community

Mo Wang, Deborah A. Olson, and Kenneth S. Shultz
Mid and Late Career Issues: An Integrative Perspective

Mark A. Wilson, Winston Bennett, Shanan G. Gibson, and George M. Alliger
The Handbook of Work Analysis: Methods, Systems, Applications and Science of Work Measurement in Organizations

Bullying in the Workplace

Causes, Symptoms, and Remedies

Edited by

John Lipinski
Middle Tennessee State University

Laura M. Crothers
Duquesne University

Routledge
Taylor & Francis Group
NEW YORK AND LONDON

First published 2014
by Routledge
711 Third Avenue, New York, NY 10017

Simultaneously published in the UK
by Routledge
27 Church Road, Hove, East Sussex BN3 2FA

Routledge is an imprint of the Taylor & Francis Group, an informa business

Library of Congress Cataloging in Publication Data
Bullying in the workplace: causes, symptoms, and remedies / edited by John Lipinski & Laura M. Crothers
pages cm
1. Bullying in the workplace. I. Lipinski, John. II. Crothers, Laura M.
HF5549.5.E43B86 2013
658.3′8–dc23 2013004844

ISBN: 978-1-84872-961-2 (hbk)
ISBN: 978-1-84872-962-9 (pbk)
ISBN: 978-0-203-79863-8 (ebk)

Typeset in Minion Pro
by HWA Text and Data Management, London

Printed and bound in the United States of America
by Edwards Brothers Malloy

Dedicated to Meredith Julia, our most precious gift,

and to my father, Conrad, who taught me how to write.

Contents

Series Foreword

Jeanette N. Cleveland
Colorado State University

Kevin R. Murphy
Landy Litigation and Colorado State University

The goal of the Applied Psychology Series is to create books that exemplify the use of scientific research, theory, and findings to help solve real problems in organizations and society. Lipinski and Crothers' *Bullying in the Workplace: Causes, Symptoms, and Remedies* does an exemplary job of bringing together research and practice insights from a variety of disciplines to address a perennial problem in organizations – i.e. bullying.

The first section of this book tackles the challenging problem of defining and measuring bullying and places it in the context of other types of misbehavior in organizations. Bullying is like pornography – people know it when they see it but have a hard time defining it. This section makes considerable progress in laying out what bullying is and why we should be concerned about it. The second section of the book asks *why* bullying exists and how it can be best understood. Developmental, evolutionary, ecological, and neurological perspectives are brought to bear to help understand this phenomenon. The third section deals with the *what* of bullying, by identifying the various forms of bullying in the workplace and by illustrating both the communalities and the unique features of different sorts of bullying in organizations. The fourth section asks *what to do* about bullying, examining strategies for managing bullying in the workplace. The final section identifies future opportunities and challenges in dealing with bullying in the workplace.

Bullying in the Workplace: Causes, Symptoms, and Remedies shows how perspectives from a number of scientific disciplines can be combined to define, understand, and manage the problem of bullying in the workplace. Bullying in the schoolyard has long been recognized as a problem; the current volume shows how this same phenomenon takes on different forms in the workplace, and how workplaces can respond to this problem. We are very happy to add *Bullying in the Workplace: Causes, Symptoms, and Remedies* to the Applied Psychology Series.

Preface

When we first started discussing our research, who would have expected a school psychologist and a management scholar to find synergy? One day, while talking about Dr Crothers' research about bullying in schools, the question arose, "What happens to school bullies when they grow up?" The obvious answer was that they enter the workforce and become a part of society. This led to the question, "Do they continue to bully?" These simple questions led to one of our first papers together, "Cliques, rumors, and gossip by the water cooler: Female bullying in the workplace."

While doing the research for the paper, we discovered that management scholars had been working on this problem in earnest for years, but much remained to be discovered, understood, and disseminated. As we concluded this paper, we believed that the next step toward addressing this problem was assembling and synthesizing the literature from psychologists and management scholars into a book in order to provide a holistic view of the issue. This volume is the result of that effort. The authors in this book cover bullying from its underlying neuropsychological roots all the way to the observations of practitioners who deal with the ramifications of peer victimization in the day-to-day management of their operations.

We believe that this book will be enlightening to practitioners and scholars alike. We hope that the lessons in this book will lead to a better handling of bullying in the workplace and will encourage researchers to develop both a greater understanding of the subject and to develop new techniques to help keep bullying out of the workplace. The effects of bullying have negative ramifications for both the individuals involved and their organizations as a whole. As companies seek ways to increase productivity, employee satisfaction, and profitability, developing better solutions to the problem of bullying will have a positive impact on workplaces and employees. We are proud to have assembled the work of this group of preeminent authors to assist in this effort.

Acknowledgments

The editors would like to extend our sincere thanks to Daniel S. Wells and Charles M. Albright, who engaged in tireless and exacting editing of the chapters in this book. We would also like to thank our editor, Anne C. Duffy, who was both encouraging and highly professional in helping us complete this project.

About the Editors

John Lipinski is an Associate Professor of Management at Middle Tennessee State University, Murfreesboro. He earned his Ph.D. in Business Administration from the University of Pittsburgh in 2007, his M.B.A. from the University of Michigan in 1997, and his B.A. from the University of Pittsburgh in 1993. Prior to starting his academic career, Dr Lipinski held managerial positions with companies such as Procter & Gamble, Warner Lambert, and PNC Bank. He continues consulting with both large, established corporations and startups. His publication record includes 19 peer-reviewed journal articles and he regularly presents at regional and international management conferences. Dr Lipinski's work explores topics in management, technology commercialization, and corporate strategy.

Laura M. Crothers is a Professor of School Psychology at Duquesne University, Pittsburgh. She received her D.Ed. in School Psychology in 2001, her Ed.S. in School Psychology in 1997, and her M.Ed. in Educational Psychology in 1995 from Indiana University of Pennsylvania. She received her B.A. in Psychology from Grove City College, Pennsylvania, in 1994. Dr Crothers has been named a national expert in childhood bullying by the National Association of School Psychologists, and serves on several journal editorial boards. Dr Crothers is the author of over 50 peer-reviewed manuscripts, monographs, and book chapters, five books, and has conducted presentations regionally, nationally, and internationally. Dr Crothers has contributed to the source literature by studying bullying in children, adolescents, and adults.

Contributors

Charles M. Albright, M.S.Ed.
Department of Counseling, Psychology, and Special Education
Duquesne University

Susan Scheller Arsht, M.B.A.
Department of Communication and Journalism
University of New Mexico

Michelle Barker, Ph.D.
Department of International Business and Asian Studies
Griffith University, Australia

Brandi Berry, M.A.
Department of Educational Psychology
University of Nebraska–Lincoln

William N. Bockanic, J.D.
Department of Management, Marketing, and Logistics
John Carroll University

Jeanette N. Cleveland, Ph.D.
Department of Industrial Organizational Psychology
Colorado State University

Vanessa A. Durand, M.S.Ed.
Department of Counseling, Psychology, and Special Education
Duquesne University

Scott Erker, Ph.D.
Senior Vice President
Development Dimensions International, Pittsburgh, PA

Dorothy L. Espelage, Ph.D.
College of Education, Child Development Division
University of Illinois at Urbana-Champaign

Eric J. Fenclau, Jr., M.S.Ed.
Department of Counseling, Psychology, and Special Education
Duquesne University

Julaine E. Field, Ph.D.
Department of Counseling and Human Services
University of Colorado at Colorado Springs

Janie Harden Fritz, Ph.D.
Department of Communication & Rhetorical Studies
Duquesne University

Alyssa M. Gibbons, Ph.D.
Department of Industrial Organizational Psychology
Colorado State University

Jeffrey Guiler, Ph.D.
Department of Business Management
Robert Morris University

Susan Harthill, J.D.
Florida Coastal School of Law

Joyce Thompson Heames, Ph.D., S.P.H.R.
Department of Business Management
West Virginia University

Jenna Hennessey, M.S.Ed.
Department of Counseling, Psychology, and Special Education
Duquesne University

Tammy L. Hughes, Ph.D.
Department of Counseling, Psychology, and Special Education
Duquesne University
David Hurlic, Ph.D.
The Hurlic Group

Charles Jaquette, M.S.Ed.
Department of Counseling, Psychology, and Special Education
Duquesne University

Jered B. Kolbert, Ph.D.
Department of Counseling, Psychology, and Special Education
Duquesne University

Jennifer Loh, Ph.D.
Department of School Psychology and Social Science
Edith Cowan University

Pamela Lutgen-Sandvik, Ph.D.
Department of Communication & Journalism
University of New Mexico

Rachel Marsh, B.A.
Department of Industrial Organizational Psychology
Colorado State University

Joey Merrin, M.A.
Department of Educational Psychology
University of Illinois at Urbana-Champaign

Jeananne Nicholls, Ph.D.
College of Business
Slippery Rock University

Kisha Radliff, Ph.D.
Department of School Psychology
Ohio State University

Sheryl Ramsay, Ph.D.
Employment Relations and Human Resources
Griffith University, Australia

Rachel Robertson, Ph.D.
Department of Counseling, Psychology, and Special Education
University of Pittsburgh

Kurt Schimmel, Ph.D.
College of Business Information and Social Sciences
Slippery Rock University

Ara J. Schmitt, Ph.D.
Department of Counseling, Psychology, and Special Education
Duquesne University

James B. Schreiber, Ph.D.
Department of Educational Foundations & Leadership
Duquesne University

Evan F. Sinar, Ph.D.
Manager in Assessment Technology
Development Dimensions International, Pittsburgh, PA

Susan M. Swearer, Ph.D.
Department of Educational Psychology
University of Nebraska–Lincoln

Renée M. Tobin, Ph.D.
Department of Psychology
Illinois State University

Edward C. Tomlinson, Ph.D.
Department of Business Management
West Virginia University

David D. Van Fleet, Ph.D.
College of Technology and Innovation
Arizona State University

Ella W. Van Fleet, Ph.D.
College of Technology and Innovation
Arizona State University

Lisa J. Vernon-Dotson, Ph.D.
School of Education
Coastal Carolina University

Daniel S. Wells, M.S.Ed.
Department of Counseling, Psychology, and Special Education
Duquesne University

Melody Wollan, Ph.D., S.P.H.R.
School of Business
Eastern Illinois University

Angela M. Young, Ph.D.
Department of Management
California State University, Los Angeles

Part I

Introduction: The Problem of Workplace Bullying

1

Organizational Misbehavior

Janie Harden Fritz
Duquesne University

INTRODUCTION

Since the 1990s, increased attention has been paid to the description of "bad" workplace conduct, and this increased awareness has spawned several conceptual families mapping the "dark side" of organizational behavior (Griffin and Lopez, 2005; Griffin and O'Leary-Kelley, 2004). In one of the first broad conceptual treatments of the area, Vardi and Wiener (1996) offered the general phrase "misbehavior in organizations" for a newly acknowledged but ubiquitous element of organizations. This phrase encompassed employee theft, unconventional practices at work, counterproductive behavior in organizations, issues of management ethics, white-collar crime, whistle-blowing, professional deviant behavior, concealing pertinent information, substance abuse, sexual harassment at work, and vandalism (Vardi and Wiener, 1996: 152).

In a later treatment, Vardi and Weitz (2004) highlighted a number of recently emergent terms that they considered part of the domain of organizational misbehavior, including aggressive, antisocial, counterproductive, deviant, and dysfunctional behavior and specific manifestations of these constructs. By that time, several of these terms had gained conceptual status in their own right. This chapter hopes to clarify the conceptual landscape of problematic interpersonal workplace behaviors by examining how theorists have grappled with the use of different labels to refer to what some researchers consider to be the same behaviors, identifying recent representative terms related to this area, and situating workplace bullying within three specific conceptual areas.

SIGNIFICANCE AND THEORY: THE MULTIPLICATION OF TERMS

The various elements in what has now become a kaleidoscopic terminological array referring to problematic behavior in the workplace differ widely in developmental status, scope, and specificity (Griffin and Lopez, 2005; O'Leary-Kelly *et al.*, 2000). O'Leary-Kelly *et al.* (2000) conceptualized antisocial work behavior to include employee deviance, organization-motivated aggression, organizational retaliatory behavior, and workplace aggression as four constructs that have been most clearly defined and developed theoretically and/or empirically. Just five years later a review of relevant literature found that the terms of deviance, workplace aggression, antisocial behavior, and violence had received the most research attention; but even with the increased attention, these terms still had the greatest likelihood for "theoretical and operational confusion and ambiguity" (Griffin and Lopez, 2005: 989).

Some researchers consider these different terms to refer to what are essentially the same phenomena (e.g. Sagie *et al.*, 2003), while others argue for their distinctiveness (e.g. Robinson and Bennett, 1995). Bennett and Robinson (2003) believe that the specific meanings of terms such as workplace aggression, antisocial behavior, counterproductive behavior, and workplace deviance are unlikely to converge. Due to the vast array of terms whose meanings are only slightly different, it is vital that researchers maintain consistency in their terminology and approach so that findings will continue to be useful and able to contribute to our knowledge of this complex and important area.

The importance of consistency and clarity is even more important today as the number of terms used to describe organizational misbehavior continues to grow through further development, refinement, and application of these concepts and their subcategories within and across disciplinary lines (e.g. Henle *et al.*, 2009; Jelinek and Ahearne, 2010; Kidwell and Martin, 2005; Kidwell and Valentine, 2009; Thau *et al.*, 2007). Additionally, more conceptualizations of problematic behaviors or umbrella terms for subsets of problematic or "detrimental behaviors and experiences in the workplace" have been newly identified or developed through reconceptualization of prior terms during the last few years, further expanding the phenomenal domain of the area and offering additional ways to frame such behaviors (Spector and Rodopman, 2010: 273).

This dilemma of labeling and definitions, or "battle of competing constructs" (Bies and Tripp, 2005: 69), has prompted calls for integration and unification necessary for systematic conceptual development (Fox and Spector, 2005; Keashly and Jagatic, 2011; Neuman and Baron, 2005; O'Leary-Kelly *et al.*, 2000; Robinson and Bennett, 1995; Robinson and Greenberg, 1998; Vardi and Weitz, 2004). In response, researchers have attempted to systematize this plethora of concepts, either as a way to refine and/or reconceptualize the general area (e.g. Griffin and Lopez, 2005; O'Leary-Kelly *et al.*, 2000; Robinson and Greenberg, 1998; Vardi and Weitz, 2004), which often takes the form of putting forth a preferred term as the domain's label (e.g. Griffin and Lopez, 2005; Neuman and Baron, 1997, 2005), or as a precursor to addressing a more specific term to provide conceptual and/or operational distinction (e.g. Fritz, 2009; Lutgen-Sandvik *et al.*, 2007).

Many different umbrella terms have been developed to help describe the broad range of actions or behaviors that comprise organizational misbehavior. Fox and Spector (2005) argue for the encompassing label "counterproductive work behaviors" as a grouping term for the several problematic behavioral phenomena in organizational settings. Under this umbrella term, they then go on to map out how other labels have been developed. They describe how an "actor" perspective of the behaviors led to the development of such terms as aggression, antisocial behavior, delinquency, deviance, retaliation, and revenge, while a "target" based perspective was responsible for the labels of abuse, bullying, incivility, and mobbing (Fox and Spector, 2005: 4).

Under the Fox and Spector (2005) conceptualization, many researchers have turned to actor-based terms to describe the negative behaviors that often occur in the workplace. Researchers have used terms such as "organizational deviance," "antisocial behavior" (Griffin and O'Leary-Kelly, 2004), "dysfunctional behavior" (Griffin and Lopez, 2005), or "workplace deviance" (Robinson and Bennett, 1995) to provide broad headings that encompass a large number of more specific negative workplace behaviors. These terms are so closely associated with each other that in the eyes of some researchers they are treated as synonymous (e.g. Van Fleet and Griffin, 2006). Recent research, however, shows that the term "workplace deviance" is gaining in popularity among researchers and has gained a prominent focus of research and application as the preferred label for the area (e.g. Kidwell and Martin, 2005).

In order to encompass specific negative behaviors, Neuman and Baron (2005: 14) argue for "workplace aggression" as the best overarching term or "integrating construct." They use this term to address such behaviors as mobbing, bullying, psychological terror, emotional abuse, petty tyranny, abusive supervision, social undermining, revenge and retaliation, counterproductive, unreliable, and deviant workplace behavior, delinquency, organizational misbehavior, and workplace incivility as instances of aggression. Bies and Tripp (2005) also note the term "workplace aggression" does not invoke any managerial bias that is inherent in terms such as "counterproductive" behavior.

Lutgen-Sandvik *et al.* (2007), in their article on workplace bullying, organize the area of problematic workplace behavior through a tripartite division of superordinate, intermediate, and subordinate phenomena of harmful communication and behavior at work (pp. 837–8). They list counterproductive workplace behavior, organizational injustice, organizational misbehavior, workplace aggression, workplace deviance, antisocial work behavior, and workplace violence as parallel superordinate categories. Workplace bullying falls into the intermediate category, along with emotional abuse, mobbing, social undermining, and workplace harassment and mistreatment. These intermediate phenomena fall under the umbrella of one or more of the superordinate phenomena and manifest elements of the subordinate phenomena, which include incivility, petty tyranny, social ostracism, verbal abuse, verbal aggressiveness, and victimization.

Given all of these terms that can range from recognizably different to functionally synonymous to painfully specific, it may seem as though understanding the theories present in this field of study is a hopeless task. Bennett and Robinson (2003) note, however, that despite differences in conceptual starting points, labels, orientations, and emphases for much of this research, the end results of the labels or definitions are highly consistent – almost all of the behaviors are perpetrated by organizational members, directed at the organization and its members, and are (potentially) harmful and intentional.

Although the "construct profusion and confusion" (Keashly and Jagatic, 2011: 43) surrounding the study of hostile work behaviors continues, Keashly and Jagatic (2011) note that the workplace aggression and workplace abuse literatures are moving toward increased connection and cohesion and that attempts at integrative work are beginning to succeed as researchers seek to understand the interrelationships among these concepts. For example, the term "emotional abuse," which seemed to measure the similar phenomena of workplace bullying, harassment, and mistreatment, was reconceptualized to incorporate the findings of related research that developed since the initial proposal of that construct (Keashly and Harvey, 2005; Keashly *et al.*, 1994), and now seems to have been subsumed under the bullying construct (Keashly and Jagatic, 2011). It is within this conceptual ferment of interpersonal problematic behaviors that research on bullying in the workplace has emerged and taken its place as a distinct scholarly and applied focus.

SALIENT FEATURES: MISBEHAVIOR IN THE WORKPLACE

Here, I adopt the organizing term "organizational misbehavior" (Vardi and Wiener, 1996; Vardi and Weitz, 2004) as a conceptual anchor for a brief review of three clusters of related terms relevant to problematic behaviors in the workplace within which workplace bullying emerges as a distinct phenomenon. Organizational misbehavior refers to "any intentional action by members of organizations that defies and violates (a) shared organizational norms and expectations, and/or (b) core societal values, mores and standards of proper conduct" (Vardi and Wiener, 1996: 153).

Conceptualized by Vardi and colleagues as a negative counterpart to the benign organizational behavior supporting managerial interests and advancing organizational goals, organizational misbehavior encompasses terms ranging from antisocial behavior and counterproductive workplace behavior through dysfunctional behavior in organizations, employee deviance, and employee misconduct to organizational and workplace aggression. Workplace misbehavior functions as organizational vice (Moberg, 1997), another broad term with connections to Spector *et al.*'s conceptualization of problematic behaviors as "counterproductive" and "deviant" (Spector and Fox, 2002; Robinson and Bennett, 1995), and Baron and Neuman's (1998) workplace aggression, inasmuch as these terms contrast with "goods" that an organization seeks to protect and promote (e.g. Arnett *et al.*, 2009), specifically, goods of productivity, place (the organization), and persons (see Fritz, forthcoming).

Workplace bullying is part of the larger context of an organization's interactive culture (e.g. Salin and Höel, 2011), a phenomenon situated within the matrix of an organization's interpersonal, structural, and communicative practices. From this perspective, the multifaceted conceptual and operational family of organizational misbehavior is a breeding ground for workplace bullying. Bullying emerges within the context of these problematic behaviors, holding a particular relationship to each term's conceptual framing. In some cases bullying is an element or subcategory of the concept, such as workplace deviance, aggression, or misbehavior. In others, bullying is a parallel phenomenon that is neither subordinate nor identical. Incivility, for example, is a low-level breach of expected interactional norms, but lacks the targeted intensity and power differential characteristic of bullying (e.g. Fritz, 2009). Incivility could, over time, transform into bullying, and bullying may involve incivility as one of its elements (Langan-Fox and Sankey, 2007).

In the remainder of the chapter, I review the organizational literature treating counterproductive work behavior, organizational deviance, and workplace aggression as types of organizational misbehavior relevant to bullying in the workplace. Each of these conceptual areas functions as a context within which bullying can be understood as a manifestation, exposing a different facet of the destructive nature of bullying, or as a byproduct, with each construct contributing to the petri dish of a bullying culture. Not only are these behaviors conceptually related – they are practically, phenomenologically, and organically interconnected in their status as creators and sustainers of practices of workplace bullying. Each of these general behavioral themes offers a different way of conceptualizing the harm done by bullies as threats to various "goods" in organizational life (Arnett *et al.*, 2009). Following Pearson *et al.* (2005), I move from the general to the specific level, from counterproductive work behavior to workplace deviance and from there to workplace aggression, which has the most direct relevance to the phenomenon of workplace bullying as an instance of organizational misbehavior.

Counterproductive Work Behavior

Counterproductive work behavior(s) (CWB) has been defined generally as "any intentional behavior on the part of an organization member viewed by the organization as contrary to its legitimate interests" (Sackett, 2002: 5) or "behavior intended to hurt the organization or other members of the organization" (Spector and Fox, 2002: 271). Sackett (2002) considers counterproductive work behavior as a facet of job performance and explores the covariance structure of behaviors considered within its domain. Spector *et al.* work from a perspective that integrates occupational stress and human aggression, focusing on CWB as an emotion-based reaction to stressful organizational conditions. Other lines of research on counterproductive work behavior explore such behaviors as employee theft and retaliation-type behaviors as cognitive responses to perceived organizational injustice (Greenberg, 1990; Sackett, 2002; Skarlicki and Folger, 1997; Spector and Fox, 2002).

Fox *et al.* (2001) offer an emotion-based model of counterproductive work behavior in an effort to integrate the latter two strands of research on counterproductive work behavior, considering organizational injustice as a type of stressor. Spector and Fox (2002) expanded the model to include CWB and organizational citizenship behaviors, exploring the role of appraisals and negative and positive emotion in relation to each of these outcomes, finding some support for the connection of positive emotion to organizational citizenship behavior and negative emotion to CWB (Miles *et al.*, 2002). More recently, Spector and Fox (2005) offered a refined model focusing only on CWB, noting a causal relation running from environment to appraisals to emotion to CWB. This more recent model takes the form of a stressor-emotion model of counterproductive work behavior, which includes individual characteristics and characteristics of the workplace (Fox and Spector, 2005: 3) as contributors to counterproductive workplace behaviors, with personality and perceived control as moderators of various relationships in the model.

Counterproductive work behavior as an organizational vice moves against the organizational "good" of productivity. Conceptualizing workplace bullying as a type of counterproductive work behavior provides a focus on the deleterious effects of this behavior on work. When someone is the recipient of bullying, productivity suffers; the focus of attention moves away from tasks and toward self-protection and related concerns. Others who observe the bullying likewise experience a similar shift of focus, with resulting decreased performance. It is possible that bullying leads to greater productivity on the part of the bully; indeed, some concerns related to institutional support of bullying rest with the perceived productivity of such persons (Sutton, 2007). However, taken as a whole, the total decrease in productivity from damage done by bullies is greater than the gains (Pearson and Porath, 2009; Sutton, 2007), and the influence on organizational climate extends this negative reach beyond its immediate influence. In terms of moving human action in organizations away from its proper end of productive contributions to human community and in terms of decreased outcomes of productivity, bullying functions as counterproductive work behavior.

Workplace Deviance

Workplace deviance is defined by Robinson and Bennett (1995: 556) in their seminal study as "voluntary behavior that violates significant organizational norms and in so doing threatens the well-being of an organization, its members, or both." Significant in their approach was the documentation of the interpersonal dimension of deviance, unacknowledged in previous work by Hollinger and Clark (1983) on deviant behavior in organizations (Sackett, 2002). Robinson and Bennett identified two major dimensions of workplace deviance: organizational vs. interpersonal and minor vs. serious. The quadrants defined by these two dimensions include (1) production deviance as a type of minor organizationally directed deviance (e.g. leaving early, intentionally working slowly); (2) property deviance as major organizationally directed deviance (e.g. stealing from the company, sabotaging equipment); (3) political deviance as minor interpersonally directed deviance (e.g. gossiping about coworkers, showing favoritism); and (4) personal aggression as serious interpersonally directed deviance (e.g. verbal abuse, sexual harassment).

In their review of research on organizational deviance, Bennett and Robinson (2003) explore deviance as the perpetrator's reactions to experiences in the workplace such as frustration, perceived injustices, lack of control, and threats to the employee. They note that different forms of perceived organizational injustice have relationships with different types of deviance (e.g. interpersonal vs. organizational deviance). For instance, people are likely to blame specific individuals rather than the organization as a whole when determining the cause of unfair outcomes, which can lead to deviance directed against a person. Also, an employee's attempts to re-establish control may lead to deviance, as illustrated by studies of perceived powerlessness as a provocation for workplace deviance, and could lead to such behaviors as sabotage, violence, and destructive behaviors. When shame or insults are used in an organization, the targets may experience lowered self-respect or self-esteem, which has been studied as a precursor to workplace violence.

In terms of the original typology of deviance (Robinson and Bennett, 1995), bullying would be a type of interpersonally directed deviance and appears to fit best in the personal aggression quadrant, although some types of bullying may involve behaviors in the political deviance quadrant (e.g. gossiping). Bullying as a vice of interpersonal deviance moves against two "goods" in the workplace – the good of place, or the organization, and the good of persons in the workplace. In terms of threats to the good of the organization, bullying as interpersonal deviance operates through its construction of a hostile work environment, culture, or climate, which is generated by means of communicative behavior (Guzley, 1992). To the extent that bullying becomes an accepted pattern of organizational culture, a once-constructive, flourishing organizational culture will have deviated or moved away from its original *telos*.

As behavior that compromises the good of persons, workplace bullying illustrates an aggressor's misguided attention to his or her coworker as other or enemy, a deviation from a constructive or healthy understanding of a fellow employee. The activity of bullying is likewise not neutral with regard to the perpetrator of bullying behavior. Bullying behaviors can actually impact the bully's self-concept, as it creates an interactive identity that invites a negative construction of self in the bully's own eyes and in the eyes of others, potentially trapping the bully in the character of a difficult person in the workplace (e.g. Duck *et al.*, 2006). Whether by intention or accident, behavioral patterns become part of unreflective conduct, shaping the nature of the place and building impressions of others as troublesome (Fritz, 2002, 2006).

Workplace Aggression

Aggression in the organizational setting has been studied by a number of different scholars from several perspectives (Martinko *et al.*, 2005).

Workplace aggression is grounded in the general aggression literature and has been applied to the organizational setting by Baron and Neuman (e.g. Baron and Neuman, 1996; Neuman and Baron, 1997, 1998, 2005). Neuman and Baron (2005: 18) define workplace aggression as "any form of behavior directed by one or more persons in a workplace toward the goal of harming one or more others in that workplace (or the entire organization) in ways the intended targets are motivated to avoid." Workplace aggression, under the rubric of hostile workplace behaviors (Keashly and Jagatic, 2011: 47), includes multiple specific subtypes of behaviors, including psychological aggression, emotional abuse, generalized workplace abuse, workplace victimization, and social undermining. This framework is perhaps the most direct, distinctive, and face valid of the three for the conceptual identity of workplace bullying.

Baron and Neuman (1998) identified three general dimensions of workplace aggression: verbal aggression (or expressions of hostility), obstructionism, and workplace violence (or overt aggression). Behaviors listed under verbal aggression/expressions of hostility (e.g. staring, dirty looks; negative or obscene gestures toward another; acting in a condescending manner toward another person; holding someone's work up to ridicule) describe behaviors commonly associated with workplace bullying (Keashly and Jagatic, 2011; Lutgen-Sandvik *et al.*, 2009). From the workplace aggression perspective, bullying is a direct counter to the good of persons in its effect of degrading the worth and value of persons and their work.

If work is an integral part of the human condition, of what it means to flourish as a human being, as Arendt (1958) suggests, then from a virtue ethics perspective, bullying is a particularly corrosive vice in its rendering of other human beings as of little account. Bullying as workplace aggression is the end result of bullying as workplace deviance in its metaphorical and literal veering away from the purpose and aims of an organization as cooperative, goal-directed human activity involving human beings as creative, productive actors in their active "work" in the world. From a virtue ethics perspective, work or productivity as a goal constitutes part of the proper ends of human life; actions that corrode that end work in the service of vice.

CONCLUSION

Workplace bullying has emerged as a distinctive conceptual entity with connections to several broad conceptual frameworks of problematic, hostile, destructive interaction in the workplace. The perspectives offered by counterproductive work behavior, workplace deviance, and workplace aggression offer rhetorical framing of the damage inflicted by bullies in the workplace in terms of several implicit or explicit goods that organizations protect and promote. The conceptual landscape of problematic interaction in the workplace is marked by multiplicity. However, as Bennett and Robinson (2003) note, such pluralism may not be a marker of theoretical or conceptual demise. The underlying philosophical ground for such terminologies adds to our stock of resources for considering why such clusters of behavior are undesirable in organizations. Attention to the dark side of workplace interaction conceptualized from many perspectives is heuristically useful, offering creative insights into more specific behaviors such as workplace bullying, which can be understood and, one hopes, decreased with further research attention.

REFERENCES

Arendt, H. (1958). *The Human Condition,* Chicago, IL: University of Chicago Press.

Arnett, R. C., Fritz, J. M. H., and Bell, L. M. (2009). *Communication Ethics Literacy: Dialogue and Difference,* Thousand Oaks, CA: Sage.

Baron, R. A., and Neuman, J. H. (1996). Workplace violence and workplace aggression: Evidence on their relative frequency and potential causes. *Aggressive Behavior,* 22, 161–73.

Baron, R. A., and Neuman, J. H. (1998). Workplace aggression – the iceberg beneath the tip of workplace violence: Evidence on its forms, frequency and targets. *Public Administration Quarterly,* 21, 446–64. Retrieved from http://www.jstor.org/stable/40861725

Bennett, R. J., and Robinson, S. L. (2003). The past, present, and future of workplace deviance research. In J. Greenberg (ed.), *Organizational Behavior: The State of the Science* (2nd edn, pp. 247–81), Mahwah, NJ: Lawrence Erlbaum.

Bies, R. J., and Tripp, T. M. (2005). The study of revenge in the workplace: Conceptual, ideological, and empirical issues. In S. Fox and P. E. Spector (eds), *Counterproductive Work Behavior: Investigations of Actors and Targets* (pp. 65–81), Washington, DC: American Psychological Association.

Duck, S., Kirkpatrick, C., and Foley, M. (2006). Uncovering the complex roles behind the "difficult" coworker. In J. M. H. Fritz and B. L. Omdahl (eds), *Problematic Relationships in the Workplace* (pp. 3–19), New York: Peter Lang.

Fox, S., and Spector: E. (2005). Introduction. In S. Fox and P. E. Spector (eds), *Counterproductive Work Behavior: Investigations of Actors and Targets* (pp. 3–10), Washington, DC: American Psychological Association.

Fox, S., Spector: E., and Miles, D. (2001). Counterproductive work behavior (CWB) in response to job stressors and organizational justice: Some mediator and moderator tests for autonomy and emotions. *Journal of Vocational Behavior*, 59, 291–309.

Fritz, J. M. H. (2002). How do I dislike thee? Let me count the ways: Constructing impressions of troublesome others at work. *Management Communication Quarterly*, 15, 410–38.

Fritz, J. M. H. (2006). Typology of troublesome others at work: A follow-up investigation. In J. M. H. Fritz and B. L. Omdahl (eds), *Problematic Relationships in the Workplace* (pp. 21–46), New York: Peter Lang.

Fritz, J. M. H. (2009). Rudeness and incivility in the workplace. In R. L. Morrison and S. L. Wright (eds), *Friends and Enemies in the Workplace: A Work Psychology Perspective* (pp. 168–94), Basingstoke: Palgrave Macmillan.

Fritz, J. M. H. (forthcoming). Interpersonal crisis communication in the workplace: Professional civility as ethical response to problematic interactions. In S. A. Groom and J. M. H. Fritz (eds), *Communication Ethics and Crisis,* Madison, NJ: Fairleigh Dickinson University.

Greenberg, J. (1990). Employee theft as a reaction to underpayment inequity: The hidden cost of pay cuts. *Journal of Applied Psychology*, 75, 561–8.

Griffin, R. W., and Lopez, Y. P. (2005). "Bad behavior" in organizations: A review and typology for future research. *Journal of Management*, 31, 988–1005.

Griffin, R. W., and O'Leary-Kelly, A. M. (eds) (2004). *The Dark Side of Organizational Behavior,* San Francisco, CA: Jossey-Bass.

Guzley, R. M. (1992). Organizational climate and communication climate: Predicators of commitment to the organization. *Management Communication Quarterly*, 5, 379–402.

Henle, C. A., Reeve, C. L., and Pitts, V. E. (2010). Stealing time at work: Attitudes, social pressure, and perceived control as predictors of time theft. *Journal of Business Ethics*, 94, 53–67.

Hollinger, R. C., and Clark, J. P. (1983). *Theft by Employees,* Lexington, MA: D. C. Heath & Co.

Jelinek, R., and Ahearne, M. (2010). Be careful what you look for: The effect of trait competitiveness and long hours on salesperson deviance and whether meaningfulness of work matters. *Journal of Marketing Theory and Practice*, 18, 303–21.

Keashly, L., and Harvey, S. (2005). Emotional abuse in the workplace. In S. Fox and P. Spector (eds), *Counterproductive Work Behavior* (pp. 201–36), Washington, DC: American Psychological Association.

Keashly, L., and Jagatic, K. (2011). North American perspectives on bullying at work. In S. Einarsen, H. Höel, D. Zapf, and C. L. Cooper (eds), *Bullying and Harassment in the Workplace: Developments in Theory, Research, and Practice* (pp. 41–71), New York: Taylor & Francis.

Keashly, L., Trott, V., and MacLean, L. M. (1994). Abusive behavior in the workplace: A preliminary investigation. *Violence and Victims,* 9, 125–41.

Kidwell, R. E. Jr., and Martin, C. L. (eds) (2005). *Managing Organizational Deviance*, Thousand Oaks, CA: Sage.

Kidwell, R. E., and Valentine, S. R. (2009). Positive group context, work attitudes, and organizational misbehavior: The case of withholding job effort. *Journal of Business Ethics*, 86, 15–28.

Langan-Fox, J., and Sankey, M. (2007). Tyrants and workplace bullying. In J. Langan-Fox, C. L. Cooper, and R. J. Klimoski (eds), *Research Companion to the Dysfunctional Workplace: Management Challenges and Symptoms* (pp. 58–74), Cheltenham: Edward Elgar.

Lutgen-Sandvik, P., Namie, G., and Namie, R. (2009). Workplace bullying: Causes, consequences, and corrections. In P. Lutgen-Sandvik and B. Sypher (eds), *Destructive Organizational Communication: Processes, Consequences, and Constructive Ways of Organizing* (pp. 27–52), New York: Routlege.

Lutgen-Sandvik, P., Tracy, S. J., and Alberts, J. K. (2007). Burned by bullying in the American workplace: Prevalence, perception, degree, and impact. *Journal of Management Studies*, 44, 837–62.

Martinko, M. J., Douglas, S. C., Harvey, P., and Joseph, C. (2005). Managing organizational aggression. In R. E. Kidwell Jr. and C. L. Martin (eds), *Managing Organizational Deviance* (pp. 237–59), Thousand Oaks, CA: Sage.

Miles, D. E., Borman, W. E., Spector, E., and Fox, S. (2002). Building an integrative model of extra role work behaviors: A comparison of counterproductive work behavior with organizational citizenship behavior. *International Journal of Selection and Assessment*, 10, 51–7.

Moberg, D. J. (1997). On employee vice. *Business Ethics Quarterly*, 7, 41–60.

Neuman, J. H., and Baron, R. A. (1997). Aggression in the workplace. In R. A. Giacalone and J. Greenberg (eds), *Antisocial Behavior in the Workplace* (pp. 35–67), Thousand Oaks, CA: Sage.

Neuman, J. H., and Baron, R. A. (1998). Workplace violence and workplace aggression: Evidence concerning specific forms, potential causes, and preferred targets. *Journal of Management*, 24, 391–419.

Neuman, J. H., and Baron, R. A. (2005). Aggression in the workplace: A social-psychological perspective. In S. Fox and P. E. Spector (eds), *Counterproductive Work Behavior: Investigations of Actors and Targets* (pp. 13–40), Washington, DC: American Psychological Association.

O'Leary-Kelly, A. M., Duffy, M. K., and Griffin, R. W. (2000). Construct confusion in the study of antisocial work behavior. *Research in Personnel and Human Resources Management*, 18, 275–304.

Pearson, C., and Porath, C. (2009). *The Cost of Bad Behavior: How Incivility is Damaging your Business and What to Do about it*, New York: Portfolio.

Pearson, D., Andersson, L., and Porath, C. (2005). Workplace incivility. In S. Fox and P. E. Spector (eds), *Counterproductive Workplace Behavior: Investigations of Actors and Targets* (pp. 177–200), Washington, DC: American Psychological Association.

Robinson, S. L., and Bennett, R. J. (1995). A typology of deviant workplace behaviors: A multidimensional scaling study. *Academy of Management Journal*, 38, 555–72.

Robinson, S. L., and Greenberg, J. (1998). Employees behaving badly: Dimensions, determinants, and dilemmas in the study of workplace deviance. In C. L. Cooper and D. M. Rousseau (eds), *Trends in Organizational Behavior* (vol. 5, pp. 1–30), Chichester: John Wiley & Sons.

Sackett: R. (2002). The structure of counterproductive work behaviors: Dimensionality and relationships with facets of job performance. *International Journal of Selection and Retention*, 10, 5–11.

Sagie, A., Stashevsky, S., and Koslowsky, M. (2003). Introduction: Misbehaviour in organizations. In A. Stagie, S. Stashevsky, and M. Koslowsky (eds), *Misbehaviour and Dysfunctional Attitudes in Organizations* (pp. 3–10). Basingstoke: Palgrave Macmillan.

Salin, D., and Höel, H. (2011). Organizational causes of workplace bullying. In S. Einarsen, H. Hel, D. Zapf, and C. L. Cooper (eds), *Bullying and Harassment in the Workplace: Developments in Theory, Research, and Practice* (pp. 227–43), New York: Taylor & Francis.

Skarlicki, D. P., and Folger, R. (1997). Retaliation in the workplace: The roles of distributive, procedural, and interactional justice. *Journal of Applied Psychology*, 82, 424–43.

Spector, E., and Fox, S. (2002). An emotion-centered model of voluntary work behavior: Some parallels between counterproductive work behavior and organizational citizenship. *Human Resource Management Review*, 12, 269–92.

Spector, E., and Fox, S. (2005). The stressor-emotion model of counterproductive work behavior. In S. Fox and P. E. Spector (eds), *Counterproductive Work Behavior: Investigations of Actors and Targets* (pp. 151–74), Washington, DC: American Psychological Association.

Spector, E., and Rodopman, O. B. (2010). Methodological issues in studying insidious workplace behavior. In J. Greenberg (ed.), *Insidious Workplace Behavior* (pp. 273–306), New York: Routledge.

Sutton, R. (2007). *The No Asshole Rule*, New York: Warner Business Books.

Thau, S., Crossley, C., Bennett, R. J., and Sczeny, S. (2007). The relationship between trust, attachment, and antisocial work behaviors. *Human Relations*, 60, 1155–79.

Van Fleet, D. D., and Griffin, R. W. (2006). Dysfunctional organizational culture: The role of leadership in motivating dysfunctional work behavior. *Journal of Managerial Psychology*, 21, 698–708.

Vardi, Y., and Weitz, E. (2004). *Misbehavior in Organizations*, Mahwah, NJ: Lawrence Erlbaum.

Vardi, Y., and Wiener, Y. (1996). Misbehavior in organizations: A motivational framework. *Organization Science*, 7, 151–65.

2

History of Bullying in the American Workplace

John Lipinski
Middle Tennessee State University

Charles M. Albright and Eric J. Fenclau, Jr.
Duquesne University

INTRODUCTION

What is Workplace Bullying/Victimization?

The definition of bullying in general, and workplace bullying in particular, has several key components. A general agreement regarding the definition of bullying concerns the frequency of the behavior, the presence of unbalanced power between perpetrator and victim (in favor of the perpetrator), and the creation of a hostile work environment (Björkqvist, 1994; Olweus, 1991). Randall (1997) defines bullying as aggressive behavior with the deliberate intent to cause physical or psychological distress to others. Bullying is a form of interpersonal aggression or antisocial behavior in the workplace that exceeds what may be considered simple incivility, and is associated with negative outcomes for both perpetrators and victims (Anderson and Pearson, 1999; Neuman and Baron, 2005; Salin, 2003).

Theoretical Background

In the 1970s, psychiatrist Carroll Brodsky interviewed over 1,000 individuals filing workers' compensation claims in California and Nevada. The results of these interviews led to the publication of *The Harassed Worker* (1976). This book is often cited as the earliest examination of workplace bullying, but it stirred little interest at the time of its publication. With this exception, before 1980, research into workplace bullying tended to be anecdotal. It was not until the research of Heinz Leymann that bullying began to be systematically studied (Zapf and Einarsen, 2005).

In the early 1980s, nursing professor Helen Cox (1991) began to study nurses' experiences of verbal abuse when one of her gifted students threatened to quit school as a result of continued abuse. Around the same time, Sheehan *et al.* explored the experience of abuse perceived by medical students (Sheehan *et al.*, 1990). However, little research was conducted that attempted to conceptualize workplace bullying in general and this research relied primarily on anecdotal and small sample size data.

But as workplace bullying research was largely ignored in the United States, Leymann and Kornbluh (1989) began a systematic exploration of bullying in the workplace in Britain and Scandinavia, and Brodsky's research was revived (Rayner, 1997; Rayner and Höel, 1998). As the topic took hold in Europe, researchers in Australia and the United States began to become interested in the topic and explore the nuances of the subject (Kieseker and Marchant, 1999).

Manifestations in the Workplace

Bullying can take many forms. Table 2.1 provides a summary of how specific forms of bullying are manifested in the workplace.

The Impact of Bullying

It is generally accepted that bullying can be considered a workplace stressor (Monks *et al.*, 2009). Individuals are at risk of experiencing several negative effects as a result of being a victim (Cooper *et al.*, 2004), and in fact, research has suggested that individuals who are bullied experience symptoms similar to post-traumatic stress disorder (Matthiesen and Einarsen, 2004). Some researchers suggest that bullying in the workplace

TABLE 2.1
Summary of Bullying Behaviors in the American Workplace

Behavior	Men	Women
Bullies	60.0%	40.0%
Victims	43.3%	56.7%
When the bully is a woman, she targets…	28.7%	71.3%
When the bully is a man, he targets…	53.5%	46.5%

Verbal Abuse (shouting, swearing, name calling, malicious sarcasm, threats to safety)	53%
Behaviors/actions (public or private) that were threatening, intimidating, humiliating, hostile, offensive, inappropriately cruel	53%
Abuse of authority (undeserved evaluations, denial of advancement, stealing credit, tarnished reputation, arbitrary instructions, unsafe assignments)	47%
Interference with work performance (sabotage, undermining, ensuring failure)	45%
Destruction of workplace relationships (among co-workers, bosses, or customers)	30%
Public humiliation of targets	54%
Behind closed doors, silently	32%
Behind closed doors, but with others' recognition	10%

has negative outcomes for the entire organization and its members, including those not directly involved in the behavior. Bullying has been shown to increase absenteeism (Kivimäki *et al.*, 2000) and push employees to resign (Quine, 1999), which raises the cost of recruiting and training to replace affected employees. Bullying also increases the risk of litigation and industrial sanctions while negatively affecting organizational effectiveness.

Workplace Bullying and Victimization Prevalence

Given the many different definitions and conceptualizations of workplace bullying in the literature, it can be difficult to pinpoint the exact prevalence rate of workplace bullying. A 2007 study of 7,740 US workers by the Workplace Bullying Institute found that 13 percent of employees reported experiencing workplace bullying in the past year. Furthermore, 24 percent of employees reported that, while they had not experienced bullying in the past year, they had been victimized at some point in their working life. Moreover, another 12 percent of employees reported that they had witnessed workplace bullying or victimization, but were not the direct victims. Given these rates of experience, 49 percent of employees sampled reported having been affected by workplace bullying. Extrapolating the Bureau of Labor Statistics employment statistics, it can be estimated that around 71.5 million American workers are affected by workplace bullying or aggression (Workplace Bullying Institute, 2007).

In a more recent investigation, the Workplace Bullying Institute studied 4,210 individuals and found similar prevalence rates of workplace bullying and aggression. This study also attempted to gather more information about what types of individuals were responsible for the bullying behavior and which individuals were being targeted. The study reported that 62 percent of bullies were men and 58 percent of targets were women. Moreover, the study found that 80 percent of female bullies target other women and 58 percent of bullying or victimization dyads are between the same gender. Furthermore, workplace bullying or aggression appears to be four times more prevalent than illegal, discriminatory harassment (Workplace Bullying Institute, 2010). While these results provide an idea of what workplace bullying and aggression looks like, including the frequency of the problem and a description of the perpetrators and victims, there is still much we do not understand.

Motivation for Workplace Bullying and Aggression

Oftentimes, when a person is bullied in the workplace, he or she may wonder about the motivation of the bully. The literature tells us that 56 percent of bullies are motivated by their own personality, 20 percent because of the target's personality, 14 percent because of the work environment, and 9 percent because of tolerance or admiration of aggression in the workplace (Workplace Bullying Institute, 2007). These statistics are striking because the 23 percent of bullying that is related to workplace factors could ultimately be changed.

The literature suggests that those involved in the bullying dyad frequently do not report the bullying to superiors, and thus the aggression continues. For example, 40 percent of victims of workplace bullying take no action, 38 percent informally complain to a supervisor, 15 percent formally complain, and 7 percent file a lawsuit (Workplace Bullying Institute, 2007). While filing a lawsuit in every instance may not be productive, a majority of victims fail to do anything, or only informally file a complaint. However, given the unstable work environment that workplace aggression often fosters, who can blame the victims for feeling helpless? Further adding to the dilemma, research has found that 72 percent of bullies are the bosses themselves (Workplace Bullying Institute, 2007). Unfortunately, the stability of the bullying and victimization dyad only serves to exacerbate the frequency of instances of bullying and inaction in the workplace to address this aggression.

Workplace Bullying and Victimization Types

When discussing workplace bullying and victimization, it is important to understand the different types of bullying or aggression that take place. Furthermore, it is critical to note that not every bullying or aggressive dyad is the same, nor is the aggressor necessarily going to engage in the same aggression all the time. Bullying and aggression are often broken down into two umbrella types: direct and indirect. Direct bullying or aggression often includes verbal and physical aggression in situations of interpersonal conflict. This is the traditional verbal, face to face altercation, or physically placing one's hands or a body part on another in an attempt to cause bodily harm.

Indirect aggression, which can be separated into relational and social aggression, is more frequently used in workplace bullying due to the less visible nature of the acts. Actions of indirect aggression can include backstabbing, excluding others from the group, spreading rumors, in addition to many other symptoms. More specifically, social aggression is often defined as attempting to manipulate group acceptance of the targeted individual and damage that target's social standing. An example of this could be excluding a coworker from an office lunch outing, putting undue pressure on someone, reducing the other's opportunity to express his or her opinions, openly dismissing the opinions of other employees, and reducing or increasing an employee's duties to hamper his or her work.

Similarly, relational aggression can be described as a group of indirect bullying behaviors that manipulate or disrupt relationships (Archer and Coyne, 2005). This manifests through the intent to harm another through exploitation of a relationship, gossiping, exclusion, spreading rumors, and sarcastic comments (Remillard and Lamb, 2005). Similarly, Crothers *et al.* (2009) report that the aim of relational aggression is to directly control an individual's behavior within a dyadic relationship. An example of relational aggression in the workplace could be influencing others to do things by making them feel guilty, blackmailing someone, withdrawing attention, and threatening to spread rumors if someone does not comply with the aggressor's demands. While the literature is presently unclear regarding which acts of aggression have the greatest impact, we do know that there are major consequences associated with all types of workplace bullying.

Workplace Bullying and Victimization Consequences

Regardless of whether the period of bullying and victimization lasts a month, a year, or many years, the consequences can be catastrophic. Victims often suffer long-term, and even permanent, psychological and occupational impairment (Crawford, 2001; Leymann and Gustafsson, 1996). Evidence suggests that bullying victimization is a "crippling and devastating problem" (Adams and Crawford, 1992: 13) with the potential to damage the victim's self-esteem, physical health, cognitive functioning, and emotional wellbeing (Einarsen and Mikkelsen, 2003; Keashly and Harvey, 2005). Research has also found that victims of workplace bullying and victimization are at an increased risk of depression (Namie, 2003), stress disorders (Scott and Stradling, 2001), alcohol abuse (Richman *et al.*, 2001; Rospenda, 2002), post-traumatic stress disorder (Leymann and Gustafsson, 1996), and even suicide (Leymann, 1990). Furthermore, because the victim often suffers from reduced self-esteem, he or she often finds himself or herself isolated, demoralized, and unable to escape the bullies' tactics (Einarsen and Mikkelsen, 2003).

While there are many documented consequences that occur in the work environment, it should also be noted that many consequences bleed into the individual's personal life and can have disastrous effects on personal relationships and family functioning (Jennifer *et al.*, 2003; Rayner *et al.*, 2002; Tracy *et al.*, 2006). Often, individuals who are bullied or victimized in the workplace displace their psychological trauma upon their family and friends, causing additional stress in the victim's life. Given that victims of workplace bullying often fail to share their experiences with friends and family, their aggression and agitation toward others may seem unfounded.

Workplace bullying and aggression does not just have negative consequences for the victim, but also can impact witnesses and the overall work environment. Barling (1996) suggests that the secondary victims of bullying, those who are not the direct target but often experience similar perceptions, fears, and expectations as a result of the vicarious exposure, are affected just as are the primary victims. Vartia (2001) suggests that those who witness the bullying of a coworker have reported significantly more stress than non-exposed workers. Additionally, coworkers who witness their colleagues' bullying or victimization are more likely to "leave their jobs as a result of their contact with bullying" than do non-exposed workers (Rayner *et al.*, 2002: 56). Furthermore, victims and non-victims of workplace bullying are at a heightened risk for feelings of negativity directed towards the workplace, often resulting in increased absenteeism, decreased productivity, decreased work satisfaction, and an overall negative work experience (Lutgen-Sandvik *et al.*, 2007).

Physical Health Problems

It has been established that one of the negative consequences of bullying is increased stress in victims (Lutgen-Sandvik *et al.*, 2007). The recurrent nature of bullying can lead to chronic stress over an extended period of time. This increase of stress in victims can have a number of short-term and long-term physical effects. The short-term effects include nausea, hand tremors, feeling uncoordinated, chills, sweating, diarrhea, rapid heartbeat and breathing, increased blood pressure, chest pain, and headaches. When bullying occurs repeatedly over time, the short-term symptoms can develop into significant long-term health problems (Lutgen-Sandvik *et al.*, 2007).

Chronic stress has been linked to an increase in gastrointestinal problems as well as an increase in sleep disturbances (Nixon *et al.*, 2011). These problems make workers uncomfortable and reduce their ability to do their work effectively. Repetitive stress in the workplace has also been associated with Chronic Fatigue Syndrome, which can contribute to decreased productivity in the workplace. Increased stress in the workplace has been linked with a diminished immune system, leaving victims more likely to contract viruses and other illnesses and increasing the likelihood that they will have to take sick days from work (Schmidt *et al.*, 2010).

The physical problems caused by increased stress in an individual's work environment can impact work performance in a number of immediate ways. It can impact the body such that the individual will suffer health concerns likely for the rest of his or her life. Chronic stress has been associated with increased blood pressure, and subsequently, an increased risk of heart disease (Carr and Vitaliano, 2012). It has also been shown to negatively impact the brain, and as a result, a worker's cognitive abilities (see Chapter 8). Stress has been associated with decreases in the mass in the hippocampus, a section of the brain that is responsible for transferring information from the worker's working memory to his or her long-term memory store (Bisaz *et al.*, 2011). These researchers also found that stress disrupted the natural flow of neurotransmitters, which also would affect the worker's ability to think and act effectively. Such negative consequences may have lifelong ramifications for the victims of bullying.

Psychological-Emotional Effects of Bullying

Although the physical repercussions for victims of bullying in the workplace are many, the psychological impact of bullying can be even greater. Chronic stress and an unsafe workplace environment can lead to the development of psychological problems and can easily exacerbate pre-existing psychological issues. The most likely outcomes of workplace bullying are an increased likelihood of symptoms of anxiety or depression (Hauge *et al.*, 2010). Symptoms of anxiety would include many of the short-term physical symptoms mentioned above, as well as heightened vigilance and a general worry that immediate threats in the office will persist, even when perpetrators of bullying are no longer present. Anxiety in the workplace can also lead to an increased risk of panic attacks (Vaughan, 2012).

Depressive symptoms include a lack of interest in activities that were previously enjoyable, including work activities, decreased motivation, feelings of hopelessness, decreased appetite, and occasionally, suicidal ideation (Matthiesen and Einarsen, 2004). As the workplace is likely one of the environments in which an individual spends most of his or her time (second only to the home environment), the psychological problems that arise at work will very likely carry over to the individual's home environment, leaving the person to feel as though there is no place where he or she can go to escape the impact of the psychological trauma faced at work.

Another troubling result of bullying in the workplace is that victims of workplace bullying will, occasionally, begin to demonstrate symptoms of post-traumatic stress disorder (PTSD). Symptoms of PTSD include: flashbacks, intrusive thoughts relating to the traumatic events, avoiding of the places and thoughts where the event occurred, and physiological as well as psychological hyperarousal (Bond *et al.*, 2010). It is particularly troubling that victims of bullying are demonstrating these types of symptoms, as they are typically associated with significant traumas such as rape, terrorism, and domestic violence (Leymann and Gustafsson, 1996). The development of these symptoms speaks to the impact that bullying can have on individuals in the workplace.

There are a number of significant physical and psychological problems that can arise and be exacerbated by bullying in the workplace. Although these issues point to the significant impact that bullying has on its victims, there are other, more fundamental problems that bullying behavior creates. The Workplace Bullying Institute (2007) states that guilt, shame, and a sense of injustice are some of the negative byproducts of bullying behavior. Such findings are revealing of the crux of the problem that workplace bullying presents. Direct and indirect aggression in the workplace denies individuals their rights to life, liberty, and the pursuit of happiness. All individuals deserve to be treated with respect, and to be able to pursue work that does not threaten their physical and psychological wellbeing.

Also, separate from the humanistic reasons that characterize bullying as a significant problem, being victimized by colleagues impact the victim's ability to be a productive part of the workplace, as a system. Feelings of guilt and shame contribute to workers feeling marginalized, which can result in employees being passive in their work environment, and thus hesitant and unwilling to contribute their talents in group settings. Feelings of injustice will likely contribute to workers feeling unsupported by their work system, which may lead to increased withdrawal from work activities and a diminished willingness to wish to contribute to the needs of the workplace. These problems ultimately decrease workplace productivity, and limit the organization's ability to adapt to changes in the workplace that are necessary for continued success. Thus, workplace bullying impedes individual workers from pursuing their fundamental rights, and also prevents organizations from reaching ideal worker productivity.

Consequences of Bullying for Perpetrators

It is clear that workplace bullying has an impact on the lives of the victims. A less clear result of workplace bullying is its indication of problems for the perpetrators of the bullying. In general, bullying is a function of either an unwillingness or inability to take part in positive social problem solving. As a result, perpetrators of workplace bullying also demonstrate increased levels of interpersonal problems (Glasø *et al.*, 2009). Balducci *et al.* (2012) found that the stress that is so detrimental to the victims of bullying is also felt by perpetrators. This suggests that the lack of positive problem-solving skills also has a negative impact on the perpetrators of bullying. Although the consequences of workplace bullying on bullies is less frequently studied than its effect on victims, given the above results, it is reasonable to conclude that the interpersonal problems that workplace bullies experience may lead to increased levels of anxiety and perhaps depression. This demonstrates that negative work environments that are created by bullying lead to negative experiences for all those involved.

Consequences for Bystanders

Bystanders of bullying behavior play complicated roles in systems that have problems with bullies. Bystanders can impact the bully/victim relationship, and are of great importance to the general office reaction to bullying in the workplace. In environments with frequent office bullying, bystanders often worry that they will be the next victims (Vartia, 2001). For this reason, the reaction of bystanders will greatly impact how specific instances of bullying affect the general social milieu of an organization. Bystanders also play an important role in mediating the impact of bullying on a victim (Paull *et al.*, 2012). If bystanders in the workplace support the victim of the bullying, then the victim is more likely to be resilient to the attack. If, however, bystanders ignore bullying behavior, then victims are likely to see their inactivity as tacit approval of the bully's behavior, and the effects of the bullying will likely be greater. For this reason, when managers are trying to prevent or stop workplace bullying, they will need to use a systems approach, and not simply consider the perpetrators and victims who are directly involved in the bullying dyad.

Legal Consequences

Workplace bullying has begun to attract the attention of the national workforce. To date, the United States' workforce does not have any specific legal protections against workplace bullying, either at the federal or state level (Coleman, 2006; Yamada, 2007). Bullying has not yet been formalized as a problem in the workforce, but has become a more frequent issue of discussion and it appears that legislation is on the horizon. Since 2003, 21 states have proposed healthy workplace bills that attempt to define and outline appropriate work behavior and limit workplace bullying behaviors (Healthy Workplace Campaign, 2012). Although there are no laws directly protecting workers against workplace bullying, there is clear evidence that workers can be protected from workplace bullying through litigation (Martin and LeVan, 2010). It will be a benefit to organizations to develop clear policies regarding workplace bullying and define the limits to appropriate workplace behavior. Such policies will not only help to create a work environment with clear behavioral expectations, but it will also help to define the rules of the office, which can help organizations protect themselves should problems with bullying lead to litigation.

SUMMARY AND CONCLUSIONS

In this chapter, the history of bullying in the American workplace in the source and popular literature is reviewed. A general agreement on the definition of bullying involves the frequency of the behavior, unbalanced power between perpetrator and victim, and the creation of a hostile work environment (Björkqvist, 1994; Olweus, 1991).

A 2007 study of 7,740 US Workers by the Workplace Bullying Institute found that 49 percent of employees had reported being affected by workplace bullying and victimization. Bullying and aggression are often broken down into two umbrella types: direct and indirect, both of which have negative effects on the victims of bullying, the perpetrators of bullying, and the organizations in which they work.

Regardless of whether the bullying and victimization dyad lasts a month, a year, or many years, the consequences can be catastrophic. Victims often suffer long-term, sometimes permanent psychological and occupational impairment (Crawford, 2001; Leymann and Gustafsson, 1996). It is clear that workplace bullying has an impact on the lives of those who are the victims of the bullying. A less clear result of workplace bullying is its indication of problems for the perpetrators of the bullying. In general, bullying is a function of either an unwillingness or inability to take part in positive social problem solving. As a result, perpetrators of workplace bullying also demonstrate increased levels of interpersonal problems (Glasø *et al.*, 2009). Finally, workplaces also suffer from bullying behavior exhibited by employees. Such consequences include diminished productivity and limits to the organization's ability to adapt to changes in the workplace that are necessary for continued success.

Since 2003, 21 states have proposed healthy workplace bills that attempt to define and outline appropriate work behavior and limit workplace bullying (Healthy Workplace Campaign, 2012). Although there are no laws directly protecting workers against workplace bullying, there is clear evidence that workers can be protected from workplace bullying through litigation (Martin and LeVan, 2010). For reasons such as including pursuing social justice for employees, maintaining or increasing levels of productivity, and avoiding litigation, it behooves organizations to prevent and assertively intervene in bullying problems in the workplace.

REFERENCES

Adams, A., and Crawford, N. (1992). *Bullying at Work: How to Confront and Overcome it*, London: Virago Press.

Anderson, L. M., and Pearson, C. M. (1999). Tit for tat? The spiraling effect of incivility in the workplace. *Academy of Management Review*, 24, 452–71.

Archer, J., and Coyne, S. M. (2005). An integrated review of indirect, relational and social aggression. *Personality and Social Psychology Review*, 9, 212–30.

Balducci, C., Cecchin, M., and Fraccaroli, F. (2012). The impact of role stressors on workplace bullying in both victims and perpetrators, controlling for personal vulnerability factors: A longitudinal analysis. *Work and Stress*, 26, 195–212.

Barling, J. (1996). The prediction, experience and consequences of workplace violence. In G. R. VanderBos and E. Q. Bulatoao (eds), *Violence on the Job* (pp. 29–50), Washington, DC: American Psychological Association.

Bisaz, R., Schachner, M., and Sandi, C. (2011). Causal evidence for the involvement of the neural cell adhesion molecule, NCAM, in chronic stress-induced cognitive impairments. *Hippocampus*, 21, 56–71.

Björkqvist, K. (1994). Sex differences in physical, verbal, and indirect aggression: A review of recent research. *Sex Roles*, 30, 177–88.

Bond, S., Tuckey, M., and Dollard, M. (2010). Psychosocial safety climate, workplace bullying, and symptoms of posttraumatic stress. *Organization Development Journal*, 28, 37–56.

Brodsky, C. (1976). *The Harassed Worker*, Lexington, MA: D. C. Health & Co.

Carr, J. E., and Vitaliano, P. P. (2012). Stress, adaptation, and stress disorders. In O. Z. Sahler, J. E. Carr, J. B. Frank, and J. Nunes (eds), *The Behavioral Sciences and Health Care* (3rd edn, pp. 52–61), Cambridge, MA: Hogrefe Publishing.

Coleman, B. (2006). Shame, rage and freedom of speech: Should the United States adopt European mobbing laws. *Georgia Journal of International and Comparative Law*, 35, 53–99.

Cooper, C. L., Höel, H., and Faragher, B. (2004). Bullying is detrimental to health, but all bullying behaviours are not necessarily equally damaging. *British Journal of Guidance and Counselling*, 32, 367–87.

Cox, H. (1991). Verbal abuse nationwide, part II: Impact and modifications. *Nursing Management*, 22, 66–9.

Crawford, N. (2001). Organizational responses to workplace bullying. In N. Tehrani (ed.), *Building a Culture of Respect: Managing Bullying at Work* (pp. 21–31), London: Taylor & Francis.

Crothers, L. M., Schreiber, J. B., Field, J. E., and Kolbert, J. B. (2009). Development and measurement through confirmatory factor analysis of the Young Adult Social Behavior Scale (YASB): An assessment of relational aggression in adolescence and young adulthood. *Journal of Psychoeducational Assessment*, 27, 17–28.

Einarsen, S., and Mikkelsen, E. G. (2003). Individual effects of exposure to bullying at work. In S. Einarsen, H. Höel, D. Zapf, and C. L. Cooper (eds), *Bullying and Emotional Abuse in the Workplace: International Perspectives in Research and Practice* (pp. 127–44), London: Taylor & Francis.

Einarsen, S., Höel, H., Zapf, D., and Cooper, C. L. (2003). The concept of bullying at work: The European tradition. In S. Einarsen, H. Höel, D. Zapf, and C. L. Cooper (eds), *Bullying and Emotional Abuse in the Workplace: International Perspectives in Research and Practice* (pp. 3–30), London: Taylor & Francis.

Glasø, L., Nielsen, M., and Einarsen, S. (2009). Interpersonal problems among perpetrators and targets of workplace bullying. *Journal of Applied Social Psychology*, 39, 1316–33.

Hauge, L., Skogstad, A., and Einarsen, S. (2010). The relative impact of workplace bullying as a social stressor at work. *Scandinavian Journal of Psychology*, 51, 426–33.

Healthy Workplace Campaign (2012). *State of the Union: State Activity*. Retrieved from http://www.healthyworkplacebill.org/states.php.

Jennifer, D., Cowie, H., and Ananiadou, K. (2003). Perceptions and experience of workplace bullying in five different working populations. *Aggressive Behavior*, 29, 489–96.

Keashly, L., and Harvey, S. (2005). Emotional abuse in the workplace. In S. Fox and P. Spector (eds), *Counterproductive Work Behaviors* (pp. 201–36), Washington, DC: American Psychological Association.

Kieseker, R., and Marchant, T. (1999). Workplace bullying in Australia: A review of current conceptualisations and existing research. *Australian Journal of Management and Organisational Behaviour*, 2, 61–75.

Kivimäki, M., Elovainio, M., and Vahtera, J. (2000). Workplace bullying and sickness absence in hospital staff. *Occupational and Environmental Medicine*, 57, 656–60.

Leymann, H. (1990). Mobbing and psychological terror at workplaces. *Violence and Victims*, 5, 119–26.

Leymann, H., and Gustafsson, A. (1996). Mobbing at work and the development of post-traumatic stress disorders. *European Journal of Work and Organization Psychology*, 5, 251–75.

Leymann, H., and Kornbluh, H. (1989). *Socialization and Learning at Work: A New Approach to the Learning Process in the Workplace and Society,* Aldershot: Gower Publishing Avebury.

Lutgen-Sandvik, P., Tracy, S. J., and Alberts, J. K. (2007). Burned by bullying in the American workplace: Prevalence, perception, degree and impact. *Journal of Management Studies*, 44, 837–62.

Martin, W., and LaVan, H. (2010). Workplace bullying: A review of litigated cases. *Employee Responsibilities and Rights Journal*, 22, 175–94.

Matthiesen, S. B., and Einarsen, S. (2004). Psychiatric distress and symptoms of PTSD among victims of bullying at work. *British Journal of Guidance and Counselling*, 32, 335–56.

Monks, C. P., Smith, P. K., Naylor, P., Barter, C., Ireland, J. L., and Coyne, I. (2009). Bullying in different contexts: Commonalities, differences and the role of theory. *Aggression and Violent Behavior*, 14, 146–56.

Namie, G. (2003). *The WBTI 2003 Report on Abusive Workplaces.* Retrieved from http://www.bullyinginstitute.org.

Nater, U. M., Maloney, E., Heim, C., and Reeves, W. C. (2011). Cumulative life stress in chronic fatigue syndrome. *Psychiatry Research*, 189, 318–20.

Neuman, J. H., and Baron, R. A. (2005). Aggression in the workplace: A social psychological perspective. In S. Fox and P. E. Spector (eds), *Counterproductive Workplace Behavior: Investigations of Actors and Targets* (pp. 13–40), Washington, DC: American Psychological Association.

Nixon, A. E., Mazzola, J. J., Bauer, J., Krueger, J. R., and Spector, P. E. (2011). Can work make you sick? A meta-analysis of the relationships between job stressors and physical symptoms. *Work and Stress*, 25, 1–22.

Olweus, D. (1991). Bully/victim problems among schoolchildren: Basic facts and effects of a school based intervention program. In D. J. Pepler and K. H. Rubin (eds), *The Development and Treatment of Childhood Aggression* (pp. 411–48), Hillsdale, NJ: Erlbaum.

Paull, M., Omari, M., and Standen, P. (2012). When is a bystander not a bystander? A typology of the roles of bystanders in workplace bullying. *Asia Pacific Journal of Human Resources*, 50, 351–66.

Quine, L. (1999). Workplace bullying in NHS community trust: Staff questionnaire survey. *British Medical Journal*, 318, 228–32.

Randall, P. (1997). *Adult Bullying: Perpetrators and Victims,* London: Routledge.

Rayner, C. (1997). The incidence of workplace bullying. *Journal of Community and Applied Social Psychology*, 7, 199–208.

Rayner, C., and Höel, H. (1998). A summary review of literature relating to workplace bullying. *Journal of Community and Applied Social Psychology,* 7, 181–91.

Rayner, C., Höel, H., and Cooper, C. L. (2002). *Workplace Bullying: What we Know, Who is to Blame, and What can we Do?,* London: Taylor & Francis.

Remillard, A. M., and Lamb, S. (2005). Adolescent girls' coping with relational aggression. *Sex Roles,* 53, 221–9.

Richman, J. A., Rospenda, K. M., Flaherty, J. A., and Feels, S. (2001). Workplace harassment, active coping, and alcohol-related outcomes. *Journal of Substance Abuse*, 13, 247–66.

Rospenda, K. M. (2002). Workplace harassment, service utilization, and drinking outcomes. *Journal of Occupational Health Psychology, 2*, 141–55.

Salin, D. (2003). Ways of explaining workplace bullying: A review of enabling, motivating and precipitating structures and processes in the work environment. *Human Relations*, 56, 1213–32.

Schmidt, D., Reber, S. O., Botteron, C., Barth, T., Peterlik, D., Uschold, N., and Lechner, A. (2010). Chronic psychosocial stress promotes systemic immune activation and the development of inflammatory Th cell responses. *Brain, Behavior, and Immunity*, 24, 1097–104.

Scott, M. J., and Stradling, S. G. (2001). Trauma, duress and stress. In N. Tehrani (ed.), *Building a Culture of Respect: Managing Bullying at Work* (pp. 33–42), London: Taylor & Francis.

Sheehan, K. H., Sheehan, D. V., White, K., Leibowitz, A., and Baldwin Jr., D. C. (1990). A pilot study of medical students' abuse. *Journal of the American Medical Association*, 263, 533–7.

Tracy, S. J., Lutgen-Sandvik, P., and Alberts, J. K (2006). Nightmares, demons and slaves: Exploring the painful metaphors of workplace bullying. *Management Communication Quarterly*, 20, 148–85.

Vartia, M. (2001). Consequences of workplace bullying with respect to the well-being of its targets and the observers of bullying. *Scandinavian Journal of Work Environment and Health*, 27, 63–9.

Vaughan, S. (2012). Ya'makasi or the art of displacement in the corporate world: A target's perspective on the impact of workplace bullying. In N. Tehrani (ed.), *Workplace Bullying: Symptoms and Solutions* (pp. 51–66), New York: Routledge.

Workplace Bullying Institute (2007). *The WBI U.S. Workplace Bullying Survey*, Washington, DC: Author and Zogby International.

Workplace Bullying Institute (2010). *The WBI U.S. Workplace Bullying Survey*, Washington, DC: Author and Zogby International.

Yamada, D. C. (2007). Potential legal protections and liabilities for workplace bullying. *New Workplace Institute*. Retrieved from www.newworkplaceinsitute.org.

Zapf, D., and Einarsen, S. (2005). Mobbing at work: Escalated conflicts in organizations. In S. Fox and P. E. Spector (eds), *Counterproductive Work Behaviour: Investigations of Actors and Targets* (pp. 237–70), Washington, DC: American Psychological Association.

3

Measurement Issues in the "Phenomenon"[1]

James B. Schreiber
Duquesne University

INTRODUCTION

This chapter focuses on the measurement and related research issues of bullying/mobbing in a variety of settings. Specifically, I focus on technical issues that I have observed within the research and are common across many psychological and sociological research agendas. I discuss issues that occur in both quantitative and qualitative studies. Finally, I provide some recommendations and future research agenda tracks that could be taken up by anyone who is interested.

SIGNIFICANCE

As any field develops, the need to increase the quality and richness of the research being conducted is increasingly important. This chapter is focused on that increase and more generally the believability of what is observed and reported. Every growing field has had this concern and as fields move forward, previous techniques are improved and former techniques, unfortunately, die off slowly. At the core, though, is measurement. Everything we measure has measurement error associated with it. Even the official US atomic clock is not perfect. The National

Bureau of Standards has to add a second to the clock about every 100 years. When you fail to take adequate steps in determining the reliability of your data, you not only introduce error into your statistical analysis or written narratives, but also decrease the reader's belief in your work and your ability to make valid arguments. If I do not believe the data (e.g. too much measurement error), nothing can be done, despite the use of a fancy statistical technique, or an overwhelming amount of participants; nothing.

RELEVANT THEORY/HISTORY

The history of workplace bullying (I will use "mobbing" henceforth) research may begin with Carol Brodksy's (1976) work in her book, "The Harassed Worker," but there is a United States Congressional Committee report from 1901 that has some indication that appointees were removed from positions and put into less desirable positions. For example, a House of Representatives driver was removed from that position and placed in a job of scrubbing "floors and cleaning spittoons" (p. 5). The report focuses, though, on abuses of employees, such as people being awarded positions for which they are not qualified. It also appears in the report that sometimes one person's salary was partially given to another person (pp. 6 and 16). Both of these could be considered bullying, harassment, or mobbing. The mobbing field did not obtain solid research grounding until Leymann's work in the mid-1980s and then hit the cultural scene with Andrea Adams's journalistic work in the United Kingdom and subsequent book publication (Adams and Crawford, 1992). In the past 10 to 15 years, the review and empirical articles across many academic fields (e.g. nursing, university faculty) that could be considered about bullying has grown exponentially.

MEASUREMENT THEORY

Issue 1: Definitions, Many with Varying Perspectives

With such a relatively young research field that is now attracting a full international research contingency, there appears to be a variety of definitions, both theoretical and operational. Because of this, it makes measurement an interesting hill to climb and creates problems about what each research group is actually measuring, or talking about. In short, one must be able to define the construct theoretically and operationally in order to measure it consistently.

Carol Brodsky's (1976) definition is quite broad because it focuses on harassment of all kinds, but particularly adult to adult behavior. Harassment for Brodksy is both generic and specific in that it "encompasses a continuum of various forms of behavior ….and involves repeated and persistent attempts by one person to torment" (p. 2). Leymann (1996) described "mobbing at work." Others have described it as "bullying at work" (Liefooghe and Olafsson, 1999). The defining attribute for work-related abuse appears to be the persistence of the abuse over a period of time, where one person is on the receiving end of negative actions from one or several others (Zapf and Einarsen, 2001) and the abused cannot defend himself or herself against these verbal, emotional, or physical insults (Einarsen, 2000). Some descriptions of the operational behaviors related to workplace bullying include teasing, being badgered, insults, exclusion from the work peer group, removal of work responsibilities, and devaluing (Einarsen *et al.*, 1994; Leymann, 1996; Zapf *et al.*, 1996).

In addition to definitions, Leymann (1996) argued that the criteria related to the operational definitions must include abuse that has lasted at least six months and occurs at least once a week. In essence, this implies a minimum of 26 incidents of mobbing. Zapf and Einarsen (2001) argue that a consensus has grown to include the following components: mobbing must be directed toward a target individual, the individual is put in an indefensible inferior position, and the mobbing occur more than once.

Rodríguez-Carbelleira *et al.* (2010) created a taxonomy in an effort to combine different operational definitions and attributes of bullying or mobbing. Their taxonomy has Type (Direct/Indirect), Nature (Work Context, Emotion, Cognition, and Behavior), and Categories (e.g. devaluation or isolation) of mobbing. Though this taxonomy is not the end of the synthesis of this work, it seems to be a good start that would allow clearer operational definitions to be created that would lead to different methods and techniques to examine the phenomenon. An agreed upon operational definition along with a taxonomy would help move the field forward. Therefore, operationally, there appear to be three aspects for mobbing (at work):

1. the time period is at least six months and once a week (Leymann, 1996),
2. it is against a target individual put in an indefensible inferior position (Zapf and Einarsen, 2001), and
3. it can be one of several categories (Rodriguez-Carballeira *et al.*, 2010).

But this may lead down a problematic road, one where word choice and specific definitions of each type and subtype, and sub-subtype are argued over, and valuable time and other resources are diverted from serious work in research about interventions and other types of programs.

Two recent reviews have also had trouble completing a definition because of the vast space the phenomenon encompasses. Crawshaw (2009) and Bartlett and Bartlett (2011) also find a definition difficult to ascertain to create their own taxonomy. Crawshaw (2009) listed all of the English words associated in this research area in alphabetical order from abuse to workplace psychological violence, with a total of 33 different words/phrases. I think the idea of Crawshaw's (2009) common nomenclature is a possible path. I believe the field, which has so many people from so many disciplines working on it, needs to have a symposium or other meeting to develop what marketers would call a consensus map (Zaltman, 2003). Finally, though, the time is now to create a common language for the field that encompasses the wide variety of the "phenomenon" (Crawshaw, 2009).

Issue 2: Reliability and Validity, Traditional Psychometric Approach

In the grand scheme, reliability and validity are not an all or nothing proposition and, most importantly, are not finalized the first time data are published (e.g. Messick, 1989). Technically, reliability and validity need to be examined and discussed with each collection of data. Within the body of literature on mobbing (and other areas), too many times the instruments used are described as reliable and valid. That is simply not accurate. No instrument is reliable or valid; the data from the instrument may be reliable, trustworthy, or believable, and the inferences from data may be appropriate, or valid (Messick, 1989; Schreiber and Asner-Self, 2011). When reliability is discussed, it is important to remember that reliability concerns measurement error, where your score on an instrument is an indicator of your theoretical true score and error ($X = T + E$; Crocker and Algina, 1986). Cronbach's alpha is the most popular indicator of reliability across the field, because it can be used with single administration quantitative surveys with Likert-type scales and is easily interpreted (Cronbach, 1951).

Most of the other types of reliabilities (e.g. test–retest, equivalence) are not used because one would need multiple administrations of the instrument, multiple versions of the instrument, or both. A common misunderstanding is that alpha is a measure of unidimensionality or homogeneity (see Cortina, 1993; Schmitt, 1996). I state this because many of the studies use high alpha values as proxies for factor dimensionality, though this occurs in every field where surveys are used. One must have interrelatedness for unidimensionality, but interrelatedness is not sufficient to argue for unidimensionality. In addition, confidence intervals (Onwuegbuzie and Daniel, 2002) and standard errors of alpha are not being included (Cortina, 1993). These are easy enough to calculate and would aid in evaluating the work being conducted.

Homogeneity or unidimensionality is the argument for a latent factor or construct. Generally, a factor analysis is used and the results from the factor analysis become evidence to make an argument for construct validity. Factor analysis, specifically exploratory factor analysis (EFA), is a *descriptive* technique that reduces a large number of items into a few groups or "factors." It is the most popular "statistical" technique that does not actually test a hypothesis. A secondary issue is that many researchers run a principal component analysis (PCA) and not a factor analysis. PCA and EFA are different in purpose and mathematics (Pohlmann, 2004); however, these are essentially the extraction techniques and not how the factors or components are related. Choosing the number of factors in PCA and EFA is generally done using Kaiser's rule, which seems to be misunderstood. At the core of the Kaiser rule is that the eigenvalues over 1.0 as the cutoff are the *lower* boundary, not the final indicator of the number of factors to retain (Gorsuch, 1983). In addition, Kanyongo (2006) observed that, looking at the scree plot (which is based on eigenvalues), researchers could not agree on the number of factors to retain as the scree plot became more ambiguous.

For inter-factor relationships, varimax rotation is popular because it makes the factors orthogonally related, thereby making the interpretation a bit easier. In reality, factors are not typically perfectly orthogonal and forcing orthogonality tends to make things worse. Overall, the worst possible combination is the use of PCA, varimax rotation, and the Kaiser 1.0 (Preacher and MacCallum, 2003). This combination was called the "little jiffy" (Kaiser, 1970), and that wording alone should have been an indicator that there was a problem in using such a combination.

Interestingly, the argument (assumption) for using PCA or EFA is that the researcher has no idea how many factors there are or where the items will load. Yet every time I have pushed a student or colleague to make a theory-based model of the written items, they have been able to do so. Therefore, surveys are generally based on an implicit theoretical model and because of that should have that model tested first using confirmatory factor analysis (CFA).

CFA

Confirmatory factor analysis should be employed more regularly because it tests a theorized model, residuals can be examined, it provides, theoretically, error-free latent constructs, and the fit values provide evidence if the data fit the model (Kline, 2011; Schreiber, 2008). If after testing the theorized model, alternative models, and then equivalent models, the CFA does not work, then EFA would be acceptable (Schreiber, 2008). For a longer discussion of CFA see Schreiber (2008) or Kline (2011). CFA allows for more detailed analyses with invariance and multi-group testing. Invariance testing examines if the structure and weights of the model results are consistent across groups (e.g. gender, race, socio-economic status; Schreiber, 2009). Work with my colleagues on bullying (see Crothers *et al.*, 2009) used CFA and a comparison of three theoretical models to examine the structure of relational aggression, social aggression, and interpersonal maturity in bullying. Subsequent testing of invariance across gender supports the original theoretical model.

An alternative approach to group differences on latent variables estimation is a MIMIC (multiple indicators multiple causes) model. In a MIMIC analysis, factors that are hypothesized to have an effect (effect indicators) are regressed on a dichotomous indicator. MIMIC models are a viable alternative because several covariates (e.g. high/low, gender, SES) can be included into the MIMIC model without having to consistently divide the data as needed in invariance testing (Schreiber, 2009).

Item Response Theory

Another way used to analyze the data in more recent years is item response theory (IRT). Initially the focus of IRT was on dichotomous test data, but theoretical and technical advances have expanded the use of IRT for survey data, especially Likert data (IRT; Bond and Fox, 2001; Fox and Jones, 1998). There are three main advantages to using an item response analysis: fulcrum, order, and category distance analysis. With Likert-type data, the assumption is the middle point, or fulcrum, is the one exactly in the middle and on the same scale the same middle for each item. If your scale goes from 1 to 5, then 3 would be assumed to be the fulcrum. In actuality, the fulcrum point is probably not in the middle. The second assumption is that the order is linear, i.e. the five-point Likert-type scale goes 1, 2, 3, 4, 5. Again, this is probably not true for every item. In actuality, items may go 1, 3, 2, 4, 5 based on the response pattern for a particular item. The last assumption is that the distance between categories on the Likert scales are equidistant. This is simply not the case, and the threshold from one category to the next can change for each item. One of the greatest benefits of this type of analysis is the evidence for item level fit and person level fit for reliability.

The IRT analysis will also allow the examination of differential item functioning (DIF). DIF is the examination of the functioning of individual items across groups. It is analogous to invariance testing in CFA. Item functioning across groups is obviously important for researchers, as discussed previously in the CFA section on invariance/multigroup analysis. Within the CFA/IRT frameworks, recent work has provided analytical techniques to combine the invariance and DIF to test scenarios in order to determine the situation where each is best (Meade and Lautenshlager, 2004; Stark *et al.*, 2006).

Reliability and Validity, Qualitative

Qualitative researchers discuss reliability and validity in terms of believability. Interestingly, this is what quantitative researchers also mean. Because of the different types that have permeated the language in quantitative research, the concept of believability was lost in the mix. The question must be asked, "Is reliability and validity even a proper topic for qualitative research?" Some argue that these two constructs are not useful topics in qualitative research and that discussing them makes qualitative data try to "act" like quantitative data for the purpose of acceptability. I understand that argument and agree with it on many levels, but I look at reliability and validity discussions in qualitative research as part of our rhetorical persuasion to guide the reader to a certain understanding of the phenomenon or situation at hand. I feel that the concept of reliability is pertinent to qualitative data (Madill *et al.*, 2000). The reader must trust the narrative he or she is reading based on the observations made (Eisenhart and Howe, 1992; Lincoln and Guba, 1985). If the narrative is not believable, then we have failed.

Inter-rater checks are the extent to which two or more observers "see" or "hear" the same or similar thing. For mobbing, what one observes or hears is crucial for the argument. Diachronic analysis refers to the stability of an observation through time and is similar to multiple administrations of the same test (test–retest reliability) in quantitative research. This analysis is uniquely aligned with the basic agreement about mobbing that it must have happened over a period of time. The greatest problem is that the observations must remain stable to the observer over time in an ever-changing world. Synchronic analysis refers to the similarity of observations within a given time period. This does not mean a perfect replication, but instead that the observer sees consistency. Trustworthiness is based on the criteria and methodological procedures for determining whether a naturalistic investigation can be trusted (Lincoln and Guba, 1985). The greater the degree of detail and procedural clarity, the more one will be likely to trust the data collected and the inferences drawn from that data. The trustworthiness of a study can be separated into credibility, transferability, dependability, and confirmability.

Credibility is similar to experimental internal validity and concerns how close the researcher's representation and the participants' views are in concert. If the researcher provides evidence of this, such as "member checks" in which the researcher asks the participant to review his or her inferences, then some assurance is provided. Transferability, analogous to external validity in experimental research, is the concern with case-to-case transfer. The researcher must provide enough information on the case studies that a reader can judge the similarity with another case. This is important for summarizing the growing body of research on mobbing. Dependability occurs when you have provided enough information that the process of your research study is logical, traceable, and documentable to the reader. This provides your readers with the ability to attempt to replicate your study if desired. Again, this is crucial for this developing field. Confirmability is the notion that you, as the researcher, provide evidence that can be examined; that you are not simply making it all up. Researchers who work on the bog people had to conclude that the late archeologist Alfred Dieck faked a large number of the 1,800 bog people cases he researched (van der Sanden and Eisenbeiss, 2006). Behavior such as this not only causes problems for your career, but also is a violation of every research organization's code of ethics, and in the long run damages and delays the advancement of the domain of interest you wanted to study.

Triangulation is a methodological procedure for arguing that the criterion of validity, good inference making, has been met. By using multiple pieces of evidence, the researcher can check the integrity or quality of the inferences being made. As Schwandt (1997: 163) wrote, "The central point of the procedure is to examine a single social phenomenon from more than one vantage point." Triangulation provides three pieces of evidence: convergence – agreement across data types; inconsistency – disagreements across data types; and contradiction – different inferences across data types (Denzin, 1978). It is important for the researcher to realize that multiple pieces of data may not lead to a triangulated theme and that the lack of consensus may be more important than the original desired consensus.

In addition to triangulation, peer review of your data and participant reading of your inferences are some of the ways in which to increase the validity of your data. These topics are typically discussed in the analysis component of qualitative work, but they are fundamentally reliability and validity components. Finally, auditing your work using such strategies as negative case analysis, thick description, peer debriefing, feedback from others, and respondent validation will increase the believability of your research to the reader and the research community as a whole. In order for the field to advance and for others to implement the conclusions from the observations, it is critical that everyone focuses on providing quality evidence.

Issue 3: Translations

Instruments are increasingly commonly translated from the original language to a target language. For example, the LIPT was not originally written in English, but its English version is the only one I have seen. The NAQ was recently translated into Japanese (Takaki *et al.*, 2010) using a back-translation method. Translating an instrument can be very problematic. I had experience with these issues when translating multiple instruments from American English to Arabic – it took a year and a good deal of personal money to make sure the translation was accurate. On another occasion, I had difficulty working on a project in which translating English to Spanish I struggled to explain the word "blue," which in the English context meant sad.

According to Brislin (1976), translating and adapting tests and instruments for cross-cultural research is a difficult task. It is necessary to establish the linguistic, technical, and measurement equivalence of the instruments. The technical equivalence of instruments refers to the requirement that original and translated versions must yield comparable data when used in two different cultures. In order to achieve this, it is important to maintain similarity in the layout and technical conventions used in both versions of the instruments. For example, (1) the placement of boxes, circles or lines for indicating responses should be the same across both forms; (2) both versions should look the same with regard to words that are underlined or in bold type; (3) both versions should use similar punctuation and syntax; and (4) both forms should have the same directions and use the same numbering system and item order. Technical equivalence also involves resolving technical difficulties of the instrument, which can make questions hard to understand and answer. For example, flawed translations may result in unclear statements. These must be identified and revised prior to using an instrument for cross-cultural comparisons.

In establishing linguistic equivalence, the main concern should be that the meaning of each item and its translated version are the same. This is rarely an easy task (Holtzman, 1968). According to Brislin's (1980) suggestion, for optimal translation accuracy a combination of translation methods should be used. Procedurally, first, a directly translated, *simple direct translation* of the source versions of the instrument should occur. Then, a comparison of the translation and target instrument reviewed by a bilingual individual should yield the closest meaning to the original. If multiple individuals can develop translated versions, this is an advantage because you can work from the best translation of each item, creating a single version. *Review by non-involved experts* of the translated instrument and the original language versions then can be completed.

Werner and Campbell (1970) recommended using back-translation to get the best translation results. Therefore, the target version of the instrument is back-translated into the original language. Now, the original instrument and the back-translated instrument can be compared. According to Brislin *et al.* (1973), back-translation is the basis of decentering, which is a translation that involves revision of both the original and target versions of the instruments. Brislin *et al.* (1973) prefer this method because it allows for both instruments to be improved; it does not focus on one language version but instead scrutinizes both language versions. Unfortunately, in most cases, the authors of instruments do not want their instruments revised, so decentering is not commonly practiced.

Issue 4: New Technique Latent Class Cluster Analysis

A new area of analysis is latent class analysis (LCA) that is used when one is not interested in testing the structure of the construct but instead the classes of people within the data (Schreiber, 2011). Recently, in academic terms, an LCA was performed on data from the Negative Acts Questionnaire (Notelaers *et al.*, 2007). Many people have used K-means cluster analysis to look for groups, but K-means is very problematic. LCA clustering is model-based and traditional cluster analysis is not. Therefore, LCA is based on a statistical model, and the model is assumed to have a population from the data sample.

The main advantage of using a statistical model is that the choice for cluster determination is not as arbitrary and there are statistical analyses to test it. For example, the Bayesian Criterion Information (BIC) is used to test the model. In general, you select the BIC with the lowest value (Magidson and Vermunt, 2000) and test whether the model is statistically significant where the provided L^2 has a number of degrees of freedom and a p-value that should be greater than .01 in large samples. An L^2 of

1 is considered as a perfect fit. Magidson and Vermunt (2000) provide a succinct description of the technique and evaluative evidence you need to use to decide about the quality of the model. Most importantly, LCA is an improvement over traditional techniques. Over the past decade, the technique seems to have gained a great deal of momentum in European-based research but not as much in US-based research.

Issue 5: Sampling

Sampling is a process in which the size of the sample needed is driven a great deal by the type of question being asked, data collected, and planned analysis technique. While the length of this chapter does not permit a delineation of all of the possible sample types, a basic separation is the larger goal of the study – generalization past the sample or a rich description of a case. If the researchers are looking to generalize, a representative sample is needed; if not, a specific case may be all that is necessary. Researchers tend to get into trouble when they have a sample that they cannot generalize but do so anyway.

Issue 6: Social Bias/Self-Report Bias

Social bias in self-report instruments has been an issue for many decades (e.g. Campbell and Griffin, 1979). The same issue pertains here, because there is no way to "get at" mobbing in any pure "objective" manner. The larger issue is that response sets confound interpretation of items. There are three core types of response sets: social desirability, acquiescence, and extremity. There are options for collecting and analyzing data to reduce the effects of response sets. For a good review, see Paulhus, 1991. During interviews, a competent interviewer can ask questions that probe the reliability of the data being provided by the participant. Survey designers have to plan for social bias in self-report instruments. A popular option is to reverse code a few of the items because of the belief that the negatively worded items encourage the participant to process the content more carefully. I am not a proponent of this approach (Weems *et al.*, 2003). Item orientation can potentially confound factor structure (Campbell and Grissom, 1979; Deemer and Minke, 1999; Eggers, 2000; Johanson and Osborn, 2000) and may often result in a separate factor for the negatively worded items (Anderson *et al.*, 1979; Magazine *et al.*, 1996; McInerney *et al.*, 1994).

RECOMMENDATIONS

For the field of bullying research, the first recommendation is to come together on an agreed upon nomenclature or definition system. There are simply too many people working in this area not to do this. Many years ago, the top researchers in intelligence came together and wrote a single piece about the known and unknowns of IQ. Those in the field may consider the same path. An agreed upon system will not only advance the field but also will provide a common language when you are talking to people outside the field (e.g. legislators, human resources departments). If you do not have a common system, you begin to sound like you do not know what you are talking about, how to measure the constructs, or how to create intervention models (e.g. progressive discipline models). I also believe there is a great deal of room for mixed method studies that combine numeric and non-numeric data that can illuminate the individual, social, and systemic components that give rise to the phenomenon. Finally, for those who are not researchers, be wary of a single study on which to base a decision. The field is large enough for you to find multiple studies and use the results to triangulate a potential decision based on your context in comparison to the study parameters (e.g. participants, instruments used, length of study, etc.).

There are many research agendas that can be taken up or expanded upon. Studies looking at both the structure of the construct in a CFA and the groups that may be within the data (LCA) is one such agenda. This may be expanded to ascertain comparisons across public and private organizations. These studies could also advance techniques in the field. Even good data visualization can help the field advance (Yau, 2011).

For practitioners, I always say be wary of single studies, or someone who said, "I read this one study that said ..." I have to bite my tongue when, in my daughter's music group, the teacher brings up a study, which I can never find, about X causing Y. Such a phenomenon is no different or less problematic in work meetings or team projects. Reading is fundamental to understanding the evolution of a field of study, and that means reading multiple studies or a credible and thorough recent review of the field.

NOTE

1. Note this word comes from Crawshaw's (2009) discussion of the problem with words and definitions associated with this topic area.

REFERENCES

Adams, A., and Crawford, N. (1992). *Bullying at Work*, London: Virago Press.

Anderson, J. P., Anderson, P. A., and Jenson, A. D. (1979). The measurement of nonverbal immediacy, paper presented at the Annual Meeting of the Eastern Communication Association, Philadelphia, PA (ERIC Document Reproduction Service no. ED 203409).

Bartlett, J. E., and Bartlett, M. E. (2011). Workplace bullying: An integrative literature review. *Advances in Developing Human Resources*, 13, 69–84.

Bond, T. G. and Fox, C. M. (2001). *Applying the Rasch Model: Fundamental Measurement in the Human Sciences*, Mahwah, NJ: LEA.

Brislin, R. W. (1970). Back-translation for cross-cultural research. *Journal of Cross-cultural Psychology*, 1, 185–216.

Brislin, R. W. (1976). Comparative research methodology: Cross-cultural studies. *International Journal of Psychology*, 11, 215–29.

Brislin, R. W. (1980). Translation and content analysis of oral and written material. In H. C. Triandis and J. W. Berry (eds), *Handbook of Cross-Cultural Psychology* (pp. 389–444), Boston, MA: Allyn & Bacon

Brislin, R. W., Lonner, W., and Thorndike, R. (1973). *Cross-Cultural Research Methods*, New York: John Wiley & Sons.

Brodksy, C. M. (1976). *The Harassed Worker*, Lexington, MA: D. C. Heath & Co.

Campbell, N. J., and Grissom, S. (1979). Influence of item direction on student responses in attitude assessment. Paper presented at the Annual Meeting of the American Educational Research Association, San Francisco, CA (ERIC Document Reproduction Service no. ED 170366).

Cortina, J. M. (1993). What is coefficient alpha? An examination of theory and applications. *Journal of Applied Psychology*, 78, 98–104.

Crawshaw, L. (2009). Workplace bullying? Mobbing? Harassment? Distraction by a thousand definitions. *Consulting Psychology Journal: Practice and Research*, 61, 263–7.

Crocker, L., and Algina, J. (1986). *Introduction to Classical and Modern Test Theory*, New York: Hold, Rinehart, & Winston.

Cronbach, L. J. (1951). Coefficient alpha and the internal structure of tests. *Psychometrika, I ft*, 297–334.

Crothers, L. M., Schreiber, J. B., Field, J. E., and Kolbert, J. B. (2009). Development and measurement through confirmatory factor analysis of the Young Adult Social

Behavior Scale (YASB): An assessment of relational aggression in adolescents and young adulthood. *Journal of Psychoeducational Assessment*, 27, 17–28.

Deemer, S. A., and Minke, K. M. (1999). An investigation of the factor structure of the teacher efficacy scale. *Journal of Educational Research*, 93, 3–10.

Denzin, N. K. (1978). *The Research Act: A Theoretical Introduction to Sociological Methods*, New York: Praeger.

Eggers, S. J. (2000). Spirituality in mid-life and late adulthood (doctoral dissertation, University of Memphis, 2000), *Dissertation Abstracts International*, 61 (3A).

Einarsen, S. (2000). Harassment and bullying at work: A review of the Scandinavian approach. *Aggression and Violent Behavior*, 5, 379–401.

Einarsen, S., Höel, H., Zapf, D., and Cooper, C. L. (2003). The concept of bullying at work: The European tradition. In S. Einarsen, H. Höel, D. Zapf, and C. L. Cooper (eds), *Bullying and Emotional Abuse in the Workplace: International Perspectives in Research and Practice* (pp. 1–30), London: Taylor & Francis.

Einarsen S., Raknes, B. I., Matthiesen, S. B. M., and Hellesøy, O. H. (1996). Bullying at work and its relationships with health complaints: Moderating effects of social support and personality. *Nordisk Psykologi*, 48, 116–37.

Eisenhart, M. A., and Howe, K. R. (1992). Validity in educational research. In M. D. LeCompte, W. L. Millroy, and J. Preissle (eds), *The Handbook of Qualitative Research in Education* (pp. 643–80), San Diego, CA: Academic Press.

Fox, C. M., and Jones, J. A. (1998). Uses of Rasch modeling in counseling psychology research. *Journal of Counseling Psychology*, 45, 30–45.

Gorsuch, R. L. (1983). *Factor analysis* (2nd edn), Hillsdale, NJ: Lawrence Erlbaum Associates.

Holtzman, W. H. (1968). Cross-cultural studies in psychology. *International Journal of Psychology*, 3, 83–91.

Johanson, G. A., and Osborn, C. J. (2000). Acquiescence as differential person functioning. Paper presented at the Annual Meeting of the American Education Research Association, New Orleans, LA. (ERIC Document Reproduction Service no. ED 441022).

Kaiser, H. F. (1970). A second generation Little Jiffy. *Psychometrika*, 35, 401–15.

Kanyongo, G. (2006). Determining the correct number of components to extract from a principal components analysis: A Monte Carlo study of the accuracy of the scree plot. *Journal of Modern Applied Statistical Methods*, 4, 120–33.

Kline, R. B. (2011). *Structural Equation Modeling* (3rd edn), New York: Guilford.

Leyman, H. (1996). The content and development of mobbing at work. *European Journal of Work and Organizational Psychology*, 5, 165–84.

Liefooghe, A., and Olafsson, R. (1999). Scientists and amateurs: Mapping the bullying domain. *International Journal of Manpower*, 20, 39–49.

Lincoln, Y. S., and Guba, E. G. (1985). *Naturalistic Inquiry*, Thousand Oaks, CA: Sage.

Madill, A., Jordan, A., and Shirley, C. (2000). Objectivity and reliability in qualitative analysis: Realist, contextualist and radical constructionist epistemologies. *British Journal of Psychology*, 91, 1–20.

Magazine, S. L., Williams, L. J., and Williams, M. L. (1996). A confirmatory factor analysis examination of reverse coding effects in Meyer and Allen's Affective and Continuance Commitment Scales. *Educational and Psychological Measurement*, 56, 241–50.

Magidson, J., and Vermunt, J. K. (2001). Latent class factor and cluster models, bi-plots and related graphical displays. *Sociological Methodology*, 31, 223–64.

McInerney, V., McInerney, D., and Roche, L. (1994). Definitely not just another computer anxiety instrument: The development and validation of CALM: computer anxiety and learning measure, paper presented at the Annual Stress and Anxiety Research Conference, Madrid, Spain (ERIC Document Reproduction Service no. ED 386161).

Meade, A., and Lautenshlager, G. J. (2004). A comparison of item response theory and confirmatory factor analytic methodologies. *Organizational Research Methods*, 7, 361–88.

Messick, S. (1989). Meaning and values in test validation: The science and ethics of assessment. *Educational Researcher*, 18, 5–11.

National Civil Service League (1901). *Abuses in the Appointment of Subordinate Officers and Employees of the House of Representatives*, Washington, DC: NCSL (LOC JK1432. N27).

Notelaers, G., Einarsen, S., De Witte, H., and Vermunt, J. K. (2006). Measuring exposure to bullying at work: The validity and advantages of the latent class cluster approach. *Work and Stress*, 20, 289–302.

Onwuegbuzie, A. J., and Daniel, L. G. (2002). A framework for reporting and interpreting internal consistency reliability. *Measurement and Evaluation in Counseling and Development*, 35, 89–103.

Paulhus, D. L. (1991). Measurement and control of response bias (pp. 17–59). In J. P. Robinson, P. R. Shaver, and L. W. Wrightsman (eds), *Measures of Personality and Social Psychological Attitudes* (pp. 17–59), San Diego, CA: Academic Press.

Pohlmann, J. T. (2004). Use and interpretation of factor analysis in the Journal of Educational Research: 1992–2002. *Journal of Educational Research*, 98, 14–22.

Preacher, K. J., and MacCallum, R. C. (2003). Repairing Tom Swift's electric factor analysis machine. *Understanding Statistics*, 2, 13–32.

Rodríguez-Carballeira, A., Escartin Solanelles, J., Visauta Vinacua, B., Garcia, C. P., and Martín-Peña, J. (2010). Categorization and hierarchy of workplace bullying strategies: A Delphi survey. *Spanish Journal of Psychology*, 13, 297–308.

Schmitt, N. (1996). Uses and abuses of coefficient alpha. *Psychological Assessment*, 8, 350–3.

Schreiber, J. (2008). Core reporting practices in structural equation modeling. *Research in Social and Administrative Pharmacy*, 4, 83–97.

Schreiber, J. (2009). Multi-group analysis in structural equation modeling. In T. Teo and M. S. Khine (eds), *Structural Equation Modeling in Educational Research: Concepts and Applications* (pp. 329–44), Rotterdam: Sense Publishers.

Schreiber, J. B. (2011). *Technical Report: Latent Cluster Class Analysis for Evaluation and Visitor Studies,* Washington, DC: Smithsonian Institution Office of Policy and Analysis.

Schreiber, J. B., and Asner-Self, K. K. (2011). *Educational Research,* New York: John Wiley & Sons.

Schwandt, T. (1997). *Qualitative Inquiry: A Dictionary of Terms,* Thousand Oaks, CA: Sage.

Stark, O., Chernyshenko, O. S., and Drasgow, F. (2006). Detecting differential item functioning with confirmatory factor analysis. *Journal of Applied Psychology*, 91, 1292–1306.

Takaki, J., Tsutsumi, A., Fujii, Y., Taniguchi, R., Hirokawa, K., Hibino, Y., Lemmer, R. J., Nashiwa, H., Wang, D-H., and Ogino, K. (2010). Assessment of workplace bullying and harassment: Reliability and validity of a Japanese version of the Negative Acts Questionnaire. *Journal of Occupational Health*, 52, 74–81.

van der Sanden, W. A. B., and Eisenbeiss, S. (2006). Imaginary people: Alfred Dieck and the bog bodies of northwest Europe. *Archaologisches Korrespondenzblatt*, 36, 111–22.

Weems, G. H., Onwuegbuzie, A. J., Schreiber, J. B., and Eggers, S. J. (2003). Characteristics of respondents with different response patterns to positively- and negatively-worded items on rating scales. *Assessment and Evaluation in Higher Education*, 26, 587–607.

Werner, O., and Campbell, D. T. (1970). Translating, working through interpreters, and the problem of decentering. In R. Naroll and R. Cohen (eds), *A Handbook of Method in Cultural Anthropology* (pp. 398–420), New York: American Museum of Natural History.

Yau, N. (2011). *Visualize This: The Flowing Data Guide to Design Visualization, and Statistics*, New York: John Wiley & Sons.

Zaltman, G. (2003). *How Customers Think: Essential Insights into the Mind of the Market*. Boston, MA: Harvard Business School Publishing.

Zapf, D., and Einarsen, S. (2001). Bullying in the workplace: Recent trends in research and practice – an introduction. *European Journal of Work and Organizational Psychology*, 10, 369–73.

Zapf, D., Knorz, C., and Kulla, M. (1996). On the relationship between mobbing factors, and job content, social work environment, and health outcomes. *European Journal of Work and Organizational Psychology*, 5, 215–37.

4

How Unaddressed Bullying Affects Employees, Workgroups, Workforces, and Organizations: The Widespread Aversive Effects of Toxic Communication Climates

Pamela Lutgen-Sandvik and Susan Scheller Arsht
University of New Mexico

INTRODUCTION

Unaddressed workplace bullying, mobbing, or employee abuse (synonymous terms for persistent, enduring interpersonal aggression at work) can have a measurably negative impact on organizations' communication climates and, by association, organizational goals (Yamada, 2000). Direct costs are associated with increased disability and workers' compensation claims, increased medical costs, and costs defending lawsuits for wrongful discharge or constructive discharge (Matusewitch, 1996). Indirect costs are low-quality work, reduced productivity, high staff turnover, increased absenteeism, deteriorated customer relationships, and loss of positive public image. A high turnover rate is one of the most frequent consequences and is commonly a sign of toxic communication climates.

Even less tangible negative effects are "opportunity costs of lowered employee commitment, such as lack of discretionary effort, commitments outside the job, time spent talking about the problem rather than working, and loss of creativity" (Bassman, 1992: 137). Problems go unsolved and can accumulate into crises, because bullying encourages "fixing the blame rather than fixing the problem" (p. 140). Terrorized workers hide mistakes rather than using them as improvement opportunities (Lockhart, 1997) in an environment of "fear and mistrust, resentment, hostility, feelings of humiliation, withdrawal, and play-it-safe strategies" (Bassman, 1992: 141). For employees who have been bullied or witnessed bullying of their peers, a kind of goal displacement occurs in which the primary goal becomes self-protection. Workers maintain a constant state of hypervigilance – a perfectly understandable response to constant threat, yet one that is corrosive to workers and workplace health (Bassman, 1992; Lockhart, 1997).

When communication climates are marked by persistent aggression (i.e. bullying), the aggression impacts all of the people in the environment and spreads outward to negatively affect not only that workgroup but the organization as a whole. When organizations allow workplace bullying to go unaddressed and solidify into a toxic communication climate, employees suffer, workgroups polarize, workforce capital thins and declines, and organizations fail to reach their potential. Too often, we recognize only the individual-level effects of bullying and do not see that bullying is systemic and not simply reflective of a few problem employees. The purpose of this chapter is to provide a better picture of these negative effects and to suggest ways to address the problem. In order to do this, this chapter explores the effects and responses with a multi-level lens ranging from individual to organizational.

Definitions key to this chapter include workplace bullying, communication climate, bullies, and targets. Workplace bullying is persistent interpersonal aggression that is both direct and indirect, verbal and non-verbal, and is aimed at one or more employees in an organization and perpetrated by one or more other members of the same organization in situations marked by power disparity.[1] Power disparity in this context means that targets nearly always feel unable to fully defend themselves against attack or end abuse. Communication climate is the social tone of interactions and relationships in a work environment (Albrecht, 1979). Communication climates involve all forms of communication: ongoing face-to-face interactions, written or verbal messages from unseen upper-managers, beliefs about the motivations behind upper-management communiqués, gossip or buzzing among workgroup members about past interactions and interactions they have heard about but not directly witnessed, and so forth.

Bullies are the perpetrators of this persistent aggression and abuse as well as those who either actively or passively support these aggressors. While this chapter will use the term "bully," some research refers to these aggressor as actors (e.g. Fox and Spector, 2005). Supporters are also referred to as henchmen/women, passive bullies, followers, or patrons (Boddy *et al.*, 2010; Lutgen-Sandvik and Fletcher, 2012; Olweus, 2003). Finally, targets are persons subjected to frequent, repetitive, enduring attacks. The bullying literature uses the term *target*, as opposed to *victim*, to shift focus from self-blame or victim-blaming to point to perpetrator responsibility.

Why Unaddressed Bullying Matters

Bullying is a genuinely horrifying experience for those targeted, but it is also traumatizing to bystanders who witness and sympathize. Bullying can be harmful to workgroup social relationships and negatively impact work output. Bullying not only hurts the organization internally, but also can damage organizational reputations and public relations. Because workplace bullying occurs at work – in front of and involving many people – we must consider it a systemic issue instead of an individual, psychological issue. When bullying is present in a workplace environment, most organizational members simply ignore the abuse and hope it will go away, or they remove the targets, hoping to end the problem, but these actions rarely help (Lutgen-Sandvik, 2006). Leadership interventions to ameliorate bullying are successful or partially successful in only a third of cases; in the other two-thirds leadership does nothing, intervenes with no effect, or intervenes in a way that worsens targets' plights (Keashly, 2001; Namie and Lutgen-Sandvik, 2010). What occurs when bullying is left unaddressed (or addressed in an ineffective way) is an embedding of aggression and bullying into organizational cultures so that over time more and more members begin displaying aggression, some from seeing peers and higher-ups model aggressive behavior and others in a sort of defeatist self-defense (Einarsen *et al.*, 2010).

There are a number of reasons why organizational members fail to effectively address workplace bullying in organizations. First, most organizational members, whether boss, peer, or subordinate, have no real idea how to deal with workplace bullying. Indeed, we go to work with a basic assumption that all will interact within the norms of polite and civil discourse; interactions only become an issue when certain members breach this assumption (Sypher, 2004). When breaches occur, organizational members do not know how to respond. Second, organizational members, including upper-managers, are put off by, shocked, and even petrified (i.e. freeze response) by interpersonal aggression and are therefore apprehensive and frightened of approaching the offending parties. In many cases, even bullies' supervisors are afraid of them and are unwilling to carry out the required discipline or even employment termination that may be required (Lutgen-Sandvik and McDermott, 2008; Pearson, 1998). Third, too many organizational members view only the micro- or individual-level features of the problem and its effects and fail to recognize that the issue is not just a few problem employees. As mentioned, workplace bullying or persistently aggressive interactions negatively affect bystanders, poison workgroups, kill teamwork, and retard meeting organizational missions or goals (Lutgen-Sandvik and Tracy, 2012).

EFFECTS OF UNADDRESSED WORKPLACE BULLYING: EMPLOYEES, WORKGROUPS, WORKFORCES, AND ORGANIZATIONS

Employees (Targets and Witnesses)

Targets

At the micro-level of work coordination, where people interact on a daily basis to get the work of an organization completed, targets suffer the most direct harm from unaddressed workplace bullying. Overwhelming evidence indicates that being persistently abused at work negatively affects all aspects of targeted workers' lives. They suffer from a number of physical ailments that targets directly associate with being bullied, including gastrointestinal programs (e.g. irritable bowel syndrome), insomnia, weight gain and loss (Namie, 2003), and musculoskeletal problems (Vranceanu *et al.*, 2009). Medical research suggests that bullying is associated with chronic stress, high blood pressure, and increased risk of coronary heart disease (De Vogli *et al.*, 2007; Kivimäki *et al.*, 2003; Lutgen-Sandvik *et al.*, 2007).

Targets' emotional health suffers as well (Duffy *et al.*, 2002). They report experiencing depression, elevated anxiety, and anxiety attacks (Kivimäki *et al.*, 2003; Namie, 2003), which they link to being abused at work. Targets say that they live with daily terror of continued attacks – abuse they characterize as *hammering away* and *chipping away* at them (Tracy *et al.*, 2006). Unabated bullying eats away at targets' self-esteem and self-worth (Price Spratlen, 1995). Many describe experiencing the symptoms of post-traumatic stress disorder (PTSD): hypervigilance, thought intrusions, and avoidance-disassociation (Leymann and Gustafsson, 1996; Mikkelsen and Einarsen, 2002; Namie, 2003). Persons abused at work report higher rates of alcohol consumption and abuse (Richman *et al.*, 2001), and more often think about suicide (Leymann, 1990) than do non-bullied workers. In fact, in his early work Leymann (1990: 122) claimed that "about 10%–15% of the total number of suicides in Sweden each year" were linked to cases of extreme mobbing.

Targets' work productivity and personal relationships also flounder when they are subjected to constant abuse. When organizations fail to intervene, targets' cognitive functioning suffer (Brodsky, 1976), and their performance dwindles (Lutgen-Sandvik *et al.*, 2008). Some targets are so damaged that they cannot reintegrate into the workforce, or can do so only after intensive rehabilitation therapy (Leymann and Gustafsson, 1996). Being abused at work also impairs relationships outside of work. Targets say that they often bring bullying home (Tracy *et al.*, 2006), and family members have reported having to face the bullied targets' displaced aggression (Hoobler and Brass, 2006).

Witnesses, Bystanders

Employees who see others abused at work but are not abused directly are alternately referred to as witnesses or bystanders (Keashly, 2010). In many cases, bystanders are considered *secondary* targets; they are "employees who themselves were not violated but whose perceptions, fears, and expectations are changed as a result of being vicariously exposed to violence" (Barling, 1996: 35). The harm that witnesses report attest to the fact that workplace bullying is a collective experience that produces increasing levels of harm when left unaddressed. For example, bystanders report increased levels of "destabilizing forces at work, excessive workloads, role ambiguity, and work relationship conflict" (Jennifer *et al.*, 2003: 495). When bullying is present in work environments, non-bullied employees report elevated negativity, stress, and lower levels of work satisfaction than non-exposed workers (Lutgen-Sandvik *et al.*, 2007). Bystanders also report increased intentions to leave the organization where bullying is taking place when they are compared to non-exposed employees (Rayner *et al.*, 2002; Vartia, 2001).

Unaddressed bullying creates a working climate drenched in dread, fear, and hypervigilance. Fear coupled with dread are the overwhelming emotions that witnesses and targets report feeling when they have to go to work each day. When coworkers see or hear about others being bullied, they make the logical assumption that they could be targeted in a similar fashion and hypervigilance becomes a permanent feature of work life (Lockhart, 1997). When witnessing coworkers pull back their support for targets because they fear being targeted themselves, the witnesses report feeling very guilty about their reactions (Lutgen-Sandvik, 2006). As bullying continues, these emotions increase and infect others. As ongoing fear, emotional exhaustion, and guilt increase, the likelihood of staff turnover goes up as well.

Workgroups

Because bullying conflicts are so volatile and aggressive, they spread fear through the entire workgroup and typically push members into one of three non-bullied bystander groups: those who cluster around and support bullies (bully allies), those who support or protect targets (target allies), and those who attempt to distance themselves from the bullying conflict (neutral or silent bystanders; Lutgen-Sandvik, 2006).

Bully allies are alternately labeled "passive bullies, followers, or henchmen" (Olweus, 2003: 67) and patrons or pawns (Boddy *et al.*, 2010). Patrons are those who help bullies ascend to positions of power and persons to whom bullies turn as third-party allies. Bullies often choose these people as a strategic support network (Boddy *et al.*, 2010). Pawns are persons initially loyal to the bullies who side with them in bullying conflicts but later feel or discover they are being used or manipulated. Pawns often emerge later as targets (Boddy *et al.*, 2010). Bully allies, especially passive bullies and followers are people "who participate in bullying but do not usually take the initiative" (Olweus, 2003: 67). Henchmen/women, on the other hand, actively take part in bullying conflicts, loyally following the bully's lead and working to undermine, remove, and sometimes even destroy targets' reputations (Lutgen-Sandvik, 2006).

Target allies and neutral bystanders are often considered *secondary* targets because, although they were not targeted, their "perceptions, fears and expectations are changed as a result of being vicariously exposed to violence" (Barling, 1996: 35). Workgroup members who side with the targets comprise the second group, typically bystanders who believe the abuse is morally wrong or members who have long-standing friendships with targets (Lutgen-Sandvik, 2006). Over time, others may join the target's side of the conflict, especially if they shift from being followers, patrons, or pawns to being targets.

The silent onlookers comprise the third group, those who take a Switzerland-type perspective of their role in the conflict. They strive to be uninvolved non-combatants. Neutral or silent bystanders want to stay out of the conflict because they see targets' experiences of being "undermined, disenfranchised, and emasculated" by the bullies and their allies (Boddy *et al.*, 2010: 124).

Membership in all groups continuously shifts and morphs. Targets' supporters become worn down and burnt out; non-involved persons suddenly become targets or begin taking sides, and persons in the bullying circle are ousted. Persons safe from targeting at one time become targets at another time when bullies' alliances shift, which they commonly do (Westhues, 2005). Bullies commonly redirect their aggression to those who look like a threat or whose actions or words place bullies in a negative light (Crawshaw, 2005; Fast and Chen, 2009).

Workforces

Given these dynamics, workplaces where bullying is left unchecked have a frightening potential to create an impoverished workplace that materializes over time as an indirect result of a series of worker-exit waves. During the crests of the waves when a bullying climate is dominating the organization, talented employees leave without a fight, or may briefly fight, give up, and then decide to leave. In the first wave, the brightest and most talented leave, taking their wealth of occupational capital (skills, technical knowledge, experience, etc.) with them to new employers (Crawford, 2001; Rayner *et al.*, 2002). A second wave of workers, who initially try to stop the bullying but find that their efforts are met with escalating abuse, ambivalence from upper management, or both, begin to leave soon after. After fighting what feels like a losing battle and finding themselves on the receiving end of escalated abuse, this second group may also exit the organization (Adams and Crawford, 1992; Zapf and Gross, 2001). In a third intermittent wave, new employees come in but frequently leave after assessing the negative workplace dynamics (Bassman, 1992), unless they lack the occupational capital to do so. Unfortunately, these waves leave behind a less talented cadre of workers with fewer occupational options and fewer organizationally valued assets (Adams and Crawford, 1992; Randall, 2001).

It is possible too that these workers have a weaker identity construct and may be more likely to suffer psychological damage as a result of bullying (Zapf *et al.*, 2003). It is also reasonable to expect that some of the people who stay and are subjected to ongoing abuse become frustrated, angry, and vengeful (Folger and Baron, 1996). For example, one of the workgroups in this study reported discussing and fantasizing about the bully's murder, and one witness in particular refused to learn first aid so that she would never be in a position to have to save the bully's life. The building rage in abused workers, erosion of human resources, and resulting increase in work distribution may contribute to a powder-keg atmosphere, with the potential for a serious explosion given the right spark. Allen and Lucero's (1996) study of insider murder is informative here and points to the potentially deadly dynamics of unchecked bullying.

Organizations

The central consequences to organizations include lost productivity, decreased worker commitment and satisfaction, increased operating costs, loss of positive public relations, and, over time, impoverished workforces. Abuse at work, particularly from supervisors, reduces organizational citizenship behaviors – discretionary acts that promote organizational effectiveness (Zellars *et al.*, 2002). Not surprisingly, facing persistent harassment and humiliation increases absenteeism. Indeed, an Equal Employment Opportunity Commission (EEOC) officer explained that one of the indicators the EEOC used to identify if problems exist in a workgroup is employee use of sick leave (P. Kendall, personal communication, 27 Sept. 2007).

Presenteeism can also be a problem in hostile work environments. This term usually means "slack productivity from ailing workers" (Cascio, 2006: 245), but can occur when bullied workers fear missing work because of what might transpire in their absence when they are not there to defend themselves (e.g. rumors, work destruction, key task removal; Rayner *et al.*, 2002). Workers in hostile environments may be present but they are not producing at their peak potential. Enormous levels of energy are necessary to cope with, defend against, and make sense of persistent harassment and humiliation (Lutgen-Sandvik, 2006).

Organizations most likely also face increased premiums for workers' compensation (Brodsky, 1976) and medical insurance (Bassman, 1992). Lawsuits associated with bullying (e.g. wrongful or constructive discharge), although rare, are costly both in legal fees and staff hours (Rayner *et al.*, 2002). Quite commonly, organizations also suffer loss of positive public images (Bassman, 1992) and find it increasingly difficult to recruit staff, especially when word spreads within a specialized group of employees about an employee-abusive organization (Lutgen-Sandvik and McDermott, 2008).

Recommendations

Given the destruction wrought by workplace bullying, this section explores ideas for both prevention and intervention at the micro- and meso-levels.[2] These recommendations draw on my earlier statement that individual-level responses are unlikely to resolve workplace bullying and typically make this much worse for suffering targets and bystanders. This is especially true when aggression has become entrenched, workers are demoralized, and widespread harm has occurred.

MICRO-LEVEL RESPONSES

Target Responses

Given my caveat about individual-level responses, I offer the following with some caution. However, in US organizations particularly and organizations in other individualistic cultures, we as organizational members often point to targets as the source of what is to be done. I offer these suggestions more to assist suffering targets than to provide substantive interventions for organizational change. Additionally, those targeted are keen to know what they can do to stop abuse, so I address some potential approaches individuals might take, including coworkers.

For targets, being able to name what is happening as *workplace bullying* is crucial for understanding and responding to the experience (Namie, 2006). Information about bullying from research studies, trade publication articles, and books bolster employee claims to upper-management and HR and make it easier for targets to externalize bullying rather than blame themselves. Targeted workers may also decide to file formal or informal complaints to unions, EEOC, the bully's boss, or attorneys (MacIntosh, 2006). But whatever actions a target decides to take against the bully or organization, ensuring self-care and social support are important as well, which might involve taking time off and spending time with supportive friends and family (Namie and Namie, 2000).

If and when individual tactics fail (which sadly is often the case), advising targets about the possibility of building collective efforts and the investment of time these efforts take can be a helpful step. If there is no such possibility and targets can find another job, targets are encouraged to leave the organizations – much in the same way as a counselor would advise a battered woman to leave a perpetrator. Just as battered women should not be advised to stay and try and change a perpetrator, a target of bullying should not stay and try and change a bully.

MESO-LEVEL RESPONSES

Meso-level responses are those that involve organizational systems or at least specific working departments/divisions. Short-term approaches such as identifying lone perpetrators (or targets) while disregarding the working environment's factors that encourage and sustain bullying will likely fail to produce meaningful lasting change. Successful efforts require the full commitment of top-level leadership, involvement of middle-management, and engagement of employees (Tehrani, 2001).

Meso-Level Commitment

Neither top–down nor bottom–up approaches are likely to meet with success. For change to occur in organizations, upper-managers, middle managers, and line workers must be involved and committed to building a respectful communication climate. Certainly, all employees will not be equally committed, but there must be someone (or hopefully many "someones") at each level who wants to make communication more respectful.

First, top-level commitment to dignity and respect for all workers is crucial because the behaviors of those perceived to be organizational representatives set the tenor for others. As Noreen Tehrani has aptly put it, "employees will quickly become cynical when … exhort[ed] … to behave in a way that bears little relationship to the action behaviors of the managers they observe in their daily life" (2001: 136). Second, middle managers must be engaged because they "have the greatest opportunity to demonstrate that a culture that respects the dignity of individual employees is possible" (Tehrani, 2001: 137). When middle managers are habitually aggressive and autocratic, they often believe this approach gives them power and will be highly suspicious of changes perceived as removing that power. If this is the case, organizations have to offer (possibly require) communication skills *training*, *encouragement*, and *reward* to help them move from their current style to one conducive to creating a dignity-based communication climate. The core element of such training is interpersonal communication skills – an area that is often most challenging during the transition.

Third, employees at all levels and from functional areas must be involved and engaged in assessing the current communication climate, determining areas for improvement, and implementing changes. Research suggests that creating a cross-level, cross-functional team (or a number of them depending on organizational size) and coupling team(s) with external researchers or experts can be especially effective (Keashly and Neuman, 2005, 2009). Together, they identify problems and outline potential solutions.

CONCLUSION

In this chapter, I have addressed the systemic outcomes associated with unaddressed workplace bullying, which includes the negative effects on employees, workgroups, workforces, and organizations. These dynamics point to frightening results for people, institutions, and society as aggression becomes a way of life.

NOTES

1 As such, this chapter excludes bullying from customers, patients, and other external people. In terms of power disparity (inability to defend fully against attacks or stop abuse), although anyone at any level can perpetrate bullying, in the US, UK, and EU managers and persons with higher organizational positions than targets are most often identified as perpetrators. In Scandinavia peers and managers are identified as bullies at approximately equal rates (Lutgen-Sandvik *et al.*, 2007; Zapf *et al.*, 2003).

2 For a discussion of the macro-level solutions, see Lutgen-Sandvik and Tracy, 2012.

REFERENCES

Adams, A., and Crawford, N. (1992). *Bullying at Work: How to Confront and Overcome it*, London: Virago Press.

Albrecht, T. L. (1979). The role of communication in perceptions of organizational climate. In D. Nimmo (ed.), *Communication Yearbook 3* (pp. 343–57), New Brunswick, NJ: Transaction Books.

Allen, R. E., and Lucero, M. A. (1996). Beyond resentment: Exploring organizationally targeted insider murder. *Journal of Management Inquiry*, 5, 86–103.

Barling, J. (1996). The prediction, experience and consequences of workplace violence. In G. R. VanderBos and E. Q. Bulatoao (eds), *Violence on the Job* (pp. 29–50), Washington, DC: American Psychological Association.

Bassman, E. S. (1992). *Abuse in the Workplace: Management Remedies and Bottom Line Impact,* Westport, CT: Quorum Books.

Boddy, C. R. P., Ladyshewsky, R., and Galvin, P. (2010). Leaders without ethics in global business: Corporate psychopaths. *Journal of Public Affairs*, 10, 121–38.

Brodsky, C. (1976). *The Harassed Worker,* Lexington, MA: D. C. Health & Co.

Cascio, W. F. (2006). The economic impact of employee behaviors on organizational performance. In E. E. I. Lawler and J. O'Toole (eds), *America at Work: Choices and Challenges* (pp. 241–56), New York: Palgrave Macmillan.

Crawford, N. (2001). Organisational responses to workplace bullying. In N. Tehrani (ed.), *Building a Culture of Respect: Managing Bullying at Work* (pp. 21–31), London: Taylor & Francis.

Crawshaw, L. (2005). Coaching abrasive executives: Exploring the use of empathy in constructing less destructive interpersonal management strategies, unpublished doctoral dissertation, Fielding Graduate University, Santa Barbara, CA.

De Vogli, R., Ferrie, J. E., Chandola, T., Kivimäki, M., and Marmot, M. G. (2007). Unfairness and health: Evidence from the Whitehall II Study. *Journal of Epidemiology and Community Health*, 61, 513–18.

DeWine, S., and James, A. C. (1988). Examining the communication audit: Assessment and modification. *Management Communication Quarterly,* 2, 144–69.

Duffy, M. K., Ganster, D. C., and Pagon, M. (2002). Social undermining in the workplace. *Academy of Management Journal,* 45, 331–51.

Einarsen, S., Höel, H., Zapf, D., and Cooper, C. L. (eds) (2010). *Workplace Bullying: Developments in Theory, Research and Practice,* London: Taylor & Francis.

Fast, N. J., and Chen, S. (2009). When the boss feels inadequate: Power, incompetence, and aggression. *Psychological Science,* 20, 1406–13.

Folger, R., and Baron, R. A. (1996). Violence and hostility at work: A model of reactions to perceived injustice. In G. R. VanderBos and E. Q. Bulatoao (eds), *Violence on the Job,* Washington, DC: American Psychological Association.

Fox, S., and Spector: (eds) (2005). *Counterproductive Work Behavior,* Washington DC: American Psychological Association.

Hoobler, J. H., and Brass, D. J. (2006). Abusive supervision and family undermining as displaced aggression. *Journal of Applied Psychology*, 91, 1125–33.

Jennifer, D., Cowie, H., and Ananiadou, K. (2003). Perceptions and experience of workplace bullying in five different working populations. *Aggressive Behavior*, 29, 489–96.

Keashly, L. (2001). Interpersonal and systemic aspects of emotional abuse at work: The target's perspective. *Violence and Victims*, 16, 233–68.

Keashly, L. (2010). From observation to engagement: Building coworker efficacy to address bullying, paper presented at the National Communication Association 96th Annual Convention, Chicago, IL, Nov.

Keashly, L., and Neuman, J. H. (2005). Bullying in the workplace: Its impact and management. *Employee Rights and Employment Policy Journal*, 8, 335–73.

Keashly, L., and Neuman, J. H. (2009). Building a constructive communication climate: The Workplace Stress and Aggression Project. In P. Lutgen-Sandvik and B. Davenport

Sypher (eds), *Destructive Organizational Communication: Processes, Consequences, and Constructive Ways of Organizing* (pp. 339–62), New York: Routledge/Taylor & Francis.

Kivimäki, M., Virtanen, M., Vartia, M., Elovainio, M., Vahtera, J., and Keltikangas-Järvinen, L. (2003). Workplace bullying and the risk of cardiovascular disease and depression. *Occupational and Environmental Medicine*, 60, 779–83.

Leymann, H. (1990). Mobbing and psychological terror at workplaces. *Violence and Victims*, 5, 119–26.

Leymann, H., and Gustafsson, A. (1996). Mobbing at work and the development of post-traumatic stress disorders. *European Journal of Work and Organizational Psychology*, 5, 251–75.

Lockhart, K. (1997). Experience from staff support service. *Journal of Community and Applied Social Psychology*, 7, 193–8.

Lutgen-Sandvik, P. (2006). Take this job and . . . : Quitting and other forms of resistance to workplace bullying. *Communication Monographs*, 73, 406–33.

Lutgen-Sandvik, P., and Fletcher, C. V. (2012). Conflict motivations and tactics of targets, bystanders, and bullies: A thrice-told tale of workplace bullying. In J. G. Oetzel and S. Ting-Toomey (eds), *Sage Handbook of Conflict Communication* (2nd edn), Thousand Oaks, CA: Sage.

Lutgen-Sandvik, P., and McDermott, V. (2008). The constitution of employee-abusive organizations: A communication flows theory. *Communication Theory*, 18, 304–33.

Lutgen-Sandvik, P., and Tracy, S. J. (2012). Answering five key questions about workplace bullying: How communication scholarship provides thought leadership for transforming abuse at work. *Management Communication Quarterly*, 26, 3–47.

Lutgen-Sandvik, P., Alberts, J. K., and Tracy, S. J. (2008). The communicative nature of workplace bullying and responses to bullying, paper presented at the Western States Communication Association Annual Convention, Denver/Boulder, CO, Feb.

Lutgen-Sandvik, P., Tracy, S. J., and Alberts, J. K. (2007). Burned by bullying in the American workplace: Prevalence, perception, degree, and impact. *Journal of Management Studies*, 44, 837–62.

MacIntosh, J. (2006). Tackling workplace bullying. *Issues in Mental Health Nursing*, 27, 665–79.

Matusewitch, E. (1996). Constructive discharge: When a resignation is really a termination. *Employment Discrimination Report*, 6, 1–5.

Mikkelsen, E. G., and Einarsen, S. (2002). Basic assumptions and post-traumatic stress among victims of bullying at work. *European Journal of Work and Organizational Psychology*, 11, 87–111.

Namie, G. (2003). The WBI 2003 report on abusive workplaces. Retrieved Oct. 2003 from www.bullyinginstitute.org.

Namie, G. (2006). *Bully Busters: Guide to Citizen Lobbying*, Bellingham, WA: Workplace Bullying Institute.

Namie, G., and Lutgen-Sandvik, P. (2010). Active and passive accomplices: The communal character of workplace bullying. *International Journal of Communication*, 4, 343–73.

Namie, G., and Namie, R. (2000). *The Bully at Work: What you Can Do to Stop the Hurt and Reclaim your Dignity on the Job*, Naperville, IL: Sourcebooks.

Olweus, D. (2003). Bully/victim problems in school: Basic facts and an effective intervention programme. In S. Einarsen, H. Höel, D. Zapf, and C. L. Cooper (eds), *Bullying and*

Emotional Abuse in the Workplace: International Perspectives in Research and Practice (pp. 62–78), London: Taylor & Francis.

Pearson, C. M. (1998). Organizations as targets and triggers of aggression and violence: Framing rational explanations for dramatic organizational deviance. *Research in the Sociology of Organizations*, 15, 197–223.

Price Spratlen, L. (1995). Interpersonal conflict which includes mistreatment in a university workplace. *Violence and Victims*, 10, 285–97.

Randall, P. (2001). *Bullying in Adulthood: Assessing the Bullies and Their Victims*, New York: Brunner-Routledge.

Rayner, C., Höel, H., and Cooper, C. L. (2002). *Workplace Bullying: What we Know, Who is to Blame, and What Can we Do?*, London: Taylor & Francis.

Richman, J. A., Rospenda, K. M., Flaherty, J. A., and Freels, S. (2001). Workplace harassment, active coping, and alcohol-related outcomes. *Journal of Substance Abuse*, 13, 347–66.

Sypher, B. D. (2004). Reclaiming civil discourse in the workplace. *Southern Communication Journal*, 69, 257–69.

Tehrani, N. (2001). A total quality approach to building a culture of respect. In N. Tehrani (ed.), *Building a Culture of Respect: Managing Bullying at Work* (pp. 135–54), London: Taylor & Francis.

Tracy, S. J., Lutgen-Sandvik, P., and Alberts, J. K. (2006). Nightmares, demons and slaves: Exploring the painful metaphors of workplace bullying. *Management Communication Quarterly*, 20, 148–85.

Vartia, M. (2001). Consequences of workplace bullying with respect to the well-being of its targets and the observers of bullying. *Scandinavian Journal of Work Environment and Health*, 27, 63–9.

Vranceanu, A.-M., Barsky, A., and Ring, D. (2009). Psychosocial aspects of disabling musculoskeletal pain. *Journal of Bone and Joint Surgery*, 91, 2014–18.

Westhues, K. (2005). *Workplace Mobbing in Academe: Reports from Twenty Universities*, Lewiston, NY: Edwin Mellen Press.

Yamada, D. (2000). The phenomenon of "workplace bullying" and the need for status-blind hostile work environment protection. *Georgetown Law Journal*, 88, 475–536.

Zapf, D., and Einarsen, S. (2003). Individual antecedents of bullying. In S. Einarsen, H. Höel, D. Zapf, and C. L. Cooper (eds), *Bullying and Emotional Abuse in the Workplace: International Perspectives in Research and Practice* (pp. 165–84), London: Taylor & Francis.

Zapf, D., and Gross, C. (2001). Conflict escalation and coping with workplace bullying: A replication and extension. *European Journal of Work and Organizational Psychology*, 10, 497–522.

Zapf, D., Einarsen, S., Höel, H., and Vartia, M. (2003). Empirical findings on bullying in the workplace. In S. Einarsen, H. Höel, D. Zapf, and C. L. Cooper (eds), *Bullying and Emotional Abuse in the Workplace: International Perspectives in Research and Practice* (pp. 103–26), London: Taylor & Francis.

Zellars, K. L., Tepper, B. J., and Duffy, M. K. (2002). Abusive supervision and subordinates' organizational citizenship behavior. *Journal of Applied Psychology*, 87, 1076–8.

Part II

Theories and Etiology

5

Schoolyard Scuffles to Conference Room Chaos: Bullying across the Lifespan

Eric Fenclau, Jr., Charles M. Albright, Laura M. Crothers, and Jered B. Kolbert
Duquesne University

INTRODUCTION

Although bullying was once considered to be a social problem unique to childhood, research conducted during the last few decades has suggested that the behaviors associated with bullying continue into adulthood. Bullying is a form of instrumental aggression, meaning that it is proactive and frequently not a response to aggressive behavior demonstrated by a victim (Espelage and Swearer, 2003). Also, a power differential exists between the perpetrator and victim, and results in the victim feeling unable to defend him or herself from the bully's aggression (Espelage and Swearer, 2003). Bullying behavior tends to be repeated over time, although in some cases, a single incident can also be seen as an instance of this type of aggression (Olweus, 1993).

As previously mentioned, although bullying has been extensively studied in childhood, less attention has been paid to adult bullying in the research literature. However, there has recently been an increased emphasis upon identifying and intervening in instances of adult bullying, particularly in the workplace. In this chapter, the authors will review the developmental progression of bullying across the lifespan with the hope that such understanding will lead to more successful prevention and intervention efforts at all age levels.

WHY A DEVELOPMENTAL PERSPECTIVE OF BULLYING IS HELPFUL IN UNDERSTANDING BULLYING IN THE WORKPLACE

Bullying has often been considered a childhood problem. Such behavior has a long history, with numerous references in classic childhood literature (e.g. Oliver Twist), and is international in both breadth and scope as it has been documented and studied in Norway, Finland, and Sweden, as well as Japan, Australia, the United Kingdom, Germany, the Netherlands, Belgium, Italy, Spain, Portugal, France, and Switzerland (Batsche, 1997; Smith and Brain, 2000). Evidence has been provided establishing the normative (routinely occurring) nature of bully–victim relationships in schools (Smith and Brain, 2000). Certainly, bullying is recognized as one of the most common and widespread forms of school violence, and involves approximately 30 percent of American students during their school careers (Nansel *et al.*, 2001). Because it has often been conceptualized as a problem of childhood and adolescence, less attention has been paid to bullying in adulthood, although research conducted in the last decade has sought to remedy that deficit by providing studies of bullying in the workplace. Nevertheless, both the theoretical and practical understanding of bullying in the workplace can be enhanced by reviewing the literature pertaining to bullying during childhood.

DEVELOPMENTAL PROGRESSION OF VERBAL AND PHYSICAL BULLYING

Indeed, bullying is a problem that may begin in childhood, but extends into adulthood. Dilts-Harryman (2004: 29) illustrates this concept by stating that "society is learning that little bullies grow into big bullies … change a few words, and the adult bully was once the young bully who sat in your classroom." Olweus (1993), the pre-eminent Norwegian bullying researcher, suggests that children who engage in direct bullying and aggressive behaviors in early childhood are likely to continue that trend into adulthood by displaying elevated levels of aggression in the workplace, in intimate relationships, and within family relationships. This sequence of direct bullying from early childhood into adulthood has distinct characteristics, which look developmentally different at various ages.

Before discussing such differences across various age populations, it is important to understand the various types of direct bullying behaviors. Episodes involving physical bullying may entail hitting, kicking, punching, pinching, slapping, destroying property (Griffin and Gross, 2004), or restraining another (Olweus, 1993). These types of behaviors are often easily observed, and tend to be reported with greater frequency than less overt forms of bullying. Moreover, physical bullying often has physiological consequences (i.e. physical injuries), which can be documented and visibly detected.

Verbal bullying is also considered to be a form of direct bullying as it often manifests itself overtly, but is observed and documented less frequently because the consequences are less evident. These behaviors involve name calling, teasing, and insults about intelligence or attractiveness (Griffin and Gross, 2004). Furthermore, researchers have found that the most common victimization involves being belittled about looks or speech (Nansel *et al.*, 2001). It is important to recognize that the descriptions presented represent a short list of possible direct bullying behaviors. Since bullies tend to choose their tactics based on their learned experiences, a wide variety of aggressive acts could be completed in order to bully others.

Regular social development follows a marked path through which all typically developing children and adults progress. When deviations or deficits occur, the individual tends to engage in age-inappropriate maladaptive behaviors in an attempt to make sense of his or her world, given his or her underdeveloped skill set (Siegler *et al.*, 2006). Typically developing children begin their maturation progression by acquiring social skills through engaging in cooperative play and developing perspective-taking abilities, permitting growth away from previous egocentric thinking (Beauchamp and Anderson, 2010; Siegler *et al.*, 2006). Moreover, these skills are practiced over time, and perfected through reinforced attempts. Thus, the development of the social skill set is directly related to a child's opportunities to interface with other children (Beauchamp and Anderson, 2010). It should be noted that physical aggression demonstrated around age 2 is considered a part of normal social development. The problem begins when children continue their successfully learned maladaptive behaviors into early childhood and beyond.

If social development deviates from the typical trajectory in early childhood, one can see elevated levels of aggression that exceed those found in normal development. These increased levels of physical aggression can manifest as a method of necessity, in an attempt to obtain or achieve whatever the child is seeking (i.e. obtaining food and toys). Troubling behaviors at this age are often ignored because they seem harmless, but if unmitigated they become a successfully learned technique. Such behavior patterns are utilized until other means of obtaining the desired results are appropriately developed. However, these behaviors tend to gradually decrease as the child ages and attains advanced language development (Alink *et al.*, 2006).

As children enter middle childhood, typically developing youth continue to utilize language as a primary method of social interaction, and decrease their levels of physical aggression (NICHD and Arsenio, 2004). Within middle childhood social development, children begin to build upon their learned language skills and start to master cognitive and social skills as a method to competently function as they enter school. This new environment creates the need to understand and adhere to rules and social norms, which enable children to interface successfully and cooperatively with their peers (Siegler *et al.*, 2006). Typically, during this developmental stage, children begin to model behaviors seen by peers and parents, and tend to incorporate the observed methods into their personal interactions with peers. This process helps children to model appropriate social interaction, but also can embed maladaptive methods to handling interpersonal conflict within a child's functioning.

Learning from parents establishes a foundation from which children interact with peers and typically carries over into adolescence and adulthood, thus determining the extent and type of aggression they will exhibit (Letendre, 2007). Moreover, when this social developmental sequence deviates from a typical trajectory, one tends to see individuals in middle childhood continuing to engage in heightened levels of physical aggression. This exhibition of direct physical aggression becomes more problematic in middle childhood because the behavior is no longer socially and developmentally acceptable. Furthermore, these maladaptive behaviors illustrate that the child cannot resolve problems appropriately, which is often associated with emotional regulation problems, conduct problems, and peer rejection (Card *et al.*, 2008).

As youth in middle childhood move into adolescence, their social development changes dramatically, typically maturing through an increase in personal independence and appropriate peer group interaction (Beauchamp and Anderson, 2010; Bowie, 2007). These behaviors are often seen through adolescents becoming more autonomous, searching for independence from their previous sources of emotional connection. Adolescents start to develop enhanced peer to peer and peer group relationships, which helps them to develop their own personal identity. Moreover, successful identity formation is related to adolescents' chosen peer groups, their understanding of social interactions, and increase in group dynamics (Siegler *et al.*, 2006).

When adolescent social development deviates from the typical trajectory, different forms of aggression begin to present themselves. If aggression was a successful method of socializing in early and middle childhood, during adolescence these methods tend to become refined and escalate if unchecked (Loeber and Hay, 1997). It is within this period of social development that forms of aggression are most distinctly divided between girls and boys (Letendre, 2007). More specifically, relational aggression is seen as more socially acceptable for females (discussed later in this chapter), and physical aggression more appropriate for males (Bowie, 2007).

To that end, at this stage of social development, girls tend to develop more interest in their relationships and interactions with others, leading to relational aggression as a method for solving problems with peers. Conversely, boys are typically goal-directed in their behavior, and maintain autonomy in their relationships, which tends to lead to more physical aggression as a method for problem solving with others (Letendre, 2007). Despite these theoretical gender differences, research has found that as adolescents age, both boys and girls tend to engage in relational aggression with similar frequency (Crothers *et al.*, 2009b). Similarly, with adolescence typically comes a decrease in physical bullying behaviors (Crothers *et al.*, 2009b).

Of course, as adolescents transition to adulthood, it is typical for them to graduate from secondary or post-secondary education to the workplace. With that change, workplace behavioral expectations and social dynamics evolve into a social hierarchy within the employment setting. A dominance hierarchy often becomes established, in which certain employees become leaders, while others assume roles that are subordinate to their peers. While perpetrators of workplace bullying may be superiors, colleagues, subordinates, or clients, bullying by superiors against subordinates is the most common form of peer aggression (71 percent; Namie, 2003a). Lutgen-Sandvik (2006: 406) suggests that "adult bullying at work is a pattern of persistent hostile discursive and nondiscursive behavior that targets perceive as efforts to harm, control or drive them from the workplace." These behaviors include "public humiliation, constant criticism, ridicule, gossip insults, and social ostracism" (Lutgen-Sandvik, 2006: 406).

Research predicts that unaddressed workplace conflict tends to lead to workplace bullying when behaviors are allowed to progress into violence and abuse (Ayoko *et al.*, 2003). Over one million individuals are the victims of violent crimes in the workplace each year, with 60 percent of these crimes being characterized as simple assault by the Department of Justice (Randall, 1998). With regard to the violent crimes in the workplace, 75 percent were fistfights or similar altercations; 17 percent were shootings; 8 percent were stabbings; and 6 percent were sexual assaults (Randall, 1998). Additionally, of the 54 percent of the incidents perpetrated by one employee against another, 13 percent were an employee against a manager; and 7 percent were incidents of customer workplace bullying. Understandably, targets of workplace bullying often anticipate the workday with dread and a sense of impending doom (Lutgen-Sandvik *et al.*, 2007). Victims of workplace bullying tend to feel profoundly ashamed of being victimized and often are upset with their inability to fight back and protect themselves (Lutgen-Sandvik *et al.*, 2007). In summary, given the prevalence of physical and verbal workplace bullying, and its significant emotional, physical, and psychological impact upon victims, intervention is imperative to ensure a safe working environment for all employees.

DEVELOPMENTAL PROGRESSION OF RELATIONAL AND SOCIAL AGGRESSION

In the workplace, like in most society, direct aggression is not typically tolerated. At an early age, children are taught that it is unacceptable to be physically aggressive, learning instead to express frustrations verbally. By elementary school, children are socialized against demonstrating verbal aggression as well. While first parental and then societal boundaries suppress most directly aggressive behaviors, such limits do not necessarily assuage the anger and frustration that can lead to directly aggressive acts (Coie and Dodge, 1998). This can cause aggressive behaviors to become covert, with the perpetrator using means that cannot immediately be identified as aggressive. Researchers speculate that this is how indirect aggression is initially developed.

Non-physical forms of aggression have primarily been given three different names: indirect aggression, relational, and social aggression. Although some debate exists regarding actual differences between indirect, relational, and social aggression (Archer and Coyne, 2005), we will discuss relational and social aggression as related but separate constructs given that Crothers *et al.* (2009b) found support for such a viewpoint.

Relationally aggressive acts are defined by their specific intent: they are directed at another individual with whom one has an existing relationship with the specific aim of causing psychological harm to that person or negatively impacting the target's social status. Relational aggression may be overt or covert and includes gossip, cruel rumors, or physically excluding another among others. The focus of the perpetrator in relational aggression is to establish power or inflict harm within a dyadic relationship. Within a female friendship, for example, an individual may wish to register her displeasure with her friend by excluding her from a social interaction, avoiding her, threatening to end the relationship, insulting her personal appearance or qualities that the perpetrator is aware of as a result of the intimacy of the relationship, initiating seemingly helpful behavior of which the purpose is to undermine the target's self-confidence (e.g. volunteer to take the target shopping to update the target's wardrobe), insulting persons who are important to the target, or withdrawing or failing to follow through on previously agreed forms of support.

In social aggression, the focus of the aggressor is to impact social status, either by diminishing the target's status, or enhancing one's own status. Behaviors that might be used to decrease the status of a victim include sharing intimate information about the target, spreading false information about the target such as questioning sexual behavior or sexual orientation, excluding the target from group interactions (e.g. social ostracizing), and organizing a group's response or view of the target. In the case of a perpetrator attempting to elevate his or her status among peers, social aggression is manifested by pursuing eminence by undermining others, engaging in deception, or pursuing power in a manner that harms another person. For example, a perpetrator may reveal intimate information about a victim in order to gain favor with peers, pursuing or stealing a coveted friend or boyfriend, and taking out the competition by belittling their qualities or undermining their qualities to better one's own achievement.

While the capacity for relational and social aggression involves a sophisticated set of social skills and cognitive complexity, there is research suggesting that relational aggression can begin early in a child's life. Generally, relational and social aggression are more likely to occur as children develop the verbal and social-cognitive skills that are necessary to execute subtle social behaviors (Björkqvist, 1994). These skills rely upon the development of language skills as well as the ability to ease away from the egocentric thought that is typical of early childhood. These developments allow the child not only to have the language skills necessary to manipulate a relationship socially, but also to have the ability to see a situation from another child's perspective, thus being able to predict potential outcomes of their behavior and understand what is likely to bother others.

These skills are likely to develop in early childhood and can lead to the development of such relationally aggressive behaviors as a child threatening to end a friendship if a friend does not do what the child wants, not inviting a child to a party, threatening to exclude a child if he or she does not do what the child wants, or refusing to listen to someone with whom he or she is angry (at this young age, perhaps even literally covering their ears; Archer and Coyne, 2005). Children learn how to execute new behaviors from observing the behaviors of those who are older than they are (Bandura, 1986). Thus, it is likely that these children are learning relationally aggressive behaviors by copying social behaviors that they observe their parents and siblings using. This provides an explanation as to how these indirectly aggressive tactics are learned by young children and also how they are perpetuated across generations.

As children move into early adolescence, their cognitive and language skills as well as social skills develop to a point where relational aggression is used with greater sophistication. It is also a period when children attempt to minimize parental influence and instead use their peers as their primary reference group (Siegler *et al.*, 2006). The intersection of these two developmental trends is a reason why early adolescence is a period in which relationally aggressive tactics flourish. Children begin to have more independence and start to engage in more adult-like social interactions. For example, they will begin to go to the mall or parties and interact with other children in situations that are not directly supervised by adults. It is during such occasions that some children begin to use their growing social repertoires to manipulate social relationships.

There is less research regarding social aggression in comparison to physical and verbal bullying, but it can be argued that adolescents' acquisition of abstract reasoning leads to the emerging capacity of social aggression. Crothers *et al.* (in press) found that there was a stronger relationship between deep and elaborative processing for social aggression than there was for relational aggression among late adolescents. Crothers *et al.* (in press) suggest that social aggression may require a higher level of cognitive-analytical abilities than relational aggression. For example, strategic social aggression often requires that a perpetrator know how to manipulate peers into targeting an individual for social isolation. This process requires the perpetrator to know what will motivate others to socially "cut off" from a target, even if tension or conflict does not currently exist between the peers and the target.

Additionally, perspective-taking is generally seen as an essential capacity for both relational and social aggression. The relational aggressor must understand the psychological worldview of the intended target to know what is likely to negatively impact the victim emotionally. Similarly, the social aggressor must attempt to understand the perspectives of the members of the peer group in order to estimate their likely responses. However, there are forms of relational aggression that do not appear to require an extremely high level of cognitive complexity, including criticizing others, threatening to end a relationship in order to obtain compliance from the target, using the silent treatment, and intentionally excluding others. In contrast, socially aggressive tactics such as gossiping, spreading rumors, backbiting, breaking confidences, criticizing behind another's back, ignoring, or deliberately excluding others from a group, may require added sophistication in that the perpetrator seeks to predict the responses of multiple members of the social setting.

The social milieu of children in early adolescence can also serve to foster the growth and expansion of relationally and socially aggressive behaviors. Girls at this age often have closer and more structured social relationships than do boys (Mazur, 1989). Adolescent girls are also typically more adept at identifying social groups, as opposed to boys who tend to have larger and looser groups (Cairns *et al.*, 1985). Having more investment in a social relationship will increase the likelihood that relational aggression will be a useful tool to manipulate others for personal gain. If these behaviors are reinforced socially through increased notoriety or status in the social group, then they likely will continue to be utilized.

Another developmental factor that leads to an increase of relationally aggressive behaviors in adolescence is language skills. It has been established that the development of relationally and socially aggressive behavior is related to the growing sophistication of language skills (Bowie, 2007). A child who is going to manipulate a relationship in an aggressive way will need strong verbal skills to be successful. Girls tend to develop verbal skills earlier than boys, so when taken into consideration with the aforementioned differences in social structure, it is not surprising that in adolescence girls tend to utilize relational aggression more than boys (Salmivalli *et al.*, 2000). Eventually males' verbal skills do catch up with females', and not surprisingly there is evidence to suggest that by adulthood males utilize relationally aggressive behaviors as often as females (Archer and Coyne, 2005; Björkqvist *et al.*, 1992).

As children grow from adolescents to adults, the behaviors that they practice grow as well. If those relationally and socially aggressive behaviors that were born on the playground were perceived as being successful in meeting the child's goals, then he or she is likely to continue to use these tactics to meet his or her objectives. Adult relational and social aggression can take on many forms. Some relationally aggressive behaviors that adults may use include: influencing others by making them feel guilty, pretending to be hurt to make others feel bad, stealing a romantic partner, withdrawing attention from a relationship, threatening to end a relationship if the other person does not comply with the person's wishes, using infidelity as revenge, and flirting with another person to make a partner jealous (Archer and Coyne, 2005; Crothers *et al.*, 2009a). Socially aggressive behaviors used by adults may include questioning a target's competency, undermining a target's alliances by questioning his or her loyalty, inflating one's virtues in comparison to the target's, etc.

For many, the workplace provides the most important social setting in the adult world, and with the high stakes atmosphere of many companies and industries, it is not surprising that relational aggression is manifested in the workplace as office bullying. Although there are cases of violence in the workplace, direct aggression typically is not tolerated in the adult employment setting. However, the naturally competitive and often frustrating nature of the office can create an environment that can easily reinforce relationally and socially aggressive behavior. Harvey *et al.* (2006)

explain that there are a number of environmental factors that lead to an increased probability that office bullying will take place. Among other factors, Harvey *et al.* (2006) stress that the growing pressure of the pace of the work day, increased office diversity, decreased office supervision, a sink or swim mentality, and threats of downsizing can all create the type of tense work environment that can foster and reinforce relationally aggressive behavior. Once such an environment is prevalent, it will likely continue to reward those who use aggressive tactics and bullying will become the rule, not the exception.

CONSEQUENCES OF OFFICE BULLYING

Workplace bullying is becoming a worldwide problem. Perpetration happens at all levels, and in many different workplace arenas, making it difficult to manage, and absenteeism is the most common outcome of workplace bullying. Harbison (2004) concluded that a company with 1,000 employees could save $720,000 annually just by reducing its absence rate from 3 percent to 2 percent. To further speak to the reasoning behind the heightened level of absenteeism, Duffy and Sperry (2007: 401) state that employees leave their workplace after being bullied often "feeling dead, wanting to be dead, feeling invisible, and abandoned." Short-term consequences of workplace bullying can result in heightened levels of anxiety, depression, irritation, physiological symptoms (Dilts-Harryman, 2004; Tracy *et al.*, 2006), decreased self-esteem and self-confidence (Einarsen, 2000; Randle, 2003), and damaged interpersonal and familial relationships (Rayner *et al.*, 2002; Tracy *et al.*, 2006).

While the short-term consequences are often the most apparent, long-term consequences are also a major concern. Research suggests that individuals who suffer pervasive workplace bullying can also experience long-term, sometimes permanent psychological and occupational impairment (Crawford, 2001), depression (Bilgel *et al.*, 2006; Namie, 2003b), prolonged stress (Dilts-Harryman, 2004), alcohol abuse (Richman *et al.*, 2001; Rospenda, 2002), post-traumatic stress disorder (Bilgel *et al.*, 2006; Fox and Stallworth, 2005; Leymann and Gustafsson, 1996), and even suicidal behavior (Leymann, 1990; Leymann and Gustafsson,

1996). Moreover, recent medical research suggests that recurrent episodes of workplace bullying can result in chronic stress, high blood pressure, increased risk of coronary heart disease (Kivimäki *et al.*, 2005), and other chronic diseases such as asthma, rheumatoid arthritis, osteoarthritis, sciatica, diabetes, or cardiovascular disease (Kivimäki *et al.*, 2003). While there are numerous individual consequences of workplace bullying, the effects on the work environment can be just as profound. Harvey *et al.* (2006) state that workplace bullying can lead to reduced flexibility, difficulty in implementing organizational change, and a diminishment in organizational commitment. These effects not only create a harmful environment for employees, but contribute to a static, inefficient workplace that can stifle organizational success.

CONCLUSION AND SUMMARY

Adults who bully others in the workplace are likely to have engaged in bullying in childhood and adolescence, although there are expected differences in the form and sophistication of aggression used by adults. A developmental perspective may provide managers with insight regarding the level of functioning of the adult perpetrator of bullying. An employee's use of rather unsophisticated forms of aggression is more typically associated with the aggressive behaviors of childhood, namely physical and verbal aggression. Such forms of aggression may be indicative of personality issues which are not likely to be readily addressed by typical managerial interventions such as increased supervision or alterations in incentives, and would instead require intensive psychotherapy. The developmental perspective of bullying provided also implies that managers may seek to focus upon those forms of workplace bullying which predominate among adults, specifically relational and social aggression.

Although possibly idealistic and outside the purview of the workplace environment, it can be argued that management should proactively seek to assist employees to develop more mature forms of interpersonal relations, since, as discussed in the chapter, such aggression impacts workers' productivity and the organizational structure of the business or company. An increased understanding of the more subtle and indirect forms of aggression typically used by adults can also help management decrease the degree of such forms of aggression that are used between employees and are part of either the explicit and implicit patterns and rules of the organization.

A developmental perspective of workplace bullying suggests that companies must use a proactive, comprehensive, and long-term approach to reduce such aggression and provide an environment that helps workers to learn more mature ways of relating to work colleagues. A developmental understanding of bullying proposes that such behaviors are an inherent part of human relations, and only through the combined efforts of the family and school environments do children gradually learn to relinquish overt and physical forms of aggression. However, during adolescence and early adulthood, aggression tends to become more subtle and indirect. The workplace environment may be seen as an extension of the family's and school's efforts to assist people in developing more principled ways for achieving personal status, while simultaneously benefitting the needs of the company and resolving conflicts.

The workplace environment can help employees by adopting policies prohibiting the use of social and relational aggression, providing specific instruction and modeling of expected forms of relating, and by fostering an environment that encourages employees to non-defensively reflect upon their tendencies and motivations for using aggression. The developmental perspective of bullying provided in this chapter implies that aggression is an inherent aspect of human relations, and that aggression is often functional, meaning that it offers advantages to the perpetrator. Given this information, it is likely that bullying behavior can only be modified slowly, with significant environmental support and reinforcement.

REFERENCES

Alink, L. R. A., Mesman, J., van Zeijl, J., Stolk, M. N., Juffer, F., Koot, H. M., van Jzendoorn, I. (2006). The early childhood aggression curve: Development of physical aggression in 10- to 50-month-old children. *Child Development*, 77, 954–66.

Archer, J., and Coyne, S. (2005). An integrated review of indirect, relational, and social aggression. *Personality and Social Psychology Review*, 9, 212–30.

Ayoko, O.B., Callan, V. J., and Hartel, C. L. (2003). Workplace conflict, bullying and counterproductive behaviors. *International Journal of Organizational Analysis*, 11, 283–301.

Bandura, A. (1986). *Social Foundations of Thought and Action: A Social Cognitive Theory*, Englewood Cliffs, NJ: Prentice-Hall.

Batsche, G. M. (1997). Bullying. In G. G. Bear, K. M. Minke, and A. Thomas (eds), *Children's Needs II: Development, Problems, and Alternatives* (pp. 171–9), Bethesda, MD: National Association of School Psychologists.

Beauchamp, M. H., and Anderson, V. (2010). SOCIAL: An integrative framework for the development of social skills. *Psychology Bulletin*, 136, 39–64.

Bilgel, N., Aytac, S., and Bayram, N. (2006). Bullying in Turkish white-collar workers. *Occupational Medicine*, 56, 226–31.

Björkqvist, K. (1994). Sex differences in physical, verbal, and indirect aggression: A review of recent research. *Sex Roles*, 30, 177–88.

Björkqvist, K., Lagerspetz, K., and Kaukiainen, A. (1992a). Do girls manipulate and boys fight? Developmental trends in regard to direct and indirect aggression. *Aggressive Behavior*, 18, 117–27.

Björkqvist, K., Österman, K., and Kaukiainen, A. (1992b). The development of direct and indirect aggressive strategies in males and females. In K. Björkqvist and P. Niemelä (eds), *Of Mice and Women: Aspects of Female Aggression* (pp. 51–64), San Diego, CA: Academic Press.

Bowie, B. H. (2007). Relational aggression, gender, and the developmental process. *Journal of Child and Adolescent Psychiatric Nursing*, 20, 107–15.

Cairns, R. B., Perrin, J. E., and Cairns, B. D. (1985). Social structure and social cognition in early adolescence: Affiliative patterns. *Journal of Early Adolescence*, 5, 339–55.

Card, N. A., Stucky, B. D., Sawalani, G. M., and Little, T. D. (2008). Direct and indirect aggression during childhood and adolescence: A meta-analytic review of gender differences, intercorrelations, and relations to maladjustment. *Child Development*, 79, 1185–1229.

Coie, J. D., and Dodge, K. A. (1998). Aggression and antisocial behavior. In N. Eisenberg (ed.), *Handbook of Child Psychology* (5th edn, vol. 3, pp. 779–862), New York: Wiley.

Crawford, N. (2001). Organizational responses to workplace bullying. In N. Tehrani (ed.), *Building a Culture of Respect: Managing Bullying at Work* (pp. 21–31), London: Taylor & Francis.

Crothers, L. M., Lipinski, J., and Minutolo, M. C. (2009a). Cliques, rumors, and gossip by the water cooler: Female bullying in the workplace. *Psychologist-Manager Journal*, 12, 97–110.

Crothers, L. M., Schreiber, J. B., Field, J. E., and Kolbert, J. B. (2009b). Development and measurement through confirmatory factor analysis of the Young Adult Social Behavior Scale (YASB): An assessment of relational aggression in adolescence and young adulthood. *Journal of Psychoeducational Assessment*, 27, 17–28.

Crothers, L. M., Kolbert, J. B., Kanyongo, G. Y., Field, J. E., and Schmitt, A. J. (in press). Cognitive processing styles and relational aggression. *Journal of Aggression, Maltreatment, and Trauma.*

Dilts-Harryman, S. (2004). When bullies grow up. *ASCA School Counselor*, 42, 28–32.

Duffy, M., and Sperry, L. (2007). Workplace mobbing: Individual and family health consequences. *Family Journal*, 15, 398–404.

Einarsen, S. (2000). Harassment and bullying at work: A review of the Scandinavian approach. *Aggression and Violent Behavior*, 5, 379–401.

Espelage, D. L., and Swearer, S. M. (2003). Research on school bullying and victimization: What have we learned and where do we go from here? *School Psychology Review*, 32, 365–83.

Fox, S., and Stallworth, L. E. (2005). Racial/ethnic bullying: Exploring links between bullying and racism in the US workplace. *Journal of Vocational Behavior*, 66, 438–56.

Griffin, R. S., and Gross, A. M. (2004). Childhood bullying: Current empirical findings and future direction for research. *Aggression and Violent Behavior*, 9, 389–400.

Harbison, G. (2004). FMLA is serious business. *Industrial Management*, 46, 28–31.

Harvey, M. G., Heames, J. T., Richey, R. G., and Leonard, N. (2006). Bullying: From the playground to the boardroom. *Journal of Leadership and Organizational Studies*, 12, 1–11.

Kivimäki, M., Virtanen, M., Vartia, M., Elovainio, M., Vahtera, J., and Keltikangas-Järvinen, L. (2003). Workplace bullying and the risk of cardiovascular disease and depression. *Occupational Environment Medicine*, 60, 779–83.

Kivimäki, M., Ferrie, J. E., Brunner, E., Head, J., Shipley, M. J., Vahtera, J., and Marmot, M. G. (2005). Justice at work and reduced risk of coronary heart disease among employees. *Archives of Internal Medicine*, 165, 2245–51.

Letendre, J. (2007). "Sugar and spice but not always nice": Gender socialization and its impact on development and maintenance of aggression in adolescent girls. *Child and Adolescent Social Work Journal*, 24, 353–68.

Leymann, H. (1990). Mobbing and psychological terror at workplaces. *Violence and Victims*, 5, 119–26.

Leymann, H., and Gustafsson, A. (1996). Mobbing at work and the development of post-traumatic stress disorders. *European Journal of Work and Organizational Psychology*, 5, 251–75.

Loeber, R., and Hay, D. (1997). Key issues in the development of aggression and violence from childhood to early adulthood. *Annual Review of Psychology*, 48, 371.

Lutgen-Sandvik, P. (2006). Take this job and . . . : Quitting and other forms of resistance to workplace bullying. *Communication Monographs*, 73, 406–33.

Lutgen-Sandvik, P., Tracy, S. J., and Alberts, J. K. (2007). Burned by bullying in the American workplace: Prevalence, perception, degree and impact. *Journal of Management Studies*, 44, 837–62.

Mazur, E. (1989). Predicting gender differences in same-sex friendships from affiliation motive and value. *Psychology of Women Quarterly*, 13, 277–91.

Namie, G. (2003a). Workplace bullying: Escalated incivility. *Ivey Business Journal*, 68, 1–6.

Namie, G. (2003b). The WBTI 2003 report on abusive workplaces. Retrieved from http://www.bullyinginstitute.org.

Nansel, T. R., Overpeck, M., Pilla, R. S., Ruan, W., Simons-Morton, B., and Scheidt, P. (2001). Bullying behaviors among US youth: Prevalence and association with psychosocial adjustment. *Journal of the American Medical Association*, 285, 2094–2100.

NICHD Early Child Care Research Network, and Arsenio, W. F. (2004). Trajectories of physical aggression from toddlerhood to middle childhood: Predictors, correlates, and outcomes. *Monographs of the Society for Research in Child Development*, 69, 1–143.

Olweus, D. (1993). *Bullying at School: What we Know and What we Can Do*, Oxford: Blackwell.

Randall, P. (1998). *Adult Bullying: Perpetrators and Victims,* London: Routledge.

Randle, J. (2003). Bullying in the nursing profession. *Journal of Advanced Nursing,* 43, 395–401.

Rayner, C., Höel, H., and Cooper, C. L. (2002). *Workplace Bullying: What we Know, Who is to Blame, and What Can we Do?,* New York: Taylor & Francis.

Richman, J. A., Rospenda, K. M., Flaherty, J. A., and Freels, S. (2001). Workplace harassment, active coping, and alcohol-related outcomes. *Journal of Substance Abuse,* 13, 347–66.

Rospenda, K. (2002). Workplace harassment, services utilization, and drinking outcomes. *Journal of Occupational Health Psychology,* 7, 141–55.

Salmivalli, C., Kaukiainen, A., and Lagerspetz, K. (2000). Aggression and sociometric status among peers: Do gender and type of aggression matter? *Scandinavian Journal of Psychology,* 41, 17–24.

Siegler, R., Deloache, J., and Eisenberg, N. (2006). *How Children Develop* (2nd edn), New York: Worth Publishers.

Smith, K., and Brain, P. (2000). Bullying in schools: Lessons from two decades of research. *Aggressive Behavior,* 26, 1–9.

Tracy, S. J., Lutgen-Sandvik, P., and Alberts, J. K. (2006). Nightmares, demons, and slaves: Exploring the painful metaphors of workplace bullying. *Management Communication Quarterly, 20,* 148–85.

6

Evolutionary Psychological Models for Predicting Bullying and Implications for Intervention

Jered B. Kolbert, Laura M. Crothers, and Daniel S. Wells
Duquesne University

INTRODUCTION

In comparison to the extensive study of childhood bullying conducted within the last few decades, the investigation of such behavior in the workplace has been less thorough, as many of the studies to date have simply focused upon the correlates and consequences of perpetration and victimization. In fact, there have been only a few publications that have presented broad theoretical frameworks for understanding workplace bullying. In one such article, White (2004) presented a psychodynamic explanation for workplace bullying, suggesting that perpetrators and victims often unconsciously manage their anxieties through the dynamics of a bully–victim relationship.

In contrast, researchers of childhood bullying have largely conceptualized the issue utilizing social learning theories, in which perpetrators are believed to acquire bullying behaviors through operant and vicarious conditioning mechanisms. Children who bully are believed to be both positively and negatively reinforced for their behavior by virtue of attaining their goals (positive reinforcement), and by the removal of threats to their power (negative reinforcement; Batsche and Knoff, 1994). Similarly, Slaby and Guerra (1988) proposed a social-cognitive model of aggression in which the aggression-supporting beliefs that perpetrators often hold may encourage their bullying behavior.

However, researchers who endorse models such as social learning theory often do not acknowledge that there may be a biological predisposition to such aggressive behavior that is maintained and reinforced through social systems. Therefore, the purpose of this chapter is to conceptualize the phenomenon of workplace bullying from an alternative framework, that of evolutionary psychology, and discuss implications for intervention from this perspective.

SIGNIFICANCE

The rationale of utilizing an evolutionary psychological perspective to understand workplace bullying in part stems from a need to explore the deep-seated motivations that contribute to the development of the behavior of aggression toward peers. Bullying has been shown to persist across time, as it was discussed in literature as early as the 18th and 19th centuries (Koo, 2007), and across nationalities and cultures, as it has been studied in countries such as Norway, Finland, and Sweden, as well as Japan, Australia, the United Kingdom, Germany, the Netherlands, Belgium, Italy, Spain, Portugal, France, and Switzerland (Batsche, 1997; Smith and Brain, 2000). This persistence and breadth of impact indicates that bullying may be viewed as an inextricable part of human nature. There is research that suggests that individuals have a variety of motivations that contribute to the expression of bullying behavior, and that while there is evidence that it is a learned behavior (e.g. Batsche and Knoff, 1994), there is also empirical support for the adaptive nature of aggression demonstrated against peers (Axelrod, 1984).

RELEVANT THEORY

Evolutionary psychology applies Charles Darwin's evolutionary theory to understand human behavior (Costello and Angold, 2000). Darwin (1859) proposed two revolutionary principles: (1) that species are in constant process of adaptation, which occurs through reproduction, and (2) that the success of such reproduction is driven by natural selection. Darwin supported Thomas Malthus's finding that populations increase exponentially but that their numbers are constrained by environmental conditions, such as the availability of food, the dangers of disease, etc. Sexual reproduction provides the subsequent generation with a combination of characteristics that have been successful for the previous generation and new characteristics that may be advantageous for surviving a changing environment.

Characteristics of species are referred to as "naturally selected" because the organisms that are more "fit" for the environment are able to survive and reproduce, passing on a greater proportion of their genetic material to the next generation. Through the repetition of this process, certain traits become more prevalent in the species, whereas less successful traits are eventually extinguished. The driving force behind the theory of evolutionary psychology is that the genes that influence our behavior were selected to be adaptive for human beings in contexts that existed long ago. Thus, to understand our current behavior, we must recognize that our behavioral tendencies were designed for the altogether different environment of our ancestors (Malik, 1996).

Evolutionary psychologists assert that common forms of behavior exist because they have provided some competitive advantage, either in terms intra-species or inter-species competition. Research indicates that all species use both cooperation and aggression (Axelrod, 1984). The adaptive value of inter-species aggression is readily evident, providing access to resources and defense against predators. Evolutionary theorists have suggested that the potential advantages of intra-species aggression include obtaining the resources of others, establishing a reputation that deters others from attacking, enhancing social status, preventing romantic partners from infidelity, pursuing new mates, or reconnecting with former mates (Buss, 2009; Campbell, 1995; Duntley and Shackelford, 2008; Smith, 2007). However, intra-species aggression is also potentially non-adaptive since it may result in death or injury to members of one's species, thus threatening their survival and reproduction (Sagan and Druyan, 1993).

Evolutionary psychologists, such as Sagan and Druyan (1993), suggest that highly cooperative species have evolved dominance hierarchies in which a "pecking order" exists among group members in order to limit the negative effects of aggression. Dominance may be considered a form of aggression, but is a type of behavior which has a more specific intent. Aggression has traditionally been defined as behavior intended to harm another individual (Archer, 2009), whereas the purpose of dominance behaviors is to increase the social status of the perpetrator, or decrease the social status of the intended target (Mazur, 1994). We propose that perpetrators of workplace bullying may be motivated by a desire for dominance, meaning that bullies want to enhance their social status at the expense of others. Social status, regardless of how it is gained, whether through an individual's merit or by other means, is likely to yield tangible benefits (e.g. higher salary, promotions, preferential work assignments, the admiration of peers) for those with higher status.

SALIENT FEATURES

The prevalence of bullying among adults in the workplace suggests that this form of aggression among adults must offer adaptive advantages. Workplace bullying appears to be widespread (Beale, 2001). A survey of Australians revealed that 74 percent of respondents reported being bullied at work (CareerOne, 2007), and a survey of Americans found that 49 percent of working people reported being victimized directly or having witnessed bullying in the workplace (Namie, 2007).

Taxonomy of Workplace Bullying

The establishment of dominance may be a function of the most common types of workplace bullying. Escartin *et al.*'s (2010) taxonomy of workplace bullying, which is one of the few models to enjoy empirical support, is comprised of six different categories: (1) isolation, (2) control and manipulation of information, (3) abusive working conditions, (4) emotional abuse, (5) professional discredit and denigration, and (6) devaluation of the professional role. While the first two categories are readily identifiable, abusive working conditions are defined as modifications in the work environment or conditions that prevent the employees from fulfilling their responsibilities or put their health at risk. Emotional abuse involves more person-oriented acts, such as criticisms about the victim's personal life and beliefs. Professional discredit and denigration of the target's professional reputation and standing typically involve attacking the employee's knowledge, experience, effort, or performance. Finally, devaluation of the professional role involves belittling the importance of the role of the employee, unjustifiably altering the employee's responsibilities, or assigning the employee responsibilities that are non-essential, unrealistic, or beneath his or her position. It is readily evident how each of these forms of workplace bullying could be used to decrease the social status of the employee.

Social Status of Workplace Bullies

There is scant research regarding the relationship between workplace bullying and social status. However, research with adolescent populations appears to support the contention that some perpetrators of bullying are motivated by dominance. Crick and Dodge's (1994) social information processing framework is probably the most commonly used theory for understanding childhood perpetrators of bullying. They proposed that chronic aggression, including bullying, is the result of consistently misperceiving ambiguous social cues on the part of the aggressor. For example, Coie *et al.* (1991) found that aggressive children, including bullies, tend to have a hostile attribution bias, meaning that they inaccurately believe that other children are responding aggressively toward them. However, Sutton *et al.* (1999) proposed an alternative theory, suggesting that perpetrators of bullying are not necessarily deficient processors of information; rather, they purposely intend to change the structure of group relationships to enhance their power. Sutton *et al.* (1999) argued that at least some perpetrators of bullying are socially intelligent and have superior theory of mind skills that they use to predict and anticipate the behavior of victims and the members of the peer group.

Initial studies indicated that childhood bullying was associated with peer rejection (e.g. Pellegrini *et al.*, 1999). However, more recent studies have found that childhood perpetrators of bullying can be disliked but also be regarded as popular by their peers (e.g. Caravita *et al.*, 2008; Cillessen and Rose, 2005; Farmer *et al.*, 2003). Estell *et al.* (2007) noted that childhood perpetrators of bullying were disliked by their peers or socially controversial, meaning that they were liked by some peers and disliked by other peers, but were perceived to be central members of the peer group.

Peeters *et al.* (2010) provide evidence that early adolescent perpetrators of bullying were a heterogeneous group, comprised of three bully subtypes for both boys and girls: a popular socially intelligent group, a popular moderate group, and an unpopular less-socially-intelligent group. These researchers also found that the high social status was associated with social intelligence and the use of relational aggression. Peeters *et al.* (2010) hypothesized that perpetrators of bullying have varying motives, with the popular, socially intelligent bullies using their skills and centrality within the group to manipulate others to ostracize the victim, thus enhancing the perpetrator's dominance. Interestingly, the results revealed that male bullies who were unpopular and lacking in social intelligence were also highly relationally aggressive, which contradicts other studies that have identified a positive relationship between relational aggression and social intelligence (e.g. Salmivalli *et al.*, 2000). As an explanation, Peeters *et al.* (2010) offers the results of a study conducted by Xie *et al.* (2002), who found that relational and social aggression were seen as different constructs by early adolescent participants. Social aggression was defined as covert aggressive attacks, including gossiping, while relational aggression involved more overt attacks, such as excluding others or ignoring. Early adolescent participants in Xie *et al.*'s study (2002) perceived social aggression to be more damaging, while relational aggression was viewed by these individuals as reactive to other forms of aggression.

Relational and Social Aggression and Workplace Bullying

There has been controversy regarding the definition and characteristics of relational aggression. Although Archer and Coyne (2005) concluded from a review of literature that indirect, relational, and social aggression are more alike than they are different, Crothers *et al.* (2009) found evidence suggesting that relational and social aggression are related but distinct constructs. Archer and Coyne (2005) believed that a primary difference between relational and social aggression is the intended motivation of the aggressor. In using relational aggression, the aggressor wants to obtain power within a dyadic relationship, whereas the motivation of the aggressor who uses social aggression is to reduce the social status of the intended victim within the social context.

Crothers *et al.* (in press) found that among college students there was an incredibly strong relationship between both relational and social aggression and two cognitive-analytic abilities, deep and elaborative processing, but that the relationship between social aggression and elaborative and deep processing was stronger than it was for relational aggression. It is possible that social aggression requires a higher level of cognitive-analytical abilities than relational aggression. For example, strategic social aggression often requires that a perpetrator know how to manipulate peers to target an individual for social isolation. This process requires the perpetrator to know what will motivate others to socially "cut off" a target from social interaction, even if tension or conflict does not currently exist between the peers and the target.

Additionally, perspective-taking is generally seen as an essential capacity for both relational and social aggression. The relational aggressor must understand the psychological worldview of the intended target to know what is likely to impact the victim emotionally, and the social aggressor must attempt to understand the perspectives of the members of the peer group in order to estimate their likely responses. However, there are forms of relational aggression that do not appear to require an extremely high level of cognitive complexity. For example, the definition of relational aggression included criticizing others, threatening to end a relationship in order to obtain compliance from the target, using the silent treatment, and intentionally excluding others. In contrast, social aggression refers to aggressive acts that are intended to impact both the intended target and the larger peer group.

It is important for organizations to differentiate between relational and social aggression, given that physical forms of bullying are rare compared to nonphysical forms of aggression (Keashly, 2001; Neuman and Baron, 1998). Most of the forms of workplace bullying in Escartin *et al.*'s (2010) taxonomy would appear to be types of social aggression. The primary function of isolation, control and manipulation of information, professional discredit and denigration, and devaluation of the professional role most likely is to reduce the social status of the intended victim. Emotional abuse is the only form of workplace bullying in Escartin *et al.*'s taxonomy that would seem to be more highly associated with the function of relational aggression, which is to obtain power within a dyadic relationship. Furthermore, it may be hypothesized that social aggression is even more prevalent among adults who are more likely to have acquired the social intelligence required for social aggression in comparison to youth. If social aggression is, in fact, more prevalent than relational aggression among adults, it can be argued that dominance is one of the primary motivators among adults who commit bullying in the workplace environment.

In further differentiating these related constructs, Peeters *et al.* (2010) suggest that relational aggression may serve a different function than social aggression. As mentioned earlier, Xie *et al.* (2002) found that early adolescents perceived relational aggression to be reactive in nature, and Peeters *et al.* (2010) revealed that unpopular male bullies lacking in social intelligence were more likely to use relational aggression. These results support Crick and Dodge's (1994) hypothesis that perpetrators of bullying have one or more deficiencies in social cognitive processing, and respond aggressively to peers due to misperceptions of social interactions.

The Adaptive Functions of Workplace Bullying

We believe that evolutionary theory implies that workplace bullying may serve two main adaptive functions. The bullying of horizontal competitors is primarily intended to communicate to the individual competitor, "Do not challenge me, I have more power than you," and this form of bullying may be more likely to be used when a perpetrator is first attempting to establish his or her position in the dominance hierarchy, or when the perpetrator perceives that his or her status is being threatened by a rival. It has been suggested that such "horizontal bullying" may occur when the perpetrator perceives the victim as threatening his or her sense of superiority (Yamada, 2000), makes the perpetrator feel vulnerable (Namie and Namie, 2000), or is likely to occur in very competitive, pressure-intense work environments (Roscigno *et al.*, 2009).

In contrast, the bullying of subordinates is intended to communicate to the group as a whole, "No one should challenge me, I am powerful;" thus, serving a maintenance function to indicate one's level of power within the organization. Roscigno *et al.* (2009) concluded from a review of the literature that victims of workplace bullying typically have less power than the perpetrator. Indeed, they found that minority and female workers were the most vulnerable to bullying, while Hodson *et al.* (2006) observed that vulnerability to bullying was associated with low job security, low-end service work, and minority status.

RECOMMENDATIONS

Dominance can be defined as the attempt to increase one's social status, or undermine the social status of a rival, through the use of aggression. We argue that bullying is a type of dominance-oriented behavior, and as discussed earlier, among adolescents, may be associated with being disliked, but it may also result in enhanced social status (e.g. Peeters *et al.*, 2010). Despite the potential risks to the popularity of perpetrators, workplace bullying appears to pose considerable threats to employees' health and well-being (Hogh *et al.*, 2011), damages organizations (e.g. Tracy *et al.*, 2006), and negatively affects financial profit (e.g. Johnson and Indvik, 2001). Thus, there are undesirable consequences of workplace bullying to perpetrators, victims, as well as the company or the organization.

Use of Eminence-Oriented Strategies

Based upon these findings, organizations are encouraged to incorporate the concept of eminence when establishing expectations of employee behavior. Eminence is defined as the acquisition of elevated rank through the use of socially valued and approved accomplishments (Kemper, 1990). Eminence requires the use of a social power base, in which an individual is able to change the beliefs and attitudes or influence someone else (French and Raven, 1959). Eminence is essentially the use of referent power, in which individuals follow another because of his or her identification with that individual and due to a desire to be associated with the leader. The pursuit of eminence requires greater maturity than does the path to dominance. First, eminence takes longer to establish than dominance, so it requires patience and consistent, sustained effort on behalf of the individual seeking status. Aggressive urges are sublimated into the pursuit of winning the respect of others.

Evolutionary psychological theorists would suggest that, since human beings appear to biologically predisposed to pursue social status through dominance-oriented behaviors, organizations must be proactive in identifying and teaching eminence-oriented strategies, providing a system structured to protect and provide restitution to the less powerful, and ensuring means for remediation and consequences for perpetrators of workplace bullying. Hodson *et al.* (2006) found that the organizational context is a significant predictor of workplace bullying committed by supervisors, and, moreover, that organizations with low job security and chaotic production procedures experienced higher levels of workplace bullying. Organizations must achieve a balance in communicating that aggression is not to be tolerated, while also recognizing that it is an inherent part of human behavior and relationships. A long-term approach is likely necessary to enable people to adopt more principled and mature ways of seeking recognition and influence within their workplace.

WORKING WITH PERPETRATORS OF WORKPLACE BULLYING FROM AN EVOLUTIONARY PSYCHOLOGICAL PERSPECTIVE

Olweus (1993) found that youth who bully are more likely to engage in criminal activities in adulthood, suggesting that perpetrators have difficulty following societal rules, identifying appropriate interpersonal boundaries, and adhering to standards of decorum even after maturing beyond their youth. In essence, bullies in childhood often continue their behavior into adulthood. Consequently, organizations must challenge perpetrators of workplace bullying, providing a firm and consistent message regarding the inappropriateness of the behavior, but also simultaneously providing perpetrators with the support to non-defensively reflect upon their behaviors and gradually learn more egalitarian ways of relating.

Managers are encouraged to adopt a long-term perspective, as perpetrators of workplace bullying are likely to first deny or minimize their behaviors as normal way of relating. The manager must consistently indicate that the behavior will not be tolerated, but continue to convey respect to the employee to increase the likelihood that the employee will self-evaluate his or her behaviors. Obviously, there is a high likelihood that the workplace employee will withdraw from the manager, and in such cases, it may be helpful for the employee to engage in activities of self-exploration with a counselor or a mentor. Managers should recognize that an early sign of progress is that the perpetrator displays ambivalence about his or her use of aggression, questions workplace behavior policies, and also expresses confusion regarding what is expected of him or her. It is understandable that perpetrators are likely to feel a desire to continue their aggressive behavior, since bullying has likely been effective for them.

The evolutionary psychology perspective may help managers in identifying the potential function of the workplace bullying. Does the perpetrator appear to be motivated by a desire for social status within the group, or a desire to undermine potential rivals for power? If the perpetrator is possibly motivated by social status within the group, the manager may help the perpetrator affirm his or her status in more socially acceptable ways. If the perpetrator believes that his or her power is being threatened by rivals, the manager may help the perpetrator to recognize the individual benefits that are likely to accrue as a result of collaboration, and clearly identify the collaborative behaviors expected of him or her. Demonstrations of social aggression may indicate that the perpetrator is motivated by social status, whereas relational aggression, which some regard as a more reactive form of aggression, may indicate that the perpetrator lacks the behavioral repertoire for mature forms of conflict resolution.

CONCLUSION AND SUMMARY

In this chapter, the authors presented the theory of evolutionary psychology and how it may be applied to help to understand bullying behavior in the workplace. A natural question that may be posed is why don't workplaces simply eliminate the dominance hierarchy? The answer is that dominance hierarchies serve an essential function, reducing conflict without devolving into altercations, in society at large and in working environments in particular.

With this reality in mind, it may be helpful to educate all employees about the dominance hierarchy, and how individuals' attempts at gaining power or prestige within the organization may be at the expense of their peers. Employees can be educated regarding the different power bases in human society and the human tendency to misuse power. One of the qualities that appears unique to our species is our capacity for consciousness, which allows us to reflect upon our behaviors, and thus learn from our mistakes and those of our ancestors. Human resource departments and management can provide opportunities for employees to discuss human nature and its tendency toward power and social status, as well as our ability to compensate for our shortcomings through cooperation and endeavors to promote social harmony.

From the perspective of evolutionary psychological theory, the foremost goal with perpetrators is to assist them in relying less on dominance and more on eminence-oriented behaviors. One technique that may be helpful is for human resource departments or managers to engage employees who bully in solution-oriented discussions in which they identify successful social encounters that did not rely upon them victimizing others or resulting in negative outcomes for themselves. Recognition for one's achievements may actually be more likely as a result of the bully's ability to work successfully on a team, thus pooling together several individuals' talents to reach a goal that would be less attainable by working alone. Emphasizing the shared benefits that result from group members' successes (e.g. pay increases, promotions, admiration of peers) may encourage perpetrators to seek out the path of eminence instead of dominance in order to reach these successes.

REFERENCES

Archer, J. (2009). Does sexual selection explain human sex differences in aggression? *Behavioral and Brain Sciences*, 32, 249–311.

Archer, J., and Coyne, S. M. (2005). An integrated review of indirect, relational, and social aggression. *Personality and Social Psychological Review*, 9, 212–30.

Axelrod, R. (1984). *The Evolution of Cooperation*, New York: Basic Books.

Batsche, G. M. (1997). Bullying. In G. G. Bear, K. M. Minke, and A. Thomas (eds), *Children's Needs II: Development, Problems, and Alternatives* (pp. 171–9), Bethesda, MD: National Association of School Psychologists.

Batsche, G. M., and Knoff, H. (1994). Bullies and their victims: Understanding a pervasive problem in the schools. *School Psychology Review*, 23, 165–74.

Beale, D. (2001). Monitoring bullying in the workplace. In N. Tehrani (ed.), *Building a Culture of Respect: Managing Bullying at Work* (pp. 77–94), London: Taylor & Francis.

Buss, D. (2009). The multiple adaptive problems solved by human aggression. *Behavioral and Brain Sciences*, 32, 271–2.

Campbell, A. (1995). *A Mind of Her Own: The Evolutionary Psychology of Women*, New York: Oxford University Press.

Caravita, S. C. S., Di Blasio, P., and Salmivalli, C. (2008). Unique and interactive effects of empathy and social status on involvement in bullying. *Social Development*, 18, 140–63.

CareerOne (2007). Australian workforce infested with bullies, 20 July. Retrieved from http://media.monster.com/CMS/auen/seeker/pdf/CareerOne-Bullies-in-the-workplace.pdf.

Cillessen, A. H. N., and Rose, A. J. (2005). Understanding popularity in the peer system. *Current Directions in Psychological Science*, 14, 102–5.

Coie, J. D., Dodge, K. A., Terry, R., and Wright, V. (1991). The role of aggression in peer relations: An analysis of aggression episodes in boys' play groups. *Child Development*, 62, 812–26.

Costello, E. J., and Angold, A. (2004). Bad behaviour: An historical perspective on disorders of conduct. In J. Hill and B. Maughan (eds), *Conduct Disorders in Childhood and Adolescence* (pp. 1–31), New York: Cambridge University Press.

Crick, N. R., and Dodge, K. A. (1994). A review and reformulation of social-information processing mechanisms in children's social adjustment. *Psychological Bulletin*, 115, 74–101.

Crothers, L., Schreiber, J. B., Field, J., and Kolbert, J. B. (2009). Development and measurements through confirmatory factor analysis of the *Young Adult Social Behavior Scale (YASB)*: An assessment of relational aggression in adolescence and young adulthood. *Journal of Psychoeducational Assessment*, 27, 17–28.

Crothers, L. M., Kolbert, J. B., Kanyongo, G. Y., Field, J. E., and Schmitt, A. J. (in press). Relational and social aggression and reflective processing in a university sample. *Journal of Aggression, Maltreatment and Trauma*.

Darwin, C. (1859). *The Origin of Species*, New York: Macmillan.

Duntley, J. D., and Shackelford, T. K. (eds) (2008). *Evolutionary Forensic Psychology*, New York: Oxford University Press.

Escartin, J., Rodriguez-Carballeira, A., Gomez-Benito, J., and Zapf, D. (2010). Development and validation of the workplace bullying scale "EAPA-T". *International Journal of Clinical and Health Psychology*, 10, 519–39. Retrieved from http://www.aepc.es/ijchp/articulos_pdf/ijchp-364.pdf.

Estell, D. B., Farmer, T. W., and Cairns, B. D. (2007). Bullies and victims in rural African American youth: Behavioral characteristics and social network placement. *Aggressive Behavior*, 33, 145–59.

Farmer, T. W., Estell, D. B., Bishop, L., O'Neal, K. K., and Cairns, B. D. (2003). Rejected bullies or popular leaders? The social relations of aggressive subtypes of rural African American early adolescents. *Developmental Psychology*, 99, 992–1004.

French, J. R. P., and Raven, B. H. (1959). The bases of social power. In D. Cartwright (ed.), *Studies in Social Power* (pp. 150–67), Ann Arbor, MI: Institute for Social Research.

Hodson, R., Roscigno, V. J., and Lopez, S. H. (2006). Chaos and the abuse of power: Workplace bullying in organizational and interactional context. *Work and Occupations*, 33, 382–416.

Hogh, A., Mikkelsen, E. G., and Hansen, A. M. (2011). Individual consequences of workplace bullying/mobbing. In S. Einarsen, H. Höel, D. Zapf, and C. L. Coopers (eds), *Workplace Bullying: Developments in Theory, Research and Practice* (pp. 107–28), New York: Taylor & Francis.

Johnson, P. R., and Indvik, J. (2001). Slings and arrows of rudeness: Incivility in the workplace. *Journal of Management Development*, 20, 706–13.

Keashly, L. (2001). Interpersonal and systemic aspects of emotional abuse at work: The target's perspective. *Violence and Victims*, 16, 233–68. Retrieved from http://search.

proquest.com.authenticate.library.duq.edu/docview/208556288/fulltextPDF/13A4B62002B79C9E123/2?accountid=10610.

Kemper, T. (1990). *Social Structure and Testosterone: Explorations of the Socio-Bio-Social Chain,* New Brunswick, NJ: Rutgers University Press.

Koo, H. (2007). A time line of the evolution of school bullying in differing social contexts. *Asia Pacific Education Review*, 8, 107–16.

Malik, K. (1996). The beagle sails back into fashion. *New Statesman*, 125, 35–6.

Mazur, A. (1994). A neurohormonal model of social stratification among humans: A microsocial perspective. In L. Ellis (ed.), *Social Stratification and Socioeconomic Inequality*, vol. 2, *Reproductive and Interpersonal Aspects of Dominance and Status* (pp. 37–45), Westport, CT: Praeger.

Namie, G. (2007). *U.S. Workplace Bullying Survey,* Washington, DC: Workplace Bullying Institute and Zogby International.

Namie, G., and Namie, R. (2000). *The Bully at Work: What you Can Do to Stop the Hurt and Reclaim your Dignity on the Job* (2nd edn), Naperville, IL: Sourcebooks.

Neuman, J. H., and Baron, R. A. (1998). Workplace violence and workplace aggression: Evidence concerning specific forms, potential causes, and preferred targets. *Journal of Management*, 24, 391–419.

Olweus, D. (1993). *Bullying at School: What we Know and What we Can Do,* Cambridge, MA: Blackwell.

Peeters, M., Cillessen, A. H. N., and Scholte, R. H. J. (2010). Clueless or powerful? Identifying subtypes of bullies in adolescence. *Journal of Youth and Adolescence*, 39, 1041–52.

Pellegrini, A. D., Bartini, M, and Brooks, F. (1999). School bullies, victims, and aggressive victims: Factors related to group affiliation and victimization in early adolescence. *Journal of Educational Psychology*, 91, 216–34.

Roscigno, V. J., Lopez, S. H., and Hodson, R. (2009). Supervisor bullying, status inequalities and organizational context. *Social Forces*, 87, 1561–89.

Sagan, C., and Druyan, A. (1993). *Shadows of our Forgotten Ancestors,* New York: Ballantine.

Salmivalli, C., Kaukiainen, A., and Lagerspetz, K. (2000). Aggression and sociometric status among peers: Do gender and type of aggression matter. *Journal of Psychology,* 41, 17–24.

Slaby, R. G., and Guerra, N. G. (1988). Cognitive mediators of aggression in adolescent offenders: 1. Assessment. *Developmental Psychology*, 24, 580–8.

Smith, D. L. (2007). *The Most Dangerous Animal: Human Nature and the Origins of War,* New York: St Martin's Press.

Smith, P. K., and Brain, P. (2000). Bullying in schools: Lessons from two decades of research. *Aggressive Behavior*, 26, 1–9.

Sutton, J., Smith, P. K., and Swettenham, J. (1999). Bullying and "theory of mind": A critique of the "social skills deficit" view of antisocial behavior. *Social Development*, 8, 117–27.

Tracy, S. J., Lutgen-Sandvik, P., and Alberts, J. K. (2006). Nightmares, demons, and slaves: Exploring the painful metaphors of workplace bullying. *Management Communications Quarterly*, 20, 148–85.

White, S. (2004). A psychodynamic perspective of workplace bullying: Containment, boundaries and a futile search for recognition. *British Journal of Guidance and Counseling*, 32, 269–80.

Xie, H., Swift, D. J., Cairns, B. D., and Cairns, R. B. (2002). Aggressive behaviors in social interaction and developmental adaptation: A narrative analysis of interpersonal conflicts during early adolescence. *Social Development*, 11, 205–24.

Yamada, D. C. (2000). The phenomenon of "workplace bullying" and the need for status-blind hostile work-environment protection. *Georgetown Law Journal*, 88, 475–536.

7

Social-Ecological Model for Predicting Workplace Bullying

Dorothy L. Espelage
University of Illinois at Urbana-Champaign

Brandi Berry
University of Nebraska–Lincoln

Joey Merrin
University of Illinois at Urbana-Champaign

Susan M. Swearer
University of Nebraska–Lincoln

INTRODUCTION AND RELEVANT THEORY

The phenomenon of bullying (i.e. intentional harmful repetitive behavior where the person being targeted cannot defend him- or herself) has received a great deal of attention in the past two decades among school-aged youth (Espelage and Swearer, 2011). In fact, many people associate bullying with child or adolescent behavior and rarely think of this phenomenon as something that can affect adults as well. But adult bullying can be just as pervasive and dangerous as child bullying; this adult aggression generally occurs at an adult's place of work and is therefore referred to as "workplace bullying." As with previous research on bullying among youth, we will conceptualize the complexity of bullying behaviors among adults from a social-ecological perspective (Espelage and Swearer, 2003, 2011; Swearer and Doll, 2001). As Kurt Lewin wrote over 75 years ago, behavior is the function of the individual's interaction with his or her environment (Lewin, 1936). Thus, workplace bullying is defined by the individual's personal interaction with the work environment.

While the term "workplace bullying" was first used in 1992 (Adams and Crawford, 1992; Namie and Namie, 2009), investigators (e.g. Crawshaw, 2009) have noted that that there are many conflicting terms and definitions of the phenomenon, workplace bullying. *Bullying* has remained the preferred term in English speaking countries whereas non-English speaking European countries tend to use the term *mobbing* (Namie and Namie, 2009). Along with the range of definitions, there are also a variety of behaviors that can be conceptualized as workplace bullying. Workplace bullying behaviors have been described as general (e.g. humiliation and social exclusion) or work related (e.g. excessive workload assignments and unfair criticism; Ólafsson and Jóhannsdóttir, 2004) and can be perpetrated against both individuals and groups of employees (Höel *et al.*, 2001).

Lee and Brotheridge (2006) also identified three more specific types of bullying behaviors that are often seen in the workplace: verbal abuse (e.g. jokes made at one's expense), work undermined (e.g. set impossible deadlines), and belittlement (e.g. ordered to stay late). While this wide range of research does not seem to agree on the specific definitions or behaviors associated with workplace bullying, almost all of the research suggests that bullying in the workplace does exist and can have many negative effects on individuals and on organizations as a whole.

Despite these many definitions and characteristics of workplace bullying, this phenomenon has received much less research attention than school bullying among youth. Therefore, in order to better understand workplace bullying, comparisons are often made to the more researched topic of school bullying. A dominant theory in the area of school bullying that has been extended to workplace bullying is the social-ecological framework. This theoretical framework of human development posits that individual attitudes and behavior are shaped by a range of nested contextual systems, including family, friends, work, and societal environments (Bronfenbrenner, 1977, 1979; Espelage and Swearer, 2003).

The *microsystem* represents the first level of the social-ecological theory of human development, which is composed of individuals and others with whom the individual has direct interactions (e.g. family, friends, coworkers) across different settings (e.g. work, home). The *mesosystem* represents the second level of the ecological theory of human development, which is defined as inter-relationships between two or more microsystems in which the individual is situated; experiences in one microsystem level or direct interactions can influence another (Bronfenbrenner, 1977). Situations in which an individual is exposed to bullying and violence in the workplace and then is violent and aggressive toward his or her family at home would be seen as a conflict on the mesosystem level. The *exosystem* comprises the third level of the ecological framework, which includes interactions between two or more interactions or settings, one of which does not directly influence the individual. In the workplace, boardroom decisions that might affect workplace policies or address work climate issues are an example of the exosystem.

The *macrosystem* may be considered the outermost layer in an individual's work environment. This layer comprises abstract influences such as cultural values, customs, and laws (Berk, 2000). The macrosystem impacts the individual through its indirect influence on the microsystem, mesosystem, and exosystem. Finally, the dimension of time is included in this framework as the *chronosystem*. This system exerts itself directly upon the individual, through external events (e.g. promotion or pregnancy) or internal events (e.g. menopause). It also can exert itself indirectly upon the individual through social and cultural trends.

SIGNIFICANCE

Although complex, the social-ecological framework provides a conceptual framework for examining the equally complex problem of workplace bullying. It is particularly relevant because it allows us to examine the combined impact and interactions of these social contexts. This chapter will use the social-ecological framework to review the literature on workplace bullying to inform our understanding of how to prevent bullying perpetration and victimization within the workplace. A brief overview of some of the microsystem level factors that have been found to be associated with workplace bullying is presented in the subsequent sections. However, no studies have examined the mesosystem or exosystem in relation to workplace bullying.

ABC Process-Oriented Theory of Workplace Bullying

Within the studies focused on the microsystem, the process-oriented antecedent–behavior–consequence (ABC) model has been utilized in order to understand and prevent workplace bullying (see LaVan and Martin, 2008). The ABC model posits that it is important to identify the factors that precede workplace bullying (antecedents), the specific bullying behaviors that emerge in the workplace and responses victims of workplace bullying employ (behaviors), and the impact on individuals and the environment as a result of workplace bullying (consequences).

Microsystem

From a prevention standpoint, it is necessary to identify the factors that allow bullying to occur in the first place. When examining the antecedents of workplace bullying, investigators have largely focused on characteristics of employees who bully, who are bullied, and factors that may lead to hostile relations between employees. These individual and interpersonal factors are perpetrated in an individual's microsystem as defined by the social-ecological theory. Bullying generally occurs between two people that come into direct contact with one another, and therefore understanding bullying behavior requires an understanding of how an individual's microsystem is constructed. Selected individual and interpersonal factors that may be relevant to the study of workplace bullying are described below.

Individual Factors

One important individual factor to consider is the person's status within the workplace. Studies have shown that victims of bullying are mostly targeted by individuals in superior positions (Höel *et al.*, 2001; McKay *et al.*, 2008). Status has been found to interact with gender, such that male workers and supervisors were more likely to be bullied than their female peers, whereas females in middle and senior management positions were more likely to be bullied than their male peers (Höel *et al.*, 2001). However, it is unclear whether overall rates of workplace bullying are different across gender. Some studies (e.g. Ólafsson and Jóhannsdóttir, 2004) have found that males appear to be more likely to be bullied in the workplace than females, whereas others (e.g. Smith *et al.*, 2003; Moreno-

Jiménez *et al.*, 2007; Zapf *et al.*, 1996) have found that females are more likely to experience workplace bullying than males.

Interestingly, individuals who are more talented and competent appear to experience workplace bullying more often than less talented and competent individuals (Strandmark and Hallberg, 2007). This phenomenon of bullying the most talented could be an indication of competition and work envy impacting the occurrence of work bullying. Similarly, having material assets and/or privileged backgrounds may increase an individual's risk for being bullied in the workplace. In addition, individuals who are new employees or working under a new manager are likely to experience bullying (Rayner, 1997). Assertiveness was found to moderate the relationship between inequity in the workplace and bullying such that, in an environment characterized by inequity, individuals who were more assertive were less likely to be bullied (Moreno-Jiménez *et al.*, 2007).

Turning from predictors of victimization to predictors of workplace bullying perpetration, holding a management position and being of an older age are two factors associated with bullying behaviors (Rayner, 1997). Regarding gender, males appear to be more likely than females to perpetrate workplace bullying (Ólafsson and Jóhannsdóttir, 2004; Rayner, 1997). Baillien *et al.* (2009) found that individuals who experienced greater personal frustrations (e.g. job dissatisfaction) and utilized ineffective coping strategies (e.g. ruminating and/or complaining) were more likely to perpetrate workplace bullying than those with greater job satisfaction or more positive coping strategies. It could be that these individuals who are frustrated and discontented with their jobs externalize these feelings by bullying others.

Interpersonal Factors

Employees who operate under a different set of values and beliefs may experience conflict, including divisions among groups and coercive behaviors (Strandmark and Hallberg, 2007). Conflicting values may also lead to power struggles and/or interpersonal problems, which often precede incidents of workplace bullying. Interpersonal problems in the workplace have been categorized into issues related to an individual or group simply having poor interpersonal skills and areas of conflict that arise over a specific work-related problem (Baillien *et al.*, 2009), both of which may be associated with greater prevalence of workplace bullying. In a finding similar to the already noted trend that the most talented workers are likely to be bullied, it also appears that those individuals who were the most highly sought after as collaborators by colleagues were more likely to be victims of workplace bullying (Coyne *et al.*, 2004). Given the variability in the research findings, it is important to draw conclusions cautiously, particularly surrounding issues of causality. The fact that the majority of studies exploring workplace bullying are cross-sectional or qualitative in nature prevents causal conclusions from being made. Clearly, more research is warranted.

Macrosystem

Macrosystem, the fourth and final level of the ecological systems, is referred to as a 'cultural blueprint', which may determine the social structures and activities in the immediate systems levels. The macrosystem level consists of organizational, social, cultural, and political contexts, which may determine the interactions within other system levels (Bronfenbrenner, 1977). Summaries of the various macrosystem level factors that lead to the development of workplace bullying will be discussed.

Organizations have been shown to display attitudes and cultures towards bullying behavior that enable, motivate, and create precipitating structures and processes that can help lead towards an aggressive, bullying-filled workplace (Salin, 2003a). Enabling factors of workplace bullying include an imbalance of power, low perceived costs of bullying, and high rates of workplace dissatisfaction and frustration. Motivating factors refer to structures or processes that encourage bullying through incentives; these include competitive work environments, reward systems or expected benefits from individualized gains, and excessive organizational bureaucracy. Precipitating factors predictive of workplace bullying refer to organizational changes such restructuring, changes in management, and changes in work assignments or workload (Salin, 2003a). As the rates of these enabling, motivating, and precipitating factors increase, it is likely that workplace bullying will in turn increase.

Next, we will provide more detail about the macrosystem factors that should be considered when assessing and preventing workplace bullying.

Organizational Culture

The culture of an organization can have a lasting impact on the development and longevity of workplace bullying (Einarsen, 1999). The organizational culture defines the work norms, rules, and expectations of an organization and acts as a source of reality for managers and employees (Harvey *et al.*, 2006). A destructive organizational culture can affect multiple levels of the workplace. In certain types of organizations, bullying behaviors are accepted and encouraged as a normative part of the organizational culture. Archer (1999) investigated a paramilitary organization in the United Kingdom in which bullying behavior was used to institutionalize new employees with the norms, rules, and expectations of the organization. Inappropriate behavior by managers, threats and use of discipline, and bullying within groups were found to be accepted norms within the organization and were used to maintain tradition while reinforcing white male dominance. This organization had strongly established hierarchies and relied heavily on a socialization process of new employees; bullying was used as a way to gain unrestricted subordination of new employees.

Research has also found that workplace environments that support workplace bullying fall along opposite ends of a continuum. First, organizations that emphasize strict conformity, power imbalances, and very formal work environments have been found to have higher rates of workplace bullying. Second, organizations with ambiguity in power structure and distinction, informal work environments, and overly tolerant managers have also been found to be risk factors for the development of workplace bullying (Baillien *et al.*, 2008). Thus, such studies have demonstrated the need for a balance in power dynamics and informal/formal interactions within an organizational culture in order to reduce the risk of workplace bullying behavior.

Furthermore, the social climate or atmosphere, which refers to the interaction and communication norms within an organization and the quality of relationships among members, can greatly impact the development of workplace bullying. Baillien *et al.* (2009) identified a "culture of gossip" as an indication of poor social climate. Workplaces in which rumors and ridicule were daily events among coworkers contributed to division of coworkers and laid the groundwork for the development of workplace bullying.

Working Conditions

Some of the strongest predictors of workplace bullying within the macrosystem of the social-ecological framework are role conflict and role ambiguity (Baillien and De Witte, 2009). When workers do not clearly understand their job roles, responsibilities, or expectations, the conditions are set for bullying behaviors to flourish. Moreover, the physical environment of the workplace can also affect the emergence of bullying behaviors. Baillien *et al.* (2008) found that working conditions with high room temperatures, unpleasant environments, and shared equipment or tools were related to increased bullying behaviors. Thus, at the very least, management practices should clearly define job roles and provide adequate working conditions for employees.

Leadership/Management

One of the signs of a bullying relationship as noted in the definition of bullying itself is that a power differential must be present. Therefore, the inherent power differences between managers and employees can easily morph into a bullying situation when the manager begins to abuse his or her power (Rayner, 1997; Zapf *et al.*, 1996). Managers who do begin to abuse their power and bully their subordinates for any reason, including minority status of the victim (e.g. gender, race), victim work performance, or factors innate to the manager, can have negative effects on individual workers as well as the larger organization. Similar to the research on overall organizational climate, both leadership styles that are coercive and those that are laissez-faire (i.e. permissive) have been related to an increase in bullying behavior (Hauge *et al.*, 2007).

In an investigation of laissez-faire leadership style, Skogstad (2007a) found that individuals who were managed by a laissez-faire leader experienced high levels of role conflict and role ambiguity and had increased conflicts with coworkers. In other words, the association between a laissez-faire leadership style and bullying involvement was partially mediated through role conflict, role ambiguity, and increased conflicts; however, a direct effect between a laissez-faire style and bullying remained. Organizations often influence leadership and managerial styles by giving preference to those who display aggressive leadership styles, claiming that those managers can "get things done." By allowing those aggressive individuals to remain in positions of power, upper management can contribute to and implicitly allow the perpetration of workplace bullying.

Organizational Factors

Many organizational factors can be viewed as motivating factors that incentivize workplace bullying behaviors throughout the organization. One important organizational factor that has been found to have a positive association with the development of workplace bullying is internal competition (Salin, 2003b). In the case of highly stressful or competitive environments, work-related conflicts can transform into personalized conflicts (Zapf, 1999). Work-related or personal conflicts that are played out at work may escalate into repeated bullying behaviors. For example, bullying behaviors could be used to attack underachieving employees in a perceived effort to boost performance, or attack high-achieving employees who may pose a threat to a bully's career goals.

Furthermore, organizational chaos (i.e. lack of coherence) and job insecurity have been linked to bullying behavior. In a qualitative study, Hodson *et al.* (2006) analyzed data on organizational culture from 148 organizations and evaluated a model of bullying based on relational power and organizational context. Results showed that bullying arose from the interaction of relational powerlessness and organizational chaos. Furthermore, results showed that coercive bureaucracy consists of a lack of autonomy and power and can lead to bullying behaviors. Facilitative bureaucracy helped reduce conflict and ambiguity and was negatively associated with bullying behavior.

Organizational Change

Organizational change is considered a precipitating process that has been found to elicit workplace bullying (Salin, 2003b). In a study of 1,260 workers from ten private Belgium organizations, Baillien and De Witte (2009) found a significant relationship between organizational change and bullying. The same study found that role conflict and job insecurity mediated the association between organizational change and bullying. It was concluded that organizational change elicits negative emotions that can lead to bullying behavior when an individual is negatively affected by the change (i.e. high role conflict and job insecurity). Moreover, Skogstad *et al.* (2007b) also found a relationship between organizational change and workplace bullying. More specifically, work environment changes, downsizing in staff, and reduced pay predicted both task-related and person-related bullying.

RECOMMENDATIONS

Future research on workplace bullying should focus on testing the components of the social-ecological framework that are predictive of workplace bullying in order to prevent its occurrence. Since much of the research in this area is cross-sectional in nature, it is difficult to examine how dynamics within a workplace are impacted by changes in the various systems that are the hallmark of work environments. The need for research aside, it appears that management needs to regularly assess the interpersonal and intrapersonal dynamics that may be promoting conditions supportive of workplace bullying. It is important to assess any vertical hierarchies (e.g. manager to subordinate, popular employee to outcast) that exist in which some employees hold more social capital and might be exerting dominance or control over others because of their social status.

It is necessary to understand that how employees cope with workplace bullying might contribute to whether or not the bullying continues. D'Cruz and Noronha (2010) found that most responses to bullying could be conceptualized by the core theme of "protecting my interests." Within that theme were four further themes: experiencing confusion (e.g. dismissing experiences of being bullied), engaging organizational options (e.g. reporting experiences of bullying to HR), moving inwards (e.g. social withdrawal), and exiting the organization (i.e. changing jobs). Although some employees may leave their jobs as a result of being bullied, one study found that most individuals kept their jobs, despite being bullied, for a variety of reasons (Hallberg and Strandmark, 2006).

Lee and Brotheridge (2006) also investigated ways individuals could choose to respond to being bullying and identified four types of employee coping: self-doubt (e.g. felt worthless), ignoring bully (e.g. stayed calm), indirect or passive (e.g. talked to another person about the behavior), and problem-solving (e.g. asked the person to stop). Three of these coping strategies do very little to stop the bullying behavior and can contribute to the development of a negative work culture, even one in which victims respond aggressively to bullying (Lee and Brotheridge, 2006). Employers should provide education and specific skills to support the development of problem-solving actions that can stop the bullying behavior from occurring and increase positive lines of communication.

It is also important for management to understand that there may be gender differences in reactions to bullying. Aggressive and confrontational responses may be more characteristic of males than females. One study found that females were more likely than males to seek help and males were more likely than females to confront the perpetrator of workplace bullying (Ólafsson and Jóhannsdóttir, 2004). This study also found that older individuals were more likely than younger individuals to report that they did nothing, perhaps because older individuals had had more experiences of being unable to stop workplace bullying. Based on these findings, managers should take especial care to identify those employees who are least likely to report bullying behavior if it occurs and provide extra support and education for those individuals.

In addition, it is in the best interest of management to recognize the serious consequences of bullying on the organizational climate and the potential for workplace bullying to increase as the risk factors across the social ecology increase. Evidence suggests that the experience of workplace bullying is significantly associated with poor mental, emotional, and physical health (Höel *et al.*, 2004). These health problems have been found to emerge within months of the first experience of bullying (Hallberg and Strandmark, 2006) and to be more severe in individuals who have experienced bullying more recently (Höel *et al.*, 2004). Common health problems associated with the experience of being bullied include anxiety, depression, and psychosomatic symptoms ranging from mild (e.g. headache) to severe (e.g. respiratory problems and pain; D'Cruz and Noronha, 2010; Hallberg and Strandmark, 2006). Other consequences associated with the experience of being bullied include symptoms of decreased self-esteem and self-confidence (Hallberg and Strandmark, 2006), post-traumatic stress (Nielsen *et al.*, 2008), and social isolation of oneself and/or one's family (Hallberg and Strandmark, 2006).

It is important to emphasize that these consequences are associated with workplace bullying and are not necessarily directly caused by workplace bullying. Some factors (e.g. sense of coherence with coworkers) may act as protective factors, reducing victims' risks of experiencing negative consequences (Nielsen *et al.*, 2008). Lee and Brotheridge (2006) found that self-doubt mediated the association between bullying and health problems whereas Moreno-Jiménez *et al.* (2007) found that social anxiety and assertiveness moderated the relationship between bullying and health problems. Therefore, the mediating and moderating variables that may affect the relationship between workplace bullying and its consequences warrant further study. In addition, although we focused on consequences for victims of workplace bullying, consequences for individuals who perpetrate workplace bullying and witness workplace bullying should also be considered and studied.

SUMMARY AND CONCLUSIONS

Workplace bullying can be understood through a social-ecological framework in which perpetration and victimization among coworkers, management, and supervisors develops from interactions between and among intrapersonal, interpersonal, and environmental factors. However, a number of gaps remain in this research area. First, we need a better understanding of how leadership styles and management techniques influence the development of workplace bullying behavior. It appears that changes made at the macrosytem level (organizational change) seem to relate to changes at the microsystem level (bullying behavior) and have the ability to reduce workplace bullying. Second, very few studies have examined how family or home conditions relate to the perpetration and victimization at work, which would be an important examination of the mesosystem. Given that aggression in the home is associated with bullying within schools and among children (Espelage and De La Rue, in press), one might suspect that this connection holds for adults in the workplace. Finally, given the hierarchical nature of many organizations, future research should examine workplace bullying as being situated within cliques, networks, and among bystanders through social network studies such as those in the school bullying literature (Espelage *et al.*, 2003).

REFERENCES

Adams, A., and Crawford, N. (1992). *Bullying at Work: How to Confront and Overcome it*, London: Virago Press.

Archer, D. (1999). Exploring "bullying" culture in the para-military organisation. *International Journal of Manpower*, 20, 94–105.

Baillien, E., and De Witte, H. (2009). Why is organizational change related to workplace bullying? Role conflict and job insecurity as mediators. *Economic and Industrial Democracy*, 30, 348–71.

Baillien, E., Neyens, I., and De Witte, H. (2008). Organizational, team related and job related risk factors for bullying, violence and sexual harassment in the workplace: A qualitative study. *International Journal of Organizational Behavior*, 13, 132–46.

Baillien, E., Neyens, I., De Witte, H., and De Cuyper, N. (2009). A qualitative study on the development of workplace bullying: Towards a three way model. *Journal of Community and Applied Social Psychology*, 19, 1–16.

Berk, L. E. (2000). *Child Development* (5th edn), Boston, MA: Allyn & Bacon.

Bronfenbrenner, U. (1977). Toward an experimental ecology of human development. *American Psychologist*, 32, 513–31.

Bronfenbrenner, U. (1979). *The Ecology of Human Development*, Cambridge, MA: Harvard University Press.

Coyne, I., Craig, J., and Smith-Lee Chong, P. (2004). Workplace bullying in a group context. *British Journal of Guidance and Counselling*, 32, 301–17.

Crawshaw, L. (2009). Workplace bullying? Mobbing? Harassment? Distraction by a thousand definitions. *Consulting Psychology Journal*, 61, 263–7.

D'Cruz, P., and Noronha, E. (2010). The exit coping response to workplace bullying: The contribution of inclusivist and exclusivist HRM strategies. *Employee Relations*, 32, 102–20.

Einarsen, S. (1999). The nature and causes of bullying at work. *International Journal of Manpower*, 20, 16–25.

Espelage, D. L., and De La Rue, L. (in press). School bullying: Its nature and ecology. *International Journal of Adolescent Medicine and Health*.

Espelage, D. L., and Swearer, S. M. (2003). Research on school bullying and victimization: What have we learned and where do we go from here? *School Psychology Review*, 32, 365–83.

Espelage, D. L., and Swearer, S. M. (eds) (2011). *Bullying in North American Schools* (2nd edn), New York: Routledge.

Espelage, D. L., Holt, M. K., and Henkel, R. R. (2003). Examination of peer-group contextual effects on aggression during early adolescence. *Child Development*, 74, 205–20.

Hallberg, L. R-M., and Strandmark, K. M. (2006). Health consequences of workplace bullying: Experiences from the perspective of employees in the public service sector. *International Journal of Qualitative Studies on Health and Well-Being*, 1, 109–19.

Harvey, M. G., Heames, J. T., Richey, R. G., and Leonard, N. (2006). Bullying: From the playground to the boardroom. *Journal of Leadership and Organizational Studies*, 12, 1–11.

Hauge, L. J., Skogstad, A., and Einarsen, S. (2007). Relationships between stressful work environments and bullying: Results of a large representative study. *Work and Stress*, 21, 220–42.

Hodson, R., Roscigno, V. J., and Lopez, S. H. (2006). Chaos and the abuse of power: Workplace bullying in organizational and interactional context. *Work and Occupations*, 33, 382–416.

Höel, H., Cooper, C. L., and Faragher, B. (2001). The experience of bullying in Great Britain: The impact of organizational status. *European Journal of Work and Organizational Psychology*, 10, 443–65.

Höel, H., Faragher, B., and Cooper, C. L. (2004). Bullying is detrimental to health, but all bullying behaviours are not necessarily equally damaging. *British Journal of Guidance and Counselling*, 32, 367–87.

LaVan, H., and Martin, M. (2008). Bullying in the U.S. workplace: Normative and process-oriented ethical approaches. *Journal of Business Ethics*, 83, 147–65.

Lee, R. T., and Brotheridge, C. M. (2006). When prey turns predatory: Workplace bullying as a predictor of counteraggression/bullying, coping, and well-being. *European Journal of Work and Organizational Psychology*, 15, 352–77.

Lewin, K. (1936). Psychology of success and failure. *Occupations: The Vocational Guidance Journal*, 14, 926–30.

McKay, R., Arnold, D. H., Fratzl, J., and Thomas, R. (2008). Workplace bullying in academia: A Canadian study. *Employee Responsibilities and Rights Journal*, 20, 77–100.

Moreno-Jiménez, B., Rodríguez-Muñoz, A., Moreno, Y., and Garrosa, E. (2007). The moderating role of assertiveness and social anxiety in workplace bullying: Two empirical studies. *Psychology in Spain*, 11, 85–94.

Moreno-Jiménez, B., Rodríguez-Muñoz, A., Salin, D., and Morante Benadero, M. E. (2007). Workplace bullying in southern Europe: Prevalence, forms and risk groups in a Spanish sample. *International Journal of Organisational Behaviour*, 13, 95–109.

Namie, G., and Namie, R. (2009). U.S. workplace bullying: Some basic considerations and consultation interventions. *Consulting Psychology Journal: Practice and Research*, 61, 202–19.

Nielsen, M. B., Matthiesen, S. B., and Einarsen, S. (2008). Sense of coherence as a protective mechanism among targets of workplace bullying. *Journal of Occupational Health Psychology*, 13, 128–36.

Ólafsson, R. F., and Jóhannsdóttir, H. L. (2004). Coping with bullying in the workplace: The effect of gender and type of bullying. *British Journal of Guidance and Counselling*, 32, 319–33.

Rayner, C. (1997). The incidence of workplace bullying. *Journal of Community and Applied Social Psychology*, 7, 199–208.

Salin, D. (2003a). Ways of explaining workplace bullying: A review of enabling, motivating, and precipitating structures and processes in the work environment. *Journal of Human Relations*, 56, 1213–32.

Salin, D. (2003b). Bullying and organizational politics in competitive and rapidly changing work environments. *International Journal of Management and Decision-Making*, 4, 35–46.

Skogstad, A., Einarsen, S., Torsheim, T., Aasland, M., and Hetland, H. (2007a). The destructiveness of laissez-faire leadership behavior. *Journal of Occupational Health Psychology*, 12, 80–92.

Skogstad, A., Matthiesen, S. B., and Einarsen, S. (2007b). Organizational changes: A precursor of bullying at work? *International Journal of Organizational Theory and Behavior*, 10, 58–94.

Smith, P. K., Singer, M., Höel, H., and Cooper, C. L. (2003). Victimization in the school and the workplace: Are there any links? *British Journal of Psychology*, 94, 175–88.

Strandmark, K. M., and Hallberg, L. R-M. (2007). The origin of workplace bullying: Experiences from the perspective of bully victims in the public service sector. *Journal of Nursing Management*, 15, 332–41.

Swearer, S. M., and Doll, B. (2001). Bullying in schools: An ecological framework. *Journal of Emotional Abuse*, 2, 7–23.

Zapf, D. (1999). Organisational, work group related and personal causes of mobbing/bullying at work. *International Journal of Manpower*, 20, 70–9.

Zapf, D., Knorz, C., and Kulla, M. (1996). On the relationship between mobbing factors, and job content, social work environment, and health outcomes. *European Journal of Work and Organizational Psychology*, 5, 215–37.

8

Neurological Contributions to Bullying Behavior

Laura M. Crothers, Jered B. Kolbert, Charles M. Albright, Tammy L. Hughes, and Daniel S. Wells
Duquesne University

INTRODUCTION

Bullying, or peer victimization, is a behavioral phenomenon that has numerous, inter-related causes. Since the 1970s, researchers have examined the psychological, behavioral, and sociological correlates of bullying, and more recently, investigators have begun to explore the biological components of peer victimization (Hazler *et al.*, 2006). The intent of this chapter is to provide readers with an understanding of the biological aspects of the commission of bullying that is part of an integrated perspective for viewing this complex issue. This chapter will explore the neurological features of perpetrators of bullying and individuals with psychological disorders in which aggression is a prominent characteristic, the neurological correlates of the experience of peer victimization, the interaction between genetics and environment, and identify recommendations for workplace managers.

SIGNIFICANCE

A biological perspective of bullying implies that perpetrators may be driven by processes that are largely outside of their conscious awareness. In other words, individuals are either biologically predisposed to be aggressive because such behavior was adaptive in our ancestral environment, or they have biological deficits that interfere with their ability to interact with others, accurately identify emotions and intentions in others, and manage their impulses. The adaptive behavior and the behavioral deficit arguments both imply that the propensity to bully others is deeply ingrained and not easy to remedy. Unfortunately, given such inclinations, perpetrators are unlikely to exhibit remorse for their behaviors as they regard interactions with others as a constant struggle for dominance.

The biological perspective appears to offer two primary implications for workplace settings. The first is that markers of biological factors that may predispose applicants to aggressive behavior may be used by human resource personnel to potentially identify individuals who may struggle in certain positions, particularly in those that require a high degree of interpersonal interaction. For example, measures of executive functioning may be used to identify applicants who possess frontal lobe deficits. However, it is important to note that these tools may be used in such a way as to violate the Americans with Disabilities Act (ADA), 1990, and thus should be used with caution.

The other implication is that perpetrators who may be predisposed to aggression require clearly identified structured interventions to address bullying in the workplace, including concrete and tangible consequences, and removal from situations that provide them with the opportunity for perpetration. Such individuals are likely to require long-term approaches to intervention in which there is a balance between providing clear and consistent consequences for problematic behavior, and support to assist perpetrators to gradually develop insight regarding the thoughts and feelings related to their motivations.

RELEVANT THEORY

Social Cognitive Theory

Bullying has typically been conceptualized as a learned behavior (e.g. social cognitive theory), in which bullying is modeled for children by adults, siblings, and peers, who in turn adopt the behavior in their own repertoire. In the social cognitive model, perpetrators are believed to acquire bullying behaviors through operant and vicarious conditioning mechanisms. Individuals who bully are believed to be both positively and negatively reinforced for their behavior by virtue of attaining their goals (positive reinforcement), and by the removal of threats to their power (negative reinforcement; Batsche and Knoff, 1994). Similarly, Slaby and Guerra (1988) proposed a social-cognitive model of aggression in which the aggression-supporting beliefs that perpetrators often hold may encourage their bullying behavior. In the workplace, perpetrators of bullying are likely to bring a set of positive beliefs about aggression with them from their childhood learning experiences, which encourages the demonstration of victimizing behaviors toward peers.

Evolutionary Psychological Theory

Another theory that may help explain bullying behavior is an evolutionary psychological perspective, in which it is believed that human beings have a biological predisposition to such aggressive behavior that is maintained and reinforced through social systems. Indeed, there is empirical support for the adaptive nature of aggression demonstrated against peers (Axelrod, 1984). Some theorists have posited that highly cooperative species have developed dominance hierarchies through evolutionary adaptation in which a "pecking order" among group members curtail the negative effects of aggression (Sagan and Druyan, 1993). Dominance may be considered a form of aggression, but the purpose of dominance behaviors is to increase the social status of the perpetrator, or decrease the social status of the intended target (Mazur, 1994). Perpetrators of workplace bullying may be motivated by a desire for dominance, essentially wishing to enhance their social status at the expense of others, since social status, regardless of the merits or lack of merits through which the status has been gained, is likely to yield tangible benefits (e.g. higher salary, promotions, preferential work assignments, the admiration of peers) for those with higher status (see Chapter 6).

Need for Including Biological Models

In attempting to provide a holistic understanding of the variables that contribute to bullying behaviors, Hazler *et al.* (2006) advocate for the integration of biological processes that both influence and are influenced by these other models of bullying behavior. One of the obstacles in exploring biological models of bullying behavior is that it is often not feasible to obtain biological measures in situ (e.g. collect salivary and blood cortisol levels during real-life situations; Hazler *et al.*, 2006; Malamud and Tabak, 1993). Of the biological variables that contribute to bullying behavior, perhaps most important are individuals' neurological features, including neuroanatomy and neurohormones. However, the neurological contributions to bullying behavior are not well understood, in part due to the impracticality of measuring these factors during actual bully–victim conflicts. Thus, in order to better understand the potential neurological contributions to bullying behavior, it may be helpful to examine the neurological correlates to conduct-disordered or antisocial behavior, which are often associated with bullying.

Relationship of Bullying with Conduct Disorder and Antisocial Behavior

Multiple investigations have found correlations between bullying, conduct disorder, and antisocial behavior. A 2003 investigation of a group of middle school students and group-matched controls found that bullying was associated more with Axis I diagnoses such as conduct disorder and oppositional defiant disorder than in matched controls (Coolidge *et al.*, 2004). In a national inquiry of the psychiatric correlates of bullying in adults, Vaughn *et al.* (2010) found significant associations between bullying, conduct disorder, and antisocial behavior, among other psychiatric conditions. In a more recent study, researchers used regression analysis to examine the relationship between perpetration of bullying (at ages 13–14) and future antisocial behavior, criminal behavior, and interaction with the police or criminal courts six to ten years later. Moderate significant associations, which were greater for males than females and for short-term versus long-term outcomes, were found between bullying perpetration and subsequent antisocial behavior. After accounting for other risk factors, perpetration of bullying remained a significant predictor of later antisocial behavior and contact with police or courts (Renda *et al.*, 2011). Given these findings, it appears logical to include the research regarding the neuropsychological correlates of conduct disorder when discussing the relationship between neurological variables and bullying.

SALIENT FEATURES

Summary of Neurological Features in Conduct Disorder and Antisocial Behavior

There appear to be several neurological features and conditions that are predictive of a vulnerability to the development of conduct disorder (CD) symptomatology. First, left amygdala activation levels appear to be lower in those with CD than in those who do not have CD in response to fear or threat. Second, researchers have found differential neural activity in the prefrontal areas of the brain in CD adolescents in comparison with control groups, specifically in the right dorsal anterior cingulated cortex (Sterzer *et al.*, 2005). Further, evidence of frontal cortex dysfunction and executive functioning deficits has been found among adolescents with CD symptomatology (Giancola and Mezzich, 2000). Third, slower brain waves, greater wave amplitude, shorter latency periods, temporal lobe seizures, and lower resting heart and electrodermal levels have been associated with CD (Bauer and Hesselbrock, 2001; Gabrielli and Mednick, 1983; Mpofu, 2002; Raine and Venables, 1987; Volavka, 1990). Additionally, lower cortisol levels have been found in those diagnosed with CD (Oosterlaan *et al.*, 2005; Pajer *et al.*, 2001). Finally, there are neurochemical factors that have been associated with CD, including low or poorly modulated levels of neurotransmitters, specifically serotonin and norepinephrine, and the behavioral activation and inhibition functions of the hypothalamic-pituitary-adrenal (HPA) axis (Mpofu, 2002). Given these findings, it is clear that there are established neurological variables that are associated with conduct disorder and antisocial behavior.

The question may be posed, how relevant are these findings to our understanding of the neurological correlates to bullying? Although the literature base investigating this topic is less extensive in comparison to that regarding the neurological variables in conduct disorder and antisocial behavior, in the next section of this chapter the neurological correlates that have been associated with bullying will be presented. Note that several of the studies that have been conducted use samples of children rather than adults. Because there are fewer studies investigating bullying in adults than in children, the presentation of the existing research will be applied to the workplace with a caution that the findings may not be directly relevant to adults. In Table 8.1 (pp. 122–3), the summary of the neurological correlates of bullying and victimization are presented for ease of reference.

Neuropsychological Variables and Bullying

Bullying has been associated with neuropsychological dysfunction in a sample of middle school students. Coolidge *et al.* (2004) found that middle school students who bullied, in comparison to a group of matched controls, scored in the clinically elevated range on three neuropsychological scales on the Coolidge Personality and Neuropsychological Inventory: executive function deficits (e.g. frontal lobe dysfunction, an area involved in decision-making, planning, and organizational problems; problems with learning, reading, memory, and concentration; and social misjudgments, including poor interpersonal decision-making and choices), general neuropsychological dysfunction, and mild neurocognitive symptoms. These researchers deduce that many bullies lack the appropriate frontal lobe functioning required to follow or carry out directions from peers or adults as well as inhibit aggressive and inappropriate verbal and physical behaviors.

Neuroanatomy and Bullying

The neuroanatomy involved in the experience of bullying has been identified in both adult and child studies, both regarding victimization from and perpetration of bullying. A series of experiments by Eisenberg and colleagues (Eisenberger *et al.*, 2003, 2007; Burklund *et al.*, 2007) suggest that activation in the dorsal anterior cingulate cortex (dACC) is more responsible for interpreting cues for social rejection, rather than the general limbic system (Burklund *et al.*, 2007). In an experiment in which adult participants were led to believe they were excluded by two others, subjects underwent an fMRI scan in order to identify the neural correlates of experiencing social exclusion. Results revealed that physical pain-related neural regions were involved in the processing of distress related to social exclusion, including the dACC, which has previously been associated with the distress of physical pain, the insula (involved in the processing of visceral sensations as well as negative affect), and the right ventral prefrontal cortex (involved in the regulation of distress associated with physical pain and negative emotional experiences).

Changes in the anterior cingulate cortex (ACC) mediated the right ventral prefrontal cortex (RVPFC) distress correlation, implying that the RVPFC structure regulates the distress of social exclusion by disrupting the activity of the ACC (Eisenberger *et al.*, 2003). Thus, the dACC appears to be an important structure in mediating an individual's experience of social distress after being bullied. A greater amount of activation in the dACC is linked with lower levels of social support and longer physiological stress responses (levels of cortisol), and consequently, the propensity to feeling excluded and rejected by others (Eisenberger *et al.*, 2007; Masten and Eisenberger, 2009). In a similar study of adolescents, the RVPFC was activated along with the ventral striatum. Researchers hypothesized that the ventral striatum becomes activated in adolescents because their prefrontal cortex is not yet fully developed, and the ventral striatum region helps to regulate adolescents' affective responses to threatening stimuli to support the underdeveloped prefrontal cortex (Masten *et al.*, 2009).

There have also been investigations of the neuroanatomical features associated with disruptive behavior disorders in children (e.g. conduct disorder and oppositional defiant disorder), of which bullying is often an associated behavior. In one of the few neuroimaging studies conducted that investigated disruptive behavior disorders in children, Li *et al.* (2005) found diminished myelination and less coherent fiber track structures in the fasciculus, which may suggest communication weaknesses among the associated cortical regions. Sterzer *et al.* (2007) discovered decreased gray matter volumes in the bilateral anterior insular cortex and the left amygdala in those with CD. Furthermore, Huebner *et al.* (2008) noted gray matter reductions in limbic brain structures in those with CD, leading them to conclude that boys with CD and AD/HD evidenced brain abnormalities in the frontolimbic areas that resemble structural brain deficits like those seen in adults with antisocial behavior (Fahim *et al.*, 2011).

TABLE 8.1
Summary of the Neurological Correlates of Bullying Behavior

Neurological Variables	Structures or Functioning	Perpetrators of Bullying	Victims of Bullying
Neuropsychological Variables		Executive function deficits	
Neuroanatomical Features	Activity in dorsal anterior cingulate cortex (dACC)	Abnormal function	Increased activity interprets cues for social rejection
	Activity in the right ventral prefrontal cortex distress correlation (RVPFC)		Increased activity regulates distress of social exclusion
	Activity in ventral striatum		Helps to regulate adolescents' affective responses to social rejection
	Diminished myelination and less coherent fiber track structures in the fasciculus	Seen along with antisocial behavior	
	Decreased gray matter volumes in the bilateral anterior insular cortex and the left amygdala	Seen along with antisocial behavior	
	Gray matter reductions in limbic brain structures	Seen along with antisocial behavior	
	Increased gray matter concentration in the medial orbitofrontal and anterior cingulate cortices	Delay in cortical maturation in brain areas implicated in decision-making morality, and empathy	
	Increased gray matter volume and concentration in the bilateral temporal lobes	Delay in cortical maturation in brain areas implicated in decision-making morality, and empathy	

	Enhanced left-sided amygdala activation	Seen along with antisocial behavior	
	Decreased overall mean cortical thickness	Diminished inhibition in anger, aggression, cruelty, and impulsivity	
	Thinning of the cingulate, prefrontal and insular cortices	Diminished inhibition in anger, aggression, cruelty, and impulsivity	
Neurohormonal Features	Testosterone	Associated with aggression	
	Cortisol	Lower levels of cortisol	Disrupted circadian rhythms, blunted, flattened, or increased cortisol
	DHEA(s)		Offsets effects of cortisol
Gene–Environment Linkages		50% genetic contribution to aggression	Risk of victimization has no genetic contribution

Boys with callous-unemotional (C/U) conduct problems have been found to have increased gray matter concentration in the medial orbitofrontal and anterior cingulate cortices, in addition to gray matter volume and concentration in the bilateral temporal lobes. The authors of this study suggest that a delay in cortical maturation in brain areas implicated in decision-making morality and empathy may be seen in boys with C/U conduct problems (DeBrito *et al.*, 2009). Functional neuroimaging revealed abnormal function of the anterior cingulate cortex in individuals with CD (Sterzer *et al.*, 2005), while in another investigation, enhanced left-sided amygdala activation was found in response to negative pictures in comparison to neutral pictures when presented to CD boys (Herpertz *et al.*, 2008). Fahim *et al.* (2011) found that, in comparison to controls, children with disruptive behavior disorders had decreased overall mean cortical thickness, thinning of the cingulate, prefrontal, and insular cortices, and decreased gray matter density in the same brain regions. These findings suggest that the thinning and decreased gray matter of the insula disorganizes prefrontal circuits, diminishing the inhibitory abilities of the prefrontal cortex on anger, aggression, cruelty, and impulsivity, thus increasing an individual's likelihood to engage in aggressive behavior, such as bullying (Fahim *et al.*, 2011).

Neurohormones and Bullying

One of the hormones associated with aggressive behavior is testosterone, which is also linked to increased size, muscle mass, and secondary sexual characteristics in men (Nelson, 2000). Testosterone also seems to interact with an individual's social situation, such as bullying, to produce behavioral consequences. Testosterone-related behavior appears to be dependent upon relationships and the social context of an individual instead of directly influencing his or her behavior (Booth *et al.*, 2003; Hazler *et al.*, 2006).

Another neurohormone, cortisol, regulates the fight or flight response (the inclination to defend oneself or retreat in the face of a threat), among other functions. In a study examining the cortisol levels of adult victims of bullying in the workplace, these individuals were found to suffer from altered circadian cycles of cortisol (Kudielka and Kern, 2004). Other research has also suggested that victimization affects cortisol levels. In an investigation of late-childhood monozygotic twins, bullied twins exhibited a blunted cortisol response compared with their nonbullied co-twins (Ouellet-Morin *et al.*, 2011).

Similarly, researchers have uncovered that being victimized by peers predicted poor health outcomes and a flattened cortisol awakening response that was also associated with health problems. In a study of adolescents who were victims of bullying, subjects exhibited higher levels of cortisol after undergoing a stressor (e.g. the Trier Social Stress Test in which they prepared and delivered a speech), and lower cortisol levels 30 minutes after the stressor, which was also associated with more health problems. These findings suggest that the relationship between peer victimization and poor physical health may be accounted for by differences in neuroendocrine functioning (Knack *et al.*, 2011). In another examination of the neuroendocrine functioning in bullied adolescents, peer victimization predicted elevated symptoms of depression, which predicted lower cortisol levels, which then predicted memory deficits (Vaillancourt *et al.*, 2011).

Carney *et al.* (2010) found an indirect relationship between cortisol and bullying exposure, which included both victimization and witnessing peer victimization, among middle school students. Namely, children's level of exposure to bullying was associated with lower cortisol levels only through its relation to children's level of anxiety. The authors surmised that bullying may function as a familiar and chronic stressor, even if the bullying is infrequent, as victims tend to ruminate about bullying experiences, fearing that it will happen again (Janson and Hazler, 2004). The authors also theorized that the lower cortisol levels of victims and witnesses may be indicative of desensitization, meaning that people become increasingly tolerant of aggression.

In terms of the perpetration of bullying, given the developmental research documenting the inverse relationship between cortisol and externalizing behavior problems (Oosterlaan *et al.*, 2005; Pajer *et al.*, 2001), it is likely that an association exists between cortisol and the commission of bullying (Hazler *et al.*, 2006). In one investigation, Vaillancourt and Sunderani (2011) found that in women, but not men, lower salivary cortisol levels were associated with higher levels of primary psychopathy (e.g. cold affect and interpersonal manipulation), with psychopathy being highly related to indirect aggression.

Another set of hormones that have an impact on behavior is DHEA and its sulfated ester DHEA(s). These hormones are positively associated with learning, memory, and externalizing problems (Majewska, 1995; Wolf and Kirschbaum, 1999) and help to protect the human body from the negative effects of overexposure to cortisol. Of key importance to bullying is that DHEA(s) offsets the effects of cortisol to help moderate excessive fight/flight responses (Hazler *et al.*, 2006; Rosenfeld *et al.*, 1971).

Hazler *et al.* (2006) explain that hormones are evaluated in terms of three categories (basal, diurnal, and reactive) in how they interact with the social, emotional, cognitive, and behavioral contexts of individuals (Booth *et al.*, 2000). Human beings appear to have different predispositions for hormonal reactions to events like bullying, which may explain why some respond differently than others. Furthermore, the severity and incidence of stressful conditions have both direct and indirect influences upon the response of these hormones and their associated behavior. In the case of bullying, reactions will likely be stronger based upon the magnitude and duration of the perceived threat. It may be assumed that chronic stressful situations, such as bullying, may affect and have lasting influences on these hormones beyond individuals' initial hormonal response.

Gene–Environment Interaction

Although there are links between neurological variables and bullying, one study sought to examine the diathesis-stress hypothesis of disease that proposes that an environmental stressor such as peer victimization should lead to maladjustment primarily in those with pre-existing genetic vulnerability. Using a sample of twins, the study evaluated whether the link between peer victimization and child aggression was moderated by children's genetic risk for such behavior.

While children's genetic risk for aggression was estimated to be a function of their co-twin's aggression and the pair's zygosity (e.g. 50 percent of the variance in aggression is accounted for by genetic contributions), the risk for peer victimization was found to be an environmentally driven variable that is unrelated to their genetic disposition (Brendgen *et al.*, 2008).

There was, however, support for a gene–environment interaction between peer victimization and the child's genetic risk for aggressive behavior for girls. Victimized girls showed high levels of aggression if they had a high genetic link of being aggressive, whereas the link between victimization and aggression was weak in girls with a low genetic risk of engaging in aggressive behavior. In boys, peer victimization was related to aggression regardless of the child's genetic risk for this behavior (Brendgen *et al.*, 2008, 2011). Essentially, a high level of peer victimization was related to a high level of aggression regardless of boys' genetic propensity to such behavior. Experiences of abuse, in any form, may be a risk factor for aggressive behavior in children with a genetic disposition to this behavior, while children without a genetic disposition to aggressive behavior may be more resistant to developing aggression when abused by others (Brendgen *et al.*, 2008). Thus, those with a preexisting genetic vulnerability to developing aggression are particularly vulnerable to becoming aggressive when bullied by peers. In a later study, Brendgen *et al.* (2011) found that a positive relationship with a teacher mitigated the genetically mediated expression of aggression. It is for this reason that insulating children from the risk of being bullied and providing protective factors to children during their formative years are important to prevent them from potentially becoming aggressive in adulthood.

RECOMMENDATIONS

To begin, it is useful to understand that, although there is an emerging literature pointing toward the biological contributions to expressed bullying behavior, it is also clear that the environmental context can and does directly shape when, how, and if bullying is likely to occur. More directly, when organizations are able to create effective working environments that are prepared to promote employees' work toward shared goals and immediately address bullying when it occurs, the opportunities for bullying diminish (Sperry, 2009). Furthermore, it is important to recognize that it is the negative effects of bullying that organizations seek to decrease, such as competitiveness that results in humiliating others – not organizational competitiveness; similarly, gossip at the expense of others – not gossip as a means of increasing connectedness or cooperation that can be used to facilitate teamwork (Kniffin and Sloan Wilson, 2010). These distinctions are necessary for organizational leaders and managers to make, as they may otherwise readily dismiss anti-bullying policies as promoting (learned or evolutionary) weakness.

It likely behooves organizations to carefully examine the nature of job tasks and note fully the requirements of the tasks to be accomplished. It is obvious to point out that hiring individuals to match the job tasks will also go a long way to decreasing bullying. However, there are many examples in which personality dynamics, such as gregariousness, are overvalued when skills such as keen social judgment and impulse control would better serve the organization in completing the job task. Indeed, optimal outcomes are more likely to be achieved when the organizational context and the selection of employees who are prepared to function in those environments are matched.

Taken together, prevention of bullying is more effective than reaction to these behaviors; organizations without widespread bullying can easily articulate behavioral expectations to employees and reward positive organizational behaviors. When bullying is present, and the biological basis for these behaviors is being considered, it is most useful to determine if there is a match between the job tasks and the skills of the individual and, furthermore, how that match contributes to group or shared goals (Bowie, 2010). Individuals who use bullying tactics because such behaviors have resulted in social status gain may instead compete in the use of altruism. Indeed, there is research showing that individual acts of altruism can be explained by the social capital rewards gained when coworkers view these acts as selfless (Choi and Mai-Dalton, 1998).

When there are deficits in a perpetrator's interpersonal behaviors (e.g. poor social skills, presence of callous/unemotional traits) or impulse control, and there is a desire to retain the employee, managers will need to: (1) limit opportunities for bullying to occur; (2) establish clear expectations and definitions for desirable and undesirable behaviors; and (3) provide tangible rewards that are consistently administered to achieve the best outcomes. As a caution, any rewards offered should also be available to others in the organization (e.g. positive praise, award recognition, etc.). Otherwise, there is a risk of creating a culture in which acting aggressively results in perks for perpetrators. The general idea is to encourage natural rewards with more frequency (e.g. productivity score card) for those who need feedback to maintain appropriate work behaviors.

CONCLUSION AND SUMMARY

The problem of workplace bullying is not easily solved. When attempting to understand bullying, there are a number of socially derived perspectives that attempt to explain why bullying persists from childhood through adulthood and into the workplace. Although it is a difficult relationship to speak about with certainty, an inquiry into the causes and functions of bullying behavior would be incomplete without discussing biological processes that potentially impact the behavior of office bullies. These factors are important, as they can be largely unconscious and out of the individual's control.

Biological considerations involve both evolutionary and neurochemical factors. From an evolutionary perspective, aggressive behaviors demonstrated toward peers are adaptive in many environments. Many of the office settings that continue to have problems with bullying create work environments where aggressive behavior is rewarded and those with an evolutionary predilection toward aggressive behavior thrive.

Along with evolutionary considerations, there are a number of neurological deficits that increase the likelihood of aggressive behavior in work settings. There is currently little research that investigates neural correlates of aggressive behaviors in adults in the workplace, but it is possible to make inferences from research done on individuals with disorders such as conduct disorder and antisocial personality disorder. Individuals with these disorders are more likely to exhibit aggressive behaviors, as well as callous and unemotional personality traits. They also demonstrate neurological deficits that are associated with aggression, such as prefrontal lobe deficits and reduced size of parts of the amygdala. Hormonal differences of individuals who tend to be aggressive include increased levels of testosterone as well as decreased baseline cortisol levels. These biological indicators are associated not only with perpetrators of bullying, but also with victims. Those who have suffered from bullying also tend to demonstrate abnormal levels of cortisol and experience many health-related consequences of their victimization.

Differentiating among factors that impact office bullying is useful as it allows intervention of these bullying practices to be more specifically informed. Recommendations for interventions will vary as to the function of the aggressors' behaviors. If the aggressive behavior is part of behavior to seek dominance in a hierarchy, then changing the criteria by which success and status are attained to more positive attributes or behaviors will likely reduce the aggressive behavior. If, however, the aggressive behaviors are the function of neurological variations, it is likely that the individual's aggressive behaviors will be more difficult to eliminate. These individuals will require close monitoring and office rules with clear consequences. No matter the source of aggressive tendencies, it will be important for organizations to be able to identify during job interviews employees who are likely to bully others, in order to try to limit bullying in their organization, as some aggressive tendencies will be difficult to change within the workplace milieu.

Creating a positive and collegial work environment is important to work productivity, and personal safety in the work environment is a fundamental human right. Office bullying is a threat to both of these. The makeup of the office bully is multifaceted, and it is unlikely that any office manager or human resources representative will be able to correctly identify every potentially aggressive employee. That being said, understanding the role that biological processes play in aggressive workers will provide insights that will help company decision-makers understand the source of bullying behavior.

REFERENCES

Axelrod, R. (1984). *The Evolution of Cooperation,* New York: Basic Books.

Batsche, G. M., and Knoff, H. (1994). Bullies and their victims: Understanding a pervasive problem in the schools. *School Psychology Review*, 23, 165–74.

Bauer, L. O., and Hesselbrock, V. M. (2001).CSD/BEM localization of P300 sources in adolescents "at-risk": Evidence of frontal cortex dysfunction in conduct disorder. *Biological Psychiatry*, 50, 600–8.

Booth, A., Carver, K., and Granger, D. A. (2000). Biosocial perspectives on the family. *Journal of Marriage and Family*, 62, 1018–34.

Booth, A., Johnson, D. R., Granger, D. A., Crouter, A. C., and McHale, S. (2003). Testosterone and child and adolescent adjustment: The moderating role of parent–child relationships. *Developmental Psychology*, 39, 85–98.

Bowie, V. (2010). Individuals, organizations and workplace violence, paper presented at the Transforming Your Organization from "Toxic" to "Welcoming" Social Justice Social Change Centre Seminar, Penrith, Australia, Sept.

Brendgen, M., Boivin, M., Vitaro, F., Girard, A., Dionne, G., and Pérusse, D. (2008). Gene–environment interaction between peer victimization and child aggression. *Development and Psychopathology*, 20, 455–71.
Brendgen, M., Boivin, M., Dionne, G., Barker, E. D., Vitaro, F., Girard, A., ... Pérusse, D. (2011). Gene–environment processes linking aggression, peer victimization, and the teacher–child relationship. *Child Development*, 82, 2021–36.
Burklund, L. J., Eisenberger, N. I., and Lieberman, M. D. (2007). The face of rejection: Rejection sensitivity moderates dorsal anterior cingulate activity to disapproving facial expressions. *Social Neuroscience*, 2, 238–53.
Carney, J. V., Hazler, R., Oh, I., Hibel, L. C., and Granger, D. A. (2010). The relations between bullying exposures in middle childhood, anxiety, and adrenocortical activity. *Journal of School Violence*, 9, 194–211.
Choi, Y., and Mai-Dalton, R. R. (1998). On the leadership function of self-sacrifice. *Leadership Quarterly*, 9, 475–501.
Coolidge, F. L., DenBoer, J. W., and Segal, D. L. (2004). Personality and neuropsychological correlates of bullying behavior. *Personality and Individual Differences*, 36, 1559–69.
DeBrito, S. A., Mechelli, A., Wilke, M., Laurens, K. R., Jones, A. P., Barker, G. J., ... and Viding, E. (2009). Size matters: Increased grey matter in boys with conduct problems and callous-unemotional traits. *Brain*, 132, 843–52.
Eisenberger, N. I., Lieberman, M. D., and Williams, K. D. (2003). Does rejection hurt? An fMRI study of social exclusion. *Science*, 10, 290–2.
Eisenberger, N. I., Way, B. M., Taylor, S. E., Welch, W. T., and Lieberman, M. D. (2007). Understanding genetic risk for aggression: Clues from the brain's response to social exclusion. *Biological Psychiatry*, 61, 1100-08.
Fahim, C., He, Y., Yoon, U., Chen, J., Evans, A., and Pérusee, D. (2011). Neuroanatomy of childhood disruptive behavior disorders. *Aggressive Behavior*, 37, 326–37.
Gabrielli, W. F., and Mednick, S. A. (1983). Genetic correlates of criminal behavior: Implications for research, attribution, and prevention. *American Behavioral Scientist*, 27, 59–74.
Giancola, P. R., and Mezzich, A. C. (2000). Executive cognitive functioning mediates the relation between language competence and antisocial behavior in conduct-disordered adolescent females. *Aggressive Behavior*, 26, 359–75.
Hazler, R. J., Carney, J. V., and Granger, D. A. (2006). Integrating biological measures into the study of bullying. *Journal of Counseling and Development*, 84, 298–307.
Herpertz, S. C., Huebner, T., Marx, I., Vloet, T. D., Fink, G. R., Stoecker, T., ... Herpertz-Dahlmann, B. (2008). Emotional processing in male adolescents with childhood-onset conduct disorder. *Journal of Child Psychology and Psychiatry*, 49, 781–91.
Huebner, T., Vloet, T. D., Marx, I., Konrad, K., Fink, G. R., Herpertz, S. C., and Herpertz-Dahlmann, B. (2008). Morphometric brain abnormalities in boys with conduct disorder. *Journal of the American Academy of Child and Adolescent Psychiatry*, 47, 540–7.
Janson, G. R., and Hazler, R. J. (2004). Trauma reactions of bystanders and victims to repetitive abuse experiences. *Violence and Victims*, 19, 239–55.
Knack, J. M., Jensen-Campbell, L. A., and Baum, A. (2011). Worse than sticks and stones? Bullying is linked with altered HPA axis functioning and poorer health. *Brain and Cognition*, 77, 183–90.
Kniffin, K. M., and Sloan Wilson, D. (2010). Evolutionary perspectives on workplace gossip: Why and how gossip can serve groups. *Groups and Organizational Management*, 35, 150–76.

Kolbert, J. B., Crothers, L. M., and Wells, D. (in press). Evolutionary psychological models for predicting bullying and implications for intervention. In J. Lipinski and L. M. Crothers (eds), *Bullying in the Workplace: Causes, Symptoms, and Remedies*, New York: Routledge.

Kudielka, B. M., and Kern, S. (2004). Cortisol day profiles in victims of mobbing (bullying at the work place): Preliminary results of a first psychobiological field study. *Journal of Psychosomatic Research*, 56, 149–50.

Li, T. Q., Matthews, V. P., Wang, Y., Dunn, D., and Kronenberger, W. (2005). Adolescents with disruptive behavior disorder investigated using an optimized MR diffusion tensor imaging protocol. *Annals of the New York Academy of Sciences*, 1064, 184–92.

Majewska, M. D. (1995). Neuronal actions of dehydroepiandrosterone: Possible roles in brain development, aging, memory, and affect. *Annals of the New York Academy of Sciences*, 774, 111–20.

Malamud, D., and Tabak, L. (eds) (1993). *Saliva as a Diagnostic Fluid*, New York: Annals of the New York Academy of Sciences, vol. 694.

Masten, C. L., and Eisenberger, N. I. (2009). Exploring the experience of social rejection in adults and adolescents: A social cognitive neuroscience perspective. In M. J. Harris (ed.), *Bullying, Rejection, and Peer Victimization: A Social Cognitive Neuroscience Perspective* (pp. 53–78), New York: Springer.

Masten, C. L., Eisenberger, N. I., Borofsky, L. A., Pfeifer, J. H., McNealy, K., Mazziotta, J. C., and Dapretto, M. (2009). Neural correlates of social exclusion during adolescence: Understanding the distress of peer rejection. *Social Cognitive and Affective Neuroscience*, 4, 143–57.

Mazur, A. (1994). A neurohormonal model of social stratification among humans: A microsocial perspective. In L. Ellis (ed.), *Social Stratification and Socioeconomic Inequality*, vol. 2, *Reproductive and Interpersonal Aspects of Dominance and Status* (pp. 37–45), Westport, CT: Praeger.

Mpofu, E. (2002). Psychopharmacology in the treatment of conduct disorder children and adolescents: Rationale, prospects, and ethics. *South African Journal of Psychology*, 32, 9–21.

Nelson, R. J. (2000). *An Introduction to Behavioral Endocrinology* (2nd edn), New York: Sinauer.

Oosterlaan, J., Guerts, H. M., Knol, D. L., and Sergeant, J. A. (2005). Low basal salivary cortisol is associated with teacher-reported symptoms of conduct disorder. *Psychiatry Research*, 134, 1–10.

Ouellet-Morin, I., Danese, A., Bowes, L., Shakoor, S., Ambler, A., Pariante, C. M., … Arseneault, L. (2011). A discordant monozygotic twin design shows blunted cortisol reactivity among bullied children. *Journal of the American Academy of Child and Adolescent Psychiatry*, 50, 574–82.

Pajer, K., Gardner, W., Rubin, R. T., Perel, J., and Neal, S. (2001). Decreased cortisol levels in adolescent girls with conduct disorder. *Archives of General Psychiatry*, 58, 297–302.

Raine, A., and Venables, P. H. (1987). Contingent negative variation, P3 evoked potentials, and antisocial behavior. *Psychophysiology*, 24, 191–9.

Renda, J., Vassallo, S., and Edwards, B. (2011). Bullying in early adolescence and its association with anti-social behaviour, criminality and violence 6 and 10 years later. *Criminal Behavioral Mental Health*, 21, 117–27.

Rosenfeld, R. S., Hellman, L., Roffwarg, H., Weitzman, E. D., Fukushima, D. K., and Gallagher, T. F. (1971). Dehydroepiandrosterone is secreted episodically and synchronously with cortisol by normal man. *Journal of Clinical Endocrinology and Metabolism*, 33, 87–92.

Sagan, C., and Druyan, A. (1993). *Shadows of our Forgotten Ancestors*, New York: Ballantine.

Slaby, R. G., and Guerra, N. G. (1988). Cognitive mediators of aggression in adolescent offenders: 1. Assessment. *Developmental Psychology*, 24, 580–8.

Sperry, L. (2009). Mobbing and bullying: The influence of individual, work group, and organizational dynamics on abusive workplace behavior. *Consulting Psychology Journal: Practice and Research*, 61, 190–201.

Sterzer, P., Stadler, C., Poustka, F., and Kleinschmidt, A. (2007). A structural neural deficit in adolescents with conduct disorder and its association with lack of empathy. *Neuroimage*, 37, 335–42.

Sterzer, P., Stadler, C., Krebs, A., Kleinschmidt, A., and Poustka, F. (2005). Abnormal neural responses to emotional visual stimuli in adolescents with conduct disorder. *Biological Psychiatry*, 57, 7–15.

Vaillancourt, T., and Sunderani, S. (2011). Psychopathy and indirect aggression: The roles of cortisol, sex, and type of psychopathy. *Brain and Cognition*, 77, 170–5.

Vaillancourt, T., Duku, E., Becker, S., Schmidt, L. A., Nicol, J., Muir, C., and Macmillan, H. (2011). Peer victimization, depressive symptoms, and high salivary cortisol predict poorer memory in children. *Brain and Cognition*, 77, 191–9.

Vaughn, M. G., Fu, Q., Bender, K., DeLisi, M., Beaver, K. M., Perron, B. E., and Howard, M. O. (2010). Psychiatric correlates of bullying in the United States: Findings from a national sample. *Psychiatric Quarterly*, 8, 183–95.

Volavka, J. (1990). Aggression, electroencephalography, and evoked potentials: A critical review. *Neuropsychiatry, Neuropsychology, and Behavioral Neurology*, 3, 249–59.

Wolf, O. T., and Kirschbaum, C. (1999). Actions of dehydroepiandrosterone and its sulfate in the central nervous system: Effects on cognition and emotion in animals and humans. *Brain Research Review*, 30, 264–88.

Part III

Forms of Workplace Incivility

9

Bullying as Workplace Incivility

Tammy L. Hughes and Vanessa A. Durand
Duquesne University

INTRODUCTION

Workplace bullying and similar harassment is recognized as a major concern for organizations and individuals (Joint Commission, 2008). When workplace aggression is present, the negative outcomes for organizations include loss of work productivity and diminished effort towards shared goals (Anderson and Pearson, 1999). While the cost of failing to address problematic workplace behaviors is significant and widely acknowledged, how to address organizational structures and individual issues within the workplace remains a challenge that companies have, at present time, not successfully answered.

Considered on a continuum, mobbing behavior sits at the aggressive extreme of behavior, while incivility sits at the mild extreme. In terms of comparison, mobbing is a severe form of bullying that is defined as a highly aggressive and coordinated attack by many on a few, or often one, individual(s), in which the removal of that individual from the organization is a clear goal of the aggressive attack (Sperry, 2009). In contrast, incivility is the case of an individual deviating from organizational norms in a manner that is considered rude, inconsiderate, disrespectful, and evidence of a lack of self-control that is otherwise warranted in the organizational context (Anderson and Pearson, 1999; Phillips and Smith, 2003). Some authors argue that productivity disruptions mark the point where incivility meets the formal definition of bullying (Porath and Erez, 2009), while others contend that the bullying threshold is met when incivility goes unchecked (Twale and De Luca, 2008). Regardless, there is a substantial literature base demonstrating that incivility is a widespread problem and it is disruptive both to organizations and employees (Porath and Erez, 2009).

The move by some authors to characterize incivility as bullying may be viewed as an effort to document the serious disruption incivility brings to the workplace. Yet, the effort to characterize incivility as equally disruptive as incidents of bullying may be largely semantic because when the constructs of abusive supervision, bullying, incivility, social undermining, and interpersonal conflict are statistically differentiated, these minor differences do not add incrementally to our knowledge of workplace aggression (Hershcovis, 2011); that is, *all* are disruptive. Indeed, what is more useful to note is that because incivility is so prevalent and the intensity – but not the impact – is low, its risk may be minimized.

This chapter describes incivility and its prevalence in the workplace. We discuss how to: (1) understand the nature of the problems that organizations face when incivility is present, (2) how to identify the environmental contexts where incivility flourishes, and (3) use findings supported by research in implementing simple, practical and low-cost interventions as well as comprehensive interventions.

INCIVILITY DEFINED

Although incivility has been defined in a variety of ways over the years, there is general consensus that incivility is: (a) low in its intensity and (b) ambiguous in its intention. Generally, incivility is distinguishable from workplace bullying, which is described as much more intense and targeted, and from abusive supervision in the workplace where there is a hierarchical relationship (Sakurai and Jex, 2012).

Incivility is described as a violation of the workplace normative culture where behaviors are considered rude, discourteous, or obnoxious (Anderson and Pearson, 1999). Examples include arriving late to a meeting, checking email or texting during a meeting, failing to respond to phone or email requests in a timely manner, and ignoring or interrupting a colleague in the workplace, among others. Although acts of incivility can be nonverbal (e.g. ignoring a coworker), researchers suggest that low-intensity verbal exchanges (e.g. gossiping, rude responding, jokes at the expense of others) are among the most common mistreatment in the work setting (Kaukiainen *et al.*, 2001).

The intent to harm is ambiguous in uncivil behaviors (Sakurai and Jex, 2012; Sayers *et al.*, 2011). First, the act itself may be equivocal. Is multi-tasking on your hand-held computer during meetings due to the need to respond to an urgent issue, due to poor time management, to pointedly ignore the presentation, or is there another explanation? Does it matter what the explanation is if the behavior is chronic and unchanged? Second, the target of uncivil behavior is often not aware of the intent of the action or if it is actually or solely directed toward him or her. The uncivil act seems to be without provocation or explanation. Continuing with the example above, is the decision to not participate in the meeting related to the presenter directly? Furthermore, not only are the motives behind the uncivil treatment often unknown to the target (Sakurai and Jex, 2012), but also they may be unknown to the aggressor (Anderson and Pearson, 1999). That is, the individual's act may be uncivil but is without conscious intent or a target. Indeed, many have argued that, because the intent is difficult to determine, incidents of incivility are more prevalent and tend to persist (Sakurai and Jex, 2012). As noted previously, incivility is reported to be present when employees feel a lack of protection from violations that result in an inability to work with each other (Twale and De Luca, 2008) and when the work environment and productivity are compromised (Anderson and Pearson, 1999).

INCIVILITY IN THE WORKPLACE

One challenge to addressing incivility is the fact that organizational normative practices and cultures vary; what characterizes incivility is specific to each organizational context. For example, such pro-social behaviors as cleaning the shared microwave after use, replenishing low office supplies, or greeting coworkers may be appreciated but not expected within one organization but considered a necessary, normative practice in another. The second, seemingly contradictory challenge is that there is generally a shared agreement regarding the nature of a normative practice within a work setting. As such, although violations are contextual and often unwritten (e.g. there is no mention in the employee handbook that says to greet people pleasantly), organizational practices are easily understood and widely held throughout the work setting.

Incivility is reported to be very common. Researchers report between 50 percent (Remington and Darden, 2002) and 71 percent (Cortina *et al.*, 2001) of workers have witnessed or experienced uncivil behavior. Similarly, 79 percent of a law enforcement sample (Cortina and Magley, 2009) and 75 percent of a university employee sample (Cortina *et al.*, 2004) indicated that they had experienced uncivil behaviors. More recently, Trudel and Reio (2011) found that workplace incivility had been experienced by 86 percent of workers in the past year. Indeed, as the interactions between people become more complex and frequent, so too is the risk for incivility (Anderson and Pearson, 1999).

Research has also shown that there are very few formal complaints made about episodes of incivility. Pearson and Porath (2009) report that only about 6 percent of targets make a report. Authors hypothesize that targets fear retaliation from the aggressor (Cortina *et al.*, 2001) or they may be discouraged from making a complaint if the aggressor has an informal power base and is well liked (Sakurai and Jex, 2012). However, it appears that it is the nature of the aggression – and specifically the ambiguity (e.g. did he or she mean to insult me?) – that keeps many from reporting.

WHO IS A TARGET OF INCIVILITY?

Most frequently, women are reported to be the targets of uncivil behavior (Cortina, 2008; Cortina *et al.*, 2002; Pearson *et al.*, 2000). One notable difference, however, is reported in a study in which non-western Asians found that men reported greater levels of incivility (Lim and Lee, 2011).

Researchers have identified some victim personality variables that are highly correlated with workplace harassment. Self-perceived victimization was predicted by reported trait anxiety and trait anger (Vie *et al.*, 2010). That is, individuals who indicate high levels of trait anxiety and identify themselves as a victim tended to perceive ambiguous situations as uncivil and/or characterized by acts of bullying. Furthermore, authors concluded that when anxiety levels are high enough to affect performance and workplace interactions, this may also lead to a tendency to interpret the work environment as uncivil and inappropriate (Vie *et al.*, 2010). An individual's coping skills and abilities to handle situations with high levels of negative emotion and low levels of positive emotion impact whether or not that individual claims to experience incivility or bullying behaviors (Glasø *et al.*, 2011).

Both targets and coworkers agree that incivility is directed toward those who are perceived to show low agreeableness (Milam *et al.*, 2009). Glasø *et al.* (2007) noted that victims in their study were described as less extroverted, less agreeable, and less conscientious; victims were also reported to be more emotionally unstable than their coworkers.

THE SIGNIFICANCE OF UNCHECKED INCIVILITY

Pearson and Porath (2009) indicate that incivility costs businesses $14,000 per year per employee in work production. Unfortunately, incivility has the potential to escalate into more intensive aggression in the workplace (Anderson and Pearson, 1999). As such, incivility that is unaddressed and leads to future episodes of workplace bullying is likely to only escalate workplace costs. Bullying is reported to cost companies more than $200 billion per year (Williams, 2011).

Targets of incivility report lower job satisfaction (Penny and Spector, 2005), difficulty focusing on their job tasks (Heuven *et al.*, 2006), low affective wellbeing (Sakurai *et al.*, 2011), and counterproductive work behaviors (Penny and Spector, 2005). Individuals who repeatedly experience acts of incivility think about quitting their jobs (Cortina *et al.*, 2001; Pearson *et al.*, 2000) and about 12 percent do leave the organization (Workplace Bullying Institute, n.d.).

There are substantial data that workplace stress leads to physiological and psychological distress (Nielsen *et al.*, 2008; Tepper, 2000) that may extend to wellbeing beyond the work setting. Lim and Lee (2011) considered how incivility affects work-to-family conflict. In their non-western Asian sample, they found an increase in family conflict when an individual experienced uncivil behavior from his or her supervisors. Researchers have equated the impact of incivility to the phenomenon documented in the psychological literature known as "hassles of daily living," which describes how more ubiquitous acts account for more distress than major life events (Baker, 2006; Jacobs *et al.*, 2006).

Causes of Incivility

Pearson *et al.* (2005) have identified shifts in social contexts and organizational pressure as the primary factors that contribute to uncivil behavior in the workplace. Contextual shifts have been attributed to changes in worker demographics, general social irreverence, and feeling that the organization is not adhering to the unwritten employee/organization contract (Pearson *et al.*, 2005). Organizational pressures can include stress associated with compressed deadlines and timelines (Pearson *et al.*, 2005), failure to adapt to technology (Reio and Ghosh, 2009), poor leadership (Blau and Andersson, 2005; Pearson *et al.*, 2005), and the perception of organizational in/justice (Sayers *et al.*, 2011).

RELEVANT THEORIES

The Affective Events Theory (AET) posits that employees' attitudes and behaviors are explained by the interaction of the employee's personality and emotional traits and the effects of workplace events (Weiss and Cropanzano, 1996). Specifically, this theory focuses on how the work environment affects the employees' emotions and attitudes. Often, it is used to explain psychological distress as a result of a work environment conducive to bullying or incivility. AET assumes that organizational structures affect the probability of workplace harassment. For example, when there is laissez-faire leadership, or the lack of definite goals, responsibilities, and management obligations, role ambiguity and role confusion can result for employees. This type of poor leadership can increase reports of a hostile work environment and bullying. Skogstad *et al.* (2007) found that laissez-faire leadership is significantly and positively correlated with bullying and workplace stresses such as role conflict and role ambiguity. Furthermore, they also demonstrated that when bullying and incivility are present in the workplace, there is an increased relationship between laissez-faire leadership and psychological distress.

Workplace variables are also related to the rates and experiences of bullying and other uncivil behaviors. Sperry (2009) describes several organizational subsystems such as organizational strategy, culture, personnel, and the external environment that can independently prevent or promote workplace abuse. Also, employees who reported they were frequently a victim or witness to bullying or incivility also reported higher perceptions of workplace demands, lower perceptions of workplace support, and lower personal control over resources (Tuckey *et al.*, 2009). In contrast, when employers in highly demanding work environments create a supportive atmosphere that meets the needs of employees (e.g. by providing the necessary management and resources), there is less of an opportunity for bullying and other workplace abuse, including incivility, to occur.

The Affect Infusion Model (AIM; Forgas, 1995) is often used to explain interpersonal behaviors in the workplace. This theory describes how social judgments and information processing are influenced by affect (Forgas, 2002). Affect infusion is the process of organizing emotionally charged information and events into our decision-making strategies for the purpose of making specific judgments about the current issue, and then generalizing these judgments to subsequent (maybe unrelated) issues or events (Forgas, 1995). The theory suggests that the influences of emotions on judgments decrease when the information from the environment is clear, matches into an already established judgment schema, and when the judgment is goal directed to a specific (workplace) motivation. Affect is more instrumental when the judgment needed requires using cognitive shortcuts, needs to integrate new material with previous learned information, and relies on memory. The more complexity presented in the situation and thus the interaction of known information to new material, the more affect has an influence (Forgas, 1995). As these judgments accumulate, they color our views on interpersonal relationships and specifically our perception of interactions, which ultimately influences our interpersonal behaviors (Forgas, 2002). AIM has been used to explain how individuals can hold both congruent and incongruent judgments regardless of their previous experience of those events or the individuals in the workplace.

The Emotion-Centered Model of Voluntary Work Behavior focuses on explaining the environmental and personal factors that result in specific types of work behaviors (Spector and Fox, 2002). Specifically, this theory examines how "emotion mediates the effects of environmental conditions on behavior" (Spector and Fox, 2002: 270). In other words, emotion changes the relationship between the environment, individual personality factors, and voluntary work behavior. Specifically, the model focuses on the environmental role (i.e. organizational constraints, role ambiguity, and role conflict) and how employees perceive it. Workers' perceptions are influenced by personality factors (i.e. agreeableness, conscientiousness, emotional stability) and control factors (i.e. control over the situation), which both affect the emotional state of the employee. Coming together, these factors then influence the behaviors of the employees, which in turn affect the workplace environment (Spector and Fox, 2002). When negative emotions are added, the likelihood of counterproductive work behaviors (behaviors that intentionally harm the organization) increases. However, when positive emotions are added, the likelihood of organizational citizenship behaviors (behaviors that intentionally better the organization) increases (Spector and Fox, 2002). In this model, it is assumed that emotion is needed, in most cases, to increase behaviors; therefore, employers should facilitate positive emotional events and decrease the exposure to negative emotional events in order to promote organization productivity.

Using these theories, researchers are now examining the antecedents to incivility. Roberts *et al.* (2011) considered how job stress might increase an individual's tendency to display uncivil behavior. Also, they considered the role that psychological capital (e.g. employee strength shown to increase positive organizational behaviors) would have in decreasing uncivil behaviors. These authors found that psychological capital does buffer the effect of job stress and is correlated with decreasing uncivil acts. Relatedly, Sakurai and Jex (2012) found that incivility is directly related to negative emotions, low work effort, and counterproductive work behaviors. These authors found that negative emotions mediated (accounted for) the relationship between incivility and work effort and for the relationship between incivility and counterproductive work behaviors. Indeed, addressing negative emotions in the workplace appears to be a promising intervention for decreasing uncivil behaviors.

SALIENT FEATURES OF INCIVILITY

Incivility is a low-level aggressive act where the intention of the act is often unknown (Anderson and Pearson, 1999). Gossiping, responding rudely, and jokes at the expense of others are the most common uncivil behaviors at work (Kaukiainen *et al.*, 2001). Incivility is highly prevalent and its negative impact is enormous (Joint Commission, 2008). Women are targets more often than men (Cortina, 2008; Cortina *et al.*, 2002) and there is some consensus that incivility is directed toward coworkers who are perceived to show low agreeableness (Milam *et al.*, 2009). The extent to how agreeable women should be may be dictated by cultural and organizational expectations. Targets and witnesses alike indicate high levels of psychological distress (Sakurai *et al.*, 2011), disrupted work activity (Heuven *et al.*, 2006), and negative health outcomes (Nielsen *et al.*, 2008; Tepper, 2000).

It is important to note that the effects of low-level bullying and incivility can be removed when a target has a sense of organizational coherence and/or perceives that his or her work environment is easy to adapt and control (Nielsen *et al.*, 2008). Additionally, higher levels of perceived supervisor support decreased the effects of negative emotions at work (Sakurai and Jex, 2012). Authors have concluded that, as the protective factors (e.g. organizational coherence) decrease, the severity of incivility and bullying increases (Nielsen *et al.*, 2008).

RECOMMENDATIONS

To begin, it is useful to identify if incivility is happening at the individual, group, and/or the organizational level (Sperry, 2009). Interventions are likely to work best before the problem is common and widespread; clearly, preventing incivility is ideal. That said, even when incivility is present, it is essential to address the entire social context instead of simply focusing on the few individuals who may be the most obvious in their incivility (Bowie, 2010). However, if significant incivility is occurring at the individual or group level, organizations may need to address individual conflicts along entire organizational programs.

Low-Cost Interventions

Simply put, incivility needs to be acknowledged and defined. Civil behaviors need to be clearly articulated and explicitly rewarded. Uncivil acts need to be addressed immediately and consistently. Managers, supervisors, and other organizational leaders need to model appropriate workplace behaviors (Pearson *et al.*, 2001, 2005). Where possible, organizations should identify policies in which employees can give input into the decision-making (thereby increasing the sense of control). Organizations should also attempt to promote and support positive relationships and interactions, particularly between supervisors and their subordinates (Nielsen *et al.*, 2008). A basic plan (compiled from Duffy, 2009; Namie, 2003; Namie and Namie, 2009) to create an anti-incivility policy within organizations would include:

- A purpose that includes explicitly stated goals of creating a positive, high care workplace environment. This includes declaring that uncivil, bullying, or similar behaviors are unacceptable. Be clear that everyone is protected from misconduct. Define incivility and bullying as a health and safety concern.
- A clear description of appropriate and inappropriate behaviors. Including examples of what the harassment behaviors look like will improve employees' understanding. The policy should describe observable behaviors rather than the intentions of the actor.
- Procedures for handling reports of incivility. That is, who is designated to take reports? What are the alternate sources for reporting, should the conflict be with the report taker? Descriptions of appropriate informal resolutions and alternative dispute resolutions should be provided, as should descriptions of what would constitute a formal complaint or grievance.
- Clear explanations of due process (for the reporter and the reported) that reassure all parties involved that confidentiality is standard, and a description of a time frame that covers all events and is yet thoroughly monitored should be established.
- Descriptions of how the organization is accountable for promoting a healthy workplace should be provided. The policy should determine how findings will be reported within the organization (e.g. the type and frequency of complaints in aggregate form; no individual names

will be identified). Finally, a method for describing employee growth and successes (e.g. type and frequency of improvements) should be established.

Comprehensive Interventions

There are several comprehensive programs designed to address incivility in the workplace. Most have similar plans that are modified slightly for each setting. The Civility, Respect, Engagement at Work (CREW) model presented here is easy to understand and presents some compelling data showing a decrease in uncivil behaviors, and improved collegiality and health care provider outcomes within health provider teams (Leiter *et al.*, 2011).

The CREW intervention has six steps that include: (1) a preparation period where incivility is defined, civility is identified as a core value, and a commitment to advancing civility through actions, writing articles for publication, etc., begins; (2) a survey measuring organizational attitudes and beliefs is given to establish baseline data; (3) facilitators and leaders from various locations (hospitals) are identified and trained in the CREW model; (4) six months of weekly CREW trainings are provided by the facilitators at their sites for 10–15 employees; (5) midway, at three months of the six-month training, facilitators reconvene to refresh; and (6) convening at six months, participants review progress data on their teams as well as refresh their training, knowledge, and skills.

The CREW program includes training in active listening, settling disputes, use of metaphors to improve conflict resolution, force field analysis of likes and dislikes within groups, and brainstorming. The toolkit activities that occur between CREW sessions request that participants renew their commitment to civil actions in the next week, maintain written logs documenting special contributions or acts of their coworkers that demonstrated civility, and provide a weekly CREW award for exceptional support by colleagues in their units. Data show not only improved civility outcomes as a result of the CREW intervention (Leiter *et al.*, 2011) but also that those gains were maintained (Leiter *et al.*, 2012). While authors show that initial gains do ebb, there is evidence for measureable long-lasting culture change (Leiter *et al.*, 2012).

CONCLUSION/SUMMARY

Despite government legislation such as Title VII of the Civil Rights Act of 1964, the Age Discrimination in Employment Act of 1967, and the Americans With Disabilities Act of 1990, bullying, mobbing, and incivility still occur within organizations. At this point, it is important to note that organizations themselves need to create and implement policies and programs to prevent and intervene in instances of workplace harassment. Incivility in the workplace is ubiquitous and many workers feel that it is on the rise. While targets of incivility are certainly affected, so too are bystanders and other witnesses. Acts of incivility cost companies millions in lost productivity; the effects of incivility diminish the psychological and physical health of employees. Indeed, the costs are cumulative and, if left unchecked, will likely increase. While there are some data to show that low-level incivility can and does escalate into more aggressive bullying or other workplace harassment, interventions can be implemented that have been shown to make a positive impact on the rates of uncivil workplace behavior.

REFERENCES

Anderson, L. M., and Pearson, C. M. (1999). Tit for tat? The spiraling effect of incivility in the workplace. *Academy of Management Review*, 24, 452–71.

Baker, S. R. (2006). Towards an idiopathic understanding of the role of social problem solving in daily event, mood, and health experiences: A prospective daily diary approach. *British Journal of Health Psychology*, 11, 513–31.

Blau, G., and Andersson, L. (2005). Testing a measure of instigated workplace incivility. *Journal of Occupational and Organizational Psychology*, 78, 595–614.

Bowie, V. (2010). Individuals, organizations and workplace violence, paper presented at the Transforming Your Organization from "Toxic" to "Welcoming" Social Justice Social Change Centre Seminar, Penrith, Australia, Sept.

Cortina, L. M. (2008). Unseen injustice: Incivility as modern discrimination in organizations. *Academy of Management Review*, 33, 55–7.

Cortina, L. M., and Magley, V. J. (2009). Patterns and profiles of response to incivility in the workplace. *Journal of Occupational Health Psychology*, 14, 272–88.

Cortina, L. M., Lonsway, K. L., and Magley, V. J. (2004). Reconceptualizing workplace incivility through the lenses of gender and race, paper presented at the annual meeting of the Society for Industrial-Organizational Psychology, Chicago, IL, April.

Cortina, L. M., Magley, V. J., Williams, J. H., and Langhout, R. D. (2001). Incivility in the workplace: Incidence and impact. *Journal of Occupational Health Psychology*, 6, 64–80.

Cortina, L. M., Lonsway, K. L., Magley, V. J., Freeman, L. V., Collinsworth, L. L., Hunter, M., and Fitzgerald, L. F. (2002). What's gender got to do with it? Incivility in the federal courts. *Law and Social Inquiry*, 27, 235–70.

Duffy, M. (2009). Preventing workplace mobbing and bullying with effective organizational consultation, policies, and legislation. *Consulting Psychology Journal: Practice and Research*, 61, 242–62.

Forgas, J. P. (1995). Mood and judgment: The affect infusion model (AIM). *Psychological Bulletin*, 117, 39–66.

Forgas, J. P. (2002). Towards understanding the role of affect in social thinking and behavior. *Psychological Inquiry*, 13, 90–102.

Glasø, L., Matthiesen, S. B., Nielsen, M. B., and Einarsen, S. (2007). Do targets of bullying portray a general victim personality profile? *Scandinavian Journal of Psychology*, 48, 313–19.

Glasø, L., Vie, T. L., Holmadal, G. R., and Einarsen, S. (2011). An application of affective events theory to workplace bullying: The role of emotions, trait anxiety, and trait anger. *European Psychologist*, 16, 198–208.

Hershcovis, M. S. (2011). "Incivility, social undermining, bullying … oh my!": A call to reconcile constructs within workplace aggression research. *Journal of Organizational Behavior*, 32, 499–519.

Heuven, E., Bakker, A. B., Schaufeli, W. B., and Huisman, N. (2006). The role of self-efficacy in performing emotion work. *Journal of Vocational Behavior*, 69, 222–36.

Jacobs, N., Rijisdijk, F., Derom, C., Vlietink, R., Delespaul, P., van Os, K., and Myin-Germeys, I. (2006). Genes making one feel blue in the flow of daily life: A momentary assessment study of gene-stress interactions. *Psychosomatic Medicine*, 68, 201–6.

Joint Commission (2008). Behaviors that undermine a culture of safety. *Sentinel Event Alert*, 40 (9 July). Retrieved from http://www.jointcommission.org/assets/1/18/SEA_40.PDF.

Kaukiainen, A., Salmivalli, C., Björkqvist, K., Österman, K., Lahtinen, A. K., Kostamo, A., and Lagerspetz, K. (2001). Overt and covert aggression in work settings in relation to the subjective well-being of employees. *Aggressive Behavior*, 27, 260–71.

Leiter, M. P., Day, A., Oore, D. G., and Spence Laschinger, H. K. (2012). Getting better and staying better: Assessing civility, incivility, distress, and job attitudes one year after a civility intervention. *Journal of Occupational Health Psychology*, 17, 425–34.

Leiter, M. P., Spence Laschinger, H. K., Day, A., and Oore, D. G. (2011). The impact of civility interventions on employee social behavior, distress, and attitudes. *Journal of Applied Psychology*, 96, 1258–74.

Lim, S., and Lee, A. (2011). Work and nonwork outcomes of workplace incivility: Does family support help? *Journal of Occupational Health Psychology*, 16, 95–111.

Milam, A. C., Spitzmueller, C., and Penney, L. M. (2009). Investigating individual differences among targets of workplace incivility. *Journal of Occupational Health Psychology*, 14, 58–69.

Namie, G. (2003). Workplace bullying: Escalated incivility. *Ivey Business Journal*, 68, 1–6.

Namie, G., and Namie, R. (2009). U.S. workplace bullying: Some basic considerations and consultation interventions. *Consulting Psychology Journal: Practice and Research*, 61, 202–19.

Nielsen, M. B., Matthiesen, S. B., and Einarsen, S. (2008). Sense of coherence as a protective mechanism among targets of workplace bullying. *Journal of Occupational Health Psychology*, 13, 128–36.

Pearson, C. M., and Porath, C. (2009). *The Cost of Bad Behavior: How Incivility is Damaging your Business and What to Do about it*, New York: Penguin Group.

Pearson, C. M., Andersson, L. M., and Porath, C. L. (2000). Assessing and attacking workplace incivility. *Organizational Dynamics*, 29, 123–37.

Pearson, C. M., Andersson, L. M., and Porath, C. L. (2005). Workplace incivility. In S. Fox and P. E. Spector (eds), *Counterproductive Work Behavior: Investigations of Actor and Targets* (pp. 177–200), Washington, DC: American Psychological Association.

Pearson, C. M., Andersson, L. M., and Wegner, J. W. (2001). When workers flout convention: A study of workplace incivility. *Human Relations*, 54, 1387–1419.

Penny, L. M., and Spector, P. E. (2005). Job stress, incivility, and counterproductive work behavior (CWB): The moderating role of negative affectivity. *Journal of Organizational Behavior*, 26, 777–96.

Phillips, T., and Smith, P. (2003). Everyday incivility: Towards a benchmark. *Sociological Review*, 51, 85–108.

Porath, C. L., and Erez, A. (2009). Overlooked but not untouched: How incivility reduces onlookers' performance on routine and creative tasks. *Organizational Behavior and Human Decision Processes*, 109, 29–44.

Reio, T. G., and Ghosh, R. (2009). Antecedents and outcomes of workplace incivility: Implications for human resource development research and practice. *Human Resource Development Quarterly*, 20, 237–64.

Remington, R., and Darden, M. (2002). *Aggravating Circumstances: A Status Report on Rudeness in America*, New York: Public Agenda.

Roberts, S. J., Scherer, L. L, and Bowyer, C. J. (2011). Job stress and incivility: What role does psychological capital play? *Journal of Leadership and Organizational Studies*, 18, 449–58.

Sakurai, K., and Jex, S. M. (2012). Coworker incivility and incivility targets' work effort and counterproductive work behaviors: The moderating role of supervisor social support. *Journal of Occupational Health Psychology*, 17, 150–61.

Sakurai, K., Jex, M. S., and Gillespie, M. A. (2011). Impact of coworker workplace incivility: Employee negative, emotion, job satisfaction, and work withdrawal behavior. *Japanese Association of Industrial/Organizational Psychology Journal*, 25, 13–23.

Sayers, J. K., Sears, K. L., Kelly, K. M., and Harbke, C. R. (2011). When employees engage in workplace incivility: The interactive effect of psychological contract violation and organizational justice. *Employee Responsibilities and Rights Journal*, 23, 269–83.

Skogstad, A., Einarsen, S., Torsheim, T., Aasland, M. S., and Hetland, H. (2007). The destructiveness of laissez-faire leadership behavior. *Journal of Occupational Health Psychology*, 12, 80–92.

Spector, P. E., and Fox, S. (2002). An emotion-centered model of voluntary work behavior: Some parallels between counterproductive work behavior and organizational citizenship behavior. *Human Resource Management Review*, 12, 269–92.

Sperry, L. (2009). Mobbing and bullying: The influence of individual, work group, and organizational dynamics on abusive workplace behavior. *Consulting Psychology Journal: Practice and Research*, 61, 190–201.

Tepper, B. J. (2000). Consequences of abusive supervision. *Academy of Management Journal*, 43, 178–90.

Trudel, J., and Reio Jr., T. G. (2011). Managing workplace incivility: The role of conflict management styles – antecedent or antidote? *Human Resource Development Quarterly*, 22, 395–423.

Tuckey, M. R., Dollard, M. F., Hosking, P. J., and Winefield, A. H. (2009). Workplace bullying: The role of psychosocial work environment factors. *International Journal of Stress Management*, 16, 215–32.

Twale, D. J., and De Luca, B. M. (2008). *Faculty Incivility: The Rise of the Academic Bully Culture and What to Do about it*, San Francisco, CA: Jossey-Bass.

Vie, T., Glasø, L., and Einarsen, S. (2010). Does trait anger, trait anxiety or organizational position moderate the relationship between exposure to negative acts and self-labeling as a victim of workplace bullying?, *Nordic Psychology*, 62, 67–79.

Weiss, H. M., and Cropanzano, R. (1996). Affective events theory: A theoretical discussion of the structure, causes and consequences of affective experiences at work. In B. M. Staw and L. L. Cummings (eds), *Research in Organization Behavior* (vol. 19, pp. 1–74), Greenwich, CT: JAI Press.

Williams, R. (2011). Workplace bullying: North America's silent epidemic. Workplace Bullying Institute. Retrieved from http://www.workplacebullying.org/2011/05/04/npost.

Workplace Bullying Institute (n.d.). Bullying contrasted with other phenomena. Retrieved from http://www.workplacebullying.org/bullying-contrasted.

10

Bullying in the Unionized Workplace: The Legal Model for the Protection of Employees and Employers from Employer and Union Intimidation

Jeffrey Guiler
Robert Morris University

Charles M. Albright
Duquesne University

INTRODUCTION

The concept of bullying in a union-represented workplace has evolved into popular urban legend that has been promulgated and exaggerated since the passage of the National Labor Relations Act (NRLA; Wagner Act) in 1935. Whether it is Marlon Brando's heroic struggles in *On the Waterfront* or Jack Nicholson's portrayal of Jimmy Hoffa in *Hoffa*, the Hollywood view of the unionized workplace as an environment of bullying and strong-arm tactics has permeated the popular culture to a point in which simply the word "Teamsters" (International Brotherhood of Teamsters; labor union) conjures for many a totally inaccurate vision of management–labor relations.

The actual picture on the shop floor is that of a far more professional relationship between management and organized labor that functions on a daily basis in unionized workplaces across the nation. Labor unions provide a structure that helps individuals to resolve issues on a timely and efficient basis. This process, while certainly adversarial, is regulated by a set of rules that govern the day-to-day relationship and protect the participating parties from intimidation or bullying by either party. In this chapter, the author will review the legal regulations pertaining to unions in detail and discuss their application through definitions and case studies.

UNFAIR LABOR PRACTICES: RULES OF THE ROAD FOR MANAGEMENT

The Wagner Act of 1935 (NRLA) set in place a process to stabilize and monitor the relationship between labor unions and management. Passed during the Depression, it established the rules by which labor and management would resolve contractual disputes and deal with requests for union representation. Declared constitutional by *NLRB v Jones and Laughlin Steel* (301 U.S. 1 575 S.Ct. 615) in 1937, the Wagner Act formalized a set of Unfair Labor Practices that would serve as the foundation for employers in their dealings with unionized bodies or those wishing to be represented by a union.

A series of regulations were imposed upon organized labor with the passage of the Taft–Hartley Act in 1947, which will be addressed later in the chapter. At this point, we will only address the Unfair Labor Practices, which we may view as the potential sins of management in this process. As we will see, this code severely limits the ability of the representatives of management to bully or intimidate their employees in the workplace. The regulations are enforced by the National Labor Relations Board (NLRB) through their representatives, known as NLRB Agents or simply "Board Agents," who are empowered to intervene in disputes between management and organized labor.

PREVENTION OF BULLYING AND INTIMIDATION OF EMPLOYEES SEEKING UNION REPRESENTATION

The process of achieving union representation or organizing, which is usually opposed by the employer, was identified as a probable point of employer bullying. Prior to the passage of the Wagner Act (1935), employees found by the employer to be engaged in a concerted activity toward or the achievement of union representation were often subject to intimidation or bullying by the employer if they were not formally disciplined, possibly leading to termination. This type of intimidation of employees engaging in activity for their mutual benefit led to the first of the Unfair Labor Practices 8a1 – Interference in the activities of employees engaged in concerted activity. An employer can be found guilty of interference of this nature when he or she engages in any of the following prohibited activities during a union organizing campaign. Specifically, the employer may not, during the period leading up to the election: (1) threaten employees engaged in concerted activity, (2) interrogate employees about such activity, (3) promise to reward employees if they support the employer in the certification election, or (4) spy on employees engaged in concerted activity. We will now review in detail each of these scenarios.

Threatening Employees

Aside from a physical attack, there is probably no more intense form of bullying than physically threatening an individual. In the workplace under possible union organization, the employer is strictly forbidden from threatening an employee's welfare or job. The prohibition of such activity would be enforced by the NLRB. If a complaint was made by the employee, a charge would be filed with the NLRB. The charge would be investigated by an NLRB agent and, if found to be valid, the employer would be found guilty of an 8a1 violation and would be forced to cease the activity as well post an NLRB poster admitting that such activity took place. This process puts a check on the employer's actions and certainly serves as a determent to employer intimidation of union supports in the workplace.

Case

The XYZ Manufacturing Corporation is in the middle of a union organizing drive. The manager of the second shift walks out onto the shop floor and approaches an employee. He says, "You know if the union gets in here, you all could find yourselves out of work because we might just close the plant just like that!" This is an obvious threat to the employee and his or her personal welfare and might cause him or her to fear for his or her future. The employer has certainly engaged in an activity designed to frighten the employee that would possibly deter him or her from voting for his or her best interest out of fear of losing his or her job.

Interrogation

The employer is not allowed to ask the employee questions concerning his or her views about the union or how he or she will vote in the upcoming election. A manager would be thought to intimidate an employee with any line of questioning concerning his or her views. As such an upcoming election is conducted through a secret ballot, questioning an employee would be seen as violating the basic premise of this election.

Case

The manager walks through the company's main floor knowing that the union organizer held a meeting at the local pizza shop the previous evening. As she walks past the time clock she says," So how did your meeting go last evening?" This would be perceived as intimidating those employees who might have been clocking in and had attended the meeting.

Promise

The employer is not allowed to promise the employees engaged in a union campaign any benefits that might be extended by the employer if the employees elected not to choose union representation. Such promises could be fulfilled as the employer has the economic power to deliver such rewards. While the union is allowed to promise benefits, the fact remains that it must bargain with the employer if the union succeeds in winning the election.

Case

The employer walks into the employee recreation room to make a purchase at the vending machine. As he puts his money in the machine he remarks, "You know, this vending food is not that good. I promise you if things turn out for the company in this election we could have a little cafeteria with real food in here." This is an example of the employer using a possible future benefit to buy the votes of the employees. While not exactly an instance of intimidation, it certainly interferes with the employees' right to a free election.

Spying

The employer is not allowed to engage in surveillance activities regarding employees engaged in concerted activity for their mutual benefit. Giving the employees the perception they "are being watched" is a subtle but effective form of intimidation. An example of this behavior could simply be the employer's presence at a public place where the union is scheduling an organizing event. The very presence of an individual connected with management identified by the employee at such a function would be intimidating for an employee.

Case

An employer is aware that the union is having meetings at a local club after work. The employer decides to send a member of the company security team to the parking lot of the club to record the license plates of the parked cars. The license plate numbers would then be matched to those cars parked in the employee parking lot the next day to determine which employees were present at the union meeting.

DISCRIMINATION AGAINST UNION SUPPORTERS

Retaliation

The NLRA (1935) took care to protect employees from becoming victims of discrimination as the result of retaliation of the employer against those who favored unionization. The 8A3 regulations forbid any employer from taking a punitive action against an employee who has openly expressed support or is perceived to be supporting the union in a pending election. Arbitrarily lowering an employee's job classification, changing his or her schedule to a less popular shift (night shift), or denying him or her accepted privileges are all examples of possible 8A3 charges. The employer would be challenged by the NLRB to show that actions taken by the employer were based on business necessity and not the result of anti-union feelings on the part of the employer.

Case

Mary is a single parent who works a 7:00 AM to 3:00 PM shift. She drops her child off at the daycare before work and then picks her up before the daycare closes at 6:00 PM. Her employer believes that Mary may be a union supporter and switches her to the 3:00 PM to 11:00 PM shift, claiming business reasons. This employer would be forced to defend the company against an 8A3 discrimination charge. In addition, any violation of 8A3 is an automatic violation of 8A1, as it is interfering with the union election process.

Discrimination

Discrimination is also illegal after a union has been certified as the exclusive bargaining agent for the employees under the National Labor Relations Act (1935). The employer may not single out union supporters for discriminatory treatment. This type of bullying against those who show support for their union would also be a violation of 8a3.

Case

John arrives at work wearing a new stadium jacket bearing the herald of his union. The manager asks him why he is wearing the jacket and the employee reminds the manager that there is no company dress code and therefore, in his opinion, the jacket is fine to wear to work. The manager sends the employee home without pay to change his attire. The fact that the employee was simply showing solidarity with his union and was disciplined with the loss of pay would probably qualify as a violation of 8a3 (NRLA, 1935).

8a4 Discrimination Against Those Who Seek their Rights Under the NLRA

This protects employees from intimidation or retaliation for participating in any NLRB hearing or providing information or testimony against the employer. Such activity, covert or open, is protected under the NLRA (1935). It is an unfair labor practice to take any action against an employee that is based upon or perceived to be based upon the employee's participation or discussion with an NLRB agent. This type of bullying strikes at the very heart of the election process and, in combination with other unfair labor practices (8a3 and 8a4), could cause the employer to forfeit the right to the election.

The Gissel Doctrine (1969) makes it clear that if an employer commits excessive unfair labor practices, the election may be cancelled. In other words, the employer would have no chance to campaign and the company would be ordered to bargain. This punishment, while possibly thought by employers to be severe, serves the purpose of providing the ultimate protection against bullying by the employer during the union campaign.

As previously noted, any violation of 8a3 and 8a4 is an automatic violation of 8a1. Coupled with the ultimate penalty of the forfeit of the election by the employer, these unfair labor practices serve as a stern warning against any employer bullying or intimidation during a union organizing campaign. Once a union is certified, the employer may not engage in any activities of retaliation against employees who have testified against the employer at the NLRB.

UNFAIR UNION CHARGES: RULES OF THE ROAD FOR THE UNIONS

The Taft–Hartley Act added the Unfair Union Practices in 1947. Passed over President Harry S. Truman's veto, the Act set out regulations for unions similar to those for management with the unfair labor practices. 8a1 of the Act is designed "to restrain or coerce employees in their exercise of their rights under the national labor relations act."

8b1 was specifically designed to protect union members from pressure from their own union. The employee, in his or her dealings with management, has the right to be represented by the union of his or her choice. It is also the duty of the union and its personnel to represent the employee, as it exists as the sole party with the responsibility of representing the employee. The individual union member's grievance or issue, no matter how trivial, cannot be ignored, nor can the union attempt to intimidate the member into dropping his or her grievance.

Equal Representation

In the case, *Louisville & Nashville Railroad v Steele* (326 U.S. 192 (1944)), the Supreme Court ruled that the union must represent all members equally. This ruling, coupled with 8b1, strictly prohibits any bullying of a union member by his or her duly designated representative. If the union member feels such pressure, he or she may file a charge with the National Labor Relations Board against his or her union. This prevents any bullying on the part of the union, as the member has recourse if such activity occurs.

Case

Mary Smith noticed that in her union contract the company and the union had previously agreed that overtime opportunities would be rotated (fairly divided) among all members of the bargaining unit, and that the individual union member should inform his or her supervisor if he or she wished to be included in the pool of employees who desired overtime. When Mary was not scheduled for overtime, she complained to her steward that she was being overlooked by management and that she was filing a grievance. The steward informed her that he would not process her grievance because, "The guys need overtime money because they have families and you don't." Mary Smith has a legitimate charge under 8b1.

8b2 "To Cause or Attempts to Cause the Employer to Discriminate Against an Individual Employee or Group of Employees"

The union is not allowed to ask the employer to deliberately discriminate against or deny a benefit to any particular group in the workplace. Whether female or male, a member of a particular ethnic group or particular individual, the union may not ask the employer to take discriminatory actions in concert with the union's request. This specifically prohibits the union from placing pressure on the employer to discriminate against one or a group of its own employees.

Case

Following the scenario of the previous case, Mary Smith's employer is asked by the union to ignore her request for overtime and the union requests that she not be scheduled for any overtime. The union petitions for the men in the unit to be given the overtime because they have families.

Section 8b4 of the Taft–Hartley Act

No part of the Taft–Hartley Act is more specific in the prohibition of bullying of the employer and his or her representatives than 8b4, "To threaten or attempt to coerce an employer engaged in commerce." This section strictly outlaws any coercion on the part of a labor organization against a company or representatives of that company. Here, the employer would file the charge with the National Labor Relations Board. Any activity on the part of the union in which the employer feels threatened may result in a charge.

Case

An employer is personally threatened by a representative. The employer feels that his or her safety is in danger or believes that the property of the company is being threatened with an illegal act. John Smith, the owner of Smith's towing, is told that he "better watch the trucks or something might happen." This would lead to a charge by Mr Smith against the union through the NLRB.

CONCLUSION AND SUMMARY

The rules established in federal labor law preclude bullying by either side in the unionized workplace. The protections built into the National Labor

Relations Act (as amended) go a long way in preventing intimidating behavior by either side in the management–labor relationship. Such activities, of course, do take place and the review procedures of the National Labor Relations Board guarantee there will be a hearing of such matters; and penalties will be imposed, if appropriate, on bullying in the unionized workplace.

REFERENCES

Louisville & Nashville Railroad v. Steele, 326 U.S. 192 (1944).
National Labor Relations Act, 29 U.S.C. §§151–69 (1935).
NLRB v. Gissel Packing Company, 395 U.S. 575 (1969).
NLRB. v. Jones & Laughlin Steel Company (301 U.S. 1, 575 S.Ct. 615, 81L Ed. 893 1937 U.S.).
Taft–Hartley Act (80–101, 61 Statute 136).

11

Physical and Verbal Bullying

Kisha Radliff
Ohio State University

INTRODUCTION

When one thinks about the military as it might relate to bullying, the picture of a drill sergeant yelling at new recruits and perhaps even targeting a new recruit and giving him or her extra unwanted attention might come to mind. Picture this scenario: John, a new recruit, steps off the bus for basic training. He just graduated from high school a few days ago, and this is the first time he has left home. He walks over to a group of young men who also appear to be new recruits. As the young men make small talk, a drill sergeant walks over and begins to bark orders. John is slow to get in line and the drill sergeant notices. He walks over to John and quickly singles him out, "I see we have a recruit with an attitude problem. Well, guess what, 'mama's boy', your attitude just bought the rest of the group a free push-up session. Everyone, please thank John here and start pushing!" As the weeks go by, John has several encounters with the drill sergeant. At times he is forced to stand and watch as everyone else does pushups due to his actions, or worse yet, told to count the reps out loud. Other times, he is berated or made to perform some exercise in front of the group as a form of punishment. This becomes a daily occurrence. John begins to develop feelings of anxiety and depression and starts to disconnect from the group. It seems as if he is singled out no matter what he does and the group has started to turn on him, too.

While the above scenario is not an actual case, it does illustrate how leadership style (or management style) can create a climate that is conducive to workplace bullying. Although once thought to be a rite of passage in childhood, bullying is still a problem for many even into adulthood (e.g. Bartlett and Bartlett, 2011). Bullying in the workplace can occur in many forms and, consistent with childhood bullying research, there are various definitions of workplace bullying in the literature. Workplace bullying can be defined broadly as a "pattern of destructive and generally deliberate demeaning of co-workers or subordinates that reminds us of the activities of the schoolyard bully" (Vega and Comer, 2005: 101). Einarsen and Skogstad (1996: 187) note that someone is being victimized when they are "repeatedly subjected to negative acts in the workplace" and "feel inferiority in defending" themselves. Thus, workplace bullying occurs when an individual is engaging in behavior with intent to harm the victim, this behavior occurs repeatedly over time, and there is a perceived power imbalance (e.g. the victim feels he or she is unable to retaliate or escape). The case of John (above) demonstrates how the behavior became repetitive, appeared to have the intent to harm (from John's perspective), and led to feelings of inferiority. Further, the negative impact on John (i.e. feelings of anxiety and depression and social disconnectedness) illustrates the potential harmful effects of bullying.

This chapter will focus on verbal and physical forms of bullying, with particular attention paid to these forms of bullying as they are used by some organizations (e.g. military and paramilitary) as forms of behavior management and leadership strategies. Bullying will be described from an ecological perspective with emphasis at the individual, departmental (e.g. direct supervisors), and organizational (e.g. superiors or organizational climate) levels. General recommendations will also be presented.

SIGNIFICANCE

Verbal bullying can be defined as an intent to harm another person through words (e.g. name calling, spreading rumors, not returning phone calls), whereas physical bullying occurs when actions (or inactions) are used against another person with the intent to harm (e.g. glaring at the individual, leaving a room when he or she enters, or destroying the individual's property; Baron and Neuman, 1996). There are two general frameworks for understanding workplace bullying that come from Namie and Namie (2000) and Buss (1961). Namie and Namie (2000) describe a ten-point continuum of harmful behavior that range from incivility (1 to 3), to bullying (also referred to as 'escalated incivility'; 4 to 9), to physical violence (e.g. homicide; 10). Incivility includes behaviors that are in poor taste and are inconsistent with social expectations (see Chapter 9 for discussion). Escalated incivility comprises a wide range of behaviors, including verbal and physical bullying, that occur on a frequent basis; even daily for some individuals. These behaviors can be considered as having "mild to severe interference with the accomplishment of legitimate business interests" (Namie, 2003: 1). Escalated incivility can mildly impact or severely affect an individual's health and economic wellbeing (Namie, 2003). The extreme end of the continuum, physical violence, can result in serious disruption to the victim and the organization and, at its utmost, can result in death (Namie, 2003).

While the focus of this chapter includes behaviors that fall under escalated incivility, it is important to recognize that behavior can begin as incivility and escalate to verbal or physical forms of bullying and that bullying can lead to physical violence. For individuals who have easy access to deadly force (e.g. military, police), escalation of bullying to physical violence is a realistic possibility (e.g. UK National Workplace Bullying Advice Line, 2008). This suggests a strong need for workplace bullying to be acknowledged and addressed.

Buss (1961) conceptualized aggression along three different dimensions: the verbal–physical dimension, the direct–indirect dimension, and the active–passive dimension. This framework creates eight different categories of behavior (e.g. verbal-direct-active, physical-indirect-passive) that have been used extensively in the workplace bullying literature. Many researchers (e.g. Baron and Neuman, 1996) suggest that most workplace bullying can be categorized as verbal-passive-indirect (e.g. not denying a false rumor about a coworker, purposefully not sharing necessary information with a coworker). Baron and Neuman (1996) describe other forms of verbal bullying that include passive-direct (e.g. giving the silent treatment), active-direct (e.g. verbal insults), and active-indirect (e.g. spreading rumors). Although verbal forms of bullying are generally more prevalent, and occur first when bullying is initiated, physical forms of bullying can and do occur in the workplace (Zapf *et al.*, 2003). Examples of physical bullying include not protecting the victim's welfare (passive-indirect), purposefully leaving a room when the victim enters (passive-direct), making obscene gestures (active-direct), and destroying the victim's property (active-indirect; Baron and Neuman, 1996).

Prevalence

Prevalence rates of workplace bullying vary for a variety of reasons, including how the construct is measured, the type of assessment used to measure the construct, as well as differences between the populations assessed. One of the most often cited studies of bullying in the workplace in the United States was completed by the Workplace Bullying Institute. This study found that 37 percent of Americans reported that they had been bullied at work, while almost 13 percent of those individuals were currently experiencing bullying (Namie, 2007). A study of workplace bullying in Europe found that 11 percent of individuals reported being victimized at work (Paoli and Merllié, 2001, as cited in Vandekerckhove and Commers, 2003). A study in Norway by Einarsen and Skogstad (1996) found that 8.6 percent of the individuals surveyed reported experiencing bullying in the workplace over the previous six months, with many of the individuals indicating that the bullying had lasted for about a year and a half. A cross-sectional study conducted by Leymann (1992) in Sweden found that about 3.5 percent of workers indicated that they had experienced workplace bullying (as cited in Einarsen and Skogstad, 1996). While the prevalence rate of workplace bullying may vary, it is clear that the issue of bullying does not go away as individuals move into adulthood.

Prevalence rates for verbal and physical types of bullying can be challenging to determine, as many studies provide general prevalence rates for workplace bullying but do not distinguish between types of bullying. Some studies do, however, mention prevalence rates for some specific bullying behaviors that could be categorized as verbal or physical bullying. Namie (2007) asked survey respondents to describe the types of bullying they experienced. Respondents indicated that they had experienced direct verbal bullying (e.g. shouting, name-calling; 53 percent), verbal bullying in the form of abuse of authority (e.g. poor evaluation; 46 percent), physical forms of bullying (e.g. actions that were humiliating or threatening; 53 percent), and indirect physical bullying that interfered with work performance (e.g. sabotaging one's work; 45 percent).

Keashly and Jagatic (2003) cited a study they presented at a conference in 2000 in which they discussed results from a statewide survey that assessed bullying experiences over a one-year timeframe. The authors reported prevalence rates for verbal and physical forms of bullying that occurred "sometimes" to "very often" on their developed Likert scale. Respondents reported several types of verbal bullying that included passive, active, indirect, and direct behaviors. The types of verbal bullying experienced most frequently (17.1–24 percent of respondents) were described as: the bully flaunting his or her status, ignoring contributions from the victim, getting blamed for others' mistakes, being talked down to, being interrupted, not having calls returned, and getting the silent treatment. Other verbal bullying experiences were reported less frequently (7.1–13 percent of respondents), and included such behaviors as: being verbally attacked, gossiped about, false rumors not denied, being yelled at, being put down in front of others, being excluded from work meetings, and being sworn at in a threatening way. Physical types of bullying were much less common, though 21.5 percent of respondents indicated that they had been glared at in a hostile manner. Approximately 7 percent of respondents also experienced mean pranks and 6 percent experienced negative or obscene gestures. Lastly, Zapf conducted a review that examined several studies and found that 3.6 to 9.1 percent of workplace bullying incidents included physical types of bullying (1999, as cited in Zapf *et al.*, 2003). These studies show that, while there is a wide range of prevalence rates for both verbal and physical types of bullying, verbal bullying generally occurs more often.

Impact of Bullying

Whether at school or at work, the bully often desires control over the victim (Namie and Namie, 2000). Workplace bullying can negatively impact the physical and mental health of those individuals who are bullied (Coyne *et al.*, 2000; Glendinning, 2001; Namie, 2003; Owoyemi, 2011). Workplace bullying can also affect the victim's livelihood (Namie and Namie, 2000), job performance (Höel *et al.*, 2003), job satisfaction (Hauge *et al.*, 2007), and even one's ability to continue at the job (Namie and Namie, 2000). If the victim is unable to continue with his or her work, this can affect his or her livelihood both economically and psychologically, but when the bullied worker does not leave the pain at work, the negative impacts of workplace bullying follow the victim home (Namie and Namie, 2000). A study by Owoyemi (2011) found that, in addition to the possible financial impact on the worker's family through lost wages due to increased days missed from work or being forced out of the job entirely, there can also be an emotional impact. Specifically, victims in this study reported withdrawing from their families (e.g. not engaging with their children).

In addition to the negative effects on the individual, workplace bullying is a significant issue for the organization as a whole (Østvik and Rudmin, 2001). When bullying is present in an organization, that workplace is more likely to experience increased absenteeism (e.g. Höel *et al.*, 2003; Vega and Comer, 2005), increased staff turnover (e.g. Höel *et al.*, 2003; Vega and Comer, 2005), a decline in productivity (Vega and Comer, 2005), and even legal repercussions (Glendinning, 2001; Höel *et al.*, 2003).

When considering the potential negative effects of bullying, bullying behavior in any organization, even in such inherently combative workplaces as the military, should be cause for considerable concern (Østvik and Rudmin, 2001). Individuals in the military are generally not free to come and go as they might be in a corporate organization; military personnel typically sign a commitment for a certain number of years or may be required to join for a certain length of time (Østvik and Rudmin, 2001). This can contribute to feelings of being trapped because the option to quit is not as available as it might be in other organizations and may lead to victims taking drastic measures in order to escape the bullying. This is cause for concern because these individuals are often in a position where they could do great harm to themselves or others.

Østvik and Rudmin (2001) discuss three characteristics specific to individuals in the military, which could also be true for individuals in paramilitary organizations such as the fire service or police service. These individuals are often isolated from "social norms and institutions" (p. 19), have access to weapons or other equipment that could be used for harm, and are trained for violence. What is implied here is that individuals with these characteristics who are experiencing the negative effects of bullying may feel that they have few options to make the bullying stop and may turn to suicide or violence against others (UK National Workplace Bullying Advice Line, 2008).

RELEVANT THEORY: CAN HIERARCHY AND POWER IMBALANCE CONTRIBUTE TO BULLYING IN THE WORKPLACE?

Schoolyard bullying generally includes a perceived imbalance of power as a part of the definition (e.g. Olweus, 1991), and workplace bullying is no different (Owoyemi, 2011; Salin, 2003). This imbalance of power is a natural part of most organizations, where more powerful bosses or supervisors have varying levels of control over their subordinates. Organizations that are particularly at risk for the development of bullying relationships are those that have established a strict hierarchical structure, such as the military (Salin, 2003). These codified hierarchical relationships found in the military or emergency service fields can be vital to the organization's success and there is a need for authoritarian leadership styles that encourage all employees to conform to group expectations so that organizational objectives can be effectively met (Salin, 2003; Vega and Comer, 2005). Thus, there is a fine line to consider when examining bullying within such workplaces. Archer (1999: 95) offered the following observation based on his study of the Fire Service in the United Kingdom, the United States, and Ireland:

> Within the operational activities [purpose of the organization] of the Fire Service is a culture based on power, that is to say rank and position with unargued obedience to orders and instructions is appropriate ... The difficulties experienced within managerial and interpersonal relationships surface within the non-operational [downtime] periods of activity where the cultures of power and bureaucracy (or role) form an uneasy alliance.

Archer is saying is that the hierarchical structure and power imbalance that exists within certain organizations (e.g. Fire Service, military) may be necessary to achieve the primary objectives of the organization. This is consistent with the observations made by Vega and Comer (2005). In the example of the Fire Service, it is important that subordinates know their role and follow orders without question so that a job (e.g. putting out a fire, rescuing an individual) can be completed quickly and efficiently. However, this same structure and power imbalance might not be as effective for those times when the organizational goals are not as relevant or important and, in these moments, a bullying relationship may begin to occur.

This power imbalance can contribute to the use of confrontation, intimidation, or strength to maintain order. When these leadership techniques are a part of the organizational culture, a climate that includes workplace bullying may be more likely to occur (Owoyemi, 2011). In a qualitative study examining bullying in a paramilitary organization, Owoyemi (2011) found that most participants were bullied by a superior. Because bullying is based, in part, on the perception and reaction of the victim, the use of tactics that are meant to keep employees in line or to create unity can quickly escalate into bullying when the individual singled out is unresponsive to the tactics, or responds in a negative way. The use of authoritarian practices and an organization's desire to emphasize conformity can create an environment that tolerates or even condones workplace bullying.

Leymann suggests that a strong hierarchy, an authoritarian leadership style and work climate, and poor communication are risk factors for the likelihood of workplace bullying (1992, as cited in Björkqvist *et al.*, 1994). Einarsen and Skogstad (1996) analyzed data from almost 8,000 individuals employed across various organizations and professions and found several organizational characteristics that were consistent with workplace bullying. Bullying was reported most frequently in organizations that employed a larger number of workers, focused on manual types of labor (such as manufacturing), and were comprised primarily of male employees. It is evident that the military, paramilitary organizations, and blue-collar organizations typically have such characteristics and may be a breeding ground for bullying.

ORGANIZATIONAL CLIMATE: IS IT WORKPLACE BULLYING OR TRADITION?

"I think it's tradition in the fire brigade that what we now class as bullying has always been teasing and it has been stuff which everybody is supposed to put up with" (Archer, 1999: 98). Within some organizations, there are certain rituals that are seen as tradition and are used to socialize new recruits (or new employees) to the group (Archer, 1999). These are activities or rituals that most individuals within the organization experienced when they first joined. For example, in Archer's (1999) study of the Fire Service, almost half (46 percent) of the respondents who self-identified as bullies indicated that the "bullying" behavior they engaged in was similar to what they experienced when they were lower in the ranks. This often means that these behaviors are overlooked or even approved of by managers and supervisors. In fact, one respondent (a senior officer in the Fire Service) indicated that the "physical abuse of individuals" was considered along the lines of teasing and was accepted as a rite of passage for "team building, character building, and bonding" (Archer, 1999: 98).

These behaviors that are often viewed as tradition but verge on bullying can present a dilemma for superiors. The camaraderie that is created by socializing new individuals to the group can be put at risk when the experiences are addressed as bullying, particularly when the behaviors are common practice and few individuals report those behaviors as bullying. Often, those who are most different from the other group members are those who report such behavior as bullying, but those individuals are also those who receive the most negative attention in an effort to force them to conform to group values (Archer, 1999). For these individuals, the bullying can be devastating and can have negative effects on their emotional, psychological, and physical health.

Similarly, it might be tradition to place value on certain leadership styles and those styles that have been perceived to be effective in the past. In most military and blue-collar professions, managers or supervisors have a unit or department that they supervise with regard to successful training, productivity, or success in meeting the goals of the organization. This responsibility generally encourages managers to take ownership over their unit. As a result, the manager has the power to create a workplace climate that does not tolerate workplace bullying or a climate that either encourages (e.g. by urging competition within the group) or allows (either directly or indirectly; e.g. by turning a blind eye to bullying of workers who are having difficulty "pulling their weight") workplace bullying to occur (Archer, 1999).

Managers who have rigid expectations or are "tough" on their subordinates might be viewed by those under their leadership as bullies, but higher ups might view the same behavior as valuable to accomplishing goals. Keashly and Jagatic (2003) suggest that, in some cases, management might view harassment as "functional" for increased productivity. In a mixed methods study that examined workplace bullying among individuals in the Fire

Service, Archer (1999: 97) found that when an officer (or individual in charge of a unit) who bullied others was reported, the response was often to look the other way because that individual "gets things done."

RECOMMENDATIONS

It is important that organizations that thrive on hierarchical power structures and authoritarian leadership styles, such as military and paramilitary organizations, take care to monitor the potential negative effects these leadership styles can have on individuals who are in lower ranks or have less power (Archer, 1999). Upper management ought to have a means to intervene for those individuals who are unable to cope with the tactics used by direct supervisors that could be perceived as bullying. Organizations should be particularly diligent in taking steps to prevent workplace bullying, such as having established processes (e.g. policies, trainings) in place so that those in leadership can effectively intervene when workplace bullying is brought to their attention. Several recommendations for addressing verbal and physical bullying are discussed below.

Anti-Bullying Policy

The first step in addressing workplace bullying is to create or adopt an anti-bullying policy for the organization. While there is currently no federal legislation, some states have introduced and/or adopted laws to address workplace bullying (see www.healthyworkplacebill.org for a detailed review of the Healthy Workplace Bill; Namie, 2011). Managers can determine if there is state legislation in their area that should be consulted and followed in developing a policy. An existing policy provides a formal means through which employees can report workplace bullying and guidelines that supervisors and managers can use to address complaints.

When creating an anti-bullying policy, leadership should take care in developing a policy that can be enforced. This policy ought to include definitions of workplace bullying and specific details as to what disciplinary actions and potential legal consequences could occur if an individual begins to bully (Wiedmer, 2011). Definitions of workplace bullying should be clear and provide examples of different behaviors that might be included (e.g. verbal types and physical types). It is also important to emphasize that bullying behaviors are those behaviors that are repetitive, occur over time, and have the intent to harm or are perceived as being harmful by the recipient. This is particularly important in military and paramilitary organizations that have an organizational culture or traditions that are akin to bullying and may use authoritarian practices that could be construed as bullying behavior.

Once a policy has been established, it is important to ensure that all existing employees are made aware of the policy (Wiedmer, 2011). Employees should be provided with a copy of the policy and instructed on how to access the policy if necessary (e.g. through HR or on the company website). This policy should also become a standard part of orientation or training for new hires or new recruits to the organization. This might include providing regular professional-development trainings that include a discussion of workplace bullying, including how it is defined, the possible negative effects on individuals involved, bystanders, and the organization, and other topics specific to the organization (e.g. prevalence of reported bullying, coping strategies, and how bullying incidents were resolved – all anonymous of course!; Bartlett and Bartlett, 2011).

It is not enough just to *have* an anti-bullying policy in place; the policy must also be *enforced*. In this regard, it is important that the process of addressing bullying issues that arise is transparent. Transparency allows victims to ensure that they were heard and that management (or human resources) will take steps to remedy the problem. The victim should be apprised of what is happening throughout the process. In most situations, society believes that adults are expected to address the issue themselves (Namie and Namie, 2003). Seeking outside help to address the bullying can be seen as a weakness and, in some cases, may actually perpetuate the bullying (Namie and Namie, 2003). Therefore, it is important that supervisors shield the victim from further bullying during the process of investigating the bullying (Wiedmer, 2011). This process can be a part of the policy and can be discussed in professional development training.

A study by the Workplace Bullying Institute found that only 33.4 percent of respondents thought that their employer had a specific policy to address workplace bullying *and* enforced that policy (Namie, 2007). However, this statistic may be an overestimation by individuals who believe that employers are benevolent, and not an accurate estimation based on actual experiences working with employers to address workplace bullying issues. This belief is supported by the fact that only 2.7 percent of individuals who reported experiencing workplace bullying believed that their employer had a policy that was enforced, and approximately 45 percent of survey respondents indicated that their employers had no policy and were not engaged in addressing workplace bullying issues (Namie, 2007). This speaks to the great need for employers to create anti-bullying policies that employees are made aware of and then enforce such policies (e.g. Wiedmer, 2011). Further, this policy should be applied consistently and each situation handled fairly, regardless of the position of the bully within the organization (Bartlett and Bartlett, 2011; Owoyemi, 2011). If employers make the process of addressing bullying issues transparent, this indicates to employees that the organizational leadership takes workplace bullying seriously and takes efforts to remedy the issue.

Creating an Organizational Climate that Does Not Tolerate Bullying

Another way to help prevent or at least reduce the likelihood of bullying is to create a work climate or culture that encourages positive relationships, does not tolerate bullying, and is supportive of individuals who are bullied. Individuals are likely at greater risk for bullying when they work in large organizations, such as the military or construction companies, due to the large size, the greater levels of hierarchy, and the reduced likelihood of social repercussions for the bullies (Einarsen and Skogstad, 1996). For example, Archer's (1999) study that examined bullying in the fire brigade found that there was a certain culture that existed within the organization and new recruits were expected to conform to that culture. One firefighter stated that those individuals who were different from the group had difficulty adjusting and were more likely to experience harassment or bullying from their superiors. This behavior is likely to be tolerated because it is often ingrained in the culture and even considered tradition or a "rite of passage."

Managers or supervisors are often the individuals who set the tone for the climate through the behaviors they model (e.g. Archer, 1999). For example, supervisors who use bullying tactics to motivate subordinates or do not report incidents create a (potentially) negative climate that suggests that bullying behavior is the norm (Wiedmer, 2011). Supervisors who model positive relationships with subordinates and address reported or suspected incidents create a supportive climate that suggests bullying is not tolerated. Managers and human resource departments can create an "environment in which targets are encouraged to speak up about the abuse" (Glendinning, 2001: 280). A work climate that indicates bullying is not tolerated and that victims will be supported may not eradicate bullying, but can reduce the likelihood that bullying will occur by creating a safe work environment (Bartlett and Bartlett, 2011).

In addition to creating a climate that clearly indicates that bullying is not tolerated, it may be helpful to identify an individual who serves as the point person for addressing workplace bullying (Wiedmer, 2011). While it might seem intuitive to have the victim report the bullying to his or her direct supervisor or manager, far too often it is precisely that individual who is perpetrating the bullying (Wiedmer, 2011). This may be particularly true in military and paramilitary organizations. Targets of workplace bullying often keep silent about workplace bullying for varying reasons, including a desire to be accepted by the group, fear of potentially making the situation worse, and the belief that senior management will not (effectively) address the bullying (Archer, 1999). In fact, reporting bullying incidents might be looked down upon by many individuals within the organization when certain behaviors are viewed as tradition or a part of the culture of the organization (e.g. Archer, 1999). Managers within these organizations may have a greater challenge in addressing workplace bullying and creating an organizational culture that supports positive relationships and does not tolerate bullying behavior.

CONCLUSION AND SUMMARY

Unfortunately, verbal bullying in the workplace is an issue that many individuals face. In some instances, verbal bullying can escalate into physical bullying. While physical bullying may be less common in the workplace, it does occur and has the potential to escalate to physical violence. As such, it is important that management acknowledges that workplace bullying exists and is likely an issue within their organization. Furthermore, it is important that prevention and intervention strategies are available. Not only is it important to have policies and services available, but it is also necessary to ensure that employees are aware of such policies and services and that these are enforced. With organizations that rely on hierarchical structure and power imbalances that are inherent within that structure, it can be challenging to identify and address bullying. It can also take time to change the culture of organizations that utilize authoritarian leadership styles due to the nature of their objectives (e.g. to protect and serve). Management should recognize these challenges while taking steps to eradicate bullying from their organization.

REFERENCES

Archer, D. (1999). Exploring "bullying" culture in the paramilitary organization. *International Journal of Manpower*, 20, 94–105.

Baron, R. A., and Neuman, J. H. (1996). Workplace violence and workplace aggression: Evidence on their relative frequency and potential causes. *Aggressive Behavior*, 22, 161–73.

Bartlett II, J. E., and Bartlett, M. E. (2011). Workplace bullying: An integrative literature review. *Advances in Developing Human Resources*, 13, 69–84.

Björkqvist, K., Österman, K., and Hjelt-Bäck, M. (1994). Aggression among university employees. *Aggressive Behavior*, 20, 173–84.

Buss, A. (1961). *The Psychology of Aggression*, New York: Wiley.

Coyne, I., Seigne, E., and Randall, P. (2000). Predicting workplace victim status from personality. *European Journal of Work and Organizational Psychology*, 9, 335–49.

Einarsen, S., and Skogstad, A. (1996). Bullying at work: Epidemiological findings in public and private organizations. *European Journal of Work and Organizational Psychology*, 5, 185–201.

Glendinning, M. (2001). Workplace bullying: Curing the cancer of the American workplace. *Public Personnel Management*, 30, 269–86.

Hauge, L. J., Skogstad, A., and Einarsen, S. (2007). Relationships between stressful work environments and bullying: Results of a large representative study. *Work and Stress*, 21, 220–42.

Höel, H., Einarsen, S., and Cooper, C. L. (2003). Organizational effects of bullying. In S. Einarsen, H. Höel, D. Zapf, and C. Cooper (eds), *Bullying and Emotional Abuse in the Workplace: International Perspectives in Research and Practice* (pp. 145–61), London: Taylor & Francis.

Keashly, L., and Jagatic, K. (2003). By any other name: American perspectives on workplace bullying. In S. Einarsen, H. Höel, D. Zapf, and C. Cooper (eds), *Bullying and Emotional Abuse in the Workplace: International Perspectives in Research and Practice* (pp. 31–61), London: Taylor & Francis.

Namie, G. (2003). Workplace bullying: Escalated incivility. *Ivey Business Journal* (Nov./Dec.), 1–6.

Namie, G. (2007). U.S. workplace bullying survey: September, 2007. Workplace Bullying Institute. Retrieved from http://workplacebullying.org/multi/pdf/WBIsurvey2007.pdf.

Namie, G. (2011). Healthy workplace bill: The healthy workplace campaign. Healthy Workplace Bill. Retrieved from www.healthyworkplacebill.org.

Namie, G., and Namie, R. (2000). *The Bully at Work,* Naperville, IL: Sourcebooks.

Olweus, D. (1991). Bully/victim problems among schoolchildren: Basic facts and effects of a school based intervention program. In D. Pepler and K. Rubin (eds), *The Development and Treatment of Childhood Aggression* (pp. 411–48), Hillsdale, NJ: Lawrence Erlbaum Associates.

Østvik, K., and Rudmin, F. (2001). Bullying and hazing among Norwegian army soldiers: Two studies of prevalence, context and cognition. *Military Psychology*, 13, 17–39.

Owoyemi, O. A. (2011). Exploring workplace bullying in a para-military organisation (PMO) in the UK: A qualitative study. *International Business Research,* 4, 116–24.

Salin, D. (2003). Ways of explaining workplace bullying: A review of enabling, motivating, and precipitating structures and processes in the work environment. *Human Relations*, 56, 1213–32.

UK National Workplace Bullying Advice Line (2008, September). Bullying in the military, suspicious suicides and non-combat deaths. Bully OnLine. Retrieved from http://www.bullyonline.org/workbully/military.htm.

Vandekerckhove, W., and Commers, M. S. R. (2003). Downward workplace mobbing: A sign of the times? *Journal of Business Ethics*, 45, 41–50.

Vega, G., and Comer, D. R. (2005). Sticks and stones may break your bones, but words can break your spirit: Bullying in the workplace. *Journal of Business Ethics*, 58, 101–9.

Wiedmer, T. L. (2011). Workplace bullying: Costly and preventable. *Morality in Education*, 77, 35–41.

Zapf, D., Einarsen, S., Höel, H., and Vartia, M. (2003). Empirical findings on bullying in the workplace. In S. Einarsen, H. Höel, D. Zapf, and C. Cooper (eds), *Bullying and Emotional Abuse in the Workplace: International Perspectives in Research and Practice* (pp. 103–26), London: Taylor & Francis.

12

Relational and Social Aggression in the Workplace

Julaine E. Field
University of Colorado at Colorado Springs

INTRODUCTION

Relationships between employees at work influence the success and productivity of any organization. Employees who communicate clearly, openly, and respectfully with one another are likely better able to foster a positive work climate in which employees feel a sense of common purpose and pride. Clear, frequent, and respectful communication also motivates employees to engage in effective task management, decision-making, and problem-solving. When work relationships are strained or problematic, work suffers, as do the employees entangled in these relationships.

Workplace bullying is defined as a repeated pattern (e.g. minimum of six months) of offensive, negative behavior at work, which is characterized by cruel and malicious attempts to undermine the confidence and/or social status of an individual employee or group of employees (Chappell and Di Martino, 2006). Workplace bullying may include work-related issues or non-work-related topics (i.e. personal) and goes beyond general conflicts or interpersonal clashes. In contrast to temporary workplace conflict, workplace bullying requires that the perpetrator has more power than the victim and that the perpetrator does not intend to stop the bullying because of the psychological rewards that are experienced while in power (Hubert *et al.*, 2001). In comparison to physical violence, there are far more victims of psychological violence or harassment in the workplace than victims of physical violence (Yildirim, 2009). Therefore, because workplace bullying is largely psychological in nature, relational and social aggression may be the best constructs to describe the nature of the bullying behaviors that adults exhibit when they engage with peer victimization with one another at work.

Relational aggression is a form of bullying in which the aggressor uses a personal connection or relationship to gain leverage and power over another person. Relational aggression often develops as a result of mounting tension between two individuals in a relationship (e.g. close colleagues, friends) and involves manipulation or a misuse of personal and/or social power to manipulate or control another person (Crick and Grotpeter, 1995). Relational aggression includes making statements that deliberately intend to undermine a person's self-confidence or sense of connection in the relationship. Behaviors that also may be involved in relational aggression include spreading rumors, engaging in gossip to specifically hurt the reputation of another person, giving someone "the silent treatment," or other social strategies that leave a person feeling isolated from individuals with whom they thought they had collegial relationships. Interestingly, the term, relational aggression, is often used to describe emotionally based bullying that occurs within the friendships of children or adolescents; however, these types of behaviors also can be witnessed among adults in the workplace (Einarsen *et al.*, 2009).

Social aggression (Underwood, 2003) involves "ganging up" behaviors, in which the aggressor seeks to compromise an employee's professional or social standing or popularity within an organization. Social aggression typically involves a main perpetrator who enlists the efforts of other employees to help spread negative rumors, give misinformation to a particular colleague for purposes of causing anxiety and confusion, engage in social shunning or isolation, and participate in caustic "group think" toward the identified target/victim. This form of bullying is organized, and often features systematic, long-term behaviors that negatively affect the culture and climate of an organization. Social aggression is successful when an employee becomes isolated and disconnected from others, when fellow employees attribute various negative characteristics to the target/victim that lack foundation or legitimacy, or when the targeted employee quits. Mobbing (Duffy and Sperry, 2007) is akin to the concept of social aggression, and is another term used to describe how a group may psychologically harass another worker to intimidate or exclude him or her from full participation in the workplace. Individuals who are victims of social aggression at work may describe a hostile work environment, while victims of relational aggression may focus on a specific work relationship as the source of their stress.

Relational aggression and social aggression are destructive behaviors in any workplace. In this chapter, the author will focus on exploring relational and social aggression at work, including how and why employees use relational and/or social aggression with their colleagues. The theoretical frameworks that will be used for these purposes are social dominance theory (Hinde, 1974) and Baillen *et al.*'s Three Way Model (2009). Specific recommendations for workplace managers will also be discussed.

SIGNIFICANCE AND RELEVANT THEORY

Despite the alarming statistics related to workplace bullying discussed in previous and subsequent chapters, very few organizations have official policies and procedures related to this phenomenon. Modern definitions of "bullying" consider the five different types of bullying, which are both overt and covert, including physical and verbal aggression, relational aggression, social aggression, and cyber-bullying. Without this differentiation, adults in the workplace may be challenged by the broad implications of the term, "bullying," and question whether or not this concept can be applied to describing dynamics in their workplace. Use of the terms relational aggression and social aggression, which are defined by specific behaviors, may help managers and employees better name and understand these behaviors as well as to provide a focus to both educate employees and warn them that there can be repercussions or reprimands for said behaviors.

While reviewing definitions of workplace bullying in the literature (see e.g. Chappell and Di Martino, 2000; Einarsen *et al.*, 2003), there is agreement on the relationship variables that are often involved in the manifestation of these behaviors. Individuals who display relational aggression at work often spread rumors about their workplace "friends", reveal confidential or personal information for the purposes of humiliating someone or lowering their social status among peers, take credit for the friend's work, or use confusing advice to intimidate someone or provoke anxiety (e.g. "I heard that the manager was unhappy about what you said in the meeting. You better watch yourself."). The challenge with relational aggression is that victims often know they are being mistreated; however, because it is within the context of a friendship, the victims may not label what they are experiencing as workplace bullying.

Victims of social aggression often wonder why they are the individuals who are singled out for such treatment. However, this is only part of the bullying equation. Baillen *et al.* (2009) state that individual-related characteristics and workplace-related characteristics must both be explored to comprehend how bullying takes shape in the workplace. Additional questions that must be posed include: why do adults bully in the workplace and what contextual variables exist that encourage bullying at work? An environment that contains a group of people who routinely interact with one another must contend with the dynamics of social power and how the possession or absence of social power influences how an individual is viewed and "ranked" within a social hierarchy.

The social dominance hierarchy (Hinde, 1974) is a theoretical window from which to view how social relationships and the behaviors used within these relationships may be portrayed, rationalized, or predicted. Employees who occupy "top" positions in a social dominance hierarchy at work are able to exercise their social power to influence fellow employees and the work environment overall. "Popular" employees with social power are often able to persuade others to view situations as they do, influence the "flow" of work to themselves and fellow colleagues, create favorable work circumstances for themselves (e.g. retaining pleasurable work tasks and delegating less favorable work tasks to others), and influence organizational decision-making. Employees who enjoy this type of power and influence may use it to bully fellow colleagues, particularly if those who enjoy social power and influence feel that their power is being threatened or is in jeopardy of being diminished. For example, if a new, hard-driving, effective salesperson joins a company, she may run the risk of "threatening" the social power of salespeople who have shaped the current culture and practice standards (i.e. power due to seniority, strong personalities being rewarded, etc.) in this company. If feelings of jealousy, competition, and/or mistrust arise and are not managed within the salespeople who occupy the top layers of the social dominance hierarchy, social aggression may be employed to consciously or unconsciously remind the new salesperson of the limits of her own social power and influence.

Rayner and Höel (1997) describe five categories of workplace bullying that are used to reinforce or maintain the social dominance hierarchy. Threatening a colleague's personal or social standing is one type of workplace bullying that may include insulting, intimidating, and/or devaluing an individual in subtle or overt ways. An example may include ridiculing an employee's appearance directly or within earshot of the victim or mocking a colleague's reaction to workplace bullying (e.g. "Can't you take it? Why are you getting upset about nothing?"). Threatening a colleague's professional standing is another tactic of the workplace bully who wants to undermine a colleague. Behaviors may include mocking a colleague's contributions during a department meeting, publicly accusing the colleague of lack of effort when it is unfounded, or belittling a colleague's education, training, or preparation to perform specific work tasks.

Isolation is another specific strategy used by an individual who is trying to socially or emotionally overpower a particular employee. Regardless of the field of work or the employee, workers often desire at least superficial connections with one another to ease feelings of social seclusion or lack of belonging. Other workers may hope to foster and maintain rich friendships or social connections with colleagues because they crave a sense of community or connection with others. For these types of employees, experiencing social isolation is extremely uncomfortable or troubling. Strategies to impose social isolation may include ignoring an employee when he or she is speaking, withholding information from a colleague, preventing access to particular work opportunities, or not inviting an employee to social events.

A fourth type of workplace bullying is deliberate overwork of an employee. Overwork includes assigning complex, labor-intensive tasks that have little purpose or value, applying undue pressure to an employee about a project, work task, or performance in general, impeding the progress of an employee's work by causing disruptions, assigning other tasks when the employee is attempting to complete a required project in a timely manner, or sending the employee on a "wild goose chase" for information that is tangential or not necessary to complete the required work.

The last type of workplace bullying, identified by Rayner and Höel (1997), is destabilization. Destabilization includes behaviors that seek to undermine an employee's sense of competence, purpose, professional direction, or role in an organization. Destabilization may include repeatedly dwelling on a minor mistake that an employee made, assigning the employee tasks that are not part of his or her scope of work, and rearranging or revoking an employee's work responsibilities for unclear reasons.

The first three forms of workplace bullying described above may involve relational and/or social aggression. Relational aggression and/or social aggression are most likely associated with the commission of threats to personal and professional standing and isolation. Also, each is also a form of bullying that can be perpetrated by an individual with equal or greater social power. However, overwork and destabilization would be more likely to be carried out by a perpetrator who has more social and organizational power than the victim (e.g. a supervisor).

As defined by Rayner and Höel (1997), these five types of workplace bullying help to reinforce a perpetrator's power in the social dominance hierarchy. Depending upon the size of the organization, there may be several groups in which individuals compete for positioning in a specific hierarchy (e.g. middle managers compete with other middle managers, administrative assistants compete with other administrative assistants, etc.). Yet, it must also be noted that Höel *et al.* (2001) found that supervisors are more likely to bully subordinates. These findings support the systemic nature of workplace bullying and how each person's behavior impacts another's behavior. The circular causality of workplace bullying makes it difficult to break the cycle of reactivity and exertion of power between individuals or change the culture where workplace bullying can thrive.

Baillen *et al.* (2009) propose a Three Way Model, which further illustrates the systemic nature of workplace bullying, as well as how relational and social aggression are involved. The researchers used qualitative inquiry to analyze 87 actual cases of workplace bullying. Baillen *et al.* (2009) identified three specific variables that contribute to the development of bullying in the work setting. First, intrapersonal frustration was found to be a contributor to the development of workplace bullying. This frustration is often manifested as active or externalizing for perpetrators, and passive or internalizing for victims. For example, when relational aggression occurs between colleagues, the perpetrator's stress and frustration regarding work is channeled into aggression toward a specific colleague with whom he or she may be close. The victim, although possibly also irritated with the circumstances at work, internalizes this annoyance, may be compromised as a result, and then ends up being the target of the colleague's aggravated state. This same reciprocal process may also be played out in scenarios involving social aggression; however, in the process of enacting one's frustration, the perpetrator garners the support, loyalty, and "buy in" of others before or while externalizing and targeting the victim.

The second variable is interpersonal conflict between colleagues that festers and is not resolved in an open, fair, and deliberate manner (Baillen *et al.*, 2009). This finding is consistent with relational and social aggression, as both forms of workplace bullying often entail the use of covert strategies (e.g. going "behind" a colleague's back and discussing personal information, spreading rumors to create distrust and confusion, voicing his/her discontent to everyone but the actual target, etc.) to vent one's frustration, gaining loyalty from others (i.e. social aggression) to justify his or her actions and operationalize anger toward the victim.

Unfortunately, these behaviors on the part of the perpetrator may be followed by a victim who overtly displays hurt, anger, confusion, and or other reactive behaviors, thus reinforcing the behaviors of the bully. In the case of social aggression, particularly malicious colleagues may find entertainment and humor in ganging up on and "pushing" the victim emotionally. This response exhibited by the victim reinforces the bullying behaviors (i.e. the social aggression worked and achieved its desired effect) making the behaviors more challenging to extinguish.

Finally, the last variable in the Three Way Model involves specific workplace environmental antecedents that help to build and maintain a bullying culture (Baillen *et al.*, 2009). For example, if administrators or company leaders frequently talk harshly or sarcastically about one another in a relationally aggressive manner, this modeling invites employees to cope with their interpersonal conflicts in indirect ways while simultaneously creating a "culture of gossip." High-pressured work environments invite employees to compete with one another for attention, validation, power, and resources; however, if that same work environment does not also emphasize teamwork and collaboration to ward off destructive competition between colleagues, or work sabotage based on jealousy, this environment may become ripe for the behaviors of social aggression. Individuals who achieve beyond their peers may become the targets of orchestrated mobbing to keep high achievers "in their place" in the social dominance hierarchy. Again, administrators or managers who model these same behaviors enable the proliferation of negativity and harsh treatment of others. Furthermore, administrators who turn a blind eye to the mistreatment of others perpetuate and preserve relational and social aggression in the workplace.

Salient Features

Case Vignette I (Based on an Actual Incident of Workplace Bullying)

Nicole is a 27-year-old nurse who works at a community health clinic. Nicole is a bright, assertive, vocal nurse with impeccable clinical skills and effective bedside manner. Recently, she talked with her supervisor, Cathy, about ideas for the agency to better monitor and manage patient caseloads. Although the supervisor thanked Nicole for her suggestions and willingness to try and problem solve on behalf of the agency, Nicole felt uneasy about Cathy's apparent defensiveness and quick dismissal from her office.

The next day, when Nicole went to Cathy's office to discuss a requested vacation day that had not yet been approved, her supervisor said very loudly, "So, you want a day off? I am not sure if we can do this. What do you think, Louis?" Louis' office is adjacent to Cathy's. Because Cathy stopped making eye contact with her and said nothing further, Nicole felt compelled to step over in front of Louis' office door. As soon as she did, Louis looked to her left and commented, "Nicole wants a vacation day, Karen. Are you going to approve this?" Karen is the director of the community health clinic, whose door was also open. Nicole then recognized the pattern of being "passed to the next person," and felt humiliated.

It was obvious that Cathy had told her administrative colleagues of the conversation that she and Nicole had the previous day related to patient caseloads. Red-faced and frustrated, Nicole stepped into Karen's office. Karen looked up from her paperwork, and in a haughty voice stated, "I will have to think about it." She then lowered her eyes and said nothing more. Both stunned and embarrassed, Nicole slowly walked down the hallway and made her way back to her desk.

Case Vignette II (Based on an Actual Incident of Workplace Bullying)

Roger is a tenured professor at a mid-size university. He works in a history department comprised of four men and four women. He is very good friends with his colleague, David, and they frequently "team up" to tackle service projects, produce scholarly works, and complete other administrative tasks in the department. They also engage in social activities with one another that involve their families. Both men are considered leaders in the department.

Recently, Roger was invited by his academic dean to apply for the Department Chairperson position upon the retirement announcement of the current chair. This information was inadvertently leaked just before a history department meeting, and Roger was nervous about the response from his colleagues. During the meeting, David would not make eye contact with Roger and sat stone-faced for the majority of the meeting. It was clear that David was tense and unhappy about the idea of Roger being promoted to Chairperson of the department.

> *Over the weekend, Roger received a phone call from David. David was having dinner at a local Irish pub and Roger could hear Sylvia and George (colleagues from the university) in the background. David sloppily explained that he was calling to congratulate Roger on his promotion and looked forward to Roger "being his new boss." Roger attempted to minimize David's statement about the power differential between them, to no avail. David hurriedly got off the phone, but prior to him hanging up, Roger overheard a colleague say "asshole" and the three of them were heard laughing before the dial tone.*

The case vignettes bring to life the nature of social aggression (Case Vignette I) and relational aggression (Case Vignette II). Although both scenarios involved more than one perpetrator or bystander in the bullying incident, the episode involving Roger was based on a perceived breach of loyalty, trust, and appearance of being "equals" with a colleague with whom he shared a friendship. Social aggression was possible in Case Vignette I because all three managers agreed to orchestrate against Nicole and participate in the humiliating process of her "going door to door" to seek permission for her request of a vacation day.

Workplace bullying is a broad construct, and the use of this term may impede employees and managers from clearly understanding and identifying the full range of bullying behaviors. Once named and defined, relational and social aggression focus on specific behaviors that may be observed in the workplace and underscore the interpersonal dynamics that exist between and among bullies and victims. Using standardized definitions such as relational and social aggression may assist managers with the development of clear workplace policies and rules that name unacceptable behaviors among colleagues. Additionally, these same policies should identify appropriate behaviors or ways of treating fellow employees to create a cohesive, productive organizational culture.

Randall (1997) found that most administrators have not been trained in how to manage workplace bullying, including relational and social aggression among employees, and may lack understanding regarding the way in which to identify, investigate, and respond to these behaviors when they are reported. Additionally, when confronted, many workplace bullies deny that they are "bullies" or do not identify their behaviors with the label. However, such individuals may not be as quick to repudiate specific behaviors outlined in workplace policy manual that are associated with relational and social aggression, as such behaviors may have been observed by colleagues or even individuals in management positions. Identifying and describing specific behaviors that are consistent with relational and social aggression may be much more damning than using a blanket term like workplace bullying to explain why the behaviors of the employee have been reported to management.

So, too, when perpetrators realize that they are going to be held accountable by management and that they must change the way in which they treat targeted individuals, they may be more open to identifying and admitting the defensive responses they have used to manage their own feelings. Bullies may be compelled to strike out when they are trying to avoid the cognitive dissonance or unpleasant feelings associated with competition, jealousy, inadequacy, incompetence, or rejection. Perpetrators of bullying who are able to identify the feelings that underlie their own behaviors may be more likely to interrupt the cycles of intrapersonal and interpersonal conflict described by Baillen *et al.* (2009).

RECOMMENDATIONS

The following section represents specific recommendations for managers and supervisors related to guarding against and managing the presence of relational and social aggression in the workplace.

Hiring

- Applicants should be asked about how they manage workplace-related frustration. This may include asking the individual to talk about how he or she would approach and talk to a colleague with whom he or she was experiencing conflict.
- Managers in the process of hiring a new employee should consider using case vignettes of relational and social bullying to gauge the reaction of the applicant. Case Vignettes I and II provide examples of cases that managers may present during the interview process. Applicants could be asked to describe the situation from both the perpetrator's and victim's perspective as well as to provide advice regarding the way in which management could intercede.
- Applicants can be asked about employee behaviors that they will exhibit to contribute to a positive, productive work environment.

Workplace Policy and Procedures

- Companies and organizations should consider the development of an anti-bullying workplace policy that specifically outlines the definitions of relational and social aggression and their associated behaviors. Organizations that have an anti-bullying workplace policy in place should periodically review it to ensure that it includes a broad range of bullying behaviors (e.g. overt physical bullying, overt verbal bullying, overt and covert behaviors related to relational aggression and social aggression, and cyber-bullying).
- The organization should outline clear procedures for reporting workplace bullying, including the option for anonymous reporting.
- The organization should outline clear procedures for investigating workplace bullying, including separate interviews with victims, perpetrators, and bystanders.
- The organization should identify clear procedures for applying penalties for employees who have been found to be engaging in workplace bullying. This may include being written up for the first offense, having a behavioral coaching session with an administrator for the second offense, and being placed on short-term leave for a third offense. It is important that the penalty be severe enough to thwart the relationally and/or socially aggressive behaviors exhibited by the bully.

Training

- Most new and current employees for any organization undergo required training (e.g. sexual harassment). Organizations should include opportunities for new and seasoned employees to learn about relational and social aggression in the workplace. Specific statistics and consequences for the victims, perpetrators, and the climate of the workplace should be addressed.
- Open discussion should be allowed for employees to discuss why relational and social aggression may or does take place within their organization. Employees should be part of the brainstorming process to enact new practices that may shift a negative workplace climate or maintain a healthy and productive workplace climate.
- Employees should be asked to sign a behavioral contract at work that specifically outlines the way in which employees should treat one another.

Intervention

- Supervisors and managers should intervene immediately when they detect that relational and social aggression is occurring.
- Victims of relational and social aggression should have the opportunity to receive support and feedback from supervisors and human resources staff. Those in power should be careful not to blame the victim; however, discussing why the victim has been targeted is an appropriate psychoeducational exercise.
- Perpetrators of relational and social aggression should also have the opportunity to receive support and feedback from supervisors and human resources staff. Strategies for working with perpetrators may be to ask them to engage in perspective taking and put themselves in the shoes of the victim, have them discuss how their behaviors impact the larger work climate, and have them describe the possible connection between their own intrapersonal and interpersonal frustration and how both may be better managed without victimizing another person.
- Perpetrators should also be made aware of the penalties involved if they continue to use their current behaviors.
- Supervisors and managers must demonstrate ego strength, assertiveness, and clear professional boundaries, as perpetrators may be quite charming and socially powerful and may attempt to use these skills to manipulate their supervisors and managers.
- Supervisors and managers must continually monitor their own approaches to conflict and work and be sure to avoid reinforcing a culture that condones relational and social aggression among colleagues.

CONCLUSION

This chapter has specially focused on relational and social aggression as forms of workplace bullying. Because most workplace bullying is psychological in nature, relational aggression and social aggression are appropriate constructs to describe how and why adults bully one another at work. These constructs are defined, discussed, and framed within social dominance theory as well as a Three Way Model of workplace bullying.

Two vignettes are used to illustrate how relational and social aggression may happen among colleagues, and specific suggestions are made for supervisors and managers who would like to address relational and social aggression in the workplace.

REFERENCES

Baillien, E., Neyens, I., De Witte, H., and De Cuyper, N. (2009). Qualitative study on the development of workplace bullying: Towards a three way model. *Journal of Community and Applied Social Psychology*, 19, 1–16.

Chappell, D., and Di Martino, V. (2000). *Violence at Work* (2nd edn), Geneva: ILO.

Crick, N. R., and Grotpeter, J. K. (1995). Relational aggression, gender, and social-psychological adjustment. *Child Development*, 66, 710–722. doi: 10.1111/j.1467-8624.1995.tb00900.x.

Duffy, D., and Sperry, L. (2007). Workplace mobbing: Individual and family health consequences. *Family Journal: Counseling and Therapy for Couples and Families*, 15, 398–404.

Einarsen, S., Höel, H., and Notelaers, G. (2009). Measuring exposure to bullying and harassment at work: Validity, factor structure and psychometric properties of the Negative Acts Questionnaire-Revised. *Work and Stress*, 23, 24–44.

Einarsen, S., Raknes, B. I., and Matthiesen, S. B. (1994). Bullying and harassment at work and their relationships to work environment quality: An exploratory study. *European Work and Organizational Psychologist*, 4, 381–401.

Einarsen, S., Höel, H., Zapf, D., and Cooper, C. L. (2003). The concept of bullying at work: The European tradition. In S. Einarsen, H. Höel, D. Zapf, and C. L. Cooper (eds), *Bullying and Emotional Abuse in the Workplace: International Perspectives in Research and Practice* (pp. 3–30), London: Taylor & Francis.

Hinde, R. A. (1974). *Biological Bases of Human Social Behaviour*, New York: McGraw-Hill.

Höel, H., Cooper, C. L., and Faragher, B. (2001). The experience of bullying in Great Britain: The impact of organizational status. *European Journal of Work and Organizational Psychology*, 10, 443–65.

Hubert, A., Furda, J., and Steensma, H. (2001). Mobbing, systematisch pestgedrag in organisaties: Twee studies naar antecedenten en gevolgen voor de gezondheid (Mobbing, systematic bullying behavior within organizations: Two studies for antecedents and health consequences). *Gedrag en Organisatie*, 14, 378–96.

Randall, P. (1997). *Adult Bullying, Perpetrators and Victims*, London: Routledge.

Rayner, C. and Höel, H. (1997). A summary review of literature relating to workplace bullying. *Journal of Community and Applied Social Psychology*, 7, 181–91.

Underwood, M. K. (2003). *Social Aggression among Girls*, New York: Guilford Press.

Yildirim, D. (2009). Bullying among nurses and its effects. *International Council of Nurses*, 56, 504–11.

13

Sexual Harassment and Bullying at Work

Alyssa M. Gibbons, Jeanette N. Cleveland, and Rachel Marsh
Colorado State University

INTRODUCTION

Whenever a social issue emerges and receives public attention, much controversy and debate occurs over its definition and boundaries (Gillespie and Leffler, 1987). Sexual harassment is no exception. Prior to 1976 (MacKinnon, 1979; cf. Farley, 1978), sexual harassment was just a part of everyday life for working women where such treatment was considered "business as usual". However, with Farley's (1978) book, *Sexual Shakedown: The Sexual Harassment of Women on the Job*, such business-as-usual behaviors were relabeled as "sexual harassment." Such is the case currently with the identification of incivility and bullying in the workplace, which emerged as a topic of importance in the 1990s (Jones, 2006). Other chapters have described bullying in greater detail. In this chapter, we discuss sexual harassment research and literature as a critical source from which we can increase our understanding of workplace mistreatment.

At present, there is little consensus regarding either the definitions of bullying and sexual harassment (SH) or the relationship between the two. To be sure, both are forms of individual and organizational mistreatment or counterproductive behavior at work, but the precise nature of their relationship is a matter of some debate. Some researchers view sexual harassment as a subtype of bullying, one that happens to be focused on sex or gender (Vartia and Hyyti, 2002). Others stress the gendered nature of SH, arguing that sexual harassment derives from a history of masculine power, sexism, and misogyny (Quinn, 2000), and that SH is therefore entirely distinct from other kinds of bullying. In our view, neither of these extremes is satisfying. Treating SH as simply a special case of bullying cannot account for the histories of sexual harassment litigation and research in the US, both of which have been heavily influenced by feminist theory (Quinn, 2000; Schultz, 1998), nor for many aspects of the experience of SH as reported by victims (Jones, 2006). However, by dismissing or overlooking the similarities between SH and bullying, we miss the opportunity to generalize potentially valuable theories or findings across domains and to understand the broader picture of incivility or hostile behavior in the workplace.

In this chapter, we present an integrated framework for defining sexual harassment and clarifying its relationship to bullying. We then use this framework to discuss how (a) theory and (b) research on sexual harassment can inform understanding of bullying

SIGNIFICANCE AND RELEVANT THEORY: AN INTEGRATED FRAMEWORK FOR UNDERSTANDING SEXUAL HARASSMENT AND BULLYING

Part of the difficulty in identifying boundaries between sexual harassment and bullying is that there are several different frameworks for defining sexual harassment, and the majority of these definitions are multidimensional (Jones, 2006). In other words, there are several distinct kinds of behavior that can be considered SH, and some of these are more clearly similar to bullying than others. In order to clarify the relationship between SH and bullying in this chapter, we propose an integrated framework based on three major existing perspectives: the legal perspective (Equal Employment Opportunity Commission (EEOC), 1990), the psychological perspective (Fitzgerald *et al.*, 1995, 1997b), and the competence-based perspective, as advocated by Schultz (1998). Figure 13.1 presents a conceptual overview of the alignments among these three frameworks and an integrated framework. Each row of the figure represents one framework (labeled in the boxes on the left), and corresponding concepts across frameworks

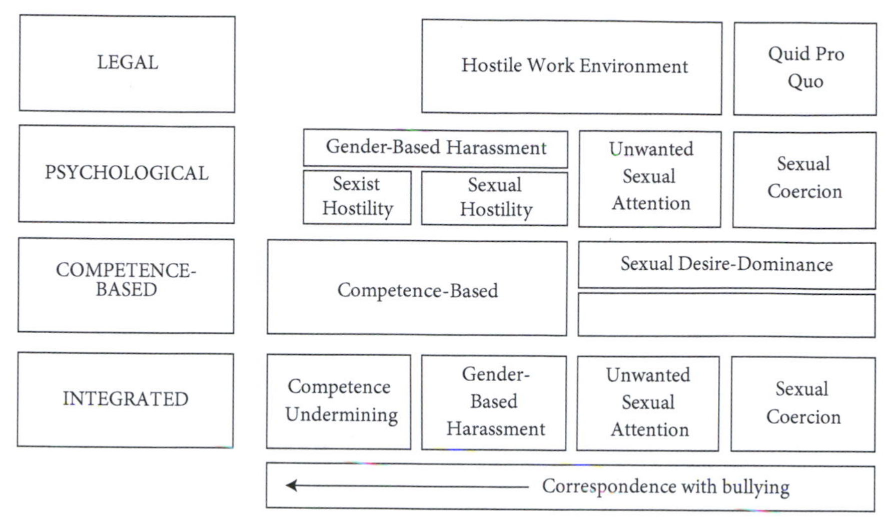

FIGURE 13.1
Alignment of frameworks for describing sexual harassment behavior

are aligned vertically. We introduce each framework briefly here, present our integrated model, and explain how the integrated model is useful in understanding SH in relation to bullying.

Legal Perspective

Although sexual harassment is a legally proscribed behavior, the term "sexual harassment" does not appear in any US federal statute. Rather, sexual harassment is considered to be a type of sex discrimination, and sex discrimination is prohibited under Title VII of the Civil Rights Act of 1964 (EEOC, 1990). Specifically, SH is considered a form of discrimination in the US because it creates different "terms, conditions, or privileges of employment" (Title VII, Sec. 2000-e2/703 (a) (1)) or "adversely affects his [sic] status as an employee" (703 (a) (2)) as a result of the victim's sex. As we consider SH in the context of bullying, it is important to remember that harassment on the basis of race, color, religion, or national origin is prohibited under the same statute for the same reasons.

At present, US law differentiates two types of sexual harassment: quid pro quo harassment and hostile work environment harassment (EEOC, 1990). These appear in the first row of Figure 13.1. Quid pro quo harassment is the archetypal case of SH, in which a person in a position of power offers job-related benefits or consequences in exchange for sexual favors. The definition of hostile work environment harassment is more subtle and complex. Hostile work environment harassment consists of a pattern of behavior, clearly based on the gender of the victim, which interferes with performance or is intimidating or offensive. Examples of behaviors that have been considered hostile work environment harassment by the courts include unwelcome sexual advances, offensive comments of a sexual nature, and the presence of pornography in the workplace (EEOC, 1990). However, neither statute nor case law regarding SH defines the issue in behavioral terms or provides a comprehensive list of behaviors that do or do not constitute harassment. Rather, SH must be determined on a case-by-case basis, taking the totality of the circumstances into account (Guidelines, 2011).

Psychological Perspective

Early SH researchers noted the inadequacy of relying on the ambiguous legal definition of SH in order to understand the phenomenon and its effects. They recognized that many employees had workplace experiences that might not lead to a finding of SH in court, but that created the same psychological experience for the victim. The psychological definition of SH (Fitzgerald *et al.*, 1995; Gelfand *et al.*, 1995) was developed as a way to assess such experiences, regardless of whether the victim filed a legal claim or even labeled the behavior as SH. This model partitions the construct into three types of harassment: sexual coercion, unwanted sexual attention, and gender-based harassment.

Sexual coercion, in which rewards or punishments are subtly or explicitly offered for sexual favors, aligns with quid pro quo harassment in the legal perspective. However, the psychological perspective extends the legal perspective by identifying two different variants of hostile work environment. Unwanted sexual attention refers to behaviors such as staring, touching, or repeated requests for dates after the recipient has made clear that these are unwelcome. Gender-based harassment includes sexist, crude, or otherwise offensive stories, remarks, or jokes. This model of SH has been replicated in military (Fitzgerald *et al.*, 1999b), workforce, and student samples (Gelfand *et al.*, 1995) as well as across cultures (Gelfand *et al.*, 1995). Some studies suggest that gender-based harassment can be further partitioned into sexual hostility (harassment that is explicitly sexual in nature) and sexist hostility (harassment that is based on gender but is not explicitly sexual; Fitzgerald *et al.*, 1999b).

The psychological perspective is represented in the second row of Figure 13.1. Fitzgerald and colleagues (1995) argue that sexual coercion corresponds clearly to quid pro quo harassment in the legal perspective, whereas gender-based harassment and unwanted sexual attention correspond to hostile work environment harassment.

Competence-Based Perspective

Schultz (1998) outlines a long history of SH cases in which courts have assumed or explicitly argued that SH is about sexual desire; that is, for a claim of SH to be upheld, courts have often required that the conduct be explicitly sexual in nature. She labels this view the sexual desire-dominance paradigm, in which it is assumed that SH stems from either the harasser's use of power to gratify sexual desire or the harasser's use of sexuality to gratify a desire for dominance, or both. However, Schultz (1998) argues that this emphasis on overtly sexual behavior means that many cases that fit the spirit of Title VII – a pattern of treatment that serves to undermine women's participation in the workplace – are denied because many of the individual behaviors that comprise them do not appear sexual. For example, in Reynolds v. Atlantic City Convention Center (1990), a woman working as a construction subforeman experienced a sustained pattern of insubordination and verbal abuse from her crew, who stated clearly that they did not wish to work for a woman. However, her claim of sexual harassment was rejected by the court because only a few of the abusive behaviors were explicitly sexual, even though the court recognized that the overall pattern of behavior was clearly based on the plaintiff's sex.

Schultz (1998) argues that assuming sexual desire-dominance is the motive for SH creates an inappropriately limited view. She suggests instead a competence-based paradigm, in which the primary explanation for SH behavior is not sexual desire but rather a desire to restrict and limit the participation of one sex in jobs and roles that have traditionally been the province of the other. Thus, in this paradigm, SH includes behaviors that are intended to undermine the perceived or actual competence of a person (male or female) who does not fit the gender stereotype of the job. These behaviors may or may not be sexual in nature (e.g. giving lower quality training to female employees), but the overall effect is to create a hostile working environment for the victims. Fitzgerald and colleagues (1999b) began to include such behaviors in their category of sexist hostility; however, in their measure, even the sexist hostility items require that the respondent attribute the behavior as occurring "because of your sex." Schultz's argument is that even those behaviors that are not obviously based on sex need to be considered in determining the overall pattern of SH.

In the third row of Figure 13.1, we link the competence-based perspective with the psychological and legal perspectives. Schultz (1998) presented the competence-based paradigm as a framework for understanding all of SH, and thus as a replacement for the sexual desire-dominance paradigm. Accordingly, competence-based harassment could be aligned with any of the types of harassment presented in the other frameworks, and this is represented in the figure. Certainly, the behaviors described by Fitzgerald *et al.* (1995, 1997a) as gender-based harassment (GBH) correspond well with the examples given by Schultz. There is room for some debate regarding whether unwanted sexual attention (USA) and sexual coercion (SC) really fit the competence-based paradigm. On the one hand, these behaviors can be ways to undermine a woman's competence in the workplace, by reducing her to a sexual object and causing others to question whether whatever success she experiences is due to her own merit or her sexual behavior. Indeed, women who report having experienced USA or SC almost universally report experiencing GBH as well (Fitzgerald *et al.*, 1999b). On the other hand, there are cases in which the sexual desire-dominance paradigm does appear to be a reasonable explanation for USA and SC behavior (e.g. Ross v. Double Diamond, 1987).

As we will discuss later on, we believe it is inappropriate to consider all instances of SH as stemming from a common motive or cause. Consequently, we have retained the sexual desire-dominance (SD-D) paradigm identified by Schultz (1998) as an alternative possible explanation for USA and SC behavior. A given instance of these behaviors could be the result of desire, dominance, threat, or a combination of these factors. However, the SD-D paradigm is not aligned with GBH, based on Schultz's finding that SH claims involving gender-based harassment were often denied when the plaintiff could not show the harassment was grounded in sexual desire.

Further, Schultz (1998) notes that competence-based harassment can also include behavior that is not explicitly sexual. As a result, in Figure 13.1, the box for competence-based harassment extends beyond the three categories of the psychological view into as-yet-undefined territory.

Integrated Perspective

In our view, each of these perspectives contributes something valuable to our understanding of SH, but the picture becomes complete only when we consider them together. The legal perspective is important for understanding the history of SH and the development of policy and research to support the law. The psychological perspective properly expands our understanding of SH to include persons and situations that might never appear in a court of law, but that nevertheless have substantial impact on the victims and their workplaces. The psychological view also has the benefit of defining SH in terms of specific, concrete behaviors, rather than more abstract terms such as "a pattern of conduct." The competence-based perspective adds theory about motives, and also broadens the set of behaviors that can be considered part of a pattern of SH.

In the final row of Figure 13.1, an integrated model synthesizes the psychological and competence-based perspectives. In addition to the three categories proposed by Fitzgerald *et al.* (1995), we have added a fourth category of "competence undermining" (CU) behavior to correspond with Schultz's (1998) argument. Such behaviors include withholding information, failing to cooperate, and other behaviors that on their face have little to no sexual content, but that make it more difficult for the target to perform her job. These four categories of behavior can be viewed as a continuum from less sexualized (CU) to more sexualized (SC) behavior.

One benefit of this integrated framework is that it offers a clear way to relate SH to bullying. Specifically, the further to the left a behavior falls on our framework, the more similar that behavior is to bullying. Although there are many definitions of bullying, most researchers appear to agree that (a) bullying is a pattern of enduring or repeated aggressive behaviors and (b) such behaviors are intended to be hostile and/or are perceived as hostile by the recipient (Einarsen and Skogstad, 1996). Examples of bullying behavior include verbal abuse; insults; offensive conduct; threatening, humiliating, or intimidating behavior; exclusionary behavior; interfering with work; and sabotage (Lutgen-Sandvik *et al.*, 2009). Such behaviors clearly overlap with CU, when the bullying happens to be based on the victim's gender (or gender nonconformity; Schultz, 1998). GBH behaviors are essentially sexualized bullying: using sex or gender content as a mechanism to undermine the victim's competence (or perceived competence).

USA and SC are not so clearly linked to bullying. As mentioned earlier in our discussion of the competence-based paradigm, these behaviors may stem from one (or more) of several possible motives. They may be extensions of a pattern of CU and GBH, intended to minimize the victim by reducing her (or him) to a sexual object rather than a competent employee. Alternately, they may be grounded in actual desire (though we suspect this is rare) or as an expression of power ("because I can get away with it"). To complicate matters, these motives may be mixed in many cases. However, the inclusion of possible motives other than threat means that these behaviors do not correspond so neatly to bullying. Further, the personally violating nature of these behaviors (which amount, in some cases, to sexual assault) may result in outcomes for the victim that are somewhat different from those associated with bullying (Dionisi *et al.*, 2012).

For this reason, we propose that SH theory and research can be applied to bullying (and vice versa) to the extent that the specific type of SH behavior falls to the left-hand side of our proposed continuum. In the following sections, we will use this framework as we discuss theory and research on sexual harassment and how it might be applied to bullying.

Prevalence of Sexual Harassment and Bullying

Considerable research has examined the prevalence of SH behavior in various domains. Much of this research is necessarily atheoretical, focused on establishing the scope and importance of the construct rather than on explaining it. Estimates of the overall frequency of SH vary depending on the sample and the method, but Fitzgerald (1993) estimates that nearly 50 percent of US women are likely to experience sexual harassment at some point in their academic or work lives. This might be considered a very broad estimate, but 44 percent of women employed by the US federal government reported SH experiences within a two-year period (US Merit Systems Protection Board, 1995).

Fitzgerald *et al.* (1999b) estimated that 78 percent of women and 38 percent of men in the military had some experience of SH. Using the typology of the psychological framework, they found that SC and USA behaviors rarely occurred alone, but nearly always occurred in conjunction with sexist hostility, sexual hostility, or both. Among women, only 13 percent had experienced SC, but 42 percent had experienced USA and 75 percent had experienced GBH. Among men, the prevalence of each type of harassment was lower, with only 2 percent experiencing SC and 8 percent experiencing USA, but 36 percent experiencing some form of GBH. Similar overlapping patterns, but different prevalence rates, occurred in Canada, where 74 percent of formal SH complaints mentioned USA and 46 percent mentioned GBH (Welsh, 2000). In Welsh's study, SC behaviors never appeared in the absence of other SH behaviors, with USA being the most frequent co-occurring behavior.

Bullying Prevalence

Estimates of the prevalence of bullying or abusive work behaviors are similarly variable, but generally higher than the estimates of prevalence for SH. One study of university employees found SH prevalence rates between 27 and 40 percent for women and 27 and 46 percent for men, but generalized workplace abuse prevalence rates between 59 and 73 percent for women and 52 and 77 percent for men (Richman *et al*., 1999). As in the SH research, more severe abusive or bullying behaviors such as physical aggression (1–13 percent) or threats (12–30 percent) were much less common than more subtle behaviors such as verbal abuse (39–58 percent) or disrespect (32–69 percent).

That bullying appears to be more widespread than SH is not surprising, considering that bullying can be based on any number of possible characteristics, whereas SH is based on gender. However, comparing the prevalence research in the two areas suggests some interesting future directions. One is the question of labeling. Numerous studies indicate that many people who report experiencing SH behaviors do not label these behaviors as harassment (i.e. they respond "no" to the question "have you ever been sexually harassed?"; e.g. Fitzgerald *et al.*, 1988). One explanation for this is that SH is an ambiguous concept (as evidenced by the varied scholarly definitions detailed above); another is that labeling oneself as a "victim" of SH may lead to negative social and psychological consequences (Fitzgerald *et al.*, 1997a; Magley *et al.*, 1999a). Both of these explanations may apply to bullying, which is also difficult to define and carries a social stigma. A nationally representative study by the Workplace Bullying Institute (WBI; 2010) found that 35 percent of individuals reported being "bullied" at work, but a study of government employees found that 71 percent reported experiencing "workplace incivility" (Cortina *et al.*, 2001). Although those findings come from different studies and cannot be directly compared, the different rates elicited by the questions asked in these two studies supports the SH literature that strongly suggests that the way questions are phrased influences respondents' willingness to report potentially stigmatizing experiences.

One recent survey study (Dionisi *et al.*, 2012) examined the co-occurrence of SH and bullying. They found that participants were as likely to report both GBH and psychological aggression (25 percent) as they were to report either alone (12 percent for GBH and 13 percent for psychological aggression). USA and SC also co-occurred with relevant measures of workplace aggression, but to a lesser degree, indirectly supporting our proposal that GBH is the most similar type of SH to bullying. Interestingly, threat aggression and physical aggression were seldom reported in the absence of the corresponding SH behavior (i.e. SC and USA, respectively). These findings highlight the need for greater integration of research on SH and bullying, as these experiences are clearly integrated in the experience of many employees.

SALIENT FEATURES OF SEXUAL HARASSMENT AND BULLYING

In this section, we will summarize major themes in the research regarding SH, with the goal of identifying what is known and what remains unclear. We will use the general framework presented above to link SH research to bullying where appropriate.

Predicting Who Will Harass

Several researchers have attempted to create profiles of the typical harasser or the likely harasser, but this research has yielded little clear success to date.

Sexual Harassment

One demographic characteristic that is often of interest in predicting harassment is the harasser's sex. Are women as likely to harass as men?

Fitzgerald and Weitzman (1990) conclude, based on their review of the literature, that although some women may engage in SH, the base rate of this behavior is extremely low. Magley *et al.* (1999b) found that military women almost exclusively reported being harassed by men; likewise, military men were more likely to be harassed by men than by women, although some men did report harassment by women.

Other demographic variables do not appear to consistently differentiate harassers from non-harassers. Fitzgerald and Weitzman (1990) found no demographic characteristics (age, rank, marital status, etc.) that distinguished between university faculty who admitted engaging in dating or sexual relationships with students (an indirect proxy for harassment; almost no respondents admitted to more egregious SH behavior) and faculty who did not. Those researchers cite a study by the National Merit Protection Board (1981; cited in Fitzgerald and Weitzman, 1990) in which SH victims generally reported that their harassers were white, older than the victim, and married, but not necessarily in a supervisory position relative to the victim. Furthermore, 43 percent of SH victims reported that they were aware that the harasser had harassed others.

In the archetypal case of SH, the harasser is in a position of power over the victim. However, considerable evidence suggests that harassers can also be peers or even organizational outsiders (e.g. Gettman and Gelfand, 2007). In a sample of military women, 32 percent reported being harassed by supervisors, but 27 percent reported being harassed by coworkers (Bostock and Daley, 2007). Chinese women were actually more likely to report being harassed by colleagues or other peers (e.g. acquaintances, neighbors) than by supervisors (Parish *et al.*, 2006), and UK police officers reported more SH from outsiders (including members of the public and offenders) than from either coworkers or supervisors (Hershcovis *et al.*, 2010).

As a more direct means of predicting harassment, Pryor (1987) developed the Likelihood to Sexually Harass (LSH) scale. This measure asks respondents to imagine themselves in various common scenarios in which they would be in a position of power relative to a woman (e.g. interviewing a female job applicant). Respondents then rate the likelihood that they would behave in various ways in each scenario. One of the possible behavioral alternatives for each scenario is a "sexual exploitation alternative" (e.g. making a job offer contingent on sexual favors), and only responses to these items are considered in the scoring. Pryor found that men with higher scores on the LSH did behave in more harassing ways, such as inappropriately touching a female confederate. Further, scores on the LSH were correlated with Malamuth's (1981) single-item Likelihood to Rape measure, beliefs that relationships between the sexes are generally adversarial, and a lack of perspective taking. In a laboratory study, Dall'Ara and Maass (1999) found support for the idea that men high in LSH were more likely to take advantage of situations that encouraged SH. Specifically, male undergraduates high in LSH were more willing to harass a (fictitious) female co-participant by sending pornographic images than were men low in LSH, but only when there were situational variables present that supported SH behavior (such as an intergroup setting rather than an inter-individual setting). Men low in LSH engaged in little harassment regardless of situational conditions.

The previously described studies of LSH included only male participants, but Perry *et al.* (1998b) compared men and women, using an adapted version of the measure for women that placed women in the positions of power. They found that women had lower average scores on the LSH than men and that women were much more likely than men to have the lowest possible score and much less likely to score above the minimum. Using exploratory factor analysis, they found somewhat different factor structures for male and female respondents, tentatively suggesting that men and women had somewhat different views about what made potential SH situations similar. Another important factor to consider about research using the LSH is that the operationalization of both the measure and the dependent variables used in subsequent studies has focused primarily on the more sexualized end of the SH spectrum (USA and SC behaviors). It is not clear whether LSH will be effective in predicting less overtly sexual behaviors such as GBH or CU.

Bullying

Although women appear to engage in SH less often than men, evidence suggests a much smaller gender gap in bullying. In two nationally representative surveys of US workers, about 60 percent of the bullies described were male (WBI, 2007, 2010). Similarly, Einarsen and Skogstad (1996) found that 49 percent of bullying victims reported men as the bully, whereas 30 percent described women bullies and 20 percent reported being bullied by individuals of both genders. Although SH is most often (though not exclusively; cf. Ryan and Kenig, 1991) directed from male harassers to female targets, bullying occurs more often between persons of the same sex. The nationally representative WBI (2010) survey found that 80 percent of female bullies targeted female victims, whereas 56 percent of male bullies targeted male victims.

An earlier WBI survey (2007) found that workplace bullies generally hold higher positions in the organization than their victims, though some bullying takes place between peers (17 percent) and some victims reported "bottom-up" bullying by subordinates (12 percent). This is consistent with comments by Einarsen (2000) that bullying typically includes some form of power asymmetry between the bully and the victim. However, Hauge *et al.* (2009) found no effect for position or decision authority in predicting those who self-identified as having bullied another person in the workplace. They found instead that the best predictor of self-identified bullying was whether the respondents also reported being bullied. Vartia and Hyyti (2002) found that women prison employees were most likely to be bullied by coworkers, whereas their male coworkers were bullied by both coworkers and supervisors. It appears that the relationship between bullying and job title is complex, and may be moderated by variables such as gender, job type, or perhaps job gender context.

Predicting Who Will Be Harassed

Sexual Harassment

There is some evidence to suggest that minority women experience more harassment than white women; however, the pattern of results is mixed. In a military sample (Fitzgerald *et al.*, 1999b), Native American women reported the highest incidence of harassment, followed by Hispanic women. White and African American women reported similar levels of harassment, and Asian American women were the least harassed. Military rank was a good predictor of harassment, with women at higher ranks reporting the least harassment. A survey of college students (Cortina *et al.*, 1998) found that, although the reported incidence of harassment experiences varied by ethnicity (with African American and Latina women reporting the most harassment), ethnicity did not predict who labeled those experiences as harassment. In the same study, lesbian or bisexual women reported a much higher rate of gender harassment compared to heterosexual women.

Although most of the existing research focuses on women, some research has examined whether and to what extent men experience SH. Fitzgerald and Weitzman (1990: 138) "conclude that although it is theoretically possible for women to harass men, it is, in practice, an extremely rare event." A large-sample study in the US military found that women consistently reported higher frequencies of all types of harassment than men did (Magley *et al.*, 1999a). Settles *et al.* (2012) found that lower-ranking military men were more likely to experience SH than higher-ranking men, and that rank differences fully mediated racial differences in the experience of SH among military men. However, Waldo *et al.* (1998) note that SH for men is qualitatively different from SH for women; the kinds of behavior that women experience as harassment may be viewed by men as relatively minor. Rather, research indicates that men may experience harassment in situations where the male gender role is strongly enforced – that is, when others criticize or belittle their masculinity (Berdahl *et al.*, 1996; Stockdale *et al.*, 1999).

Waldo *et al.* (1998) expanded on these findings by developing a version of the SEQ that was directly applicable to men (the Sexual Harassment of Men scale). The primary difference between this measure and the original SEQ was the inclusion of items in the gender harassment scale about perceived enforcement of the male gender role (e.g. "made you feel like you were not a man if you did traditionally female activities" (p. 66)). Across three samples, they found that men reported experiencing harassment from other men more often than harassment from women. Male perpetrators were more likely to engage in lewd comments and enforcement of the male gender role, whereas women perpetrators were more likely to engage in derogatory remarks about men. Interestingly, unwanted sexual attention and sexual coercion were equally likely to come from male and female perpetrators, contrasting the findings of Stockdale *et al.* (2004), who found that women were more likely than men to display USA to male victims. In one sample, Waldo *et al.* also asked about the degree to which each experience was upsetting to the participants. Enforcement of the male gender role was viewed as the most upsetting, while lewd comments were the least upsetting. Among participants who described specific incidents of harassment, the most common response was that the incident was "not at all" upsetting. This supports the argument by Fitzgerald and Weitzman (1990) that men may view many SH behaviors as normal; however, it also supports the argument by Berdahl *et al.* (1996) that simply applying SH definitions developed for women to men's experiences is inappropriate and incomplete.

The gender of the victim also appears to interact with other predictors of SH, such that the factors that predict SH for women are quite different from those for men. Risk for USA appears to decline with age for women, but not for men (Jackson and Newman, 2004). Somewhat counterintuitively, Jackson and Newman found that women (but not men) in higher pay grades and with higher levels of education reported more USA; they note that this may reflect a greater willingness to report SH rather than a greater frequency of experiencing it.

Some (e.g. Feldman-Schorrig and McDonald, 1992) have suggested that previous victimization may predispose some women to perceive SH more readily or react more negatively to behavior that others might find inoffensive. However, Fitzgerald *et al.* (1999a) found no differences whatsoever in affective responses to a number of harassment scenarios between women who had and had not experienced childhood sexual abuse. They also found no differences in the mental health outcomes (or degree of psychological distress) following SH between women who had experienced previous sexual victimization and women who had not. Fitzgerald and colleagues dismiss the "hypersensitivity" explanation for SH as "junk logic."

Bullying

Demographic factors are also limited in predicting who will experience bullying (for a thorough review, see Samnani and Singh, 2012). Though some studies find that women are bullied more often than men (e.g. WBI, 2010), other studies find no overall gender differences (e.g. Einarsen and Skogstad, 1996; Vartia and Hyyti, 2002). Some evidence suggests that older workers may be more likely to experience bullying (Einarsen and Skogstad, 1996), but these findings have not been consistently replicated. Samnani and Singh (2012) provide a substantial discussion of efforts to link bullying to personality characteristics of victims, and note a consistent finding that bullying victims tend to be higher in neuroticism than non-victims.

Predicting Where Harassment Will Occur

Another line of research has taken the perspective that identifying individuals who will harass or be harassed is the wrong approach to a systemic problem.

Sexual Harassment

Fitzgerald *et al.* (1997a) argue that job- and organization-level variables are more appropriate predictors of SH, and more appropriate targets for interventions to prevent and reduce SH. Specifically, they propose that the job gender context (i.e. the gender ratio within the job and the degree to which the job is gender-typed) and the organizational climate for sexual harassment best predict the likelihood that an individual will be harassed. In their model, characteristics of the victim influence the effects of the harassment for that specific individual, but such personal characteristics do not determine who will be harassed. In other words, the direct cause of harassment is a job and organizational climate that promotes it, not anything about the victim. In a large-sample empirical test of the model, they found that both job gender context and organizational climate were in fact significant predictors of SH, with organizational climate the strongest by far.

Similarly, Jackson and Newman (2004) found that both men and women experienced more USA when their daily work environment was dominated by persons of the opposite gender. Cogin and Fish (2007) found that an unbalanced gender ratio in the overall healthcare work environment (rather than only among people with the same job title) made SH more likely. Employees with negative perceptions of their leaders reported more SH, although the direction of causality cannot be determined. In their study of nurses, most who reported SH indicated that they had little to no prior working experience with the perpetrator of the harassment.

Bullying

Similar to SH, bullying is more likely to occur when there are power differences between bully and target, a competitive organizational culture, an aggressive interpersonal style, and a male-dominated organization (Einarsen and Skogstad, 1996). A large-scale study of the Norwegian workforce found that employees reported the highest prevalence of bullying in organizations that were large, male-dominated, and in industrial sectors (Einarsen and Skogstad, 1996). Bullying also appears to be more prevalent in organizations with more negative climate factors, such as poor leadership, high role conflict, and high levels of interpersonal conflict (Hauge *et al.*, 2007; Vartia and Hyyti, 2002). In contrast, organizations with positive psychosocial safety climates (climates in which employees perceive the organization as valuing the psychological health of employees) had a lower incidence of bullying and fewer negative employee outcomes when bullying did occur (Law *et al.*, 2011). Interpersonal and social climate factors, rather than task climate factors (e.g. job demands), appear to be the best workplace-level predictors of bullying (Skogstad *et al.*, 2011). Further, a number of researchers have argued for the importance of leadership and management factors in preventing or permitting bullying (Samnani and Singh, 2012).

The SH literature has identified a specific climate of organizational tolerance for sexual harassment (Hulin *et al.*, 1996), whereas the bullying literature has generally focused on broader climate variables, as described above. Future research should consider whether these different kinds of climate constructs offer differential or incremental value in predicting bullying and SH.

Sexual Harassment and Bullying Have Consequences

Perhaps the majority of research has focused on identifying the consequences of SH and bullying for the targets who report or experience it.

Impact on Individuals: Sexual Harassment

SH is associated with poorer psychological health and may have indirect effects on physical health (Fitzgerald *et al.*, 1997a), up to and including post-traumatic stress disorder (PTSD; Larsen and Fitzgerald, 2011; Palmieri and Fitzgerald, 2005). College students who experience SH report less satisfaction with their educational experience (Cortina *et al.*, 1998), and individuals who experience harassment in the workplace report lower job satisfaction (e.g. Fitzgerald *et al.*, 1997a; Magley *et al.*, 1999b). Both men and women experience negative psychological and physical outcomes as a result of SH (Magley *et al.*, 1999b), although the relationship appears to be more complex for women than for men. Magley *et al.* (1999b) found that for victims of either gender, the harassment need not be severe; even moderate levels of harassment are associated with negative consequences. Further, both men and women consciously linked negative outcomes to their harassment experiences. A laboratory study by Woodzicka and LaFrance (2005) suggests that even a mild episode of harassment may have immediate negative effects on the victim's performance. Women who were asked inappropriate, sexually charged questions in a job interview performed more poorly than women who were asked questions that were unusual but not sexual in nature.

Impact on Individuals: Bullying

Similar individual effects have been found for bullying, which is negatively associated with psychological wellbeing (Einarsen and Raknes, 1997; Leymann and Gustafsson, 1996) and a number of physical health symptoms (Björkqvist *et al.*, 1994; Niedhammer *et al.*, 2009). The relationship between bullying and health has been demonstrated not only with self-report measures, but also with direct physical measures such as reduced cortisol (Hogh *et al.*, 2012). As with SH, bullying victims may meet criteria for PTSD (Leymann and Gustafsson, 1996). Employees who do not experience bullying directly, but who witness it in the workplace, report more negative job attitudes than those who do not witness bullying (Einarsen *et al.*, 1994).

Dionisi *et al.* (2012) examined outcomes of SH and bullying together. Although they found substantial co-occurrence between the two (as described earlier), after controlling for the overlap, SH consistently produced stronger negative effects than bullying on psychological wellbeing and work withdrawal behavior. However, non-physical forms of bullying had stronger negative effects on job attitudes than did non-physical SH (e.g. GBH and CU). This lends strength to the argument that SH should not be subsumed as a subtype of bullying behavior; there is something distinctive about the personal nature of SH that substantially impacts employee outcomes.

Impact on Organizations: Sexual Harassment

Women who experience SH are more likely than those who do not experience SH to engage in both work withdrawal (e.g. absenteeism) and job withdrawal (e.g. looking for work elsewhere) behaviors (Fitzgerald *et al.*, 1997a; Magley *et al.*, 1999a). A similar trend occurs for men who are harassed (Magley *et al.*, 1999a). These negative outcomes persist over time, not just over weeks or months but over years (Glomb *et al.*, 1999). Further, victims of SH are not the only ones who experience negative outcomes. Ambient SH (SH experiences reported by members of an individual's workgroup, *excluding* the individual) is independently related to job satisfaction and psychological distress, over and above the effects of the individual's own SH experiences (Glomb *et al.*, 1997). Job satisfaction is a good predictor of work and job withdrawal; thus, SH may cause organizations to lose productivity and valuable employees even beyond those directly involved.

Impact on Organizations: Bullying

In one study, more than half of the respondents indicated that they had lost productivity at work because of time spent worrying about incivility or avoiding the bully (Pearson *et al.*, 2000). Trust is undermined when incivility is present throughout an organization and, as a result, employees often withdraw from the workplace emotionally and ultimately do so physically when trust is undermined by incivility. Further, employees who experience bullying report intentionally decreasing their willingness to engage in organizational citizenship behavior as well as their commitment to the organization (Pearson *et al.*, 2000).

RECOMMENDATIONS FOR APPROACHING PREVENTION AND INTERVENTION: LESSONS FOR BULLYING FROM SEXUAL HARASSMENT

One important way in which sexual harassment is qualitatively different from bullying is that SH is explicitly prohibited by law. In the US, employers are aware of their responsibility to prevent SH, as outlined by the EEOC: "an employer should take all steps necessary to prevent sexual harassment from occurring, such as affirmatively raising the subject, expressing strong disapproval, developing appropriate sanctions, informing employees of their right to raise and how to raise the issue of harassment under title VII, and developing methods to sensitize all concerned" (Guidelines, 2011). Many employers address this responsibility by developing a formal SH policy, a reporting or grievance procedure, and/or an SH prevention training program (Zugelder *et al.*, 2006).

Anti-bullying advocates have looked to SH laws and guidelines as models for workplace bullying legislation, in hopes of raising similar awareness of broader issues of bullying in the workplace. This begs the question, however, of whether SH laws have had their intended effect, and whether approaches to SH prevention and intervention are likely to be effective if adapted to address bullying. In this section, we discuss research on the effectiveness of SH prevention strategies, in light of the issues raised in previous sections.

Grievance and Complaint Procedures

Grievance or complaint procedures are focused on responding to SH incidents after the fact, but they may be important elements of a long-term prevention strategy because they (a) send important messages about the organization's tolerance for SH (Fitzgerald *et al.*, 1997b) and (b) have the potential to prevent repeat offenses by offering appropriate corrective measures and sanctions (Best *et al.*, 2010).

However, grievance procedures appear to be an insufficient solution to SH in the workplace. Grievance systems are reactive measures; for anything to be done, the victim (or another person in the workplace) must be willing to make a claim. This is particularly problematic when the procedure requires the claimant to notify an immediate supervisor, as the supervisor may be the harasser or have created the climate that allows SH to occur (Best *et al.*, 2010; Zugelder *et al.*, 2006). Even when the procedure allows reporting to an independent party, grievances still require that the victim label the experience as harassment. As we have discussed earlier, many individuals who experience SH behavior do not label it as such (e.g. Fitzgerald *et al.*, 1988; Magley *et al.*, 1999a). Formal complaints or grievances must be specific, but Thomas and Kitzinger (1994) note that many women perceive sexist or sexually offensive behavior in the workplace as so prevalent that it is difficult to single out a particular situation as being an instance of SH.

Even if an individual is confident that what she or he has experienced is SH, the difficulty and perceived cost (emotional and financial) of pursuing a claim may be a deterrent. Indeed, some researchers have gone so far as to argue that, rather than redressing grievances, the legal process actually revictimizes women who have experienced SH (Fitzgerald *et al.*, 1999a). Quinn (2000) points out that a major function of SH is to exclude the victim from informal networks in the workplace, and that making a formal claim (or even an informal one) of SH in no way solves the problem of exclusion. Rather, it reinforces it, by directly pitting the victim against others in the organization. Quinn (2000) notes that even the act of stating that a behavior is offensive or unwelcome (a key test of whether the behavior can be considered SH) calls attention to the very difference of the victim, acknowledging that she (or occasionally he) is an outsider in the group. Thus, the recommended solution to the symptoms of SH (i.e. complaining about it) actually reinforces the root cause (i.e. that a woman is perceived as not belonging in the workplace). Yet a woman who does not complain, and complain immediately, often loses legal standing due to the requirement that the harassment must be shown to be unwelcome (see also Schultz, 1998).

Finally, from a management-oriented viewpoint, Dobbin and Kelly (2007) comment that the existence of a grievance procedure (or training) does not necessarily or even generally shield employers from liability in SH cases. Rather, what matters is a prompt and appropriate response to the claim of SH, consistent with the recommendations of Best and colleagues (2010) that SH claims be handled individually rather than with a one-size-fits-all policy. Some form of grievance policy and some form of training in how to use it are necessary first steps (Zugelder *et al.*, 2006), but it is equally clear that a policy alone is no panacea for addressing SH, let alone preventing it.

Training Potential Victims

Early research on SH prevention suggested that the responsibility to address and remedy harassment resided with the individual target by making clear to the harasser that the behavior was unwelcome and reporting the harassment through organizational channels. However, Gutek (1985) and other researchers in this area quickly pointed out that this approach was akin to "blaming the victim" for handling a situation incorrectly, particularly if the harassment is repeated. Although there are a number of strategies that individual employees can take to mitigate or avoid situations where harassment (or bullying) may occur, individual strategies often are ineffective in halting the negative behaviors. Goldberg (2007) found that women who experienced training about recognizing SH and the likely consequences of potential responses expressed no more intention to report the harassment, and *less* intention to confront the harasser, than women in a control group who received no training. Further, as Quinn (2000) notes, confrontation can be extremely risky as the abuse may escalate or the employee may become a target for retaliation by either the harasser or coworkers.

Training Potential Harassers

Other approaches to SH training focus on prevention by training potential harassers to avoid engaging in SH. Many of these training programs seem to be grounded in the assumption that SH is largely unintentional and due to ignorance about appropriate workplace behavior (e.g. Keyton and Rhodes, 1999). Accordingly, they focus on factual knowledge regarding SH (e.g. laws, policies, behavioral definitions; see Perry *et al.*, 1998a) as a means of conveying expectations about acceptable and unacceptable behavior.

When this type of training is evaluated with respect to short-term outcomes, such as knowledge or attitudes, it appears to have some effect. For example, Lonsway *et al.* (2008) found that both men and women who had previous SH training were less likely to endorse common myths about SH (e.g. verbal harassment is not really SH). Perry *et al.* (1998a) found that men who were low in LSH demonstrated high factual knowledge of SH, regardless of whether they viewed a SH training video or a control video. Men who were high in LSH demonstrated poor knowledge of SH when they viewed the control video, but when they viewed the SH training video, they performed as well as low LSH men. Further, men high in LSH who viewed the control video were more likely than low LSH men to behave inappropriately with a female confederate, but behaved similarly to the low LSH men after viewing the SH training video.

These results seem to demonstrate a positive effect of SH training on not only knowledge, but also behavior, for those who need training most. However, the positive effects found by Perry *et al.* (1998a) did not persist to a second measure of LSH administered at a later point in time, implying that, although the high LSH men were able to change their behavior in the lab setting, where they knew it was expected, their long-term views regarding SH remained unchanged. As evaluation of SH training programs tends to be minimal and short-term-oriented (Perry *et al.*, 2009), this raises substantial concerns that such evaluations may lead to inaccurate conclusions.

Further, this type of SH training seems to correspond best to the sexual desire-dominance paradigm of SH, in which harassers are ignorant about either appropriate ways to express attraction or appropriate norms for workplace behavior. As we have discussed, this view may explain some instances of SH, but it is not sufficient to explain the full range of SH experiences. It is unclear how knowledge-based training of this type would create a meaningful deterrent for competence-based (Schultz, 1998) or rejection-based (Stockdale *et al.*, 2004) harassment. If harassment is motivated by a desire to exclude or drive away the harassed party, it seems unlikely that this motivation would be substantially influenced by increased factual knowledge about SH. Such training might perhaps redirect the harassment into less sexualized channels (e.g. to CU rather than USA), but not eliminate it. As bullying is better aligned with the competence-based and rejection-based views of SH than with the desire-dominance view, this has important implications for bullying prevention as well. Simply improving knowledge about permitted and prohibited behavior may not change outcomes; it is imperative to understand and influence potential bullies' motivations and attitudes.

Changing the Organizational Climate

The aforementioned prevention strategies tend to assume that sexual harassment and bullying are largely due to characteristics of individual harassers or bullies ("bad apples"), rather than features of the organization or workplace ("bad barrels"). However, there may be greater opportunities for organizations to change facets of the workplace or the work itself than to alter inherent tendencies, personalities, or traits of individual bullies or harassers. In light of the substantial evidence supporting the role of organizational climate factors in SH, organizational-level interventions are likely to be a useful addition to the prevention toolkit.

Ultimately, top management is responsible for addressing and preventing harassment and bullying (Fitzgerald *et al.*, 1997a; Liefooghe and Davey, 2001). As discussed earlier, bullying is likely to take place in organizations with highly competitive cultures (Einarsen and Skogstad, 1996), but passive tolerance of aggressive behavior is also damaging. There is an empirical relationship between "weak" or laissez-faire style leadership by the most senior managers and SH or workplace bullying (Cogin and Fish, 2007; Einarsen *et al.*, 1994; Höel *et al.*, 2001; Leymann, 1996). Further, organizations with high levels of ambiguity, such as layoff concerns and poor accountability, enable bullies to proliferate (Hodson *et al.*, 2006). On the other hand, few bullying behaviors occur in a workplace climate characterized by fairness and respectful treatment (Cortina *et al.*, 2001).

Both sexual harassment and bullying fit the definition of dysfunctional organizational behavior (Bell *et al.*, 2002). As such, we believe that organizationally based interventions have the greatest potential for managing and eliminating both SH and bullying behaviors. Taken together, it seems that effective prevention (not just management) of SH and bullying requires a multifaceted, proactive, and multilevel approach. Some form of grievance policy is needed so that organizations can handle formal reports consistently and appropriately, but grievance procedures alone are not really preventive. Knowledge-based training may help to start an organizational conversation about civility and appropriate workplace communication. This may help to prevent lower level incivility or insensitive comments, "joking," and ineffective interpersonal communications, particularly if supplemented with skills-based training on constructive interpersonal interactions. However, it is important to remember that training is ineffective when it occurs in a vacuum and that long-term changes are unlikely in the absence of supervisor support (Perry *et al.*, 2009). Accordingly, interventions should also target the supervisory level, with a focus on promoting a positive and supportive climate.

It is important to note that we do not view the "bad apples" and "bad barrels" theories as mutually exclusive. We have tried to make the argument throughout this chapter that there appears to be theoretical and empirical support for multiple causes of SH and bullying behavior, and that harassers or bullies act from different motives. Some motives may arise from or be reinforced by organizational factors; others may be more deeply linked to personality or values and thus more resistant to change (e.g. Perry *et al.*, 1998a). If a perpetrator intentionally and repeatedly bullies or harms employees, the most severe consequences should follow, including legal action and termination from the organization. Overall, however, we believe that the organizational approach – clear top-level organizational statements and follow-up training or organizational development as to what constitutes expectations about positive, healthy communications and collegial interactions – is the most effective path for addressing harassment, bullying, and incivility at work. Rather than punishing after negative behaviors occur, employees at all organizational levels should have clear expectations about appropriate and productive communications and exchanges.

REFERENCES

Andersson, L. M., and Pearson, C. M. (1999). Tit for tat? The spiraling effect of incivility in the workplace. *Academy of Management Review*, 24, 452–71.

Bell, M. P., Cycyota, C. S., and Quick, J. C. (2002). An affirmative defense: The preventive management of sexual harassment. In D. L. Nelson and R. J. Burke (eds), *Gender, Stress, and Health*, Washington, DC: American Psychological Association.

Berdahl, J. L., Magley, V. J., and Waldo, C. (1996). The sexual harassment of men? Exploring the concept with theory and data. *Psychology of Women Quarterly*, 20, 527–47.

Best, C. L., Smith, D. W., Raymond Sr., J. R., Greenberg, R. S., and Crouch, R. K. (2010). Preventing and responding to complaints of sexual harassment in an academic health center: A 10-year review from the Medical University of South Carolina. *Academic Medicine*, 85, 721–7.

Bies, R. J., and Tripp, T. M. (1995). The use and abuse of power: Justice as social control. In R. Cropanzano and M. Kacmar (eds), *Politics, Justice, and Support: Managing Social Climate at Work* (pp. 131–45), New York: Quorum Press.

Björkqvist, K., Österman, K., and Hjeltbäck, M. (1994). Aggression among university employees. *Aggressive Behavior*, 20, 173–84.

Bostock, D. J., and Daley, J. G. (2007). Lifetime and current sexual assault and harassment victimization rates of active-duty United States Air Force women. *Violence Against Women*, 13, 927–44.

Cogin, J., and Fish, A. (2007). Managing sexual harassment more strategically: An analysis of environmental causes. *Asia Pacific Journal of Human Resources*, 45, 333–52.

Cortina, L. M., Magley, V. J., Williams, J. H., and Langhout, R. D. (2001). Incivility in the workplace: Incidence and impact. *Journal of Occupational Health Psychology*, 6, 64–80.

Cortina, L. M., Swan, S., Fitzgerald, L. F., and Waldo, C. (1998). Sexual harassment and assault: Chilling the climate for women in academia. *Psychology of Women Quarterly*, 22, 419–41.

Dall'Ara, E., and Maass, A. (1999). Studying sexual harassment in the laboratory: Are egalitarian women at higher risk? *Sex Roles*, 41, 681–704.

Dionisi, A. M., Barling, J., and Dupré, K. E. (2012). Revisiting the comparative outcomes of workplace aggression and sexual harassment. *Journal of Occupational Health Psychology*, 17, 398–408.

Dobbin, F., and Kelly, E. L. (2007). How to stop harassment: Professional construction of legal compliance in organizations. *American Journal of Sociology*, 112, 1203–43.

Einarsen, S. (2000). Harassment and bullying at work: A review of the Scandinavian approach. *Aggression and Violent Behavior*, 5, 379–401.

Einarsen, S., and Raknes, B. I. (1997). Harassment in the workplace and the victimization of men. *Violence and Victims*, 12, 247–63.

Einarsen, S., and Skogstad, A. (1996). Bullying at work: Epidemiological findings in public and private organizations. *European Journal of Work and Organizational Psychology*, 5, 185–201.

Einarsen, S., Raknes, B., and Matthiesen, S. (1994). Bullying and harassment at work and their relationships to work environment quality: An exploratory study. *European Work and Organizational Psychologist*, 4, 381–401.

Equal Employment Opportunity Commission (1990). *Policy Guidance on Current Issues of Sexual Harassment*, EEOC Notice No. N-915-050, Washington, DC: Author. Retrieved from http://www.eeoc.gov/eeoc/publications/index.cfm.

Farley, L. (1978). *Sexual Shakedown: The Sexual Harassment of Women on the Job*, New York: McGraw-Hill.

Feldman-Schorrig, S. P., and McDonald, J. J. (1992). The role of forensic psychiatry in the defense of sexual harassment cases. *Journal of Psychiatry and Law*, 20, 5–33.

Fitzgerald, L. F. (1993). Sexual harassment: Violence against women in the workplace. *American Psychologist*, 48, 1070–6.

Fitzgerald, L. F., and Weitzman, L. M. (1990). Men who harass: Speculation and data. In M. A. Paludi (ed.), *Ivory Power: Sexual Harassment on Campus* (pp. 125–40), Albany, NY: State University of New York Press.

Fitzgerald, L. F., Gelfand, M. J., and Drasgow, F. (1995). Measuring sexual harassment: Theoretical and psychometric advances. *Basic and Applied Social Psychology*, 17, 425–45.

Fitzgerald, L. F., Swan, S., and Magley, V. J. (1997b). But was it really sexual harassment? Legal, behavioral, and psychological definitions of the workplace victimization of women. In W. O'Donohue (ed.), *Sexual Harassment: Theory, Research, and Treatment* (pp. 5–28), Needham Heights, MA: Allyn & Bacon.

Fitzgerald, L. F., Magley, V. J., Drasgow, F., and Waldo, C. R. (1999b). Measuring sexual harassment in the military: The Sexual Experiences Questionnaire (SEQ—DoD). *Military Psychology*, 11, 243–63.

Fitzgerald, L. F., Shullman, S. L., Bailey, N., and Richards, M. (1988). The incidence and dimensions of sexual harassment in academia and the workplace. *Journal of Vocational Behavior*, 32, 152–75.

Fitzgerald, L. F., Buchanan, N. T., Collinsworth, L. L., Magley, V. J., and Ramos, A. M. (1999a). Junk logic: The abuse defense in sexual harassment litigation. *Psychology, Public Policy, and Law*, 5, 730–59.

Fitzgerald, L. F., Drasgow, F., Hulin, C. L., Gelfand, M. J., and Magley, V. J. (1997a). Antecedents and consequences of sexual harassment in organizations: A test of an integrated model. *Journal of Applied Psychology*, 82, 578–89.

Gelfand, M. J., Fitzgerald, L. F., and Drasgow, F. (1995). The structure of sexual harassment: A confirmatory analysis across cultures and settings. *Journal of Vocational Behavior*, 47, 164–77.

Gettman, H. J., and Gelfand, M. J. (2007). When the customer shouldn't be king: Antecedents and consequences of sexual harassment by clients and customers. *Journal of Applied Psychology*, 92, 757–70.

Gillespie, D. L., and Leffler, A. (1987). The politics of research methodology in claims-making activities: Social science and sexual harassment. *Social Problems*, 34, 490–501.

Glomb, T. M., Munson, L. J., Hulin, C. L., Bergman, M. E., and Drasgow, F. (1999). Structural equation models of sexual harassment: Longitudinal explorations and cross-sectional generalizations. *Journal of Applied Psychology*, 84, 14–28.

Glomb, T. M., Richman, W. L., Hulin, C. L., Drasgow, F., Schneider, K. T., and Fitzgerald, L. F. (1997). Ambient sexual harassment: An integrated model of antecedents and consequences. *Organizational Behavior and Human Decision Processes*, 71, 309–28.

Goldberg, C. B. (2007). The impact of training and conflict avoidance on responses to sexual harassment. *Psychology of Women Quarterly*, 31, 62–72.

Guidelines on Discrimination Because of Sex, 29 C. F. R. pt 1604 (2011).

Gutek, B. A. (1985). *Sex and the Workplace: Impact of Sexual Behavior and Harassment on Women, Men and Organizations*, San Francisco, CA: Jossey-Bass.

Hauge, L. J., Skogstad, A., and Einarsen, S. (2007). Relationships between stressful work environments and bullying: Results of a large representative study. *Work and Stress*, 21, 220–42.

Hauge, L. J., Skogstad, A., and Einarsen, S. (2009). Individual and situational predictors of workplace bullying: Why do perpetrators engage in the bullying of others? *Work and Stress*, 23, 349–58.

Hershcovis, M. S., Parker, S. K., and Reich, T. C. (2010). The moderating effect of equal opportunity support and confidence in grievance procedures on sexual harassment from different perpetrators. *Journal of Business Ethics*, 92, 415–32.

Hodson, R., Roscigno, V. J., and Lopez, S. H. (2006). Chaos and the abuse of power: Workplace bullying in organizational and interactional context. *Work and Occupations*, 33, 382–416.

Höel, H., Cooper, C. L., and Faragher, B. (2001). The experience of bullying in Great Britain: The impact of organisational status. *European Journal of Work and Organizational Psychology*, 10, 443–65.

Hogh, A., Hansen, Å. M., Mikkelsen, E. G., and Persson, R. (2012). Exposure to negative acts at work, psychological stress reactions and physiological stress response. *Journal of Psychosomatic Research*, 73, 47–52.

Hulin, C. L., Fitzgerald, L. F., and Drasgow, F. (1996). Organizational influences on sexual harassment. In M. S. Stockdale (ed.), *Sexual Harassment in the Workplace: Perspectives, Frontiers, and Response Strategies* (vol. 5, pp. 127–50), Thousand Oaks, CA: Sage.

Jackson, R. A., and Newman, M. A. (2004). Sexual harassment in the federal workplace revisited: Influences on sexual harassment by gender. *Public Administration Review*, 64, 705–17.

Jones, C. (2006). Drawing boundaries: Exploring the relationship between sexual harassment, gender and bullying. *Women's Studies International Forum*, 29, 147–58.

Keyton, J., and Rhodes, S. C. (1999). Organizational sexual harassment: Translating research into application. *Journal of Applied Communication Research*, 27, 158–73.

Larsen, S. E., and Fitzgerald, L. F. (2011). PTSD symptoms and sexual harassment: The role of attributions and perceived control. *Journal of Interpersonal Violence*, 26, 2555–67.

Law, R., Dollard, M. F., Tuckey, M. R., and Dormann, C. (2011). Psychosocial safety climate as a lead indicator of workplace bullying and harassment, job resources, psychological health and employee engagement. *Accident Analysis and Prevention*, 43, 1782–93.

Leymann, H. (1996). The content and development of mobbing at work. *European Journal of Work and Organizational Psychology*, 5, 165–84.

Leymann, H., and Gustafsson, A. (1996). Mobbing at work and the development of post-traumatic stress disorders. *European Journal of Work and Organizational Psychology*, 5, 251–75.

Liefooghe, A. P. D., and Davey, K. M. (2001). Accounts of workplace bullying: The role of the organization. *European Journal of Work and Organizational Psychology*, 10, 375–92.

Lonsway, K. A., Cortina, L. M., and Magley, V. J. (2008). Sexual harassment mythology: Definition, conceptualization, and measurement. *Sex Roles, 58*, 599–615.

Lucero, M. A., Allen, R. E., and Middleton, K. L. (2006). Sexual harassers: Behaviors, motives, and change over time. *Sex Roles*, 55, 331–43.

Lutgen-Sandvik, P., Namie, G., and Namie, R. (2009). Workplace bullying: Causes, consequences, and corrections. In P. Lutgen-Sandvik and B. D. Sypher (eds), *Destructive Organizational Communication: Processes, Consequences, and Constructive Ways of Organizing* (pp. 27–52), New York: Routledge/Taylor & Francis.

MacKinnon, C. A. (1979). *Sexual Harassment of Working Women: A Case of Sex Discrimination*, New Haven, CT: Yale University Press.

Magley, V. J., Hulin, C. L., Fitzgerald, L. F., and DeNardo, M. (1999a). Outcomes of self-labeling sexual harassment. *Journal of Applied Psychology*, 84, 390–402.

Magley, V. J., Waldo, C. R., Drasgow, F., and Fitzgerald, L. F. (1999b). The impact of sexual harassment on military personnel: Is it the same for men and women? *Military Psychology*, 11, 283–302.

Malamuth, N. M. (1981). Rape proclivity among males. *Journal of Social Issues*, 37, 138–57.

Masuch, M. (1985). Vicious circles in organizations. *Administrative Science Quarterly*, 30, 14–33.

Niedhammer, I., David, S., Degioanni, S., Drummond, A., and Philip, P. (2009). Workplace bullying and sleep disturbances: Findings from a large scale cross-sectional survey in the French working population. *Sleep: Journal of Sleep and Sleep Disorders Research*, 32, 1211–19.

O'Leary-Kelly, A. M., Paetzold, R. L., and Griffin, R. W. (2000). Sexual harassment as aggressive behavior: An actor-based perspective. *Academy of Management Review*, 25, 372–88.

Palmieri, P. A., and Fitzgerald, L. F. (2005). Confirmatory factor analysis of posttraumatic stress symptoms in sexually harassed women. *Journal of Traumatic Stress*, 18, 657–66.

Parish, W. L., Das, A., and Laumann, E. O. (2006). Sexual harassment of women in urban China. *Archives of Sexual Behavior*, 35, 411–25.

Pearson, C. M., Andersson, L. M., and Porath, C. L. (2000). Assessing and attacking workplace incivility. *Organization Dynamics*, 26, 123–37.

Perry, E. L., Kulik, C. T., and Field, M. P. (2009). Sexual harassment training: Recommendations to address gaps between the practitioner and research literatures. *Human Resource Management*, 48, 817–37.

Perry, E. L., Kulik, C. T., and Schmidtke, J. M. (1998a). Individual differences in the effectiveness of sexual harassment awareness training. *Journal of Applied Social Psychology*, 28, 698–723.

Perry, E. L., Schmidtke, J. M., and Kulik, C. T. (1998b). Propensity to sexually harass: An exploration of gender differences. *Sex Roles*, 38, 443–60.

Pryor, J. B. (1987). Sexual harassment proclivities in men. *Sex Roles*, 17, 269–90.

Quinn, B. A. (2000). The paradox of complaining: Law, humor, and harassment in the everyday work world. *Journal of Social Inquiry*, 25, 1151–85.

Reynolds vs. Atlantic City Convention Center, U.S. Dist. LEXIS 17016 (1990).

Richman, J. A., Rospenda, K. M., Nawyn, S. J., Flaherty, J. A., Fendrich, M., Drum, M. L., and Johnson, T. (1999). Sexual harassment and generalized workplace abuse among university employees: Prevalence and mental health correlates. *American Journal of Public Health*, 89, 358–63.

Ross v. Double Diamond, 672 F. Supp. 261 (1987).

Ryan, J., and Kenig, S. (1991). Risk and ideology in sexual harassment. *Sociological Inquiry*, 61, 231–41.

Samnani, A. K., and Singh, P. (2012). 20 years of workplace bullying research: A review of the antecedents and consequences of bullying in the workplace. *Aggression and Violent Behavior*, 17, 581–9.

Schultz, V. (1998). Reconceptualizing sexual harassment. *Yale Law Journal*, 107, 1683–1805.

Settles, I. H., Buchanan, N. T., and Colar, B. K. (2012). The impact of race and rank on the sexual harassment of Black and White men in the U.S. military. *Psychology of Men and Masculinity*, 13, 256–63.

Skogstad, A., Torsheim, T., Einarsen, S., and Hauge, L. J. (2011). Testing the work environment hypothesis of bullying on a group level of analysis: Psychosocial factors as precursors of observed workplace bullying. *Applied Psychology: An International Review*, 60, 475–95.

Stockdale, M. S., Visio, M., and Batra, L. (1999). The sexual harassment of men: Evidence for a broader theory of sexual harassment and sex discrimination. *Psychology, Public Policy, and Law*, 5, 630–64.

Stockdale, M. S., Berry, C. G., Schneider, R. W., and Cao, F. (2004). Perceptions of the sexual harassment of men. *Psychology of Men and Masculinity*, 5, 158–67.

Thomas, A. M., and Kitzinger, C. (1994). "It's just something that happens": The invisibility of sexual harassment in the workplace. *Gender, Work, and Organization*, 1, 151–61.

US Merit Systems Protection Board (1995). *Sexual Harassment in the Federal Workforce: Trends, Progress, and Continuing Challenges*, Washington, DC: Author.

Vartia, M., and Hyyti, J. (2002). Gender differences in workplace bullying among prison officers. *European Journal of Work and Organizational Psychology*, 11, 113–26.

Waldo, C. R., Berdahl, J. L., and Fitzgerald, L. F. (1998). Are men sexually harassed? If so, by whom? *Law and Human Behavior*, 22, 59–79.

Welsh, S. (2000). The multidimensional nature of sexual harassment: An empirical analysis of women's sexual harassment complaints. *Violence Against Women*, 6, 118–41.

Woodzicka, J. A., and LaFrance, M. (2005). The effects of subtle sexual harassment on women's performance in a job interview. *Sex Roles*, 53, 67–77.

Workplace Bullying Institute (2007). 2007 WBI U.S. workplace bullying survey. Retrieved from http://www.workplacebullying.org/wbiresearch/wbi-2007.

Workplace Bullying Institute (2010). 2010 WBI U.S. workplace bullying survey. Retrieved from http://www.workplacebullying.org/wbiresearch/2010-wbi-national-survey.

Zugelder, M. T., Champagne, P. J., and Maurer, S. D. (2006). An affirmative defense to sexual harassment by managers and supervisors: Analyzing employer liability and protecting employee rights in the United States. *Employee Responsibilities and Rights Journal*, 18, 111–22.

14

Workplace Cyber Bullying: A Research Agenda

Kurt Schimmel and Jeananne Nicholls
Slippery Rock University

INTRODUCTION

The topic of bullying is in the forefront of education. Teachers and administrators are increasingly aware of the problem and its potential negative effects on all parties involved as suggested by Olweus (1993) and Wang *et al.* (2009). The concept of cyber bullying, however, has received large amounts of research only within the last decade, and those initial investigations revolved largely around children and their experiences (Campbell, 2005). The realization that cyber bullying occurs in the workplace is an even more recent revelation. In a search of the EBSCO-Host newspaper database, the term "cyber bully" was first coined in the popular press in 2004 with an article titled "Cyberbullies cause real pain" in the *New York Times* (Linn *et al.*, 2004). That year there were only three articles found that contained the term. In 2011, however, there were 47 articles in the database containing the term "cyberbully" or "cyber bully." This increase in the number of times the term is used would indicate that public awareness growing.

SIGNIFICANCE

New media and new forms of communication have always had the possibility of use for both good and bad. The internet and its relative anonymity, along with the relative impersonal nature of the exchanges, provide a medium that can easily be abused. Boundaries that are normally not crossed in face-to-face interactions are crossed in the virtual world – in part because there is no immediate feedback from the victim. That is, a poster places comments onto the web without ever seeing the reaction of or impact on the recipient. Normal cues that may occur in face-to-face interpersonal communication and would normally create a threshold to indicate a line has been crossed, are not available online, thus creating a free-fire zone for rants and incivility (Pujazon-Zazik and Park, 2010).

With cyber bullying, an aggressor can attack with anonymity and the target may not know who is responsible for causing them harm. Furthermore, due to the electronic nature of the attack, bullying can occur at any time and has no spatial boundaries. That is, the attack occurs online anywhere the victim logs on, either at home or at work. There is no refuge from the attack as opposed to regular bullying, in which a targeted individual may find some escape while at home. A cyber bully can attack even when the target believes he or she is safe. This anonymity and persistence makes cyber bullying more insidious in some respects. Also, the target of cyber bullying can experience the negative effects of the same attack multiple times. Since the attack is media based, the material that is intended to cause harm to the target does not go away as it is saved and can continue to be accessed in cyberspace beyond the initial posting and can therefore cause harm again and again (Tokunaga, 2010).

Academic research in cyber bullying has focused largely on teens and students (e.g. Agatston *et al.*, 2007; Griezel *et al.*, 2008; Wang *et al.*, 2009). These researchers have revealed the pervasive nature of the problem. According to Wang *et al.* (2009) and Li (2007), between 13 and 40 percent of students have experienced cyber-bullying behavior. As these students grow up and become part of the adult workforce, they will bring these generational bad habits and incivility issues with them. Therefore, understanding that cyber bullying is an important avenue of the larger phenomenon of workplace bullying is vital to organizations as they attempt to build productive, civil workplaces, free of the powerful negative effects of bullying.

RELEVANT THEORY

Workplace Bullying

Workplace bullying is slowly gaining the attention of companies and academic researchers. In part, this recognition is due to negative consequences to organizations such as absenteeism and employee turnover (Raynor and Höel, 1997). Li (2007) defines workplace bullying as a form of aggression that may include both verbal and physical harassment. Li (2007) further notes that bullies intentionally inflict injury or discomfort on their targets by using such behaviors as hitting, pushing, hostile gesturing, threatening, humiliating, degrading, teasing, name-calling, put-downs, sarcasm, taunting, staring, silent treatment, manipulating friendships, and ostracizing.

Workplace bullying is more prevalent than many might think. In a 1997 study by Raynor and Cooper, 53 percent of respondents reported being bullied. However, official reported incidences are much lower. Why? The reason may be that a stigma exists against reporting incidences of workplace bullying in an official manner (Raynor and Höel, 1997). Namie (2010) suggests several possible inter-related explanations of this stigma. One explanation states that low reporting is due to a cultural bias against appearing weak. The target of a workplace bully may feel that, if he or she were to alert someone of the abuse, there would be a risk of appearing weak and dependent, which would further negatively impact his or her standing and experiences at work. A second possibility is the economic conditions in which employees find themselves. In a sluggish job market, some people feel lucky just to have a job, and they may be embarrassed or ashamed to complain about work issues and fear that by speaking out they may hurt their chances of keeping their job. Furthermore, to expose being bullied at work requires a certain level of independence, pride, and self-assurance, as suggested by Namie (2010), and those psychological constructs are the very qualities most damaged during an experience of bullying!

Organizations should care more about bullying among their employees. Workplace bullying not only impacts victims, but also those who simply witness the bullying taking place (Namie, 2010). This impact could be especially dangerous in the case of cyber bullying. Due to the anonymous nature of cyber bullying, individuals who witness incidents of cyber bullying may constantly fear that they will be next to fall victim to the faceless terror of the cyber bully and will feel helpless to do anything to prevent the attack because the attacker is unknown. Bullying therefore has a greater impact for organizations, including impact on morale, culture, and productivity beyond the traditional aggressor–aggressed dyad.

Cyber Bullying

At this time, there is no generally accepted definition of cyber bullying. Broadly speaking, most researchers will agree that cyber bullying is aggression that is perpetrated by individuals utilizing electronic devices or environments such as cell phones, email, text messaging, internet websites, chat rooms, blogs, and online videos. The bully uses these instruments as tools to insult, mock, threaten, intimidate, or spread rumors about a victim. When cyber bullying is closely examined, however, a multiplicity of issues and opinions emerge, largely because so little is understood about this phenomenon due to an absence of research. Current thought and evidence both seem to indicate that cyber bullying is more than simply an electronic version of bullying. The difference appears to stem, in part or in whole, from the fact that electronic acts of aggression do not occur face-to-face, but from a distant vantage point by individuals who can remain unidentified. It involves covert rather than physical aggression, and this can add important elements of ambiguity to the bully–victim dynamic.

Cyber bullying can occur anywhere the aggressor has access to electronic communications. Therefore, unlike traditional bullying, there is no way to escape. The attacks invade one's privacy and traditional areas of safety at home, work, or even during the commute (Tokunaga, 2010). Li (2007) provides seven broad categories of cyber-bullying behaviors:

- Flaming – angry, rude, or vulgar messages about a person sent to an online group or to the target directly via email or other text messaging.
- Online harassment – repeatedly sending offensive messages via email or other text messaging to the target directly.
- Cyber stalking – online harassment that includes threats of harm or is excessively intimidating.
- Denigration – sending harmful, untrue, or cruel statements about a target to other people or posting such material online.

- Masquerade – pretending to be someone else and sending or posting material that makes the target look bad.
- Outing – sending or posting material about a person that contains sensitive, private, or embarrassing information, including forwarding private messages or images.
- Exclusion – cruelly excluding a target from an online group.

These seven different types of aggressive, cyber-bullying behaviors can be completed both overtly and covertly, meaning that the victim may or may not know the identity of the individual who is causing him or her harm. For this reason, cyber bullying is postulated to be more appealing to the bully, as he or she is protected from any negative repercussions of his or her actions and because of the increased worry and confusion the target experiences, as it is unclear who is responsible for the attack (Pujazon-Zazik and Park, 2010).

In extreme cases, those who experience cyber bullying have committed suicide as a result of the abuse. In a recent, widely publicized case, a Rutgers University student, Tyler Clementi, killed himself in 2010 after his roommate streamed his sexual encounter with another man via his webcam. In another case in 2006, Megan Meier also committed suicide after several episodes of online taunting. While most targets of cyber bullying do not resort to such behaviors, the negative effects for each of the targets are clear.

SALIENT FEATURES

There is very little academic research in the area of cyber bullying in the workplace. However, the work that has been done demonstrates the occurrence of cyber bullying is not something that should be ignored. In a study of workplace bullying, 40 percent of union workers experienced bullying in general, while 10 percent of those experienced cyber bullying. Of those who experienced cyber bullying at work, 100 percent also experienced face-to-face bullying (Privatera and Campbell, 2009). The increase in cyber bullying in the workplace should not be a surprise since the adolescents who grew up using the new technologies to bully are now entering the workforce and bringing their norms and behaviors with them. In addition, those that bully face-to-face certainly have no reservations about taking a less direct tack, so as more and more emphasis is placed on virtual communication and interaction, the more aggressive individuals will turn to cyber bullying. No work environment is safe from cyber bullying, including academe (Gupta, 2008).

There has been increased attention on cyber bullying in the workplace in the popular press and these resources have attempted to describe what cyber bullying practices are and ways to avoid them (Duram, 2010; Tsikoudakis, 2011). These articles not only serve as resources for the targets of cyber bullying, but they provide important considerations for organizations as a whole. One area that these articles highlight is the legal risks corporations face when cyber bullying occurs. Currently, 21 states are debating legislation that would make workplace bullying an unlawful practice (http://www.healthyworkplacebill.org). These regulations would extend beyond current US laws addressing hostile work environments.

The impact of cyber bullying at work is noted by Privatera and Campbell (2009) on several levels. The immediate impact on the individual is diminished physical and psychological health and wellbeing. Continued abuse can begin to affect the target's personal relationships and self-esteem. These in turn affect future career advancements as well as the level of productivity at the target's current position, as the target is more likely to miss days of work.

To date, research on cyber bullying in the workplace has focused on describing the actions and consequences of the abusive behaviors. The following sections provide a more theoretically based series of propositions to explore cyber bullying in the workplace as well as its underlying causes. The constructs of trait anger, narcissism, approval of aggression, behavioral ethics, job dissatisfaction, interpersonal conflict, and the demographic construct of gender are presented as possible areas for a robust, more theoretically grounded stream of research to pursue in explaining the underlying roots of cyber bullying in the workplace.

Trait Anger

Trait anger refers to an individual's propensity to anger as a personality trait (Deffenbacher, 1992). Persons with high trait anger have higher predispositions to respond in a hostile manner and perceive situations as frustrating (Hershcovis *et al.*, 2007). Trait anger is shown to be related to workplace aggression (Douglas and Martinko, 2001). Fox and Spector (1999) demonstrate that a relationship between trait anger and both work frustration and workplace aggression exists, and is directed at the individual target of aggressive actions and towards the organization as a whole. The importance of trait anger (and other individual difference variables such as self-control and negative affectivity) is demonstrated by Hempworth and Towler (2004), who found these constructs to account for 27 percent of the variance in workplace aggression. Given the strength of the relationship between trait anger and general workplace bullying, future researchers should continue to examine the relationship between trait anger and workplace cyber bullying in particular. Based on these past findings, it would seem as though perpetrators of workplace cyber bullying would have higher levels of trait anger than individuals who do not bully. It may also be important to investigate if those who participate in cyber bullying have different levels of trait anger when compared to individuals who choose to bully face-to-face.

Narcissism

Narcissism is a multidimensional construct and includes a sense of grandiosity and superiority, a sense of entitlement, exploitation of others for personal gain, lack of empathy for others, and an excessive need for admiration from others (Ang *et al.*, 2009). Lubit (2004) notes that narcissistic managers devalue others, feel exempt from the normal rules of society, display a lack of empathy, and have little, if any, conscience. Narcissism is related to relational aggression in adolescents, which can carry over into adulthood (Kerig and Stellwagen, 2010). Narcissism is shown to be related to aggression specifically in the form of a reprisal. Ang *et al.* (2009) note that, when a narcissistic bully felt as though he or she had been insulted or slighted, that individual directed a greater amount of aggressive behavior toward the person or persons who the bully felt had wronged them. Further, in the workplace, if a negative evaluation or interpersonal encounter is perceived as threatening, it is likely that narcissists will perceive bullying behavior as legitimate and justifiable (Ang *et al.*, 2009). Challenges to a narcissist's grandiose self-image can also lead to a rage that is destructive both to themselves and their victims. Thus, even constructive feedback can result in inappropriate retaliation that harms both parties (Lubit, 2004). Due to these findings, future research should investigate if narcissism is positively related to cyber-bullying behavior.

Approval of Aggression

Normative beliefs are shown to influence behavioral intentions as well as observable behaviors. Normative approval of aggression is a construct that is shown to be directly related to aggressive behaviors and to mediate the relationship between other constructs that are positively related to aggression. Research indicates that children and adolescents who approve of the use of aggression are considered to be more aggressive by their parents, teachers, and peers than individuals who do not approve of the use of aggression (Ang *et al.*, 2009).

Huesmann and Guerra (1997) longitudinally studied normative beliefs that are supportive of aggression and found that eventually, aggressive, bullying behavior resulted. Their results indicate that normative beliefs become stable by fourth and fifth grade and, once stable, these beliefs predict aggressive, bullying behavior through adolescence and beyond. In a similar finding, Bellmore *et al.* (2005) demonstrated that adolescents who believe in the appropriateness of aggression chose hostile and aggressive response options that resulted in subsequent physical, verbal, and indirect bullying behavior. Therefore, since cyber bullying is another method of aggressive, bullying behaviors, future research would likely conclude that the approval of aggression is positively related to cyber bullying in the workplace.

Gender

Gender has also been found to be related to aggression. Some studies indicate that men are more aggressive than women (Green, 1990; McFarlin *et al.*, 2001). However, in specific situations, women have been found to be more aggressive than men (Namie and Namie, 2000). Such is the case in the instance of cyber bullying where females are more likely to be both the victim and perpetrator of the aggressive behavior (Tokunaga, 2010). Gender differences also exist in regard to who is the perpetrator of bullying at work. Men are more likely to be bullied by their superiors, while women are just as likely to be bullied by a superior or a peer (Salin, 2005). For women, workplace bullying affects their beliefs about the world, people, and themselves. Additionally, women have greater symptoms of post-traumatic stress disorder than males (Rodríguez-Muñoz *et al.*, 2010).

Within the acts of cyber bullying, gender differences also exist. In males, gender visual cues can be considered good indicators of severe cyber bullies and cyber victims (Menesini *et al.*, 2011). These findings show that our knowledge of the effects of gender and bullying behavior is mixed. Therefore, it is recommended that future researchers should examine the specific relationship between gender and workplace cyber bullying.

Job Dissatisfaction

Job dissatisfaction is a function of how much people dislike their job (Spector, 1997). Several studies have linked job dissatisfaction and frustration to bullying behavior at work. Stress is shown to increase job dissatisfaction and to lower aggression thresholds for the concerned individuals – partly due to the fact it does not allow for time-consuming conflict-solving (Salin, 2005). For example, bullying may result from individuals' inefficient coping with frustration (Baillien *et al.*, 2009). Einarsen *et al.* (1994) and Vartia (1996) found a significant correlation between bullying and low satisfaction with the social climate at work.

Dissatisfied employees are more likely to behave destructively and act out through workplace aggression (Herscovits *et al.*, 2007). This aggression may be an effort to assert or regain some level of control over their job (Judge *et al.*, 2006). Interestingly, Rodríguez-Muñoz *et al.* (2010) demonstrate that bullying may also be a cause (and not a result) of job dissatisfaction. Thus, understanding the direction of the relationship between job satisfaction and bullying as well as the impact that job satisfaction has on the occurrence of cyber bullying will be important topics for further research.

Interpersonal Conflicts

Interpersonal conflict has been a known work stressor for over four decades, after Boulding (1963) described it as discrepant views or perceived incompatibilities between two or more individuals at work. Aggression has been shown to be a reaction to work stressors (Hershcovis *et al.*, 2007). Pearson *et al.* (2000) suggest that time pressure reduces the "niceties" of business life and increases the risk for strong and spiraling interpersonal conflicts. These spiraling conflicts may result in workplace bullying behaviors. Workplace incivility may then escalate into a pattern of bullying and, specifically, cyber bullying (Anderson and Pearson, 1999). A better understanding of the nature of interpersonal conflicts that are most likely to lead to instances of cyber bullying would be important findings that could help stop cyber-bullying behaviors before they are able to start.

Behavioral Ethics

Another area for examination is the relationship between cyber bullying at work and behavioral ethics. Behavioral ethics provide a contextual theoretical framework for future research. The definition by researchers Trevino *et al.* (2006) of behavioral ethics includes individual behavior that is subject to or judged according to generally accepted moral norms of behavior. In addition, behavioral ethics tend to be primarily concerned with explaining individual behavior that occurs in the context of larger social prescriptions. The ethical decision-making process itself is believed to have several stages, the first of which is moral awareness or moral identification (Rest, 1986), in which the person identifies circumstances or situations in which a moral standard, principle, or problem exists. These situational factors (such as job context) were also found by Trevino (1986) to moderate the moral judgment process and include the individual's cognitive stage as a response to an ethical dilemma in the person–situation interactionist model for organizations. Similarly, Ferrell and Gresham (1985) found that agreement of proper ethical conduct varies based on the issue involved and, regarding ethical decision-making, Strong and Meyer (1992) found a relationship with an individual's demonstrated moral reasoning.

At the second stage, the moral judgment stage, Rest (1986) argued that the ethical judgment process is activated once a person becomes aware of the ethical issue. This activation is also noted by Bandura (1999), where if one's personal standards of ethical behavior are activated, a person then regulates his or her behavior to avoid behaving unethically. Accordingly, avoiding or morally "disengaging" from the process of acknowledging or activating one's personal standards at this point allows a person to avoid the guilt that violating their personal standards of ethical behavior would otherwise create.

In the next stage, it makes sense then that the degree of motivation or commitment a person possesses in deciding whether or not to take a moral course of action or take responsibility for moral outcomes will be influenced by his or her degree of moral engagement. Such a process may begin to explain bullying behavior. If moral motivation is defined as a person's "degree of commitment to taking the moral course of action, valuing moral values over other values, and taking personal responsibility for moral outcomes" (Rest *et al.,* 1999: 101) and a person does not see his or her bullying behavior as morally or ethically wrong, perhaps even sees it as justified, he or she will not regulate his or her behavior. In fact, a moderate correlation has been found between moral cognition and behavior (Kohlberg, 1969; Trevino and Youngbood, 1990). Furthermore, if an organization's ethical climate (shared perception among organization members regarding criteria and focus; Trevino *et al.*, 2006) is such that unethical behavior such as bullying is not challenged, individuals participating in or receiving such behavior will have little recourse or support to thwart the behavior. Therefore, an understanding of an individual's stage of ethical reasoning should provide valuable insights into his or her level of bullying behaviors in general, as well as his or her cyber-bullying behaviors more specifically.

CONCLUSION

This chapter has developed ten research propositions that independently or in combination provide a theoretically grounded explanation of cyber bullying in the workplace. The current literature is in the descriptive stage and focuses on what cyber bullying in the workplace is and how frequently it happens. Researchers have begun to look at the consequences of this form of cyber bullying. For a greater understanding of cyber bullying to be developed, a robust theoretical framework needs to be employed to allow description, but also to include prediction and intervention. Thus, this chapter serves as a call for theoretically based research utilizing existing constructs to explain behaviors related to cyber bullying.

REFERENCES

Agatston, P. W., Kowalski, R., and Limber, S. (2007). Students' perspectives on cyberbullying. *Journal of Adolescent Health*, 41, 559–60.

Anderson, L. M., and Pearson, C. M. (1999). Tit for tat? The spiraling effect of incivility in the workplace. *Academy of Management Review*, 24, 452–71.

Ang, R. P., Ong, E. Y. L., Lim, J. C. Y., and Lim, E. W. (2009). From narcissistic exploitativeness to bullying behavior: The mediating role of approval of aggression beliefs. *Social Development*, 19, 721–35.

Baillien, E., Neyens, I., De Witte, H., and De Cuyper, N. (2009). A qualitative study on the development of workplace bullying: Towards a three way model. *Journal of Community & Applied Social Psychology*, 19, 1–16.

Bandura, A. (1999). Moral disengagement in the perpetration of inhumanities. *Personality and Social Psychology Review*, 3, 193–209.

Bellmore, A. D., Witlow, M. R., Graham, S., and Juvonen, J. (2005). From beliefs to behavior: The mediating role of hostile response selection in predicting aggression. *Aggressive Behavior*, 31, 453–72.

Boulding, K. E. (1963). *Conflict and Defense: A General Theory*, New York, NY: Harper Tourchbooks.

Campbell, M. A. (2005). Cyber bullying: An old problem in a new guise? *Australian Journal of Guidance and Counselling*, 15, 68–76.

Deffenbacher, J. L. (1992). Trait anger: Theory, findings, and implications. In C. Spielberger and J. N. Butcher (eds), *Personality Assessment* (vol. 9, pp. 177–201), Hillsdale, NJ: Lawrence Earlbaum Associates.

Douglas, S. C., and Martinko, M. J. (2001). Exploring the role of individual differences in the prediction of workplace aggression. *Journal of Applied Psychology*, 4, 547–59.

Duram, J. (2010). *Cyber bullying at work*. http://www.safeworkers.co.uk/cyber-bullying-work.html.

Einarsen, S., Raknes, B. I., and Matthiessen, S. B. (1994). Bullying and harassment at work and their relationships to work environment quality: An exploratory study. *European Work and Organizational Psychologist*, 4, 381–401.

Ferrell, O. C., and Gresham, L. G. (1985). A contingency framework for understanding ethical decision making in marketing. *Journal of Marketing*, 49, 87–96.

Fox, S., and Spector, P. E. (1999). A model of work frustration-aggression. *Journal of Organizational Behavior*, 20, 915–31.

Green, R. G. (1990). *Human Aggression*, Pacific Grove, CA: Brooks/Cole Publishing.

Griezel, L., Craven, R. G., Yeung, A. S., and Finger, L. R. (2008). The development of a multi-dimensional measure of cyberbullying, paper presented at the Australian Association for Research in Education, Brisbane, Dec.

Gupta, U. G. (2008). Cyber-harassment in academia. *University Business*. Retrieved from http://www.universitybusiness.com/article/cyber-harassment-academia.

Hempworth, W., and Towler, A. (2004). The effects of individual differences and charismatic leadership on workplace aggression. *Journal of Occupational Health Psychology*, 9, 176–85.

Hershcovis, M. S., Turner, N., Barling, J., Arnold, K. A., Dupré, K. E., Inness, M., … Sivanathan, N. (2007). Predicting workplace aggression: A meta-analysis. *Journal of Applied Psychology*, 92, 228–38.

Huesmann, L. R., and Guerra, N. G. (1997). Children's normative beliefs about aggression and aggressive behavior. *Journal of Personality and Social Psychology*, 72, 408–19.

Judge, T. A., Scott, B. A., and Ilies, R. (2006). Hostility, job attitudes, and workplace deviance: Test of a multilevel model. *Journal of Applied Psychology*, 91, 126–38.

Kerig, P. K., and Stellwagen, K. K. (2010). Roles of callous-unemotional traits, narcissism, and Machiavellianism in childhood aggression. *Journal of Psychopathology and Behavioral Assessment*, 32, 343–52.

Kohlberg, L. (1969). Stage and sequence: The cognitive developmental approach to socialization. In D. A. Goslin (ed.), *Handbook of Socialization Theory* (pp. 347–480), Chicago, IL: Rand McNally.

Li, Q. (2007). Bullying in the new playground: Research into cyberbullying and cyber victimisation. *Australasian Journal of Educational Technology*, 23, 435–54. Retrieved from http://www.ascilite.org.au/ajet/ajet23/li.html.

Linn, E., Fagin, A., Hussey, M., Sher, D. M., and Hartmann, I. (2004). Cyberbullies cause real pain [Letters to the editor]. *New York Times* (30 Aug.), A18.

Lubit, R. (2004). The tyranny of toxic managers: Applying emotional intelligence to deal with difficult personalities. *Ivey Business Journal*, 68, 19–27.

McFarlin, S. K., Fals-Stewart, W., Major, D. A., and Justice, E. M. (2001). Alcohol use and workplace aggression: An examination of perpetration and victimization. *Journal of Substance Abuse*, 13, 303–21.

Menesini, E., Nocentini, A., and Calussi, P. (2011). The measurement of cyberbullying: Dimensional structure and relative item severity and discrimination. *Cyberpsychology, Behavior, and Social Networking*, 14, 267–74.

Namie, G. (2010). *The WBI U.S. Workplace Bullying Survey*, Washington, DC: Workplace Bullying Institute and Zogby International.

Namie, G., and Namie R. (2000). *The Bully at Work: What you Can Do to Stop the Hurt and Reclaim your Dignity on the Job*, Naperville, IL: Sourcebooks.

Olweus, D. (1993). *Bullying at School: What we Know and What we Can Do*, Cambridge, MA: Blackwell.

Pearson, C. M., Andersson, L. M., and Porath C. L. (2000). Assessing and attacking workplace incivility. *Organizational Dynamics*, 29, 123–37.

Privatera, C., and Campbell, M. A. (2009). Cyberbullying: The new face of workplace bullying? *CyberPsychology and Behavior*, 12, 395–400.

Pujazon-Zazik, M., and Park, M. J. (2010). To tweet, or not to tweet: Gender differences and potential positive and negative health outcomes of adolescents' social internet use. *American Journal of Men's Health*, 4, 77–85.

Raynor, C., and Cooper, C. (1997). Workplace bullying: Myth or reality – can we afford to ignore it? *Leadership and Organizational Development Journal*, 18, 211–14.

Raynor, C., and Höel, H. (1997). A summary review of literature relating to workplace bullying. *Journal of Community and Applied Social Psychology*, 7, 118–91.

Rest, J., Narvaez, D., Bebeau, M. J., and Thoma, S. J. (1999). *Postconventional Moral Thinking: A Neo-Kohlbergian Approach*, Mahwah, NJ: Lawrence Erlbaum.

Rest, J. R. (1986). *Moral Development: Advances in Research and Theory*, New York: Praeger.

Rodríguez-Muñoz, A., Moreno-Jiménez, B., Sanz Vergel, A. I., and Hernández, E. G. (2010). Post-traumatic symptoms among victims of workplace bullying: Exploring gender differences and shattered assumptions. *Journal of Applied Social Psychology*, 40, 2616–35.

Salin, D. (2005). Workplace bullying among business professionals: Prevalence, gender differences and the role of organizational politics. *Pistes*, 7, 1–11. Retrieved from http://www.pistes.uqam.ca/v7n3/articles/v7n3a2en.htm.

Spector, P. E. (1997). *Job Satisfaction: Applications, Assessment, Causes, and Consequences*, Thousand Oaks, CA: Sage.

Strong, K. C., and Meyer, G. D. (1992). An integrative descriptive model of ethical decision making. *Journal of Business Ethics*, 11, 89–94.

Tokunaga, R. S. (2010). Following you home from school: A critical review and synthesis of research on cyberbullying victimization. *Computers in Human Behavior*, 26, 277–87.

Trevino, L. K. (1986). Ethical decision making in organizations: A person-situation interactionist model. *Academy of Management Review*, 11, 601–17.

Trevino, L. K., and Youngblood, S. A. (1990). Bad apples in bad barrels: A causal analysis of ethical decision making behavior. *Journal of Applied Psychology*, 75, 378–85.

Trevino, L. K., Weaver, G. R., and Reynolds, S. J. (2006). Behavioral ethics in organizations: A review. *Journal of Management*, 32, 951–90.

Tsikoudakis, M. (2011). Stay mindful of cyber bullying in the workplace. Retrieved from http://workplaceviolencenews.com/2011/04/05/stay-mindful-of-cyber-bullying-in-the-workplace.

Vartia, M. (1996). The sources of bullying: Psychological work environment and organizational climate. *European Journal of Work and Organizational Psychology*, 5, 203–14.

Wang, J., Iannotti, R. J., and Nansel, T. R. (2009). School bullying among adolescents in the United States: Physical, verbal, relational, and cyber. *Journal of Adolescent Health*, 45, 368–75.

15

Considerations Regarding the Workplace Bullying of Persons with Disabilities

Ara J. Schmitt
Duquesne University

Rachel Robertson
University of Pittsburgh

Jenna Hennessey and Charles Jaquette
Duquesne University

Lisa J. Vernon-Dotson
Coastal Carolina University

INTRODUCTION

Recent epidemiological data suggest that there are 11.3 million persons with disabilities working in the United States (National Organization on Disability, 2011). Therefore, it is likely that any given manager or employer will work with a person with a disability across one's career. As explained below, it is essential that employers understand the needs of employees with disabilities, not only to allow the employee with a disability to reach his or her on-the-job potential, but also to create a work climate that minimizes the risk of bullying as a subtype of discrimination. Employers must invest interest in preventing bullying, and intervening when it does occur, because lack of responsiveness may be interpreted as a violation of legislation aimed at reducing discrimination against workers with disabilities. As such, it is important to highlight two laws in particular in which employers should be well versed.

LEGISLATION PROVIDING PROTECTIONS FOR PERSONS WITH DISABILITIES

Two legislative mandates that provide protections for persons with disabilities in the workplace are the Americans with Disabilities Act (ADA), 2008, and Section 504 of the Rehabilitation Act of 1973. Due to the significant overlap in the rationale behind and requirements of these two laws, we will review the two together. The interested reader is referred to Russo and Osborne (2009) for a detailed review of both pieces of legislation. Important to note is that Section 504 and ADA are both considered civil rights laws that prohibit discrimination on the basis of a disability in the workplace. In order to qualify for Section 504 and ADA protections, the employee must have physical or mental impairments that substantially limit a major life activity, including work. The definition of a physical or mental impairment as provided by Section 504, and echoed by ADA, follows:

> *Physical or mental impairment means* (A) any physiological disorder or condition, cosmetic disfigurement, or anatomical loss affecting one or more of the following body systems: neurological; musculoskeletal; special sense organs; respiratory, including speech organs; cardiovascular; reproductive, digestive, genito-urinary; hemic and lymphatic; skin; and endocrine; or (B) any mental or psychological disorder, such as mental retardation, organic brain syndrome, emotional or mental illness, and specific learning disabilities.
>
> (34 C.F.R. § 104.3(j)(2)(i))

If the employee meets the definition of having a physical or mental impairment, he or she is entitled to what the law refers to as reasonable accommodations. ADA directly states that employers may be responsible for: (1) making existing facilities accessible, (2) job restructuring, (3) part-time or modified work schedules, (4) acquiring or modifying equipment,

(5) changing tests, training materials, or policies, (6) providing qualified readers or interpreters, and (7) reassignment to a vacant position.

The Legislative–Managerial Link

As noted elsewhere in this book, the perception that one is different from the larger group puts a person at risk of being the victim of bullying. This appears to be the case for employees with disabilities. Being regarded as having a disability puts an employee at risk for discrimination (Draper *et al.*, 2011). For example, Louvet *et al.* (2009) documented that employers found interviewees who were identified as having a disability, when a disability was not actually present, to be less competent than interviewees who were not labeled as having a disability. Gewurtz and Kirsh (2009) also found that the mere presence of disability can be seen as disruptive to the organization and be met with managerial resistance.

It appears, then, that the social judgment experienced by persons with disabilities begins with the mere knowledge that a disability is present. This resistance also appears to extend into the process of determining what, if any, workplace accommodations are reasonable. Foster (2007) found that negotiating reasonable accommodations with an employer can be a stimulus for bullying. A specific example of bullying included in this study involved an employee who used a wheelchair being told that the "disabled spaces were only for disabled people" as she sat in her chair next to her car. On the other hand, it does appear that positive attitudes toward persons with disabilities in the workplace are related to perceived reasonableness of accommodations, favorable relationships with coworkers, and positive outcomes for employees (Copeland *et al.*, 2010; Guwurtz and Kirsh, 2009).

We argue that raising general awareness of disabilities, and the manifestations of disabilities, is necessary to promote positive attitudes towards persons with disabilities in the workplace. Furthermore, illustrative examples of specific disability considerations are needed in order for managers to effectively prevent bullying and intervene when it does occur. In order to accomplish this goal, this chapter will present employment issues related to two disability types - physical disability and social/developmental disability - and offer specific prevention and intervention strategies.

BULLYING OF PERSONS WITH PHYSICAL DISABILITIES

Physical disabilities are generally characterized as conditions that cause impairments in mobility, vision, or hearing, or otherwise disrupt an employee's ability to perform activities of daily living such as self-care. Clearly, there is a wide array of physical disabilities that may be present in the workplace, and reviewing each of them would be outside the scope of this chapter. In order to illustrate the unique challenges that employees with one-type physical disability face, we will consider the example of spinal cord injuries (SCI).

The impairments caused by a spinal cord injury can vary greatly depending upon the location of the injury on the spine and the severity of the injury. Many employees who receive a SCI do not return to work (Lidal *et al.*, 2007) and those who do are faced with assorted challenges, such as decreased mobility within the work environment and, if necessary and deemed reasonable, adjusting to different job responsibilities. In order to illustrate domains of personal functioning that can be impacted by a disability, Table 15.1 includes the physical, health, and emotional characteristics of persons with SCI that have vocational implications.

Collectively, these facts put an employee with a SCI at a higher risk for being the target of workplace bullying. This is largely because applying the federal protections of (1) making existing facilities accessible, (2) job restructuring, (3) part-time or modified work schedules, (4) acquiring or

TABLE 15.1
Characteristics of Persons with Spinal Cord Injuries

Physical Characteristics	Health Characteristics	Emotional Characteristics
Paralysis, numbness, weakness in lower / upper body	Loss of bowel and bladder control	Depression
Use of wheelchair	Trouble breathing independently or clearing secretions from lungs	Low self-esteem
Loss of manual dexterity	High risk for pneumonia or other respiratory problems	Anxiety
	Increased risk for pressure sores and blood clots	

modifying equipment, (5) changing tests, training materials, or policies, (6) providing qualified readers or interpreters, and (7) reassignment to a vacant position may draw the ire of employers and fellow employees who might perceive these to be unfair or unjust. As discussed in other chapters within this book, employers should be aware that bullying is often subtle and consciously concealed by other employees, and even managers. These facts complicate the prevention and intervention of bullying of persons with disabilities.

In order to reduce the risk of bullying, managers and human resource department personnel need to consider the specific needs of employees with physical disabilities, like SCI, that may become the focus of peer victimization. The Occupational Safety and Health Administration (OSHA) enforces regulations designed to ensure that employees with disabilities have appropriate access to amenities and resources to be successful in the workplace. As a regulatory example, OSHA requires that employees with physical disabilities have wheelchair access to all areas of the workplace, including kitchens, bathrooms, all workspaces, doorways, and emergency exits. Not having access to these areas requires the employee with a disability to seek the assistance of other employees and managers who may not be sympathetic to their colleague's mobility needs. By ensuring reasonable access to common areas, employers not only promote the independence of their employee, but also eliminate the necessity for the employee to call attention to his or her physical limitations and become open to being a possible target of bully behavior. In brief, managers should meet with the employee with a physical disability from the outset of their employment or return to work to proactively address their mobility and other physical needs.

The perceived burden of assisting another employee with physical activities is only one source of bullying in the workplace. Bullying may also result from the belief that the victim has special benefits or privileges to which other employees do not have access. These perceived benefits may consist of the following: allowing employee with a SCI to shift work hours for a medical appointment, permitting reduced work hours, providing the opportunity to take multiple breaks throughout the work day, and varying the employee's workload in order to alleviate high physical demands. Contingent on the severity of the physical impairment, employees with SCI may also need the support of a personal care attendant to provide assistance with personal needs such as toileting, grooming, and eating.

Managers should be prepared to recognize potential bullying risk factors and actively attempt to mitigate those risks.

Bullying Prevention

Aside from creating a work climate where all employees are valued and accepted, the primary means by which organizations can attempt to prevent the bullying of employees with disabilities is through policies and procedures. General strategies for the prevention of bullying of persons with disabilities can involve a comprehensive anti-bullying policy, training for employees on the anti-bullying policy, actively encouraging reporting of bullying incidents, and creating awareness of disabilities in the workplace (Office of the Commissioner for Public Employment, 2005). Maintaining a comprehensive anti-bullying policy and resolution process is essential to prevent and effectively manage the bullying of employees with physical disabilities. The policy should clearly communicate what behaviors constitute bullying, that bullying will not be tolerated, and the specific consequences of workplace bullying. To add saliency to the anti-bullying policy, the guidelines should be integrated into the company's existing policies. This will also communicate to employees that the anti-bullying policy will be enforced.

Once a comprehensive bullying policy has been created, employee training will be required to clearly communicate the guidelines. Formal trainings, staff meetings, bulletins, and company intranet could be considered as avenues to educate staff employees regarding the bullying policy. Specific content of the training should include full details of the anti-bullying policy, how to comply with the policy, measures used in the workplace to prevent and investigate bullying, to whom bullying should be reported, the processes by which bullying will be investigated, and the consequences of bully behavior (Office of the Commissioner for Public Employment, 2005).

We recommend two points of emphasis regardless of training method. One emphasis should be the encouragement of confidential reporting of bullying incidents, and especially incidents involving employees with disabilities due to the complex legal ramifications. The second point should be that it is the managers' and human resource personnel's duty to respond promptly and confidentially to all situations in which bullying behavior is alleged to have occurred. This will set the tone that all reports will be taken seriously and fully investigated. For work settings with high employee turnover, human resource personnel could aid prevention efforts by infusing the anti-bullying policies and procedures into new employee orientations.

Finally, organizations can be proactive by providing managers and employees with disability-related information. Borrowing from the school-based disability literature, providing teachers with disability-related information increased educators' ability to generate interventions to improve the performance of students (Cunningham and Wodrich, 2006). It stands to reason that providing employees with disability-related information can at a minimum increase coworkers' sensitivity to their coworker with a disability, if not facilitate coworkers' ability to anticipate and address the needs of their colleague at work.

In the case of an employee with a SCI, a manager should first consult with the employee to gain knowledge concerning his or her physical limitations and what information would be helpful to share with coworkers. For example, it may prove useful to share with coworkers the location of the injury on the spinal cord and what degree of paralysis is present. This can lead to a personalized discussion of what accommodations will be necessary for the employee with a SCI to integrate into the workplace and, perhaps more importantly to reduce coworker hostility that can lead to bully behavior, why those accommodations are required (e.g. frequent breaks are for toileting purposes). This is not to say that sharing such information is meant to make managers and coworkers feel sorrow for the employee with a SCI. This can unintentionally lead to managers decreasing or changing the employee's job responsibilities "for their own good" (Vickers, 2009).

Bullying Intervention

In order to intervene when bullying is taking place, a manager must be able to identify the misbehavior, or the misbehavior must be brought to the manager's attention. Bullying can be difficult to identify, as it is often difficult to "catch" bullies in action in the workplace. Not only is bullying hard to detect, but also incidents may not always be reported due to fear of retribution from the bully, or the belief that no one will act on the problem if it is reported. Managers may also remain unaware of the misbehavior because the victim and the offender may not appreciate that the inappropriate behavior constitutes bullying (Namie and Namie, 2000). Furthermore, employees with disabilities may be particularly hesitant to report bullying because to do so would highlight their employee differences and potentially alter their employer's impression of their competence.

There is limited research regarding effective ways of intervening when bullying is taking place in the workplace. Overall, managers may attempt to intervene at the levels of the target/bully dyad, the immediate work environment (including coworkers), or the entire organization as a whole. Saam (2010) outlines three approaches to intervention that have been used by consultants who specialize in workplace bullying intervention and may also be applied to the workplace bullying of employees with disabilities: (1) conflict moderation/mediation, (2) coaching/education, and (3) organization development. The pervasiveness and severity of the bullying will likely dictate which approach is most appropriate for employers to pursue.

Conflict Moderation/Mediation

On the surface, mediation between the bully and the target appears to be an appropriate technique to resolve the existence of bullying. Conflict mediation typically requires the bully and the victim to informally meet with a neutral third party to find a solution to an interpersonal problem. Saam (2010) argues that this technique may be inappropriate in order to resolve workplace bullying, and we suggest that this may be particularly true when the victim has a disability. By definition, there is a power imbalance between the victim and the perpetrator when bullying is taking place. In the case of an employee with a physical disability, the victim is unable to alter the nature and implications of his or her disability in the workplace. A premise of conflict mediation, however, is that both parties have equal power and the ability to defend themselves (Saam, 2010). This is clearly not the case in a bullying situation (Ferris, 2004) that involves a person with a disability. Employers should also use conflict mediation techniques with caution as the secretive nature of informal mediation may be unsatisfying to the target who may interpret it as an attempt to hide the presence of discrimination in the form of bullying (Saam, 2010).

Coaching/Education

In lieu of conflict mediation, coaching by mental health and/or organizational specialists may be a useful strategy to resolve incidents of bullying. The recipient of coaching can be the victim or the bully himself or herself. With respect to the employee with a disability who is the target of bullying, coaching can be used to empower the employee to lower his or her personal risk by increasing assertiveness with coworkers. For example, the employee with a SCI can be coached to provide relevant information regarding his or her disability to coworkers and assertively explain his or her workplace needs before a conflict arises that could then be the catalyst for bullying. Furthermore, coaching can be used to teach the victim strategies, such as humor, to deflect bullying behavior.

Namie and Namie (2009) suggest that coaching can also be an effective intervention for the bully, so long as the workplace has a pre-existing bullying prevention policy. The policy should be used as the framework through which mental health professionals and organizational experts focus on the explicit behavioral changes the bully must make. Namie and Namie (2009) also suggest that it must be made clear to the bully that the needs of the company and the basic rights of other employees take precedence over a personal agenda. Particularly for the victim with a disability, the bully might be provided with education regarding the victim's disability, and reviewed earlier, the victim's rights as an employee with a disability according to federal legislation. The organization should require that the bully commit to clear, observable behavior change, or else face termination (Namie and Namie, 2009). To do less may be viewed as an indication that bullying and violations are tolerated within the organization.

Organizational Development

In cases where workplace bullying is widespread and a clearly articulated behavior code, that includes bullying behavior, is not present, intervention approaches that target the organization as a whole become necessary. First, the organization must create a comprehensive prevention and enforcement policy that is supported by all company stakeholders (Saam, 2010). This policy should operationally define what constitutes bullying, instruct victims to whom instances of bullying should be reported, and clearly articulate the consequences of victimizing others. Furthermore, the organization should create a plan to address the bullying with witnesses. Witnessing bullying can be a traumatizing experience for bystanders who are often fearful to intervene (Vartia, 2001). Counseling/employee assistance services should be made available for bystanders, if desired, and the victim, as post-traumatic stress is a common outcome (Mikkelsen and Einarsen, 2002; Tehrani, 2004). The organizational plan should include a mechanism to provide counseling. Counseling services are particularly crucial for employees with disabilities, such as SCI, as such employees are already at increased risk for emotional problems, like anxiety and depression.

WORKPLACE BULLYING OF PERSONS WITH SOCIAL/DEVELOPMENTAL DISABILITIES

Next, we turn to a discussion of a disability with unique workplace manifestations to highlight how prevention and intervention efforts, some of which reviewed above, can be tailored to the particular disability. Employees diagnosed with social and developmental disabilities, such as high-functioning autism (HFA) and Asperger Syndrome (AS), have the potential to be skilled, productive, and innovative employees (Grandin, 2008). However, these employees may be at increased risk for bullying due to the characteristics of their disability. HFA and AS are neurobiological disorders on the autism spectrum in which an employee may demonstrate average to above average intelligence and verbal ability, while experiencing severe deficits in social awareness and social interaction (Attwood, 1998). These social deficits may include difficulty viewing situations from another person's perspective, noticing or accurately reading the social cues of others, interpreting subtle uses of language, and displaying body language and facial expressions appropriate to a given situation, such as making eye contact and shaking hands when meeting a new person.

Along with social difficulties, employees with HFA/AS may demonstrate a variety of other issues, such as obsessive-compulsive behavior, oversensitivity to sensory stimuli such as light or sound, and difficulties comprehending complex verbal instructions. Due to these behaviors, employees with HFA/AS sometimes behave in ways that seem bizarre or confusing to others, which may in turn place them at elevated risk of being targets of bullying. Although little research currently exists regarding workplace bullying of adults with HFA/AS, school-based studies of children and adolescents indicate these individuals to be frequent victims of severe and persistent bullying, primarily due to their social deficits (Attwood, 2004; Dubin, 2007; Humphrey and Lewis, 2008). Since these deficits are lifelong, it is likely that adults with HFA/AS are at an increased risk of being bullied in the workplace. Furthermore, in contrast to employees with physical disabilities, employees with HFA/AS show no outward physical indicators of having a disability (i.e. have a "hidden" disability). Furthermore, they may be more likely to encounter bullying in the workplace due to other employees not realizing that they have a disability (Unger, 2002).

Factors that place employees with HFA/AS at risk for bullying may manifest in the workplace in a variety of ways. Some employees with HFA/AS may not recognize the social importance of cleanliness and grooming and may come to work appearing disheveled or dirty (Hendricks, 2010). For this reason, coworkers may keep their distance or make impolite or rude comments to the employee with HFA/AS. Due to their social deficits, employees with HFA/AS may also make requests or provide feedback to coworkers in a manner that may appear rude or demanding and thereby unintentionally create strained relationships with coworkers (Hurlbutt and Chalmers, 2004). Some employees with HFA/AS engage in unusual repetitive behaviors while working due to issues with sensory processing (i.e. making sense of sounds, images, or touch), or obsessive-compulsiveness, such as humming, rocking, clapping, or touching objects, which may also make them targets of harassment (Dubin, 2007). Breaks, lunch, and other social periods during the work day also tend to present challenges to employees with HFA/AS, as these are times during which social conversation and interaction is expected (Hurlbutt and Chalmers, 2004). The employee with HFA/AS who avoids social interaction during these times may be targeted because of his or her social isolation, while the employee who attempts to socialize with others may inadvertently insult or irritate others, due to misreading others' social cues or displaying inappropriate social cues him- or herself.

Unfortunately, the bullying faced by employees with HFA/AS may be further compounded by their social deficits, as they may be unlikely to recognize the harassment, confront the bully, or report the bully's behavior.

Such social naiveté may then elicit more bullying from coworkers who realize that negative consequences are unlikely (Attwood, 2004). Still further escalating the likelihood of workplace bullying is the fact that, despite their social difficulties, many employees with HFA/AS desire friendship and social interaction and may continue to initiate interactions with aggressors despite the harassment they receive (Humphrey and Lewis, 2008).

Bullying Prevention

A number of prevention strategies aimed at reducing the likelihood of employees with HFA/AS becoming involved in workplace harassment situations are available to employers. If the employee with HFA/AS is willing to disclose his or her diagnosis to coworkers, then educating coworkers on the characteristics of employees with HFA/AS should be a top priority. This information can increase coworkers' understandings of the employee differences and prevent frustration toward the unusual behavior (Muller *et al.*, 2003). Specifically, coworkers should be informed that the employee has a neurobiological disability affecting skills in social interaction, which may result in communication in an extremely direct, unintentionally blunt manner, incorrect interpretation of subtle cues, and the need for clear and direct instructions (Hurlbutt and Chalmers, 2004).

It may also be useful to inform coworkers of any particular sensory issues experienced by the employee, as they may involve unusual displays of seemingly unusual repetitive behavior (Hendricks, 2010). Secondly, it is important to directly inform employees with HFA/AS of the implicit aspects of the workplace's social culture and of norms which if broken might place the employee at increased risk of harassment. It is best to do this through writing, as written instructions cater to the common strength of visual processing over auditory processing in people with HFA/AS.

If the employee with HFA/AS prefers to avoid social interaction, it may be useful for the employee to take breaks, or arrive at and leave work at different times than coworkers. It may also be beneficial to position his or her office, desk, or cubicle in an area farther away from other coworkers, if he or she prefers, and/or removed from aversive sensory stimuli, such as high traffic, noisy areas. Established, clear mechanisms for early intervention and mediation of the situation is necessary in order to prevent it from devolving into harassment, such as a channel for reporting disputes or problems and/or a workplace mentor who is understanding of the disability and willing to provide occasional feedback and guidance regarding social interactions (Hurlbutt and Chalmers, 2004).

Bullying Intervention

If the employee with HFA/AS becomes involved in a coworker bullying situation, some commonly used and successful school-based intervention (Myles, 2003) could be employed. If the harassment is caused or influenced by characteristics related to HFA/AS, the bully should be further educated and sensitized as to the nature of the employee's disability and how related deficits may be influencing the situation. Clearly explain to the employee with HFA/AS, in writing, which behavior he or she is engaging in that is triggering the harassment, as he or she may not be aware of it. If the behavior must change, the written statement should explicitly address it, as well as what behavior the employee needs to perform instead, and the rationale for the behavioral change. It may be helpful to turn the letter into a contract that is signed by all important parties (Houmanfar *et al.*, 2009). Such a contract is unlikely to be effective unless the employee with HFA/AS genuinely agrees to what it states.

If it is deemed best that the coworkers involved avoid interacting with each other altogether, if possible, it may be useful to create a simple daily schedule for the coworker with HFA/AS that indicates when and where to take breaks in such a way that minimizes the likelihood of the employee interacting with the bully. If a workplace mentor has been established, he or she can also be effective in intervening both on the part of the employee with HFA/AS, who may have difficulty self-advocating, and to guide the employee toward behaving in ways that reduce the likelihood of bullying.

SUMMARY AND CONCLUSIONS

Employees with disabilities are at an increased risk for becoming the victims of bullying in the workplace. The stimulus for workplace bullying will likely vary given the nature of the disability. In this chapter, we have attempted to raise awareness of how physical disability and social-developmental disabilities may manifest at work, and offer organizational prevention and intervention strategies. The principles included in this chapter can be applied across disability types and work settings. Mediation, when appropriate, education, coaching, and organizational responsiveness may all be required to address bullying of employees with disabilities. Readers of this chapter should be aware that managers may be responsible for the prevention and intervention of bullying of employees with disabilities not only out of organizational responsibility, but also out of legal need.

REFERENCES

Americans with Disabilities Amendment Act of 2008, Pub. L. 110–325 (2008).

Attwood, T. (1998). *Asperger Syndrome: A Guide for Parents and Professionals,* London: Jessica Kingsley Publishers.

Attwood, T. (2004). Strategies to reduce the bullying of young children with Asperger syndrome. *Australian Journal of Early Childhood*, 29, 15–23.

Copeland, J., Chan, F., Bezyak, J., and Fraser, R. T. (2010). Assessing cognitive and affective reactions of employers toward people with disabilities in the workplace. *Journal of Occupational Rehabilitation*, 20, 427–34.

Cunningham, M. M., and Wodrich, D. L. (2006). The effect of sharing health information on teachers' production of classroom accommodations. *Psychology in the Schools,* 43, 553–64. Retrieved from http://web.ebscohost.com.authenticate.library.duq.edu/ehost/pdfviewer/pdfviewer?vid=63&sid=41401845-c591-4c08-b76f-9cae98cb3d11%40sessionmgr10&hid=13.

Draper, W. R., Reid, C. A., and McMahon, T. (2011). Workplace discrimination and the perception of disability. *Rehabilitation Counseling Bulletin*, 55, 29–37.

Dubin, N. (2007). *Asperger Syndrome and Bullying: Strategies and Solutions,* London: Jessica Kingsley Publishers.

Ferris, P. (2004). A preliminary typology of organizational response to allegations of workplace bullying: See no evil, hear no evil, speak no evil. *British Journal of Guidance and Counseling*, 32, 389–95.

Foster, D. (2007). Legal obligation or personal lottery? Employee experiences of disability and the negotiation of adjustments in the public sector workplace. *Work, Employment, and Society*, 21, 67–84.

Gewurtz, R., and Kirsh, B. (2009). Disruption, disbelief, and resistance: A meta-synthesis of disability in the workplace. *Work*, 34, 33–44.

Grandin, T. (2008). *Careers for Employees with Asperger Syndrome and High-Functioning Autism,* Shawnee Mission, KS: Autism Asperger Publishing.

Hendricks, D. (2010). Employment and adults with autism spectrum disorders: Challenges and strategies for success. *Journal of Vocational Rehabilitation*, 32, 125–34.

Houmanfar, R., Maglieri, K., Roman, H., and Ward, T. (2009). Behavioral contracting. In W. O'Donohue and J. Fisher (eds), *General Principles and Empirically Supported Techniques of Cognitive Behavior Therapy* (pp. 151–7), Hoboken, NJ: John Wiley & Sons.

Humphrey, N., and Lewis, S. (2008). "Make me normal": The views and experiences of pupils on the autistic spectrum in mainstream secondary schools. *Autism*, 12, 23–46.

Hurlbutt, K., and Chalmers, L. (2004). Employment and adults with Asperger syndrome. *Focus on Autism and Other Developmental Disabilities*, 19, 215–22.

Lidal, I., Huynh, T., and Biering-Sørensen, F. (2007). Return to work following spinal cord injury: A review. *Disability And Rehabilitation: An International, Multidisciplinary Journal*, 29, 1341–75.

Louvet, E., Rohmer, O., and Dubois, N. (2009). Social judgment of people with a disability in the workplace: How to make a good impression on employers. *Swiss Journal of Psychology*, 68, 153–9.

Mikkelsen, E., and Einarsen, S. (2002). Relationships between exposure to bullying at work and psychological and psychosomatic health complaints: The role of state negative affectivity and generalized self-efficacy. *Scandinavian Journal of Psychology*, 43, 397–405.

Muller, E., Schuler, A., Burton, B., and Yates, G. (2003). Meeting the vocational support needs of employees with Asperger syndrome and other autism spectrum disabilities. *Journal of Vocational Rehabilitation*, 18, 163–75.

Myles, B. (2003). Behavioral forms of stress management for employees with Asperger syndrome. *Child and Adolescent Psychiatric Clinics of North America*, 12, 123–41.

Namie, G., and Namie, R. (2000). *The Bully at Work*, Naperville, IL: Sourcebooks.

Namie, G., and Namie, R. (2009). U.S. workplace bullying: Some basic considerations and consultation interventions. *Consulting Psychology Journal: Practice and Research*, 61, 202–19.

National Organization on Disability (2011). *A Catalyst for the Disability Employment Movement*. Retrieved from: http://www.nod.org/about_us.

Occupational Safety and Health Administration (2011). *OSHA Field Safety and Health Manual*, Washington, DC: Government Printing Office.

Office of the Commissioner for Public Employment (2005). *Preventing and Eliminating Workplace Bullying in the Northern Territory Public Sector Framework*, Darwin NT: Office of the Commissioner for Public Employment.

Russo, C. J., and Osborne, A. G. (2009). *Section 504 and the ADA*, Thousand Oaks: CA: Corwin Press.

Saam, N. J. (2010). Interventions in workplace bullying: A multilevel approach. *European Journal of Work and Organizational Psychology*, 19, 51–75.

Section 504 Amendment to the Rehabilitation Act of 1973 (enacted under the Workforce Investment Act of 1998, Pub. L. 105–220, 112 Stat. 936 [1998]).

Tehrani, N. (2004). Bullying: A source of chronic post-traumatic stress? *British Journal of Guidance and Counseling*, 32, 357–66.

Unger, D. (2002). Employers' attitudes toward persons with disabilities in the workforce: Myths or realities? *Focus on Autism and Developmental Disorders*, 17, 2–10.

Vartia, M. (2001). Consequences of workplace bullying with respect to the well-being of its targets and the observers of bullying. *Scandinavian Journal of Work, Environment and Health*, 27, 63–9.

Vickers, M. H. (2009). Bullying, disability and work: A case study of workplace bullying. *Qualitative Research in Organizations and Management*, 4, 255–72.

Part IV

Managing Workplace Bullying

16

The Role of Human Resource Departments in Addressing Bullying Behavior

Jennifer Loh
Edith Cowan University

INTRODUCTION

Workplace bullying affects both organizations and individuals. At the individual level, workplace bullying affects the safety, welfare, and health of employees. Studies have found that targets (i.e. individuals who are bullied) reported higher levels of anxiety and depression (Namie, 2003) than did non-bullied workers. Individuals who are persistently bullied for an extended period of time also exhibited symptoms of post-traumatic stress disorder (PTSD). Individuals who are not bullied but are witnesses to such aggression reported higher levels of stress and lower work satisfaction than individuals who were not witnesses (Lutgen-Sandvik *et al.*, 2007). At the organizational level, workplace bullying results in reduced productivity, low morale, high absenteeism, escalating staff turnover, and costly workers compensation claims or legal actions (Einarsen and Mikkelsen, 2003; McCarthy and Mayhew, 2004; Zapf and Einarsen, 2001; Zapf *et al.*, 2003). Workplace bullying can also lead to adverse publicity for a company and/or affect the company's public image (Bassman, 1992). As a consequence, workplace bullying is increasingly being recognized as an important workplace issue by researchers, managers, human resource (HR) departments, and HR professionals.

Given the detrimental impact that workplace bullying can have on both the individual and the organization, managers have often recruited the help of HR departments to assist them in handling bullying concerns. Furthermore, HR departments are the first port of call for many individuals who are bullied (Lewis and Rayner, 2003). However, apart from some advice on how to deal with workplace bullying (Hubert, 2003; Mathieson *et al.*, 2006), there is limited research on the kind of measures used by organizations to combat bullying.

Many scholars believe that HR should be involved actively in the prevention and management of workplace bullying (Lewis and Rayner, 2003; Mathieson *et al.*, 2006; Namie, 2003; Salin, 2008). However, very little is known about the precise role of HR in relation to this insidious problem. Therefore, this chapter will discuss the role of HR departments in addressing bullying behaviors in the workplace. This chapter will also provide a brief discussion on potential measures that HR professionals can adopt to develop an anti-bullying workplace program.

HR CONTEXT

Traditionally, HR departments are primarily concerned with the recruitment (i.e. recruiting and paying) and the management of employees. Modern HR work also involves compensation, performance management, organization development, employees' safety, wellness, motivation, communication, administration, and training (Armstrong, 1999; Roberts *et al.*, 1991). HR is not only about hiring, developing, and retaining workers; it is also about aligning the goals of the workforce with the goals of the organization. It aims to develop an organizational culture that is conducive to cooperation and organizational success (Armstrong, 1999).

Effective HR management is about risk management within the organization; and ensuring compliance with federal laws and legislation to protect the health as well as the safety of workers in the workplace. These maintenance activities generally include initiating, developing, evaluating, and implementing policies that are aimed to prevent potential workplace hazards. Workplace bullying is one such workplace grievance which is associated with misconduct in the workplace (Gubman, 1996).

In order to combat workplace bullying, HR should be responsible for the initiation and development of an anti-bullying policy. The aim of this policy is to increase employees' awareness about the commitment the organization has towards a bully-free workplace. This policy should clearly define the nature of deviant workplace behaviors and what disciplinary actions will be taken against individuals found guilty of such offences. This anti-bullying policy should then be disseminated to all staff through various corporate programs such as job selection, induction, and performance planning review.

The assessment and management of workplace bullying should form HR second initiation. In other words, appropriate assessment and management strategies for workplace bullying should be developed and put in place. These strategies should include data collection (e.g. who was bullied, who was the accused, when did the incident take place, impact of the incident on the victim, etc.), incident reporting procedures, and procedures for implementing appropriate disciplinary actions. More crucially, HR professionals should instruct and train managers on the proper implementation of these strategies and procedures. Whenever possible, HR professionals should assist managers with the implementation of these strategies. Lastly, an evaluation process on the effectiveness of these strategies/policies should be conducted to ascertain what worked and what did not work.

Finally, to ensure continuous organizational and employee improvement, HR should engage in capacity building. Capacity building provides the organization with the opportunity to improve its current circumstances and future goals. Capacity building also involves strengthening the skills, competencies, and abilities of its employees. This is especially important in today's diversified work environment, with different stakeholders possessing competing needs and objectives.

WHAT IS WORKPLACE BULLYING?

There is no consistent definition of workplace bullying in the literature (Lutgen-Sandvik, 2003). Indeed, there is considerable confusion and conflicting definitions of what bullying in the workplace means (Barron,

1998; Namie and Namie, 2000). Nevertheless, the term workplace bullying generally refers to negative forms of interactions which are "repeated and persistent negative acts towards one or more individual(s), involve a perceived power imbalance and create a hostile work environment" (Salin, 2003: 1215). These negative behaviors are directed towards one or more workers with the intention to hurt, offend, or humiliate (Einarsen, 1999; Einarsen *et al.*, 2003). A one-off incident or inappropriate behavior may also be considered bullying, particularly if the incident is serious and causes intense emotional or psychological problems in the victims (Crawford, 1997). Bullying can also take more subtle forms, such as excluding or separating the victim from his or her group members (Leymann, 1996; Zapf *et al.*, 1996).

An equally important aspect in defining bullying is specifying which behaviors do not constitute bullying. According to the Occupational Health and Safety Act 2000 (OHS Act) and the Occupational Health and Safety Regulation 2001 (OHS Regulation), reasonable managerial actions taken in a fair and equitable way to counsel, transfer, dismiss, or not to promote an employee are not considered bullying. In addition, constructive criticisms or feedback about work-related behaviors and performances are not considered bullying as long as they are given in a positive and non-humiliating or non-threatening manner.

FACTORS CONTRIBUTING TO WORKPLACE BULLYING

There are a number of reasons why workplace bullying can occur. Research has found that organizational factors and organizational systems such as corporate change or downsizing, exploitative, restrictive work practices, job insecurity, role conflict or ambiguity, and poor leadership can lead to workplace bullying (Hodson *et al.*, 2006; Liefooghe and Davey, 2001). Other researchers suggest that power imbalances (e.g. supervisor versus subordinate or physical dominance over someone perceived to be weaker) between targets and perpetrators can lead to workplace bullying (Keashly and Nowell, 2003; Namie, 2007; Salin, 2003, 2008). Research has also found that individuals who are bullied tend to possess negative personality traits such as lack of self-control, lack of self-esteem, lack of self-confidence, poor social and communication skills (Coyne *et al.*, 2000; Douglas and Martinko, 2001; Neuman and Baron, 1998; Tepper, 2000; Zapf and Einarsen, 2003). Finally, the culture of the organization may contribute to workplace bullying.

An organization's culture can be defined as the values and behaviors shared by people or groups in the organization (Schein, 1999). Organizational culture develops over time and provides a guide to what constitutes appropriate workplace behaviors in various situations (Ravasi and Schultz, 2006). Studies have found that bullying is more prevalent in organizations or management styles that value adversarial and aggressive work practices (Höel and Cooper, 2000; Höel and Salin, 2003). Adversarial and aggressive work practices are competitive or hostile ways in which members approach tasks in order to protect their status and security (Cooke and Rousseau, 1988). Generally, organizations with aggressive cultures have heightened levels of hostility and conflict (Cooke and Rousseau, 1988).

THE ROLE OF HR IN ADDRESSING WORKPLACE BULLYING

Policy Development

Benjamin Franklin aptly stated that an ounce of prevention is worth a pound of cure. Researchers and practitioners recommend that an effective way to prevent and increase general awareness of appropriate work behaviors is to develop an organizational policy of anti-bullying in the workplace (Hubert, 2003; Mathieson *et al.*, 2006; Richards and Daley, 2003). According to Baron and Kreps (1999), organizational policies are explicit statements about what an organization stands for on a certain issue. Policies are useful because they provide guidance to organizations, managers, and employees about the accepted behaviors within organizations (Baron and Kreps, 1999). It is important that anti-bullying policies be developed in consultation with all staff and are customized to the specific needs of the organization involved. These policies should make explicit the commitment the organization has towards an anti-bullying work environment (Richards and Daley, 2003), a clear definition of what constitutes bullying and what does not constitute bullying in the workplace, a description of the factors that may contribute to workplace bullying, and the impact that bullying can have on both the individual and the organization.

For instance, in defining what workplace bullying is, the policy should state clearly that workplace bullying is repeated inappropriate behaviors, direct or indirect, and which can be aimed at one or more individuals. It is important to include that workplace bullying can be verbal, physical, or subtle acts with the intention to hurt, offend, or humiliate someone. An isolated incident will also be considered bullying and is unacceptable because it can cause severe psychological problems in victims, especially if it develops into repeated bullying. In addition, organizations should develop a culture that encourages open communication across all departmental levels. Such an organizational culture means that its members can speak out freely against bullies without fear of any negative repercussions. As part of the anti-bullying policy, there should be a statement that the organization is committed to open communication. Thus, there will be no negative repercussion for those who report inappropriate workplace behaviors.

I THINK I AM BEING BULLIED: WHAT SHOULD I DO?

Consultation

The HR department should appoint, in writing, contact officers to be the point of contact for employees' complaints. These officers must be properly trained in handling bullying issues. These contact officers should have good investigative skills, people management skills, communication skills, and mediation skills. Assurances must be provided to complainants to assure them that what they say will be kept strictly in confidence. As part of the consultation process, complainants are also assured that prompt, confidential, and impartial action will be taken in response to their reports of bullying.

The role or responsibilities of the contact officer is to provide confidential assistance and support to individuals who believe they may have been bullied. For example, they listen, provide appropriate information, and suggest viable options that the complainant may wish to take. It is important to stress that contact officers do not provide counselling services to the complainant, nor do they advocate or become involved in the investigative processes. They act simply as a point of contact to support and to provide appropriate information for the complainant.

Strategies for Assessing and Managing Workplace Bullying

In order to effectively assess and manage workplace bullying, HR departments should develop a process whereby information on the risk or hazard (i.e. workplace bullying) can be collected systematically. This includes measures such as: (1) a workplace audit on organizational systems and structures, (2) a checklist for warning signs of workplace bullying, and (3) consultations with employees. For instance, workplace audits can be conducted periodically to determine if any recent organizational changes such as major restructuring, technological changes, or management change have taken place. Organizational change when undertaken without due care can lead to high levels of job uncertainty and dissatisfaction among staff. Bullying can often occur when there are high levels of job uncertainty and dissatisfaction among staff (Hodson *et al.*, 2006; Liefooghe and Davey, 2001). A workplace audit can also be used to determine whether any department within the organization is suffering from staff shortages and whether appropriate workloads exist for all levels of employees.

Training and Instructing Managers

Very often, individuals who are bullied do not exhibit any physical signs of injury. Thus, managers should be educated and trained about the warning signs of an employee being bullied. These signs may include staff withdrawal, high levels of staff turnover, physical injuries, absenteeism, and reports of poor working relationships between coworkers (Höel *et al.*, 2003; Littler, 1996). These warning signs can be collected through a number of methods such as observations, surveys, or consultations with staff. For example, a survey may be conducted anonymously to determine how employees feel about their organization (i.e. organizational culture) and what if any challenges they are currently encountering. Surveys, when used appropriately, are excellent data collection tools, as they provide an opportunity for staff to voice their concerns. Similarly, managers can conduct a field trip to check for warning signs of workplace bullying. A record of the frequencies and intensities of these warning signs should be kept and compared over time to see if there is a pattern of escalating warning signs.

Identifying, Assessing, and Reporting of Workplace Bullying

As part of the policy package, proper procedures for identifying and assessing whether workplace bullying actually exists or has the potential to occur must be developed and made available to all staff. In other words, the HR department must work with other departments in the organization to establish clear identification, assessment, and reporting of workplace bullying. For example, when a complaint about workplace bullying is received, the hazard must first be identified and its seriousness to the health, safety, and welfare of both the organization and individual assessed. A survey may be conducted to identify who was bullied, who was the accused, when did the incident occur, the impact of the incident on the victim, length of incident, etc. When possible, the data collection phase should preferably be conducted externally so as to be independent from supervisors or the departments involved. This will ensure transparency and encourage individuals who are bullied to come forward.

Once the hazard has been identified, it needs to be assessed in terms of its seriousness. In other words, an assessment of how the hazard has affected the complainant and organization should be conducted. For example, days absent from work, the complainant's productivity level, and the complainant's physical and psychological health would be considered measurements of the effects of bullying. A proper assessment will provide some ideas for the most appropriate course of action to take. If the complaint is less serious, it is advisable that an informal resolution procedure be taken. For instance, asking the bully to stop his or her negative bullying actions. However, if the assessor deems that the allegations are more serious or that there is actual physical or psychological harm involved, then a formal investigation should be undertaken. In this case, an inspector independent of the department and organization should be engaged.

The anti-bullying policy should also clearly describe the investigative and disciplinary procedures. For instance, the policy might state that disciplinary actions will be taken against anyone who bullies a colleague. Depending on the severity of the bullying, disciplinary actions such as a warning, transfer, counseling, demotion, or dismissal may be taken against individuals who are found to have engaged in bullying. This procedure should include complaint handling, investigation, resolution, and grievance procedures. Finally, this policy should be included in job selection, induction, performance planning review, the Equal Employment Opportunity (EEO) policy, as well as the Occupational Safety and Health policy (OS&H). Documented risk management processes are valuable because they provide a systematic way of controlling for risks. In doing so, the organization is sending a clear message that it is committed to a bully-free work environment (Glendon *et al.*, 2006) and that everyone has a duty to report any workplace hazards when they see or hear them.

RESOLUTION PROCEDURES

Informal Complaint Procedure

The HR department must clearly set out the rules and regulations for resolving workplace bullying. Following discussion with an assessor, complainants must be notified of the resolution options they have. For example, depending on the assessment results, the complainant may be notified that he or she has two resolution options: (i) an informal or (ii) formal resolution procedure. If the complainant decides to opt for the informal procedure, he or she can simply approach the alleged bully by himself or herself or with a mediator and ask the bully to stop bullying or make the bully aware that his or her behaviors are causing distress. No disciplinary or investigative action is to be taken if the complainant decides to use an informal resolution procedure. A mediator is a third party who can facilitate a face-to-face discussion and reach a solution acceptable to both parties. Therefore, a manager or supervisor may not be the most appropriate person to take part in this process.

Formal Complaint Procedure

However, if the informal procedure is unsuccessful or if the allegation is more serious, then an inspector should be engaged to conduct a formal investigation into the allegation. It is important that the complainant understands what is involved in the formal investigative process. For example, information to be included in the written complaint form should include specific details of the allegation such as dates, times, names of witnesses, etc. A formal process generally consists of several steps and these steps should be made clear to the complainant and the alleged bully: (1) the complainant is informed that the investigation will start only when a formal written complaint is received; (2) correctly lodging the written complaint to the appropriate department or officer in charge; (3) making sure all the information required of the incident(s) is included in the form; (4) an initial meeting is set up with both the complainant and the alleged bully and both are briefed about the investigation process, their rights, their responsibilities, how and when the investigation process will proceed as well as end; (5) an appointment of an independent investigator who is fully aware of his or her role, the rights of both of the alleged bully and complainant, what a formal complaint procedure entails, and what the expected outcomes may be, and finally, (6) the investigator should provide a written report on the findings of the investigation to the HR department and the appropriate supervisor(s). The supervisor will then meet with both parties individually to explain the findings of the investigation verbally and in writing. There should be an appeal mechanism in place which will enable either the alleged bully or the complainant to appeal against the findings if he or she considers this necessary.

Finally, the HR department or professional should make available information regarding access to counselling and/or rehabilitation during as well as after the investigation process. For instance, the alleged bully may be instructed to undertake some counseling to help him or her recognize and change his or her bullying behaviors. Bullies may also be instructed to attend training to improve their communication skills, cultural awareness, interpersonal skills, and/or conflict resolution skills. The education of these skills should form part of HR planning.

EVALUATION

Evaluation sessions should be established to monitor and review the effectiveness of the implemented strategies. Evaluation is important because it uses empirical data to determine the effectiveness (i.e. strengths and weaknesses) of policies, products, programs, people, and organizations (Rossi *et al.*, 2004). The resulting findings can then be used to determine whether the policy or program has been implemented to plan and the extent to which it has achieved its outcome objectives. It can also be used to determine the longer term organizational needs. This ensures that the organization is on track for continual improvement. For example, some of the questions to ask in setting up an evaluation process may consist of the following. (i) Since the introduction of the anti-bullying policy, has the incident of workplace bullying decreased? If yes, what works? If not, what went wrong? (ii) How many staff are aware of the policy? (iii) Has the educational training, such as improving offender's cultural awareness and communication skills, worked? If yes, what works? If not, what went wrong? (iv) Is there a need to conduct leadership training? Finally, these evaluation findings and recommendations should be written down in a report and presented to relevant stakeholders for future decision-making.

TRAINING AND CAPACITY BUILDING

HR departments and HR professionals are seen as active players in preventing and managing bullying activities in the workplace (Liefooghe and Davey, 2001; Vega and Comer, 2005). In order to achieve these goals, HR professionals and HR departments must start at the top. In other words, they must educate, train, and build managers' capacity to develop a holistic and cooperative workplace, and deal appropriately with bullying complaints.

One way to ensure this is to have all managers undergo a leadership training course. These leadership learning experiences will encourage training managers to more effectively communicate, listen, express, and manage interactively with their subordinates (Dick, 1991; Kaye, 1994). For example, HR professionals may conduct training sessions on the use of interaction management skills which aim to improve the abilities of managers to address issues such as productivity, conflict resolution, and performance improvement in employees. Another strategy is to educate managers about the effectiveness of using "soft" people skills (Karpin,

1995) which include empathy and trust. In doing so, managers are better equipped to deal with the emotional needs of others in an empathetic way, rather than using coercive or intimidating behavior. The use of these strategies should also be included as part of the leadership training course.

The second task involved in capacity building is to increase employees' awareness about the harmful impact of workplace bullying. Educational and training courses on identifying workplace bullying, knowing what to do if bullying occurs, knowing what procedures to take in response, and where to seek help should be made available to all staff as part of their education. Finally, the organization should actively encourage and treat its employees with dignity. In other words, creating and developing a culture that treats employees as partners and as the organization's most important asset is of utmost importance to the success of a business or company (Peters and Waterman, 1982).

CONCLUSION

This chapter provides a discussion on the role of HR in addressing workplace bullying. It has also proposed measures that HR managers may adopt to help them develop an anti-bullying workplace program. It is important to stress that the proposed strategies and recommendations will only be effective if managers and seniors managers support them. Therefore, training and educating managers and upper management about the importance of a bully-free work environment is a most critical component of action when addressing workplace bullying.

REFERENCES

Armstrong, M. (1999). *A Handbook of Human Resource Management Practice,* Philadelphia, PA: Kogan Page.

Baron, J., and Kreps, D. (1999). *Strategic Human Resources: Frameworks for General Managers,* New York: Wiley.

Barron, O. (1998). The distinction between workplace bullying and workplace violence and the ramifications for OHS. *Journal of Occupational Health and Safety – Australia and New Zealand*, 14, 575–80.

Bassman, E. S. (1992). *Abuse in the Workplace: Management Remedies and Bottom Line Impact,* Westport, CT: Quorum Books.

Cooke, R. A., and Rousseau, D. M. (1988). Behavioral norms and expectations: A quantitative approach to the assessment of organizational culture. *Group and Organization Studies*, 13, 245–73.

Coyne, I., Seigne, E., and Randall, P. (2000). Predicting workplace victim status from personality. *European Journal of Work and Organizational Psychology*, 9, 335–49.

Crawford, N. (1997). Bullying at work: A psychoanalytic perspective. *Journal of Community and Applied Social Psychology*, 7, 219–25.

Dick, B. (1991). *Helping Groups to be Effective* (2nd edn), Brisbane: Interchange.

Douglas, S. C., and Martinko, M. J. (2001). Exploring the role of individual differences in the prediction of workplace aggression. *Journal of Applied Psychology*, 86, 547–59.

Einarsen, S. (1999). The nature and causes of bullying at work. *International Journal of Manpower*, 20, 16–27.

Einarsen, S. E., and Mikkelsen, E. G. (2003). Individual effects of exposure to bullying at work. In S. Einarsen, H. Höel, D. Zapf, and C. L. Cooper (eds), *Bullying and Emotional Abuse in the Workplace: International Perspectives in Research and Practice* (pp. 127–44), London: Taylor & Francis.

Einarsen, S., Höel, H., Zapf, D., and Cooper, C. (2003). The concept of bullying at work: The European tradition. In S. Einarsen, H. Höel, D. Zapf, and C. Cooper (eds), *Bullying and Emotional Abuse in the Workplace: International Perspectives in Research and Practice* (pp. 1–30), London: Taylor & Francis.

Glendon, A. I., Clarke, S. G., and McKenna, E. F. (2006). *Human Safety and Risk Management* (2nd edn), Boca Raton, FL: CRC Press/Taylor & Francis.

Gubman, E. L. (1996). The gauntlet is down. *Journal of Business Strategy*, 17, 33.

Hodson, R., Roscigno, V. J., and Lopez, S. H. (2006). Chaos and the abuse of power: Workplace bullying in organizational and interactional context. *Work and Occupations*, 33, 382–416.

Höel, H., and Cooper, C. L. (2000). *Destructive Conflict and Bullying at Work*, Manchester: School of Management, University of Manchester Institute of Science and Technology.

Höel, H., and Salin, D. (2003). Organizational antecedents of workplace bullying. In S. Einarsen, H. Höel, D. Zapf, and C. L. Cooper (eds), *Bullying and Emotional Abuse in the Workplace: International Perspectives in Research and Practice* (pp. 203–18). London and New York: Taylor & Francis.

Höel, H., Einarsen, S., and Cooper, C. L. (2003). Organizational effects of bullying. In S. Einarsen, H. Höel, D. Zapf, and C. L. Cooper (eds), *Bullying and Emotional Abuse in the Workplace: International Perspectives in Research and Practice* (pp. 145–61), London: Taylor & Francis.

Hubert, A. B. (2003). To prevent and overcome undesirable interaction: A systematic approach model. In S. Einarsen, H. Höel, D. Zapf, and C. L. Cooper (eds), *Bullying and Emotional Abuse in the Workplace: International Perspectives in Research and Practice* (pp. 299–311), London: Taylor & Francis.

Karpin, D. (1995). *Enterprising Nation: Executive Summary,* Canberra: Australian Government Publishing Services.

Kaye, M. (1994). *Communication Management,* Sydney: Prentice-Hall.

Keashly, L., and Nowell, B. L. (2003). Conflict, conflict resolution and bullying. In S. Einarsen, H. Höel, D. Zapf, and C. L. Cooper (eds), *Bullying and Emotional Abuse in the Workplace: International Perspectives in Research and Practice* (pp. 339–58), London: Taylor & Francis.

Lewis, D., and Rayner, C. (2003). Bullying and human resource management: A wolf in sheep's clothing? In S. Einarsen, H. Höel, D. Zapf, and C. L. Cooper (eds), *Bullying and Emotional Abuse in the Workplace: International Perspectives in Research and Practice* (pp. 370–82), London: Taylor & Francis.

Leymann, H. (1996). The content and development of mobbing at work. *European Journal of Work and Organizational Psychology*, 5, 165–84.

Liefooghe, A., and Davey, K. (2001). Accounts of workplace bullying: The role of the organization. *European Journal of Work and Organizational Psychology*, 10, 375–92.

Littler, C. (1996). Downsizing: A disease or a cure? *HR Monthly* (Aug.), 8–12.

Lutgen-Sandvik, P. (2003). The communicative cycle of employee emotional abuse: Generation and regeneration of workplace mistreatment. *Management Communication Quarterly*, 16, 471–501.

Lutgen-Sandvik, P., Tracy, S. J., and Alberts, J. K. (2007). Burned by bullying in the American workplace: Prevalence, perception, degree, and impact. *Journal of Management Studies,* 44, 837–62.

Mathieson, S., Hanson, M., and Burns, J. (2006). Reducing the risk of harassment in your organization. In M. O. Moore, J. Lynch, and M. Smith (eds), *The Way Forward: Proceedings from the 5th International on Bullying and Harassment in the Workplace* (pp. 129–31), Dublin: Trinity College.

McCarthy, P., and Mayhew, C. (2004). *Safeguarding the Organisation Against Violence and Bullying: An International Perspective,* Basingstoke: Palgrave-Macmillan.

Namie, G. (2003). Workplace bullying: Escalated incivility. *Ivey Business Journal,* 68, 1–6.

Namie, G. (2007). U.S. Workplace Bullying Survey. Retrieved Aug. 2011 from http://www.bullyinginstitute.org/research/wbiresearch.html.

Namie, G., and Namie, R. (2000). *The Bully at Work: What you Can Do to Stop the Hurt and Reclaim your Dignity on the Job,* Naperville, IL: Sourcebooks.

Neuman, J. H., and Baron, R. A. (1998). Workplace violence and workplace aggression: Evidence concerning specific forms, potential causes, and preferred targets. *Journal of Management*, 24, 391–411.

Peters, T., and Waterman, R. (1982). *In Search of Excellence,* Sydney: Harper & Row.

Ravasi, D., and Schultz, M. (2006). Responding to organizational identity threats: Exploring the role of organizational culture. *Academy of Management Journal,* 49, 433–58.

Richards, J., and Daley, H. (2003). Bullying policy: Development, implementation and monitoring. In S. Einarsen, H. Höel, D. Zapf, and C. Cooper (eds), *Bullying and Emotional Abuse in the Workplace: International Perspectives in Research and Practice* (pp. 247–58), London: Taylor & Francis.

Roberts, G., Seldon, G., and Roberts, C. (1991). *Human Resources Management,* Washington, DC: Small Business Administration, n.a.

Rossi, P. H., Lipsey, M. W., and Freeman, H. E. (2004). *Evaluation: A Systematic Approach* (7th edn), Thousand Oaks, CA: Sage.

Salin, D. (2003). Ways of explaining workplace bullying: A review of enabling, motivating, and precipitating structures and processes in the work environment. *Human Relations,* 56, 1213–32.

Salin, D. (2008). The prevention of workplace bullying as a question of human resource management: Measures adopted and underlying organizational factors. *Scandinavian Journal of Management*, 24, 221–31.

Schein, E. (1999). *The Corporate Culture Survival Guide,* San Francisco, CA: Jossey Bass.

Tepper, B. J. (2000). Consequences of abusive supervision. *Academy of Management Journal,* 43, 178–90.

Vega, G., and Comer, D. R. (2005). Sticks and stones may break your bones, but words can break your spirit: Bullying in the workplace. *Journal of Business Ethics*, 58, 101–9.

Zapf, D., and Einarsen, S. (2001). Bullying in the workplace: Recent trends in research and practice. *European Journal of Work and Organizational Psychology*, 10, 369–73.

Zapf, D., and Einarsen, S. (2003). Individual antecedents of bullying. In S. Einarsen, H. Höel, D. Zapf, and C. L. Cooper (eds), *Bullying and Emotional Abuse in the Workplace: International Perspectives in Research and Practice* (pp. 165–84), London: Taylor & Francis.

Zapf, D., Knorz, C., and Kulla, M. (1996). On the relationship between mobbing factors, and job content, social work environment, and health outcomes. *European Journal of Work and Organizational Psychology*, 5, 215–37.

Zapf, D., Einarsen, S., Höel, H., and Vartia, M. (2003). Empirical findings on bullying in the workplace. In S. Einarsen, H. Höel, D. Zapf, and C. L. Cooper (eds), *Bullying and Emotional Abuse in the Workplace: International Perspectives in Research and Practice* (pp. 103–26), London: Taylor & Francis.

17

Strategies for Managers in Handling Workplace Bullying

Melody Wollan
Eastern Illinois University

INTRODUCTION

By design, managers are a conduit for interpreting organizational expectations of performance and behavior from practices, policy, and top management to the individual employees. Thus, a pivotal actor in the fight against workplace bullying is the bullying employee's supervising manager. It is the manager who serves as the lynchpin figure in directing employee behaviors through training, goal-setting, assignment of duties, performance management, and discipline.

This chapter emphasizes that, in an effort to eliminate workplace bullying, a manager should attempt to alter the bullying employee's behavior and not the employee as a whole. Most managers, however, are neither equipped nor in the appropriate position to address the psychological underpinnings of motives, which might be argued as the most effective long-term solution. I use the term bullying as a verb, and henceforth avoid the use of labeling the focal employee as "the bully." In this way, managers can feel empowered to address the problem as a behavior, rather than focusing on what is "good" or "bad". Managers can invest their efforts by providing boundaries of what is acceptable or unacceptable behavior in their workplace. Once the behavior of bullying is seen as adverse behavior similar to tardiness, non-performance, or making illegal racial or gender comments, it becomes a manageable act that can be addressed as openly as other undesirable behaviors.

The manager has four foci to address bullying in their workplace (see Figure 17.1). First, the manager must consider preventive measures. During the selection process, managers can attempt to identify behaviors that are red flags of potential bullying later in employment. Managers should develop organizational policies or clarify existing policy related to harassing behavior (McCrory, 2011). Most recommendations for prevention of any type of undesirable employee behavior also include a training component for both employees and managers. Second, the organizational environment is an important aspect of an employee's day-to-day activities that affects their job satisfaction and underlying commitment to the organization. This encompasses organizational culture, communication styles, and structural elements, such as job design and the physical workstation arrangement that might enable the bullying employee to isolate his or her target without others noticing (Harvey *et al.*, 2009).

Third, managers must examine the interactions between themselves and employees. Employees observe managerial behavior and model what *is* done rather than what *should* or *could* be done as stated in policy or by terminal values (Rokeach, 1973). This role modeling is a powerful tool when used positively for mentoring, training, developing employee self-efficacy, and for motivational purposes. However, managers must also realize and examine negative influences that originate from them that could be contributing to the bullying behavior.

The fourth and final focus, when bullying does occur, is for managers to develop an action plan that intervenes within and remedies the bullying crisis. While researchers have suggested various approaches that can be taken in this process, managers ultimately rely on their own judgment. Understanding and preparing to make those judgments provides managers with the confidence to act decisively depending on the organizational need and severity of the bullying behavior. Bullying necessitates a candid conversation between the manager and the offending employee (Meinert, 2011). Managers should be coached, practice, and possibly engage in role-playing to be effective when addressing bullying behavior. Thus, being able to recognize bullying when it occurs, holding the focal employee accountable for his or her bullying behaviors, and taking disciplinary or termination steps are key intervention strategies for managers.

Further, the practices recommended in this chapter are not suggested as tools that managers can sample at random. Rather, every manager is

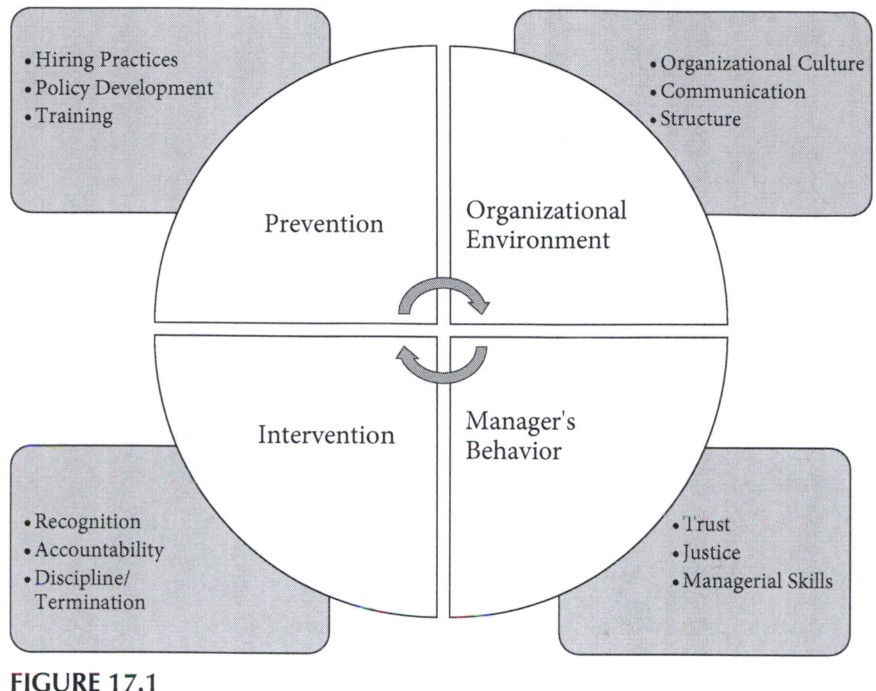

FIGURE 17.1
Managerial actions to address bullying behaviors

encouraged to systematically evaluate his or her organization, his or her own practices as a manager, and his or her employees in order to address potential problem areas before bullying reaches a crisis point (Sidle, 2009). Like others (Meinert, 2011; Parzefall and Salin, 2010), I advocate for the existence of a systemic anti-bullying strategy: developing, implementing, and enforcing anti-bullying policies, training employees and managers, maintaining a culture that promotes respect and dignity, mediating bullying related conflicts, and organizational design solutions. However, in addition to these, I also recommend prevention strategies at the hiring stage, examination of managerial behaviors, and multiple intervention options based on theory and best practices from the management field.

RELEVANT THEORY AND RECOMMENDATIONS

Prevention

In the prevention stage, managers should confront the possibility that potential for bullying exists in their work environment. Reading texts with breadth of knowledge and examples such as this book can help illustrate bullying behavior and its effects. There are three aspects of management that can aid in the prevention of bullying significantly: examining hiring practices, developing policies to address expectations of conduct and discipline, and training both employees and supervisors about workplace bullying.

Hiring Practices

The nature versus nurture argument emerges in recent literature to address bullying in the workplace (Heames *et al.*, 2006). The nature aspect reflects recommendations (e.g. MacIntosh, 2006; Vega and Comer, 2005) to evaluate applicants for potential bullying tendencies. Detert *et al.* (2008) have suggested hiring supervisors with a broader scope of justice and those who are less likely to demonstrate hostility towards others. Interpersonal skills questionnaires may be administered as a selection test to assess how applicants behave in interpersonal settings. For example, the Fundamental Interpersonal Relations Orientation-Behavior (FIRO-B®) developed initially by Schutz (1958) provides an assessment of inclusion, control, and affection (emotional affirmation, liking, approval) as they are expressed and as they are wanted by the respondent. This and other personality assessments can provide valuable information about an applicant's processing and interpersonal style that can lead to important insights regarding the individual's likelihood to bully in the workplace.

Observing an applicant interacting with a receptionist and other employees during face-to-face interviews can be informative in identifying dismissive or condescending behaviors that may be indicators of potential bullying behavior (Workplace Bullying, 2010). Research findings have suggested that such workers may display low levels of empathy. These low-empathy workers were more likely to perceive that others deserve harmful treatment (Detert *et al.*, 2008) than other employees who exhibited higher levels of empathy. Thus, applicants who appear to engage in antisocial behaviors during the brief interview process (Heames *et al.*, 2006; Robinson and O'Leary-Kelly, 1998), such as criticizing others, describing situations where they purposefully said or took some action to hurt someone, or making rude statements about others or previous work environments, should be screened and their potential risk assessed during the selection process. Background investigations, reference checking, and requiring letters of reference are other screening methods that can be utilized, as bullying individuals often have more difficulty in obtaining positive references from others whom they may have alienated (Bryant, 2010; Workplace Bullying, 2010).

One important caution: attempts at identifying employee personalities, values, beliefs, and statements that would warrant ending further consideration of an applicant can be ambiguous and potentially illegal under the Americans with Disabilities Act and the Civil Rights Act of 1964 (Edwards, 2011). Having established job-related criteria that identify standards of unacceptable and acceptable behaviors expected at work and applying these standards consistently to all applicants may minimize an employer's liability exposure. Rejecting a candidate for poor interpersonal skills that are demonstrated by his or her confrontation style during the selection process is acceptable. Simply rejecting a candidate for his or her personality is much more difficult to validate during a judicial process.

Policy Development

Some managers have a misconception that bullying behaviors are addressed in the Civil Rights Act of 1964 and by the Equal Employment Opportunity Commission (EEOC) as a form of sexual harassment. However, it has been noted that "despite behavioral similarities, bullying and discrimination have somewhat different underlying determinants" (Parkins *et al.*, 2006: 2554). Bullying often does not meet the threshold of being a discriminatory workplace action, and thus, legal remedies reserved for sexual or racial harassment may not apply (Hirschfeld and Dalhgren, 2010). By developing anti-bullying policies at an organizational level, organizations can alleviate the "need for legislative or judicial involvement" (Hirschfeld and Dalhgren, 2010: para. 12).

Creation of a bullying policy should have four major facets. First, the policy should "explicitly (state) that bullying will not be tolerated" (Vega and Comer, 2005: 107). Second, the organizational code of conduct or the policy needs to include specific examples that employees might encounter related to actual organizational practices that demonstrate acceptable versus unacceptable behaviors (Hubert, 2003; Vega and Comer, 2005). This would include defining workplace bullying. One recent study by Carbo and Hughes (2010: 387) identifies that a major problem with workplace bullying definitions is that they are "too narrow" and need to address specific elements, "including the requirement of repetitiveness, the requirement of intent, and the role of power." Carbo and Hughes (2010) point out that bullying varies in the levels of severity and less severe bullying behaviors may need to be more pervasive or repetitive to be defined as workplace bullying.

Third, the policy should indicate the level at which bullying behaviors will be addressed, and where an intervention will take place when brought to the attention of management (Djurkovic *et al.*, 2006). Consistently enforcing these policies and practices is key to the credibility of the policy and its effectiveness long-term (LaVan and Martin, 2008). Fourth, effective policies to address workplace bullying should include progressive disciplinary actions (warning, counseling, and dismissals), and include appropriate documentation at each step (MacIntosh, 2006) (Figure 17.2).

Lastly, there may be some debate about who should be included in crafting a bullying policy and its enforcement. In one British study of mid-level executives, involving line management was important to 90 percent of respondents, but 79 percent felt employee involvement was also essential (*Management Science*, 2005). Contrast that with findings in a US study of executives and human resource professionals in which employee involvement in creating policy in an employee taskforce, with department managers or with human resource (HR) departments, was identified as being preferred by only 19 percent of respondents (McCrory, 2011). Rather, McCrory's study indicated a much stronger preference (36 percent) for anti-bullying policies to be developed by or with HR departments, with 21 percent favoring policy development by or with department managers (Figure 17.3).

Training

Like sexual harassment, safety, or diversity training, a component of new employee orientation and ongoing annual training should include education and skill building regarding the prevention of bullying and what steps to take when bullying does occur (Djurkovic *et al.*, 2006). In a

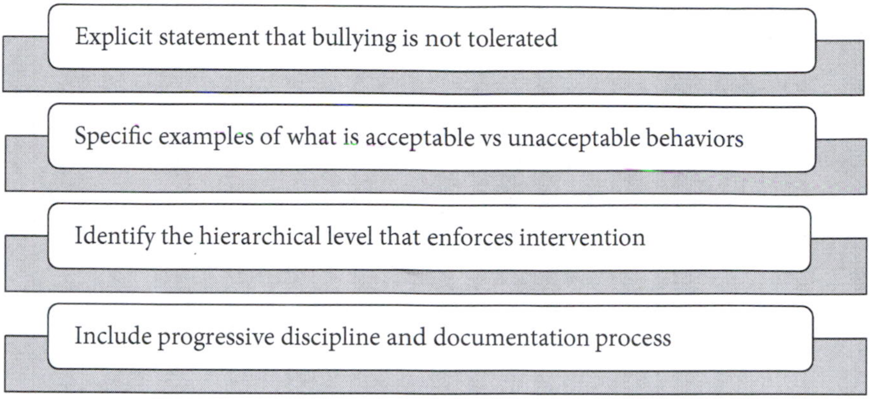

Explicit statement that bullying is not tolerated
Specific examples of what is acceptable vs unacceptable behaviors
Identify the hierarchical level that enforces intervention
Include progressive discipline and documentation process

FIGURE 17.2
Components of anti-bullying policies

21%
Department
Managers
36%
Human Resource
Professionals
19%
Employee
Involvement
24%
No Preference

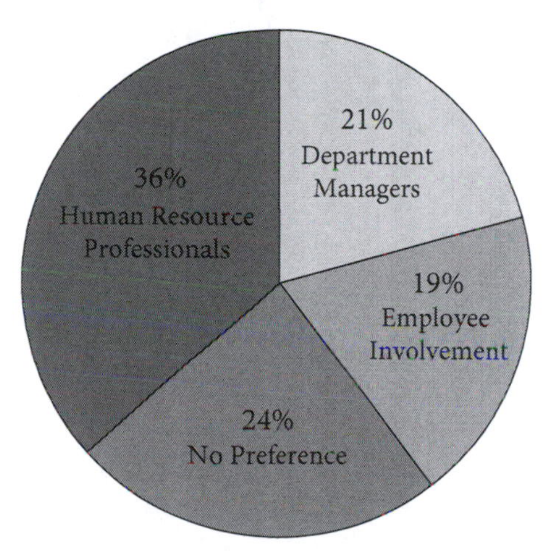

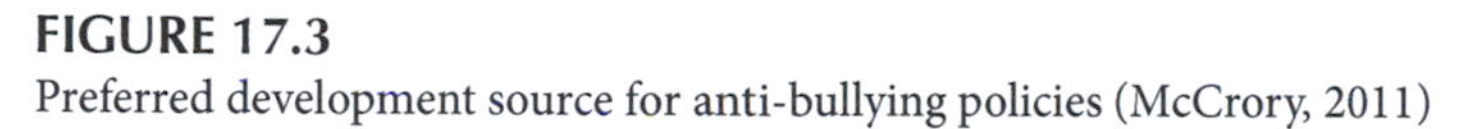

FIGURE 17.3
Preferred development source for anti-bullying policies (McCrory, 2011)

survey of executives in the United Kingdom, in combination with existing policies, training was identified as the most effective action taken to address bullying, with 83 percent of respondents rating their organizations as quite or very effective at deterring bullying (*Management Science*, 2005). Managers can be trained to increase their awareness of warning signs such as building tensions with or between employees and be observant of potential conflicts that may arise in workflow, particularly with employees that have highly interdependent tasks (MacIntosh, 2006).

Organizational Environment

In order to address bullying behaviors preemptively or in response to an existing bullying situation, examining the context of the organizational environment is an important step. The organizational environment has many components, but those most related to addressing bullying behaviors are the organizational culture, communications between employees, and structural arrangements of the organizational unit.

Organizational Culture

Most significant to reducing bullying behavior is the culture created and fostered within the organization or work unit. Organizational culture is "the pattern of basic assumptions that a given group has invented, discovered, or developed" (Schein, 1983: 14) that form the foundation for development of organizational values, artifacts, and the behavior patterns of employees.

In the nature versus nurture debate of workplace bullying, nurture refers to the creation of an environment of intolerance for bullying (Heames *et al.*, 2006). Two important characteristics of environments that nurture bullying are those that have low morale (Townend, 2008), or where employees have opportunities to utilize position power, personal power, and/or control to influence their coworkers (Carbo and Hughes, 2010). Thus, the opportunity for bullying is ubiquitous in environments that encourage empowerment, boundary-free organizational design, cross-functional teams, and participative management approaches. During in-depth interviews conducted by Carbo and Hughes (2010: 394), one participant discussed the "culture of meanness" that was a pervasive form of workplace bullying.

The abusive supervision literature is rich with theory and research findings to provide context for the genesis of workplace bullying. The first explanation of behavior is the *flows downhill* theory. This theory states that the bullying employee is simply acting towards others, generally subordinates, in the same way that they have been treated by those superior to them (Aryee *et al.*, 2007; Hoobler and Brass, 2006; Tepper *et al.*, 2006). Bullying might start at the top of the organizational chart, and as reporting employees see that the behavior is acceptable, they adopt the approach in their own work units.

A second explanation is the *causal approach*. Proponents of this theory believe that the bullying employee perceives "deep-level dissimilarity (that) evokes perceived relationship conflict, which produces lower evaluations of subordinate performance, which, in turn, lead to higher levels of abusive supervision" (Tepper *et al.*, 2011: 288). These dissimilarities may be entirely subjective and include perceived differences in values, attitudes, and personality.

Communication

While much can be discussed with regard to communications in the workplace, three aspects that are considered critical to long-term organizational functioning if bullying behavior occurs are counseling and mentoring conversations, the apology as a method of defusing a workplace bullying situation (Fox and Stallworth, 2006), and communication openness (Ayoko, 2007).

Survey data illustrate a strong preference by employees to utilize others in the process of addressing bullying (*Management Science*, 2005). Respondents agreed that organizational attempts to establish a contact person to obtain advice (82 percent), arrange internal confidential counseling (82 percent), or develop a system of external mediation (81 percent) would all help make their experience of workplace bullying shorter and less painful. These numbers make the point that employees expect discussion opportunities to be provided by the organization to address bullying behaviors. Assigning a staff employee as an official designee to respond to bullying confidentially and to put in place a process in which employees can whistle-blow, report their own or others' bullying, and provide an outlet for counseling services would be one approach to developing these types of communication outlets.

Next, if bullying does occur, it is often difficult to determine if an apology by the bullying employee to his or her target would be enough to mollify the target or if more formal complaint steps should be taken. According to Fox and Stallworth (2006), men are more willing than women and Whites are more willing than African Americans to accept an apology in regards to episodes of workplace bullying. If the bullying employee is in a managerial or supervisory position, employees are less likely to accept the apology. Of greater consequence to many organizational leaders and human resource management professionals is how the apology might mollify employees to the point where an EEOC complaint would not be pursued or even be withdrawn if already filed. On that point, Fox and

Stallworth (2006) found that managers are more willing than employees to withdraw their EEOC complaint if given an apology. Relatedly, if bullying behavior involves racial or ethnic comments by a coworker, respondents indicated they were more likely to accept an apology and withdraw an EEOC charge.

Finally, in the communications of the organization, Ayoko (2007) points out that evidence suggests that increasing communication openness will lead to fewer destructive reactions to conflict, including when workplace bullying occurs. Communication openness is particularly important when group members are experiencing difficulty in settling conflict or have the inability to move away from the conflicting situation (Ayoko, 2007).

Structure

Sidle (2009: 91) identified that "chaotic, poorly structured organizations tend to become breeding grounds for bullies." Rigid hierarchical structures contribute to communication patterns where strong and inhumane power differences become embedded, further complicating conflicts and workplace bullying (Crawford, 1997). In fact, Crawford (1997: 221) extends even further into critique of the organizational environment by saying "bullying is a symptom of organizational dysfunction." Conditions such as work overload, monotonous and unchallenging work, lack of possibilities to monitor and control one's own work, lack of clear and non-conflicting goals, and lack of constructive leadership have been identified as situations that lead to bullying by employees (Einarsen *et al.*, 1994). Recommendations by a workplace safety commission to address bullying through work design are to "structure the work environment to incorporate a sense of autonomy, individual challenge/mastery, and clarity of task expectations for employees" and to "include employees in decision-making processes" (Safety and Health Assessment and Research for Prevention, 2008: 4). Other environmental characteristics that may lead to the development of workplace bullying would include areas where there is a lack of supervision provided on a regular basis (i.e. behavior monitoring) and physical spaces where employees can bully with relatively little attention drawn to the negative behavior (Harvey *et al.*, 2009).

Manager's Behavior

There is no actor in the bullying environment that is more important than the manager. Managers have position power that creates opportunity for them to bully, to ignore bullying, or to induce punishment and consequences for bullying behaviors of their subordinates. Managers implement policies, procedures, and influence organizational culture. When effective, managers become agents leading the organizational unit to profitability, success, and goodwill among employees, suppliers, and customers. But when managers are less effective, or lack appropriate managerial skills or communication abilities, there are more possibilities for damage to occur due to the manager's level of control and influence. Thus, in this section, recommendations are offered for managers to focus on the managers themselves, to see if they are contributing to an environment that condones bullying behavior. First, the section will discuss how developing and maintaining trust and justice lessens the likelihood for bullying to occur. Then, the focus will turn to specific managerial skills that can be developed and improved to alleviate a bullying-ready environment.

Trust

An important tool for any manager is trust. In work environments, trust serves as a substitute for control, policies, monitoring, and discipline (Rousseau *et al.*, 1998). Building a trusting work environment is particularly beneficial between coworkers, where formal hierarchical expectations of relationships are less likely to be identified by policy and procedures, but rather built into culture and norms of the workgroup.

Ultimately, trust is a psychological state that is a combination of calculation of predictability with a dose of understanding others' wants and needs. Trust is built over time, and demonstrates respect and understanding for one another. That type of relationship is less likely to end up in a bullying relationship (i.e. "causal approach" as identified by Tepper *et al.*, 2011). Greenberg (2010) makes several suggestions for managers to develop and maintain trust in work relationships which can be adopted by managers and employees alike. First, always meet deadlines. Besides reducing frustration between coworkers, meeting deadlines provides coworkers with a signal of your respect for them and their work. Second, fulfill promises that you have made. By narrowing the gap between promises (intentions) and what is delivered (behavior), there is a greater likelihood of being seen as trustworthy. Third, share personal values and goals. By doing so, employees are able to develop much stronger identification with others and develop an appreciation for their approach to problem-solving, goal accomplishment, or viewpoint.

Justice

Concepts of socially constructed justice extend into managerial practice even more than trust. Just and fair treatment of all employees and tolerance of diversity demonstrates to employees that managers are serious about processes and decision-making where more than one voice will be heard (Djurkovic *et al.*, 2006). I am suggesting here that bullying is one possible side effect of injustice in the workplace.

In order to manage with fairness and justice, Greenberg (2010) summarizes a number of findings from research. Paying employees what they deserve reduces the need for employees to take action to resolve inequities they feel between their worth and their pay (Cortina, 2008). Actions that might be taken in the equity-balancing process might involve bullying of coworkers or subordinates as part of the "flows downhill" approach (Aryee *et al.*, 2007; Hoobler and Brass, 2006; Tepper *et al.*, 2006). Next, take efforts as managers to explain "decisions thoroughly and in a manner demonstrating dignity and respect" (Greenberg, 2010: 41). Providing information and explanations helps employees to understand that managerial actions are not as arbitrary as they might seem, and creates a common basis of knowledge that can be interpreted in determining future behaviors related to what is acceptable and what is unacceptable in the work environment.

Third, openly follow fair procedures as a manager. Employees emulate managerial behavior. While it is easy to make declarations of what should be done and said, it is far easier for employees to take observations of managerial behavior as a cue to organizational norms. Fourth, provide workers with a voice as part of a fair process approach to managing. Employees are more likely to accept the decision-making process and outcomes if they are part of the discussion. Providing opportunity for input openly should reduce the need for politicking, harassing, or other bullying-like influence techniques between employees.

Managerial Skills

Numerous authors have suggested that managerial skills and abilities contribute to a potential bullying environment. More than two-thirds of managers reported that they spent one day or less addressing bullying in the past year (*Management Science*, 2005) and, at that level of infrequency, it is not surprising that managers may feel ill-equipped to address bullying in the workplace when it arises. A lack of managerial skills has been cited as the top reason (66 percent) for bullying in the workplace, along with personality of bullies (57 percent), and authoritative management style (55 percent; *Management Science*, 2005). This lack of skills means that managers often resort to poor procedures for managing employee performance (Sidle, 2009), developing unreasonable expectations and excessive workloads (Rayner and Höel, 1997), and using communication patterns that include ignoring, intimidation, and belittling remarks (Foster *et al.*, 2004).

Managerial training that includes the organization's stance on pursuing reported incidents of bullying, discipline, and termination has been effective in some organizations when led by top managers (Pate and Beaumont, 2010). Requiring training for all employees regarding expectations of behavior and the code of conduct has also been shown to have a positive impact on bullying and harassment (Pate and Beaumont, 2010). Broadly, training managers in organizational policies and procedures that address bullying, being alert for potential bullying behaviors in the hiring process, enhancing trust, providing justice and fairness in work units, and monitoring and assessing the organizational environment for variables such as culture, communication, and physical arrangements are managerial skills that can be reinforced to ameliorate bullying behaviors in the present and future.

Intervention

When bullying does occur, it is important for managers to develop an action plan that intervenes in and remedies the bullying crisis. While researchers have suggested various approaches that can be taken in this process, managers ultimately rely on their judgment. Understanding and preparing to make those judgments provides managers with the confidence to act decisively depending on the organizational need and severity of the bullying behavior. Thus, managers should be coached and have an opportunity to practice by engaging role-plays in order to develop effective strategies for addressing bullying behavior, since bullying necessitates a candid conversation between the manager and the offending employee (Meinert, 2011).

A provocative statement made by Namie and Namie (2011: 73) is critical to managerial understanding of their importance in the intervention of workplace bullying: "Not acting – doing nothing – is not a neutral act." Managers must do something and not simply ignore bullying as a minor or insufficient cause of concern by itself. Some interventions are informal and may be as simple as coaching a bullying employee to make him or her aware of his or her offending actions and/or words (Hubert, 2003; Johnson and Indvik, 2001) and teaching employees appropriate ways to vent emotions in the workplace (Johnson and Indvik, 2001). Other interventions, such as transferring the bullying employee to a position where there will be less opportunity to bully (Glendinning, 2001) can be a more clear demonstration of intolerance of workplace bullying and procedurally part of discipline and/or termination (Johnson, 1998).

Recognition

While minimized in this chapter's discussion focusing on managerial actions, an underlying assumption has been that managers realize and respect that workplace bullying is a serious issue. Research has found that targets of bullies often experience numerous health problems, such as anxiety and physical issues (Mikkelsen and Einarsen, 2001), insomnia (Greenberg, 2006), increased risk of depression (Namie, 2003), alcohol abuse (Richman *et al.*, 2001), and even suicide (Leymann, 1990). Organizations should be concerned about the effects of workplace bullying on their employees and make changes to ensure that workplace bullying is not only addressed, but not tolerated in the future. Because bullying can have a "ripple effect" across the organization, it is not something to be ignored (Coyne *et al.*, 2000).

At the same time, managers must recognize their responsibilities in addressing bullying by assuming two roles: the role of diagnostician and the role of interventionist (LaVan and Martin, 2008). LaVan and Martin (2008) suggest using the ABC model, identifying antecedents, behaviors, and consequences, as a guide to recognize bullying. First, it is necessary to identify the antecedents, triggers, or causes of the specific incident of workplace bullying. As discussed in this chapter, antecedents might include the organizational policies, organizational culture, communication norms, structure and work design, and managerial behavior. Next, a manager should describe the behaviors associated with workplace bullying in terms of frequency, duration, intensity, and appropriateness. With this information, an intervention plan can be formulated and quickly implemented.

Altering behaviors via accountability

As with other influencing mechanisms, having the bullying employee approach the behavioral change from an internalized position of *want to* is likely to be more sustainable than those that *have to* amend their tactics based on compliance. Thus, the underlying issue for managers when addressing bullying in the workplace is accountability for the organization, for the manager, and for the bullying employee. The accountability perspective makes two assumptions about the workplace environment: (1) organizational culture has established a no-bullying context as being fair and just for all employees, and (2) that the organization embeds formal evaluation of behavior related to the appropriate treatment of others. Accountability theory at the individual level places the emphasis on an external review of behavior (in this case, by the manager), with appropriate rewards and punishments resulting from the results of the review (Ferris *et al.*, 1995).

Accountability becomes a mid-range goal that is monitored by the manager and the bullying employee, rather than remaining a mere incident report in a personnel file. This approach should be recognizable to managers, as it is a customary approach of most due process-related employee improvements such as tardiness, inadequate performance, or probationary periods for new employees. Managers are setting the expectation that change in behavior is required from the bullying employee, including specific examples related to the work setting that are problematic for that employee, and perhaps engaging in interpersonal skills-related coaching for the bullying employee. Focusing on accountability changes the locus of control from an external to an internal focus. That is, instead of focusing on the punishments associated with violation of a bullying policy, accountability is perceptual and encompasses the bullying employee's feelings about accountability (Cummings and Anton, 1990) and his or her perceptions of workforce characteristics (Tetlock *et al.*, 1989). Thus, an accountability approach should have longer lasting effects when utilized.

Discipline and Termination

As with most serious undesirable workplace behaviors, discipline and termination must be potential consequences of workplace bullying (MacIntosh, 2006). Given the nature of bullying behaviors, there is also the possibility of legal action that may involve external agencies and the legal system, depending on the severity of behavior and local regulations (LaVan and Martin, 2008). Extensive coverage of discipline and termination procedures is beyond the scope of this chapter, but in the following paragraph, a few guidelines for managers will be discussed.

When providing feedback to the employee, deliver your message fully, candidly, and in a timely manner, while making it readily usable to the employee (Sulkowicz, 2007). Avoid shaming the employee by giving feedback in front of others, and instead demonstrate dignity and respect for the employee in the process. If the bullying behavior is evaluated to be less severe but might be repeated over time, termination is still possible with documentation, warnings, and due process similar to guidance given for negative or destructive attitudes or being insubordinate (Harvard Business School Press, 2007). On the other hand, bullying may create conditions that endanger coworkers' health or safety, or are harassing or threatening to coworkers to the extent that it prevents them from doing their work. In those situations, there will likely be cause for immediate dismissal (Harvard Business School Press, 2007).

CONCLUSION

In this chapter, I have addressed the action steps that managers should consider when addressing bullying in their workplace. These are steps that are prescribed to multiple levels of management in the organization, as evidence exists that the bullying employee is often in a managerial position (Edwards, 2011; Hirschfeld and Dalhgren, 2010). Thus, if the bullying employee is a supervisor or mid-level manager, the steps are suggested for the director, unit, or executive-level manager in addressing the undesirable behavior. If the bullying is occurring higher in the organization chart, these steps remain applicable for the Board of Directors or owners to take in remedying the bullying situation. Finally, in the debate on whether nature and nurture affects bullying behaviors, I side with Harvey *et al.* (2009) in identifying both as important components that can be addressed with a four-pronged approach: (1) Prevention, (2) Evaluating the Organizational Environment, (3) Observation of the Manager's Behavior, and (4) Intervention.

REFERENCES

Aryee, S., Chen, Z. X., Sun, L., and Debrah, Y.A. (2007). Antecedents and outcomes of abusive supervision: Test of a trickle-down model. *Journal of Applied Psychology*, 92, 191–201.

Ayoko, O. B. (2007). Communication openness, conflict events and reactions to conflict in culturally diverse workgroups. *Cross Cultural Management: An International Journal*, 14, 106–24.

Bryant, M. R. (2010, July 28). Dealing with violence in the workplace. SHRM Online Toolkits. Available to SHRM members at http://www.shrm.org/templatesTools/Toolkits/Pages/DealingWithViolenceintheWorkplace.aspx.

Carbo, J., and Hughes, A. (2010). Workplace bullying: Developing a human rights definition from the perspective and experiences of targets. *WorkingUSA: The Journal of Labor and Society*, 13, 387–403.

Cortina, L. M. (2008). Unseen injustice: Incivility as modern discrimination in organizations. *Academy of Management Review*, 33, 55–75.

Coyne, I., Seigne, E., and Randall, P. (2000). Predicting workplace victim status from personality. *European Journal of Work and Organizational Psychology*, 9, 335–49.

Crawford, N. (1997). Bullying at work: A psychoanalytic perspective. *Journal of Community and Applied Social Psychology*, 7, 219–25.

Cummings, L. L., and Anton, R. J. (1990). The logical and appreciative dimensions of accountability. In S. Srivastva, D. L. Cooperrider, and Associates (eds), *Appreciative Management and Leadership* (pp. 257–86), San Francisco, CA: Jossey-Bass.

Detert, J. R., Trevino, L. K., and Sweitzer, V. L. (2008). Moral disengagement in ethical decision making: A study of antecedents and outcomes. *Journal of Applied Psychology*, 93, 374–91.

Djurkovic, N., McCormack, D., and Casimir, G. (2006). Neuroticism and the psychosomatic model of workplace bullying. *Journal of Managerial Psychology*, 21, 73–88.

Edwards, M. H. (2011). Dealing with workplace bullies. *SHRM Legal Report*. Available to SHRM members at http://www.shrm.org/Publications/LegalReport/Pages/WorkplaceBullies.aspx.

Einarsen, S., Raknes, B. I., and Matthiesen, S. B. (1994). Bullying and harassment at work and their relationships to work environment quality: An exploratory study. *European Work and Organizational Psychologist*, 4, 381–401.

Ferris, G. R., Mitchell, T. R., Canavan, P. J., Frink, D. D., and Hopper, H. (1995). Accountability in human resource systems. In G. R. Ferris, S. D. Rosen, and D. T. Barnum (eds), *Handbook of Human Resource Management* (pp. 175–96), Cambridge, MA: Blackwell.

Foster, B., Mackie, B., and Barnett, N. (2004). Bullying in the health sector: A study of bullying of nursing students. *New Zealand Journal of Employment Relations*, 29, 67–83.

Fox, S., and Stallworth, L. E. (2006). How effective is an apology in resolving workplace bullying disputes? An empirical research note. *Dispute Resolution Journal, 61,* 54-63. Retrieved from http://lamontstallworth.com/Articles/PDFS/How_Effective_is_An_Apology.pdf.

Glendinning, P. M. (2001). Workplace bullying: Curing the cancer of the American workplace. *Public Personnel Management*, 30, 269–86.

Greenberg, J. (2006). Losing sleep over organizational injustice: Attenuating insomniac reactions to underpayment inequity with supervisory training in interactional justice. *Journal of Applied Psychology*, 91, 58–69.

Greenberg, J. (2010). *Managing Behavior in Organizations* (5th edn), Upper Saddle River, NJ: Prentice Hall.

Harvard Business School Press (2007). *Dismissing an Employee: Expert Solutions to Everyday Challenges,* Boston, MA: Harvard Business School Publishing Corporation.

Harvey, M., Treadway, D., Heames, J., and Duke, A. (2009). Bullying in the 21st century global organization: An ethical perspective. *Journal of Business Ethics*, 85, 27–40.

Heames, J. T., Harvey, M. G., and Treadway, D. (2006). Status inconsistency: An antecedent to bullying behaviour in groups. *International Journal of Human Resource Management,* 17, 348–61.

Hirschfeld, S. J., and Dalhgren, A. (2010). Like the schoolyard, the workplace has its bully. *The Recorder.* Retrieved from http://www.law.com/jsp/ca/PubArticleCA.jsp?id=1202471199971&slreturn=1.

Hoobler, J., and Brass, D. (2006). Abusive supervision and family undermining as displaced aggression. *Journal of Applied Psychology*, 91, 1125–33.

Hubert, A. B. (2003). To prevent and overcome undesirable interaction: A systematic approach model. In S. Einarsen, H. Höel, D. Zapf, and C. L. Cooper (eds), *Bullying and Emotional Abuse in the Workplace: International Perspectives in Research and Practice* (pp. 299–311), London: Taylor & Francis.

Johnson, C. (1998). Controlling hostility. *HR Magazine*, 43, 65–8.

Johnson, P., and Indvik, J. (2001). Slings and arrows of rudeness: Incivility in the workplace. *Journal of Management Development*, 20, 705–14.

LaVan, H., and Martin, W. (2008). Bullying in the U.S. workplace: Normative and process-oriented ethical approaches. *Journal of Business Ethics*, 83, 147–65.

Leymann, H. (1990). Mobbing and psychological terror at workplaces. *Violence and Victims*, 5, 119–26.

MacIntosh, J. (2006). Tackling work place bullying. *Issues in Mental Health Nursing*, 27, 665–79.

Management Science (2005). Bullying amongst managers rockets as organisations fail to take action. *Management Science*, 49, 12–13.

McCrory, C. A. (2011). The office at your office: Head of the committee against workplace bullying, paper presented at the Institute of Behavior and Applied Management, Orlando, FL, Oct.

Meinert, D. (2011). When bullying hits home. *HR Magazine*, 56, 18.
Mikkelsen, E., and Einarsen, S. (2001). Bullying in Danish work-life: Prevalence and health correlates. *European Journal of Work and Organizational Psychology*, 10, 393–413.
Namie, G. (2003). Workplace bullying: Escalated incivility. *Ivey Business Journal*, 68, 1–6.
Namie, G., and Namie, R. F. (2011). *The Bully-Free Workplace: Stop Jerks, Weasels and Snakes from Killing your Organization*, Hoboken, NJ: John Wiley & Sons.
Parkins, I. S., Fishbein, H. D., and Ritchey, P. N. (2006). The influence of personality on workplace bullying and discrimination. *Journal of Applied Social Psychology*, 36, 2554–77.
Parzefall, M., and Salin, D. M. (2010). Perceptions of and reaction to workplace bullying: A social exchange perspective. *Human Relations*, 63, 761–80.
Pate, J., and Beaumont, P. (2010). Bullying and harassment: A case of success? *Employee Relations*, 32, 171–83.
Rayner, C., and Höel, H. (1997). A summary review of literature relating to workplace bullying. *Journal of Community and Applied Social Psychology*, 7, 181–91.
Richman, J., Rospenda, K., Flaherty, J., and Freels, S. (2001). Workplace harassment, active coping, and alcohol-related outcomes. *Journal of Substance Abuse*, 13, 347–66.
Robinson, S. L., and O'Leary-Kelly, A. M. (1998). Monkey see, monkey do: The influence of work groups on the antisocial behavior of employees. *Academy of Management Journal*, 41, 658–72.
Rokeach, M. (1973). *The Nature of Human Values*, New York: Free Press.
Rousseau, D. M., Sitkin, S. B., Burt, R., and Camerer, C. (1998). Not so different after all: A cross-discipline view of trust. *Academy of Management Review*, 23, 1–12.
Safety and Health Assessment and Research for Prevention (SHARP) (2008). *Workplace Bullying: What Everyone Needs to Know*, Report #87-2-2008, Olympia, WA: State Department of Labor and Industries.
Schein, E. H. (1983). The role of the founder in creating organizational culture. *Organizational Dynamics*, 12, 13–28.
Schutz, W. C. (1958). *FIRO: A Three Dimensional Theory of Interpersonal Behavior*, New York: Holt, Rinehart, & Winston.
Sidle, S. D. (2009). Is your organization a great place for bullies to work? *Academy of Management Perspectives*, 23, 89–91.
Sulkowicz, K. (2007). Straight talk at review time. *Business Week*, 4049 (10 Sept.), 16.
Tepper, B. J., Moss, S. E., and Duffy, M. K. (2011). Predictors of abusive supervision: Supervisor perceptions of deep-level dissimilarity, relationship conflict, and subordinate performance. *Academy of Management Journal*, 54, 279–94.
Tepper, B. J., Duffy, M. K., Henle, C. A., and Lambert, L. S. (2006). Procedural injustice, victim precipitation, and abusive supervision. *Personnel Psychology*, 59, 101–23.
Tetlock, P. E., Skitka, L., and Boettger, R. (1989). Social and cognitive strategies for coping with accountability: Conformity, complexity, and bolstering. *Journal of Personality and Social Psychology*, 57, 632–40.
Townend, A. (2008). Understanding and addressing bullying in the workplace. *Industrial and Commercial Training*, 40, 270–3.
Vega, G., and Comer, D. R. (2005). Sticks and stones may break your bones, but words can break your spirit: Bullying in the workplace. *Journal of Business Ethics*, 58, 101–9.
Workplace Bullying (2010). Workplace bullying: Tips on prevention and taking appropriate action. *YourABA E-newsletter*, Dec. Retrieved from http://www.abanow.org/2011/01/workplace-bullying0tips-on-prevention-and taking-appropriate-action.

18

Workplace Bullying: Remedies for Victims

Edward C. Tomlinson and Joyce Thompson Heames
West Virginia University

William N. Bockanic
John Carroll University

INTRODUCTION

One of the more commonly accepted definitions of workplace bullying is:

> the repeated actions and practices (of a perpetrator) that are directed to one or more workers, which are unwanted by the victim, which may be done deliberately, or unconsciously, but clearly cause humiliation, offense, distress, may interfere with job performance, and/or cause an unpleasant working environment.
>
> (Einarsen, 1999: 17)

More specifically, bullying behaviors range from gossiping about, yelling at, or ignoring a person, to socially isolating an individual. The effects of workplace bullying on the careers and personal lives of the victims tend to be consistent and severe. Indeed, researchers have characterized workplace bullying as "an extreme type of social stress" (Zapf and Einarsen, 2005: 239) that may be "a more crippling and devastating problem for employees than all other work-related stress put together" (Einarsen, 1999: 17). Bullying research shows a clear connection with adverse health, and these stress-related illnesses can have seriously negative career implications (Gardner and Johnson, 2001). Davenport *et al.* (1999) view bullying as an escalating process, yet the physical and mental health effects of bullying can be quite pronounced even in the early stages of a bullying scenario.

Clearly, the effects of workplace bullying can be devastating to the targets of such behavior, but the effects on key organizational outcomes are similarly disastrous. The harmful effects of workplace bullying on employee turnover, organizational productivity, and profitability have been well documented (Einarsen and Skogstad, 1996; Leymann, 1990; Rayner, 1997; Rayner and Cooper, 1997; Salin, 2001). One study found that 25 percent of bullying victims eventually quit their jobs (Sheehan *et al.*, 1999). Another survey of bullying targets indicated that more than half lost work time as a result of the bullying, more than one-third reduced their commitment to the organization, more than a quarter lost work time trying to avoid the bully, nearly a quarter decreased their effort at work, and 12 percent actually changed jobs as a direct result of the bullying (Pearson *et al.*, 2000). In terms of lost productivity alone, victims of bullying often estimate that they are working at only about 85 percent of their normal capacity (Höel *et al.*, 2001) and by some estimates $5–6 billion dollars is lost annually in the US alone due to "real or perceived abuse of employees by employers" (Keashley and Neuman, 2004: 353). Finally, employee lawsuits can pose yet another negative organizational outcome associated with workplace bullying (Gardner and Johnson, 2001).

The responsibility for recognizing and managing the deviant behaviors that develop within the organization lies with organizational leadership, as it shapes the culture of the organization. Some suggest that, by not taking action, organizations "legitimize" and "institutionalize" bullying (Ashforth, 1994; Liefooghe and Davey, 2001). Indeed, scholars often affirm that organizations have a clear responsibility to reduce bullying behavior among its members (Dietz *et al.*, 2003; Paine, 1994) and often offer guidance to managers in this regard. Notwithstanding the extensive literature whereby scholars have quantified the prevalence and impact of bullying in the workplace, to date, research-based prescriptions have only been addressed to managers, and not the victims who actually endure such abuse.

SIGNIFICANCE

We view prescriptive advice to victims as imperative for several reasons. First, victims know about bullying before anyone else; in fact, they know about it when no one else does (due to fear of reporting it, etc.). Second, there are a number of useful steps that can be advised, based on behavioral science and legal frameworks. Thus, the recommendations we present offer more substantive justification than what typically appears in other sources. Finally, we believe it is essential for those who believe they are bullied at work to find a sense of empowerment that comes from choosing efficacious ways to cope successfully with bullying.

RELEVANT THEORY

As with any form of human behavior, the dynamics surrounding workplace bullying (from both bully and target perspectives) are complex and multifaceted (Langan-Fox and Sankey, 2007). Given the space considerations here, along with the current state of research in this area, we cannot provide an exhaustive analysis of each of the myriad possibilities of how bullying at work might unfold (e.g. with the various combinations of personality traits of the actors involved, etc.). However, we can offer more general guidance based on extant behavioral science and legal frameworks.[1]

Salient Features

We will draw from these frameworks in more detail in the following section, where we outline a series of steps that victims can take to redress the bullying they experience at work. Notably, we leave it for others to give advice that is not directly focused on remedying the bullying problem (e.g. counseling, stress management techniques, etc.). Furthermore, these steps are arranged in an iterative and sequential manner, such that victim responses begin at a relatively low level and then escalate in intensity as needed until the problem is resolved. We adopt this approach for two reasons. First, our prescriptions make it clear that victims should not condone bullying behavior; rather, we argue that victims can learn to successfully manage the situation, at least in many situations. Second, dysfunctional conflict in organizations often has a way of spiraling out of control. Thus, our approach takes into consideration findings that victim efforts to stop the bullying appear to be most effective when conducted early in the bullying process (UNISON, 2000), and that victim efforts may be less likely to remedy the problem when they escalate the conflict (Zapf and Gross, 2001). Our guidance is tailored to calibrate victim responses in such a way as to avoid over-reacting, yet still provide research-based guidance on how to diminish bullying behavior.[2]

RECOMMENDATIONS

Look in the Mirror

Without condoning the bullying behavior of others, you should begin by carefully and objectively considering whether the bullying you are receiving might in some way be a response to what others perceive as bullying behavior *from you*. Conflict management researchers have extensively studied how reciprocation dynamics invoke destructive conflict spirals. Self-serving biases allow us to attribute the cause of others' aggression in a manner that places the blame entirely on them, thus preventing us from seeing problems that we may have in fact caused (Vega and Comer, 2005). In short, bullying and being bullied are not mutually exclusive (Douglas, 2001), and a key first step is to understand one's own degree of culpability for this type of dysfunctional conflict.

Manage Your Work-Related Behaviors

Again, without condoning the bullying behavior of others, it may be that others perceive deficiencies in your work-related behaviors. Unfortunately, many individuals in the workplace do not know how to handle such issues constructively (including managers). These individuals may respond with bullying-type behaviors simply because they have not learned more constructive techniques to use in addressing such issues. So, *examine your own job performance* to see where there are opportunities for improvement. Some researchers have acknowledged that bullying can serve constructive purposes such as performance enhancement (Vega and Comer, 2005). Ensuring that your performance is as high as possible also helps you later, both for making a business case to your manager why the bullying behaviors must stop, and/or pursuing employment elsewhere.

You should also *consider how much you follow the norms within your organization* (Vega and Comer, 2005). The term "norms" refers to shared standards of behavior within a work group or organization, and these behavioral standards can be formal or informal, explicit or implicit. Failure to adhere to group or organizational norms can elicit strong sanctions from other organizational members (Mayo, 1933). Finally, *look for other clues within the conflict that may point to how you might have unwittingly contributed to the problem*, so you can help the other person work with you in a more constructive manner that resolves the issue. Bear in mind that because some people don't handle conflict very well, the types of signals they send concerning the conflict (such as teasing about the way you dress) is not indicative of the real issue (such as a problem with how you routinely yet unintentionally postpone action on their requests).

Enhance Your Power

Several researchers indicate that a key feature of bullying is an imbalance of power (Rayner and Keashly, 2005; Zapf and Einarsen, 2005). Bullies often wield greater power than the targets, such that targets believe they are defenseless and cannot retaliate. Because bullies target weakness (Vega and Comer, 2005), movement toward a solution entails making yourself more powerful. There are multiple strategies to achieve this (Lewicki *et al.*, 2010). One way of making a weak position stronger is to *form alliances with others* (Malhotra, 2005). Other coworkers who will join your cause will enhance your confidence and lessen the chances of reprisal from the bully (Bramson, 1992); they might also learn to respond to the bully in ways that lessen the psychological rewards for such untoward behavior (see next point below). Another fundamental strategy is to *enhance the bully's dependence on you* (Malhotra, 2005). This can be accomplished to the extent that you understand and can uniquely satisfy interests that are of critical importance to the bully. Having access to or control over information or other key resources that cannot come from other sources can provide a source of power.

Similarly, *accumulating expertise in a vital area* can also provide an important base of power (Lewicki *et al.*, 2010). Finally, *it is important to understand that power is much like beauty, such that it lies in the eyes of the beholder* (Lewicki *et al.*, 2010). Many bullying victims in organizations experience a sense of helplessness because they believe that others wield more power over them than is actually the case. For example, victims of bullying bosses often conclude that their bosses have absolute power over them. The reality of the situation tempers this conclusion in two compelling ways: (1) managers must accomplish their duties through others, so in a very real sense, managers are indeed dependent on their subordinates to a nontrivial degree; and (2) managers often have restrictions on their power (i.e. they often cannot administer employee discipline without approval from their supervisor or human resources (Bramson, 1992)).

Confront the Bully Directly

It is absolutely essential to stand up for yourself (Bramson, 1981; Solomon, 1990), rather than acquiesce to the bully's power plays. In short, "bullies lose their power if you don't cower" (Solomon, 1990: 7), whereas bullies feel more empowered when others show weakness. It is just as essential to stand up for yourself in a manner that does not come across as retaliation or "fighting" back (Bramson, 1981), as bullies also feel psychologically rewarded when their victims lose control (Bramson, 1992). In other words, while cowering to the bully or responding in an explosion of your own anger are natural tendencies, they are ineffective and should be substituted with a response that denies bullies the reinforcement they receive from submission or retaliation (Bramson, 1992). When bullies are not reinforced for their hostile behavior, they are prompted to engage in more functional and constructive behavior. Successfully standing up for yourself entails several components (Douglas, 2001). First, *approach the individual to set up a time to discuss a private matter.* Be sure to do this in a calm, confident, and assertive manner. Second, *describe the problematic behavior in specific and observable terms, and communicate why you find it to be offensive.* Finally, *firmly communicate that you want this behavior to stop immediately.* An example of this type of confronting response might be:

> John, I want to talk about what happened at the staff meeting this morning. Only one minute into my presentation, you interrupted by saying that I'm an "idiot" and my proposal is worthless. I am very upset about this. Quite frankly, your personal opinion of me has no relevance in a formal business meeting, and the norms of professionalism call for you to hear my proposal in its entirety before rendering a judgment. I don't expect your agreement with me in every instance, but I do expect from you the same courtesy

> and professionalism I extend to you. Anything less is unprofessional and a distraction from the sound working relationship we need to have with each other moving forward. I will expect better treatment from you in the future.

It is worth elaborating on other notable features of this type of response. You should avoid being overly personal: address the bullying behavior, without ascribing negative traits to the bully. Instead of saying "you're so rude," say "you interrupted me during the meeting." You should also avoid generalizing; be specific and precise. Instead of saying "you always interrupt me" or "you never listen to my opinions," say "you interrupted me three times during the staff meeting today." In other words, go heavy on the facts (such as what was said, what actually happened, what other people witnessed) and lighter on any global conclusions you might have drawn about the behavior (such as the offender's motives or personality characteristics). The more you are able to describe the offensive behavior in specific and observable terms, the harder it is for the bully to dismiss the behavior by denying its occurrence.

As mentioned earlier, there is also some research suggesting that a response should be given quickly – after the first or second instance of bullying (UNISON, 2000). Other research further suggests that bullying is a "gradually evolving process" (Zapf and Einarsen, 2001), a form of conflict escalation that it might be beneficial to resolve at an early stage. Notwithstanding, some prior research suggests that active efforts to engage the bully in constructive problem solving is not successful; neither is a competitive approach that attempts to force the bully to stop (Zapf and Gross, 2001; but for an exception to the latter point, see UNISON, 2000). However, the study reported by Zapf and Gross relied on small samples and apparently on relatively coarse measures of victim responses that do not appear to correspond to the highly specific prescriptions we offer here. We also note that our advice emphasizes victim efforts to *gain more power first*, and then confront the bully. This important sequencing is not captured by Zapf and Gross. Moreover, the specific nature of our recommendation does not fit neatly into the traditional conception of problem solving. Our advice stresses victim assertiveness (after gaining more power) without any attempt to collaborate with the other *per se*. Our advice merely takes steps to avoid escalating the conflict by measures that communicate firmness on the issue, yet maintain a degree of courteous treatment to the bully (by not generalizing, by pointing to specific behavior as the problem instead of personalizing the conflict, etc.).

Report the Bullying Internally

This may entail speaking to the bully's boss or to the human resources department, ombudsman, or other internal reporting mechanism (e.g. 1-800 number or intranet site). It is critical at this point to have maintained sufficient documentation. That is, be prepared to describe specific behaviors that occurred on specific days and times. In as much detail as possible, describe what was actually said or done, and who else might have witnessed the bullying behaviors. The best strategy is to rely on the facts and not engage in a personal attack on the bully (as discussed above). Meglich-Sespico *et al.* (2007) recommend that, before filing a complaint, you must be willing to state your position as a victim and be confident that your report will do some personal good (i.e. make your situation better). If you decide to move forward with a complaint, follow the company's policies and protocols in reporting and create a paper trail. You also need to be timely in reporting. Six months to a year, guided by the severity of the bullying and after trying other strategies to rectify the situation, is a reasonable time frame to report bullying behavior. The positive side is that your follow-through may help the company solve an employment problem and give them the documentation they need to address the bullying situation.

Take Legal Action

If your efforts concentrated within the organization to remedy bullying behavior fail, you may need to be prepared to take action outside of the organization. Although some nations do address workplace bullying legislatively, in the United States there is currently no federal law, nor do the overwhelming majority of states have any laws dealing specifically with workplace bullying. Nonetheless, there are a variety of potential legal responses that may be used to address the issue. An ounce of prevention is often far less expensive than a pound of cure; and while legal action may be available as a means of redress for bullying behavior, it may not be the most prudent approach. As discussed above, the aggrieved employee is most often interested in merely having the bullying behavior cease. This, of course, will be a win-win situation for employer and employee alike, hopefully leading to a more productive, healthy, and content employee. Also, a healthy employee may be less likely to access the employer's healthcare provider, thus having the collateral benefit of helping prevent health-care premiums from escalating. In a perfect world, problems would be resolved without the need to access the legal system, thus avoiding expense, time, and limiting use of the court system to only the most egregious cases not capable of resolution amicably. In our imperfect world, however, an employer may either refuse to – or be unable to – successfully resolve the bully's aberrant behavior. Thus, resorting to litigation may be the bullied employee's only hope. In Table 18.1, we have presented a brief overview of potential legal theories that may be utilized to provide redress for physical and/or mental injuries caused by bullying behavior. Please see Chapter 21, this volume, for additional information on legal remedies in particular.[3]

Look for Another Job

Sometimes your best efforts will not be enough to stop the bullying behavior or neutralize the effects on you at your current workplace. An exit strategy would involve a voluntary separation or transfer on your part initiated to seek personal relief (Meglich-Sespico *et al.*, 2007). At that point, it becomes necessary to find another job. However, you should be a savvy job-seeker, looking for particular features in your new company that will dramatically reduce the likelihood of future bullying behavior (see Langan-Fox and Sankey, 2007, for an extended discussion). Such features should include a specific anti-bullying policy incorporated into a general code of conduct *and* policy enforcement with top-management support. Other aspects of the organization's culture should also be examined, such as the power structure and reward system. Is the power structure a rigid hierarchy or is it more egalitarian? Are rewards based on competition or cooperation? Some organizations (especially the military) have a reputation for bullying that is ingrained in their socialization practices, rendering these behaviors part of a normalized tradition. Finally, smaller and less bureaucratic organizations may tend to have less bullying. Be aware that large global companies tend to have a fast-paced and high-intensity culture that may seem overbearing to some. Thus, choose wisely in selecting your next job opportunity to ensure that the new company has a culture that best fits your personality and skill set.

TABLE 18.1
Potential Legal Theories (Causes of Action) to Redress Bullying

Assault	Battery	False Imprisonment	Defamation	Intentional Infliction of Emotional Distress	Workers' Compensation
Must prove:	Must prove:	Must prove:	Must prove:	Must prove:	Must prove:
Intent to cause apprehension (fear) of imminent/immediate harmful/offensive bodily contact.	Intent to cause harmful/offensive bodily contact.	Intent to cause confinement within fixed boundaries with no reasonable means of escape. Confined person must be aware of confinement.	(For Libel) An intentional untruthful defamatory communication which is published to a third party via writing, radio, or television and to which the publisher can assert no privilege. (For Slander) An untruthful defamatory communication which is orally published to a third party and to which the publisher can assert no privilege.	Intentional or reckless conduct which is outrageous and offensive within the context of generally accepted standards of decency and morality. Must also prove that there was a causal connection between the wrongful conduct and the resulting emotional distress, and further that the emotional distress is severe.	Physical or Stress-related Injury which occurs in the course of (i.e. during working hours) and in the scope of (i.e. within nature of job) employment. For workers' compensation to apply, injury must not be intentionally self-inflicted by employee or intentionally caused by employer.

Title VII Civil Rights Act of 1964	Age Discrimination in Employment Act of 1967	Americans with Disabilities Act 1994	Occupational Safety and Health Act	Various State Anti-discrimination Laws
Must prove: Discrimination with respect to hiring, firing, compensation, or terms and conditions of employment based upon race, color, sex, religion and national origin. Includes protection against harassment with respect to the above protected classes.	Must prove: Discrimination with respect to hiring, firing, compensation, terms and conditions of employment based upon age and that the plaintiff is 40 years of age or older.	Must prove: Discrimination with respect to hiring, firing, compensation, terms and conditions of employment with respect to a person with a disability. Employer is required to make reasonable accommodations for the disabled individual provided such do not cause undue hardship to the employer.	Must prove: Physical injury resulting from violation of federal workplace safety regulations. Does not currently cover occupational stress, thus short of an employer intentionally attempting to injure a worker to harass him/her currently has little utility with respect to bullying issues.	Generally fills in the gap where federal laws do not apply due to requirements of minimum number of employees or otherwise do not afford protection. Many states protect against discrimination based upon sexual preference or identity including gay, lesbian, bi-sexual and transgender individuals. Title VII currently provides no protection against discrimination based upon sexual preference or identity.

CONCLUSION AND SUMMARY

In this chapter, we have tackled the very sensitive issue of how targets of workplace bullying might go about attempting to remedy their situation. We based our recommendations on a broad base of extant research in behavioral science (e.g. perception and attribution, conflict management, group norms, power and influence, organizational culture) as well as the current state of jurisprudence in the United States. Notwithstanding, we believe that future academic research on workplace bullying should begin to systematically examine how targets might successfully remedy bullying situations, including the viability of the suggestions we put forth here.

NOTES

1 For the interested reader, there are several useful guides that categorize different types of bullying behaviors, and specific coping techniques customized to each type. See e.g. Bramson, 1981, 1992.
2 Note that this may entail recognizing and effectively dealing with bullying behaviors *before* they persistently occur for six months in duration or more (which is a frequently adopted criterion for "bullying" among researchers).
3 While the authors have been reasonably careful to assure the accuracy of the material contained herein, this paper should not be relied upon for or construed as the offering or rendering of legal advice and the reader should seek competent legal counsel to evaluate the merits of their proposed or intended actions.

REFERENCES

Ashforth, B. (1994). Petty tyranny in organizations. *Human Relations*, 47, 755–78.
Bramson, R. M. (1981). *Coping with Difficult People*, Garden City, NY: Anchor Press/Doubleday.
Bramson, R. M. (1992). *Coping with Difficult Bosses*, New York: Carol Publishing Group.
Davenport, N., Schwartz, R. D., and Elliot, G. P. (1999). *Mobbing: Emotional Abuse in the American Workplace*, Ames, Iowa: Civil Society Publishing.
Dietz, J., Robinson, S. J., Folger, R., Baron, R. A., and Schulz, M. (2003). The impacts of community violence and an organization's procedural justice climate on workplace aggression. *Academy of Management Journal, 46*, 317–26.

Douglas, E. (2001). *Bullying in the Workplace: An Organizational Toolkit*, Basingstoke: Gower.

Einarsen, S. (1999). The nature and causes of bullying at work. *International Journal of Manpower*, 20, 16–27.

Einarsen, S., and Skogstad, A. (1996). Bullying at work: Epidemiological findings in public and private organizations. *European Journal of Work and Organizational Psychology*, 5, 185–202.

Gardner, S., and Johnson, P. R. (2001). The leaner, meaner workplace: Strategies for handling bullies at work. *Employment Relations Today*, 28, 23–36.

Höel, H., Sparks, K., and Cooper, C. L. (2001). *The Cost of Violence/Stress at Work and the Benefits of a Violence/Stress-Free Working Environment*, Geneva: International Labour Organization.

Keashley, L., and Neuman, J. H. (2004). Bullying in the workplace: Its impact and management. *Employee Rights and Employment Policy Journal*, 8, 335–73.

Langan-Fox, J., and Sankey, M. (2007). Tyrants and workplace bullying. In J. Langan-Fox, C. L. Cooper, and R. J. Klimoski (eds), *Research Companion to the Dysfunctional Workplace: Management Challenges and Symptoms* (pp. 58–74), Cheltenham: Edward Elgar.

Lewicki, R. J., Barry, B., and Saunders, D. M. (2010). *Negotiation* (6th edn), Boston, MA: McGraw-Hill Irwin.

Leymann, H. (1990). Mobbing and psychological terror at workplaces. *Violence and Victims*, 5, 119–26.

Liefooghe, A. P. D., and Davey, K. M. (2001). Accounts of workplace bullying: The role of the organization. *European Journal of Work and Organizational Psychology*, 10, 375–92.

Malhotra, D. (2005). Make your weak position strong. *Negotiation* (July), 3–5.

Mayo, E. (1933). *The Human Problems of an Industrial Civilization*, New York: Macmillan.

Meglich-Sespico, P., Faley, R., and Knapp, D. (2007). Relief and redress for targets of workplace bullying. *Employee Responsibilities and Rights Journal*, 19, 31–43.

Paine, L. S. (1994). Managing for organizational integrity. *Harvard Business Review* (March/April), 106–17.

Pearson, C. M., Andersson, L. A., and Porath, C. L. (2000). Assessing and attacking workplace incivility. *Organizational Dynamics*, 29, 123–37.

Rayner, C. (1997). The incidence of workplace bullying. *Journal of Community and Applied Social Psychology*, 7, 199–208.

Rayner, C., and Cooper, C. (1997). Workplace bullying: Myth or reality – can we afford to ignore it? *Leadership and Organization Development Journal*, 18, 211–14.

Rayner, C., and Keashly, L. (2005). Bullying at work: A perspective from Britain and North America. In S. Fox and P. E. Spector (eds), *Counterproductive Work Behavior: Investigations of Actors and Targets* (pp. 271–96), Washington, DC: American Psychological Association.

Salin, D. (2001). Prevalence and forms of bullying among business professionals: A comparison of two different strategies for measuring bullying. *European Journal of Work and Organizational Psychology*, 4, 425–41.

Sheehan, M., Barker, M., and Rayner, C. (1999). Applying strategies for dealing with workplace bullying. *International Journal of Manpower*, 20, 50–6.

Solomon, M. (1990). *Working with Difficult People*, Englewood Cliffs, NJ: Prentice Hall.

UNISON (2000). *Police Staff Bullying Report*, London: UNISON.

Vega, G., and Comer, D. R. (2005). Bullying and harassment in the workplace. In R. E. Kidwell, Jr. and C. L. Martin (eds), *Managing Organizational Deviance* (pp. 183–204), Thousand Oaks, CA: Sage.

Zapf, D., and Einarsen, S. (2001). Bullying in the workplace: Recent trends in research and practice – an introduction. *European Journal of Work and Organizational Psychology,* 10, 369–73.

Zapf, D., and Einarsen, S. (2005). Mobbing at work: Escalated conflicts in organizations. In S. Fox and P. E. Spector (eds), *Counterproductive Work Behavior: Investigations of Actors and Targets* (pp. 237–70), Washington, DC: American Psychological Association.

Zapf, D., and Gross, C. (2001). Conflict escalation and coping with workplace bullying: A replication and extension. *European Journal of Work and Organizational Psychology,* 10, 497–522.

19

Strategies for Treating Bullies

Daniel S. Wells, Laura M. Crothers, and Jered B. Kolbert
Duquesne University

Renée M. Tobin
Illinois State University

Ara J. Schmitt
Duquesne University

INTRODUCTION

What can be done to address bullying in the workplace? Is it worthwhile to provide interventions for the perpetrator, the victim, or both? Is workplace bullying a larger systemic issue to be addressed beyond the individual or dyad? As discussed in earlier chapters, the workplace is a complex social environment with changing status relations, expectations, and politics. Negotiating bullying, like all interpersonal relations in this context, depends on multiple factors and levels within the ecological system, as discussed in Chapter 7, and not simply a particular individual or dyad. Similarly, interventions for workplace bullying may be addressed at different levels and with different methods within the organizational system.

Bullying in the workplace takes on many forms, from subtle to blatant, covert to overt, organizationally unnoticed to sanctioned, indirect to direct, inconsequential to destructive, physical to relational, and role-based to personal. Each of these aspects of workplace bullying contributes to the challenges of prevention and intervention in the workplace. The importance of addressing bullying in the workplace is clear as the deleterious effects of workplace bullying are numerous and significant. Victims report a range of negative consequences that cyclically affect both the individuals and the organization in terms of productivity and work climate. Effectively eliminating, or better yet preventing bullying in the workplace is therefore critical.

This chapter presents the extant literature regarding the significance of workplace bullying, reviews relevant theory and features of workplace bullying, and provides recommendations for the treatment of bullying behavior in the workplace. Interventions for workplace bullying are reviewed at the level of the individual, dyad, subgroup, and organization. Measures can be taken to prevent bullying through refined selection processes that help screen for aggressive behaviors. Once an individual has been hired for a position, direct feedback for any questionable behavior should be provided, coupled with limits and expectations for future behavior. Workplace bullying can also be reduced or eliminated through increased supervision and monitoring of the perpetrator's communications. Intervention strategies may likewise include changes to personnel assignments and resources. Furthermore, addressing workplace bullying can also draw on traditional psychological treatment methods such as psychoeducation and cognitive-behavioral techniques for both perpetrators and victims separately. Finally, mechanisms within the workplace, including performance appraisals, serve as an opportunity for organizations, managers, and coworkers to intervene in workplace bullying.

SIGNIFICANCE

Bullying in the workplace has been described as an epidemic (Namie, 2010). A Zogby International survey initiated by the Workplace Bullying Institute found that 35 percent of American workers have been bullied at work, while another 15 percent of workers have witnessed bullying in the workplace. Given these statistics regarding exposure to bullying, an estimated 53.5 million Americans have been bullied in the workplace (Namie, 2010). The victims of bullying have been shown to experience severe negative effects such as depression, decreased self-esteem, the development of post-traumatic stress disorder symptoms, as well as increased rates of alcohol abuse and suicide (Martin *et al.*, 2010).

Despite these wide-ranging effects, workplace leaders often find it unclear how to bring an end to bullying among those in the organization. Unfortunately, the individual who is being targeted is often left attempting to stop the bullying him- or herself. This scenario may be perpetuated by popular anti-bullying resources that recommend that victims confront the bully and simply tell that person to stop engaging in the harassment (Tyrell, 2012). However, research has demonstrated that these target-led interventions rarely work and often lead to that individual being revictimized, thus worsening the situation (Lutgen-Sandvik, 2006).

Due to the ineffective outcomes of directly confronting the bully, some victims will report the abuse to their supervisors, assuming that the supervisor is not the individual perpetrating the bullying behavior, or to the human resource (HR) department. However, merely reporting the presence of bullying typically results in little change in the unwanted behavior. Namie (2003) found that, when alerted to instances of workplace bullying, only 18 percent of bosses and 17 percent of HR departments did something helpful to stop the abuse. Counter to the expectations of the victim, after reporting the bullying, the reaction of 42 percent of bosses and 32 percent of HR departments resulted in an intensified bullying experience.

These statistics intuitively suggest that abused workers risk feeling helplessness and discouragement in the face of bullying. As the helplessness grows, individuals may feel justified in resorting to bullying behaviors themselves in an attempt to stop the harassment. In fact, some internet resources actually suggest this approach. One such site advises abused workers to "[dig] into the bully's past, including their personal life, [to] unearth some unsavory facts that the bully would prefer not to be made public" (Field, 2006b). Although the author admits that "under normal circumstances making these facts [known] might be considered unethical," if an individual is being bullied at work, the "circumstances are not normal."

This approach is not recommended, as research has found that the perpetuation of workplace bullying can institute a vicious cycle of abusive behavior. Samnani and Singh (2012) report that workplace bullies often report being victims of bullying themselves. This finding may indicate that bullying behaviors can be initiated as a form of revenge against the individual who began the bullying (Samnani and Singh, 2012). Alternatively, this may be an artifact of trickle-down aggression, whereby a middle manager is bullied by a boss or supervisor and in turn bullies those he or she supervises (Appelbaum *et al.*, 2012). Sutton (2007: 55) notes that exposure to aggressive individuals may cause an increase in the aggressive behavior of others. Consequently, workplace bullying should be viewed as "a contagious disease."

Effective interventions to stop workplace bullying are needed, given the rates of bullying and negative effects on individuals and the organization. Although some research has been devoted to the organizational antecedents of bullying, as well as to understanding the effects of bullying upon victims and on the organization as a whole, a limited amount of research has focused on predicting, identifying, and treating the perpetrators of bullying (Samnani and Singh, 2012).

RELEVANT THEORY

The first step in trying to understand the perpetrators of workplace bullying is to recognize what internal and situational factors might cause an individual to engage in instrumental aggression toward peers. One of the most basic considerations about an individual's aggressive behavior is whether the behavior is a result of a gene-based abnormality or organic brain injury. Some researchers have focused on the development and function of an aggressive individual's brain to see if physical abnormalities are associated with bullying behavior.

Harvey *et al.* (2006) list three of the most popular theories of the way in which brain function might impact bullying behavior. The first theory refers to decreased development of the frontal lobes, areas of the brain associated with being able to inhibit behavior and aggression. Individuals with these abnormalities often display decreased self-control and maturity, as well as diminished social judgment and tactfulness. A second reason for increased aggression and antisocial behavior is a gene mutation that affects the production of the enzyme monoamine oxidase-A (MAO-A), which is responsible for metabolizing several neurotransmitters in the brain. Third, those with an overdeveloped immune system have been found to be more aggressive than their peers.

These brain-based theories suggest that such individuals are "wired" toward aggression and that, without intervention, such individuals are not likely to change their behavior. At a minimum, training will be necessary that is devoted to the topics of controlling aggressive tendencies and practicing the use of pro-social interactions through role-playing. Such predispositions may be detected during pre-hiring interviews or through a thorough review of an individual's references. By training HR representatives to notice the signs of aggressive behavior, organizations may be able to identify potential bullies before they can enter the workplace, and eliminate them from a pool of applicants, an intervention discussed later in the chapter.

Just as brain-based theories suggest that individuals may be prone to aggression through hereditary or organic influences upon their neurological functioning, evolutionary and social dominance theories suggest that aggression, and bullying by extension, is likely inherent in human social interactions. Evolutionary theories of bullying propose that aggressive, dominating behaviors were adaptive for our ancestors because those who bullied were more likely to survive and thrive in the world; traits that were then passed to successive generations (Kolbert and Crothers, 2003). Social dominance theory argues that individuals are drawn to form social hierarchies within their peer groups. These hierarchies are necessary to maintain group order and protect the group from outside forces (Nishina, 2004).

Each of these theories assumes that there is an innate drive and desire for individuals to dominate and take control of their social interactions. Daniel (2006) compares a bully's perspective and goals in interpersonal relationships to the way in which a general or coach would think about a war or competitive game; the desire of the bully is to "win" or "dominate" in his or her social interactions. In order to combat this inclination, specific training in cooperation and team building skills may help individuals who bully become more capable of participating in a collaborative and helpful environment that organizations would likely wish to develop.

Other theories of bullying and aggression purport that bullies are not wired for such behavior, but rather bullies learned to display that behavior. Bandura's (1977) theory of social learning described how individuals learn through watching how other people are reinforced or punished for their behavior, also known as vicarious learning. Bandura posited that when an individual views a role model's actions resulting in positive outcomes, and believes that if he or she acts in the same way he or she too will be successful, that person will choose to act in that way.

Some studies have shown this learning by observing the development of aggressive behaviors. One such area of research focuses on the outcomes of individuals who were abused as children. In comparison to peers who were not abused, abused children have been shown to grow up to be more aggressive and more likely to abuse others (Harvey *et al.*, 2006). Similarly, Chan (2006) describes how aggressive behaviors tend to run in families, especially among siblings, as aggressive older siblings model bullying behavior to younger siblings, who in turn, bully others. In both cases, the development of aggressive behavior is thought to occur because these children are taught that interpersonal relationships are based on aggression and domination. Therefore, as adults entering the workforce, the individuals who have observed aggressive bullying behaviors and have seen those behaviors result in positive outcomes will likely conduct themselves similarly with peers or subordinates at work.

While these broad theories speak to the development of aggressive behavior and how an individual may learn or be predisposed to workplace aggression, there are also likely contributing factors in an organizational environment. Understanding the organizational antecedents to workplace bullying are valuable to managers in potentially recognizing potential bullies and where bullying may occur. Work situations that are high in role ambiguity, job insecurity, or place high demands and stress on the employees contribute to bullying in the workplace (De Cuyper *et al.*, 2009; Hauge *et al.*, 2011).

Another correlate to workplace bullying is best described by Field's (2006a) quotation, "those who can do, those who can't bully." There are several research studies that suggest that individuals may turn to bullying when they are threatened by or jealous of other workers' success in the workplace. Gardner and Johnson (2001) report that one reason an individual bullies is that he or she is jealous of the competence or skills of his or her target, while Strandmark and Hallberg (2007) note that those workers who are nominated as the most talented at their jobs experience higher rates of bullying than their less talented coworkers. By targeting the most talented, bullies can have an enormous impact upon the success of an organization. While managers should be concerned about bullying targets in their organization no matter their skills or position, the realization that this aggression is affecting the best and the brightest should only serve as a heightened incentive to stop peer victimization.

SALIENT FEATURES

A significant problem that organizations face in the attempt to reduce the rates and negative effects of workplace bullying is recognizing which kinds of behaviors constitute workplace bullying (LaVan and Martin, 2008). Labeling activities as bullying is difficult because there are many different ways a workplace bully may choose to cause harm to his or her selected target.

Types of Bullying

One type of bullying behavior is known as direct aggression. This occurs when the bully and the target are face to face and the target is immediately aware of the bullying taking place (Richardson and Green, 2006). Direct acts of bullying can be fairly obvious and are often observed by coworkers. Aggressive actions such as hitting and slapping, as well as physically intimidating behaviors such as invading personal space or pounding a desk, would all be examples of physical bullying in the workplace (De Cuyper *et al.*, 2009; Sutton, 2007). Even more common forms of direct workplace bullying are perpetrated verbally. Such actions as being yelled at, publicly humiliated, and personally insulted are examples of direct verbal bullying (Queensland Government, 2007; Tracy *et al.*, 2006). These behaviors are generally meant to damage the target's self-esteem or self-worth as the bully directly dominates the chosen individual.

Other types of bullying, such as social or relational aggression, are not as obvious to the victim and workplace observers. These behaviors are generally defined by their intended outcomes, which are to affect the target's individual peer relationships or standing in a larger peer group (Archer and Coyne, 2005; Crothers *et al.*, 2009). These actions can be committed overtly, such as when the target is given dirty looks, actively ignored, or is treated as if he or she does not exist (Queensland Government, 2007; Tracy *et al.*, 2006). Alternatively, a bully could choose to act covertly, involving such behaviors as gossiping about the target, excluding the target from important groups or meetings, and purposefully isolating the target from supportive peers (Hauge *et al.*, 2011; Hutchinson *et al.*, 2010). With these behaviors, a bully likely intends to isolate the victim, resulting in nowhere to turn for support until the victim chooses to submit to the bully's desires or leaves the organization.

While all of these behaviors can, and do, occur at work, much of the research regarding these types of aggression applies to situations outside of the work environment. However, there are examples of bullying behavior that are truly unique to the workplace. Hutchinson *et al.* (2010) mention two broad types of bullying behaviors that directly impact an individual's ability to function in the workplace. The first type of bullying is referred to as "erosion of professional competence and reputation" (p. 2323). A bully could choose to constantly question his or her target's abilities to do his or her job or withhold opportunities for training and development of skills that leaves the target belittled but also unprepared to seek work outside of the negative environment. The other broad type of bullying described is called "attack through work roles and tasks" (p. 2324). In perpetrating this type of victimization, bullies often place impossible demands on their targets, who are subsequently likely to fail, schedule the target to work unfair hours, or even remove necessary equipment that the target needs to perform his or her job. Understanding these workplace-specific bullying behaviors is likely to be important in identifying workplace bullying in an organization.

Causes of Workplace Bullying

Research suggests that workplace bullying develops from multiple causes, including both individual-related and work-related characteristics. Perpetrators are more likely to be male (e.g. De Cuyper *et al.*, 2009; Hauge *et al.*, 2009; Hershcovis *et al.*, 2007), and to be managers and supervisors more often than subordinates (e.g. Höel *et al.*, 2001). That being said, Scandinavian studies have typically found no difference between supervisors and subordinates in use of bullying in the workplace (e.g. Hauge *et al.*, 2009; Zapf *et al.*, 2003). The relationship between age and the rate of bullying perpetration is mixed, with some studies finding a negative relationship (e.g. De Cuyper *et al.*, 2009; Inness *et al.*, 2005), while other investigations identified no significant relationship between age and commission of workplace bullying (e.g. Glomb and Liao, 2003; Hauge *et al.*, 2009).

A variety of personality characteristics are associated with the perpetration of workplace bullying. Perpetrators are more likely to be socially dominant and score low in social desirability (Parkins *et al.*, 2006) and social competence (Einarsen *et al.*, 1994). Glaso *et al.* (2009) found that perpetrators were more likely to be domineering, cold, socially avoidant, vindictive, intrusive, more distrustful than non-victims, and less exploitable and overly nurturing than victims, leading the researchers to conclude that perpetrators are similar to sociopaths. Further highlighting the need for effective prevention and intervention, Hauge *et al.* (2009) found that being a victim was the strongest predictor of engaging in workplace bullying.

Bowling and Beehr (2006) conducted a meta-analysis of studies examining the environmental contributions of perpetration of workplace bullying. Role conflict and role ambiguity were found to be the strongest potential antecedents of workplace bullying. Role conflict refers to the simultaneous occurrence of two more sets of contradictory expectations. Role ambiguity derives from inadequate role-related information, resulting in a lack of understanding about responsibilities. In one of the few longitudinal studies of environmental contributions of workplace bullying conducted to date, Balducci *et al.* (2012) found that role stressors were a common antecedent to perpetration of workplace bullying. Similarly, Hauge *et al.* (2009: 355) found that role conflict predicted engagement in workplace bullying, concluding that role conflicts in the work environment produce tension in individuals which they project onto others in the work environment, and that targets of such projection respond in kind, resulting in a "spiraling effect from relative mild forms of uncivil behavior into increasingly more intense and aggressive behavior." As reviewed below, there are workplace factors that protect against bullying. For example, Hodson *et al.* (2006) analyzed 148 organizational ethnographies and concluded that coherent production procedures establish an environment in which bullying is unnecessary and not accepted.

TREATMENT APPROACHES FOR PERPETRATORS OF BULLYING

As with most behavioral problems, prevention of bullying appears to be the most effective way to manage peer victimization in the workplace. Prevention efforts include primary, proactive interventions such as establishing an anti-bullying culture (Bentley *et al.*, 2011; Duffy, 2009; Needham, 2003; Yamada, 2008) that facilitates a change in values, attitudes, verbal expressions, and ways of interacting (Bentley *et al.*, 2011; Cassitto *et al.*, 2004). Such a culture should include an authentic organizational commitment to culture change, effective education and policies, and attention to people and behavior. It is of utmost importance that senior managers or business owners act as role models and use open, honest, and mutually respectful communication (Bentley *et al.*, 2011; Yamada, 2008).

Furthermore, policies for workplace bullying should be developed. Anti-bullying policies should contain a definition of bullying, a statement of the organization's commitment to eliminating or reducing bullying, the duties of managers, a procedure by which complaints are handled, and the potential for disciplinary actions (Bentley *et al.*, 2011; Duffy, 2009; Holme, 2006; Pate and Beaumont, 2010; Rayner and Lewis, 2011; Vartia and Leka, 2011). Despite such fundamental primary intervention approaches, however, there will inevitably be a need for more reactive interventions to address the behaviors of workplace bullies, as more intractable perpetrators tend not to respond to low-intensity interventions.

Employee Selection Techniques

Avoiding the hiring of individuals who have a high potential to become bullies in the workplace is a first-line prevention strategy. As such, it is important to encourage Human Resource departments to use staff selection systems to screen out potential employees with undesirable traits or motives (Bentley *et al.*, 2011; Blackman and Funder, 2002; Fodchuck, 2007; Gardner and Johnson, 2001; Glendinning, 2001). However, such techniques should be evaluated for their potential for adverse and unintended consequences. Moreover, all selection methods should be related to the job in question and proven to be reliable and valid (Bentley *et al.*, 2011).

Notification and Sanctions

Once a bully has demonstrated aggression toward peers in the workplace, managers should inform him or her which behavior(s) is not acceptable, first verbally, and then in writing. In these discussions, a factual, non-blaming tone should be used. Prior to this meeting, the supervisor should have gathered objective evidence from victims and bystanders. Once this information has been assembled, the manager should begin the meeting with the identification of the bullying and the consequences of this behavior for the bully, since a straightforward delivery assures the employee that he or she will not be "trapped" into a lie by asking for his or her version of events (Crothers and Kolbert, 2008). At the end of the meeting, the supervisor should clearly state the next level of consequences for future bullying behaviors evidenced by the perpetrator, which may include termination from the job.

Increased Supervision and Changing of Job Responsibilities

Another step that should be taken once a bully has been identified is to increase the monitoring of his or her activities, which should be communicated directly to the perpetrator. Increased supervision may include monitoring of email and other forms of communication, verifying to the manager that meetings have been communicated in advance, with everyone being adequately notified, and notifying the perpetrator that gossip about or exclusion of colleagues will not be tolerated. Another supervisory intervention is to change the bully's job description to prevent future direct contact with likely victims in the organization. Such a change may include reducing the bully's supervision responsibilities while increasing the time these individuals spend without interacting with colleagues or subordinates (Harvey *et al.*, 2006).

Individual Treatment: Psychoeducation and Cognitive Behavioral Techniques

Supervisors should not assume that perpetrators of bullying are aware of what specific actions constitute bullying. Consequently, training should be provided to perpetrators to encourage increased awareness of bullying behavior and the consequence of these behaviors upon victims and colleagues. Additionally, although research has found that elements of cognitive behavioral therapy (specifically, a cognitive-rehearsal training program; Stagg *et al.*, 2011) have been helpful in assisting individuals in managing the problem of bullying in the workplace, the same technique may also be valuable in working with perpetrators. Programs can be developed in which bullies are presented with scenarios in which there are ambiguous interpersonal interactions that could potentially result in conflict. A coach can help to work with participants to alter irrational beliefs that may lead to aggressive behavior demonstrated toward peers, as well as encouraging perpetrators to gain insight into the impact of their behaviors upon victims and colleagues (Harvey *et al.*, 2006).

Performance Review

Once a bully has been identified in the workplace, he or she should expect frequent formative and summative performance reviews. These should include an evaluation of his or her behavior toward colleagues and subordinates. Formative assessment is used to provide feedback to the employee to guide improvements in his or her behavior on an ongoing basis. Conversely, summative assessment is used to measure the level of proficiency of the employee at the end of a prescribed amount of time, such as a quarterly or end-of-year review, by comparing his or her behavior to a set of standards. Summative evaluations should provide information that may lead to reinforcement of behavior (such as pay increases) that should be tied to the diminishment or elimination of bullying.

CONCLUSION AND SUMMARY

Workplace bullying is a growing concern within organizations. Bullying within the workplace is difficult to define, in part because it manifests in various forms. In terms of theory, bullying is commonly explained by general theories of aggression. That is, biological, social dominance, social learning, and evolutionary theories have been used to explain workplace bullying. These theories address the social, behavioral, physical, and cognitive aspects of bullying and help guide understanding of the behavior as well as subsequent treatment for it.

The treatment of these complex interpersonal conflicts can take many forms and may be implemented at different system levels, depending on the nature of the bullying. Methods of treatment may include utilizing traditional personnel evaluation mechanisms (e.g. written formal reprimands) as well as more psychological approaches (e.g. cognitive-behavioral therapy). Ideally, prevention efforts, such as creating an anti-bullying work climate, establishing clear policies to guide employee behavior, and providing positive role models within management, will reduce or eliminate the need for further intervention. Although there is not an abundance of research specifically examining the treatment of workplace bullying, the literature suggests that a combination of prevention, organizational management, and psychotherapeutic methods are well suited for these issues. Future research examining specific techniques for these behaviors within different work cultures would be a welcome addition and guide to organizations.

REFERENCES

Appelbaum, S. H., Semerjian, G., and Mohan, K. (2012). Workplace bullying: Consequences, causes and controls (Part one). *Industrial and Commercial Training*, 44, 203–10.

Archer, J., and Coyne, S. M. (2005). An integrated review of indirect, relational, and social aggression. *Personality and Social Psychology Review*, 9, 212–30.

Balducci, C., Cecchin, M., and Fraccaroli, F. (2012). The impact of role stressors on workplace bullying in both victims and perpetrators, controlling for personal vulnerability factors: A longitudinal analysis. *Work and Stress*, 26, 195–212.

Bandura, A. (1977). *Social Learning Theory*, Oxford: Prentice-Hall.

Bentley, T. A., Catley, B., Cooper-Thomas, H., Gardner, D., O'Driscoll, M. P., Dale, A., and Trenberth, L. (2011). Perceptions of workplace bullying in the New Zealand travel industry: Prevalence and management strategies. *Tourism Management*, 33, 351–60.

Blackman, M. C., and Funder, D. C. (2002). Effective interview practices for accurately assessing counterproductive traits. *International Journal of Selection and Assessment*, 10, 109–16.

Bowling, N. A., and Beehr, T. A. (2006). Workplace harassment from the victim's perspective: A theoretical model and meta-analysis. *Journal of Applied Psychology*, 9, 998–1112.

Cassitto, M. G., Fattorini, E., Gilloli, R., Rengo, C., and Gonik V. (2004). *Raising Awareness of Psychological Harassment at Work*, Geneva: World Health Organization.

Chan, J. H. F. (2006). Systemic patterns in bullying and victimization. *School Psychology International*, 27, 352–69.

Crothers, L. M., and Kolbert, J. B. (2008). Tackling a problematic behavior management issue: Teachers' interventions in childhood bullying problems. *Intervention in School and Clinic*, 43, 132–9.

Crothers, L. M., Lipinski, J., and Minutolo, M. C. (2009). Cliques, rumors, and gossip by the water cooler: Female bullying in the workplace. *Psychologist-Manager Journal*, 12, 97–110.

Daniel, T. A. (2006). Bullies in the workplace: A focus on the "abusive disrespect" of employees. Society for Human Resource Management White Paper. Retrieved from http://thepeoplegroup.com/wpcontent/uploads/2008/04/article-bullies-in-the-workplace1.pdf.

De Cuyper, N., Baillien, E., and De Witte, H. (2009). Job insecurity, perceived employability and targets' and perpetrators' experiences of workplace bullying. *Work and Stress*, 23, 206–24.

Duffy, M. (2009). Preventing workplace mobbing and bullying with effective organizational consultation, policies, and legislation. *Consulting Psychology Journal: Practice and Research*, 61, 242–62.

Einarsen, S., Raknes, B. I., and Matthiesen, S. B. (1994). Bullying and harassment at work and their relationships to work environment quality: An exploratory study. *European Work and Organizational Psychologist*, 4, 381–401.

Field, T. (2006a). Bullying at work. Bully OnLine. Retrieved from http://www.bullyonline.org/workbully.

Field, T. (2006b). The serial bully. Bully OnLine. Retrieved from http://www.bullyonline.org/workbully/serial.htm.

Fodchuk, K. M. (2007). Work environments that negate counterproductive behaviors and foster organizational citizenship: Research-based recommendations for managers. *Psychologist Manager Journal*, 10, 27–46.

Gardner, S., and Johnson, P. R. (2001). The leaner, meaner workplace: Strategies for handling bullies at work. *Employment Relations Today*, 28, 23–36.

Glaso, L., Nielsen, M. B., and Einarsen, S. (2009). Interpersonal problems among perpetrators and targets of workplace bullying. *Journal of Applied Social Psychology*, 39, 1316–33.

Glendinning, P. M. (2001). Workplace bullying: Curing the cancer of the American workplace. *Public Personnel Management*, 30, 269–86.

Glomb, T. M., and Liao, H. (2003). Interpersonal aggression in work groups: Social influence, reciprocal, and individual effects. *Academy of Management Journal*, 46, 486–96.

Harvey, M. G., Heames, J. T., Richey, R. G., and Leonard, N. (2006). Bullying: From the playground to the boardroom. *Journal of Leadership and Organizational Studies*, 12, 1–11.

Hauge, L. J., Skogstad, A., and Einarsen, S. (2009). Individual and situational predictors of workplace bullying: Why do perpetrators engage in the bullying of others? *Work and Stress*, 23, 349–58.

Hauge, L. J., Einarsen, S., Knardahl, S., Lau, B., Notelaers, G., and Skogstad, A. (2011). Leadership and role stressors as departmental level predictors of workplace bullying. *International Journal of Stress Management*, 18, 305–23.

Hershcovis, M. S., Turner, N., Barling, J., Arnold, K. A., Dupré, K. E., and Inness, M. (2007). Predicting workplace aggression: A meta-analysis. *Journal of Applied Psychology*, 74, 561–7.

Hodson, R., Roscigno, V. J., and Lopez, S. H. (2006). Chaos and the abuse of power: Workplace bullying in organizational and interactional context. *Work and Occupations*, 33, 382–416.

Höel, H., Cooper, C. L., and Faragher, B. (2001). The experience of bullying in Great Britain: The impact of organizational status. *European Journal of Work and Organizational Psychology*, 10, 443–65.

Holme, C. A. (2006). Impact not intent. *Industrial and Commercial Training*, 38, 242–7.

Hutchinson, M., Vickers, M. H., Wilkes, L., and Jackson, D. (2010). A typology of bullying behaviours: The experiences of Australian nurses. *Journal of Clinical Nursing*, 19, 2319–28.

Inness, M., Barling, J., and Turner, N. (2005). Understanding supervisor-targeted aggression: A within-person, between-jobs design. *Journal of Applied Psychology*, 90, 731–9.

Kolbert, J. B., and Crothers, L. M. (2003). Bullying and evolutionary psychology. *Journal of School Violence*, 2, 73–91.

LaVan, H., and Martin, W. M. (2008). Bullying in the U.S. workplace: Normative and process-oriented ethical approaches. *Journal of Business Ethics*, 83, 147–65.

Lutgen-Sandvik, P. (2006). Take this job and … : Quitting and other forms of resistance to workplace bullying. *Communication Monographs*, 73, 406–33.

Martin, W., Lopez, Y., and LaVan, H. (2010). What legal protections do victims of bullies in the workplace have? *Journal of Workplace Rights*, 14, 143–56. Retrieved from http://works.bepress.com/helen_lavan/5.

Namie, G. (2003). Workplace bullying: Escalated incivility. *Ivey Business Journal*, 68, 1–6.

Namie, G. (2010). *The WBI U.S. Workplace Bullying Survey,* Washington, DC: Workplace Bullying Institute and Zogby International.

Needham, A. A. (2003). *Workplace Bullying: The Costly Business Secret,* Auckland: Penguin Books.

Nishina, A. (2004). A theoretical review of bullying: Can it be eliminated? In C. E. Saunders and G. D. Phye (eds), *Bullying: Implications for the classroom* (pp. 36–62), San Diego, CA: Elsevier.

Parkins, I. S., Fishbein, H., and Ritchey, P. N. (2006). The influence of personality on workplace bullying and discrimination. *Journal of Applied Social Psychology*, 36, 2554–77.

Pate, J., and Beaumont, P. (2010). Bullying and harassment: A case of success? *Employee Relations*, 32, 171–83.

Queensland Government (2007). Employee assistance fact sheet: Workplace bullying. Organizational Health Unit, 1–2. Retrieved from http://education.qld.gov.au/health/pdfs/employee/ass-info1.pdf.

Rayner, C., and Lewis, D. (2011). Managing workplace bullying: The roles of policies. In S. Einarsen, H. Höel, D. Zapf, and C.L. Cooper (eds), *Bullying and Harassment in the Workplace: Developments in Theory, Research, and Practice* (2nd edn, pp. 327–40), Boca Raton, FL: CRC Press.

Richardson, D. S., and Green, L. R. (2006). Direct and indirect aggression: Relationships as social context. *Journal of Applied Social Psychology*, 36, 2492–508.

Samnani, A. K., and Singh, P. (2012). 20 years of workplace bullying research: A review of the antecedents and consequences of bullying in the workplace. *Aggression and Violent Behavior*, 17, 581–9.

Stagg, S. J., Sheridan, D., Jones, R. A., and Speroni, K. G. (2011). Evaluation of a workplace bullying cognitive rehearsal program in a hospital setting. *Journal of Continuing Education in Nursing*, 42, 395–403.

Strandmark, K. M., and Hallberg, L. R. M. (2007). The origin of workplace bullying: Experiences from the perspective of bully victims in the public service sector. *Journal of Nursing Management*, 15, 332–41.

Sutton, R. (2007). Building the civilized workplace. *McKinsey Quarterly*, 2, 47–55. Retrieved from http://www.changing-minds.eu/resources/bob+sutton+building+the+civilised+workplace.pdf.

Tracy, S. J., Lutgen-Sandvik, P., and Alberts, J. K. (2006). Nightmares, demons, and slaves: Exploring the painful metaphors of workplace bullying. *Management Communication Quarterly*, 20, 148–85.

Tyrell, M. (2012). How to handle a bully. Uncommon Knowledge. Retrieved from http://www.uncommon-knowledge.co.uk/articles/handle-bully.html.

Vartia, M., and Leka, S. (2011). Interventions for the prevention and management of bullying at work. In S. Einarsen, H. Höel, D. Dapf, and C. L. Cooper (eds), *Bullying and Harassment in the Workplace: Developments in Theory, Research, and Practice* (2nd edn, pp. 359–79), Boca Raton, FL: CRC Press.

Yamada, D. C. (2008). *Workplace Bullying and Ethical Leadership,* Legal Studies Research Paper Series, 08-37, Boston, MA: Suffolk University Law School.

Zapf, D., Einarsen, S., Höel, H., and Vartia, M. (2003). Empirical findings on bullying in the workplace. In S. Einarsen, H. Höel, D. Zapf, and C. L. Cooper (eds), *Bullying and Emotional Abuse in the Workplace: International Perspectives in Research and Practice* (pp. 103–26), London: Taylor & Francis.

20

Policies for Workplaces

David Hurlic
The Hurlic Group

Angela M. Young
California State University, Los Angeles

INTRODUCTION AND SIGNIFICANCE

The reality and scope of organizational bullying has been well documented over the past two decades (Adams, 1992; Field, 1996), but no formal policy or legal mandates to protect employees from bullying behavior have been instituted. Academic research finds that bullying exists on many levels (Roscigno *et al.*, 2009), is manifested in various behaviors (Escartín *et al.*, 2009), and cuts across many industrial sectors and geographic regions (Agervold and Mikkenlsen, 2004; Harvey *et al.*, 2007; Hume *et al.*, 2006; Randle, 2003). When combining the multifaceted environment of bullying with the operational challenges faced by organizations, the task of creating a comprehensive response to systemic bullying is daunting.

Given the importance of understanding and preventing bullying in the workplace, however, organizational leaders must pay attention to policy development and to developing an organizational context that prevents bullying behavior. Therefore, the focus of this chapter is twofold. First, we will describe the nature of bullying and define the specific bullying behaviors which establish the necessity of the foundation for developing useful anti-bullying policy. Second, information is presented to design an organizational context that is conducive to cooperative and productive relationships in which bullying is less likely to occur.

SALIENT FEATURES AND RELEVANT THEORY

Background

Recent research has demonstrated that bullying in the workplace is common in many organizations in the United States and that a large number of workers experience bullying (Cowen, 2011; Lutgen-Sandvik *et al.*, 2007; Salin, 2008). For example, Lutgen-Sandvik *et al.* (2007) discovered that almost 30 percent of workers surveyed stated that they had been bullied at least one time during their career. Bullying is not limited to organizations in the US, however, and researchers examining bullying in global organizations found that bullying is prevalent in many regions across the globe (Agervold and Mikkelsen, 2004; Harvey *et al.*, 2007, 2008). One study by Harvey *et al.* (2008) found that the multifaceted global business environment that has recently developed actually increases the opportunity for bullying to occur more frequently.

Much of the research on bullying links the occurrence of bullying to power. In a study by Roscigno *et al.* (2009), the researchers examined the connection between power and organizational chaos. Chaos, according to the authors, typically refers to a lack of organization and poor or inconsistent decision-making, which results in a general uncertainty that permeates the work environment. The authors concluded that power differentials and organizational context contributed to the likelihood that bullying behaviors would be exhibited by supervisors. Supervisors were found to be the most likely individuals to perpetrate bullying in the workplace because of their greater amount of power in the organization in comparison to general employees. Due to this tendency to bully those with less power, minorities and women often are bullied more frequently, as are other employees who may be perceived as lower in status and pay. These less powerful employees are at an even greater risk of being bullied when work areas are poorly supervised, as the authors show that bullying behavior is far more likely to occur in such environments (Roscigno *et al.*, 2009).

Even in light of these findings that indicate that bullying is a dangerous problem in many organizations, Cowen (2011) found that most organizations only scratched the surface of understanding how organizational communication and implementation of bullying policies could affect the rates of bullying in the workplace. For example, in a survey of HR professionals from 18 organizations, many respondents reported that their organizations had policies that addressed bullying. Yet a review of those organizational policies showed that there were no policies that referred to "bullying" specifically. An alarming pattern that Cowen noticed was that policies on anti-bullying were often developed by simply taking wording from other organizations' policies rather than developing a policy to fit the specific needs of their organization.

Given this tendency of organizations to be superficial and vague when it comes to their anti-bullying policies, where should an organization begin the process of developing and implementing a viable anti-bullying policy? Clearly, a policy specific to the organization that reflects the nature of that organization's work and environment is important, but even more than that, designing an organizational context that hinders bullying behavior and supports vulnerable employees is also needed. Hickling (2006) proposed a theoretical framework for understanding how organizations can establish a culture in which bullying in the workplace is not accepted. For example, Hickling's (2006) model identified various organizational activities to combat bullying, which include providing employees with social support and ensuring that anti-bullying policies are enforced. Hickling (2006) also noted several organizational antecedents that serve as precursors to workplace bullying. These antecedents primarily concern the specific situation in which bullying takes place and the general context or climate of the organization as a whole. Based on these findings, it is clear that organizations must address both the specific instances in which bullying is occurring and also the organizational climate at large that is responsible for allowing bullying behaviors to exist and persist.

Bullying Defined

Researchers agree that bullying is different from harassment because the negative behaviors are perpetrated indiscriminately and are not initiated as a consequence of a target's possible status as a "protected class" (Cowen, 2011; Randle *et al.*, 2007; Willborn *et al.*, 2007). The bullying behaviors themselves can consist of a wide range of behaviors, many of which are difficult to differentiate from personality or communication style. Because of the indiscriminate targets and unspecific behaviors, defining bullying is difficult and sometimes very problematic.

Terms such as bullying and harassment are subjective and can be based on each individual's values and experiences. Randle *et al.* (2007: 50), citing Adams (1992), define workplace bullying as "persistent criticism and personal abuse in public or private, which acts to either humiliate or demean the person." Field (1996) labels bullies as psychopaths and states that bullies are typically male who tend to engage in behavior that is physically and verbally aggressive. Often, bullies lack social sensitivity and appropriate interpersonal skills (Hickling, 2006). Cowen (2011) identifies employee bullying by five characteristics of communication: (1) extreme and intense, (2) persistent and prolonged, (3) resulting in harmful effects, (4) perceived as intentional, and (5) perceived as a behavior against which victims cannot defend themselves.

With little legal guidance for employers to rely upon, a formal anti-bullying policy can be difficult to develop and implement. However, it is likely that bullying behaviors in the workplace will be addressed more formally through the Occupational Safety and Health Association (OSHA) in the future, which may provide a more structured and consistent framework from which to develop policy. In fact, in OSHA's *Field Safety and Health Manual* for its own employees, bullying behavior and anti-bullying policy is presented in chapter 10 on workplace violence (Occupational Safety and Health Association, 2011).

The difficulty of formally addressing bullying behavior comes from the many variations in human communication, both verbal and nonverbal, that can be perceived as intimidating or belittling. Gross acts of violence or a threat can easily be identified, but often perpetrators lurk in solitude and cloak themselves in polite interaction. Similarly, harassment of protected-class employees can be overt, obvious, and even systematic within organizations, and therefore easily discovered and proved. However, discriminatory decisions or interactions with unprotected employees may take place in front of peers or managers without any visible indication that something more insidious is happening. Therefore, having a clear definition that encompasses all types of employees and possible aggressive behaviors is important in being able to develop relevant anti-bullying policies.

RECOMMENDATIONS

Developing an Anti-Bullying Policy

From previous research, the first step in developing an anti-bullying policy should be to establish an agreement among organizational leaders about the state of the workplace and what behaviors constitute bullying. The message the organization wants to send about its level of tolerance needs to be clearly agreed upon and understood. This is the time to broaden the view of leadership and involve representatives from Human Resource, legal counsel, and top managers but also to involve employees and supervisors who will be closest to the daily implementation of the policy. Time spent developing an understanding of bullying and obtaining top management support and input from all levels of employees in the organization will serve well the implementation of the policy.

Once organizational leaders understand and agree upon the best means of describing bullying behaviors in the workplace, a formal anti-bullying policy can be developed. The policy should be written to include a clear statement of the organization's stand on bullying behavior and a concrete description of what constitutes bullying and what does not. While an exhaustive list of behaviors is impossible, illustrative explanations of types of behaviors that are inappropriate should be included. Keeping Cowen's (2011) five characteristics of bullying behavior in mind may serve as a framework from which to describe scenarios or behaviors that are: (1) extreme and intense, (2) persistent and prolonged, (3) resulting in harmful effects, (4) perceived as intentional, and (5) perceived as a behavior against which victims cannot defend themselves. Using language that is as precise as possible and fitting the organization's specific environment and organizational makeup will help to make the policy understandable, clear, and enforceable.

The process by which the policy will be implemented and the specific steps that a victim should take and to whom to report bullying should also be clearly defined. Listing such information as whom employees should contact first, subsequent steps, and likely outcomes of the process should show everyone, from managers to low-level employees, that bullying will not be tolerated and that the victim has the power to make the abuse stop. As with complaints of harassment, supervisors are typically the first contact, but if the victim's supervisor is the alleged bully, which is often the case, a secondary contact should be identified. The procedures for reporting incidents of bullying and investigating situations should be consistent and well-defined. Information and reports should be gathered from as many relevant and involved sources as possible. As with harassment claims, human resource managers are typically responsible for such investigations, with the cooperation of the supervisor and other relevant employees.

Consequences of engaging in bullying should also be clearly spelled out and relevant and appropriate for the bullying offenses. Again, following processes used in harassment cases, training and education of bullies may be enough to stop them from targeting others. In more extreme cases, however, disciplinary actions are necessary and those consequences should be clearly outlined and enforced. Policy without consequences is not effective, but consequences that are never enforced are equally pointless.

With a formal policy on bullying in place, organizational leaders have a better chance of making change throughout the organization. However, even with the best policies in place, nothing in the workplace can change without day-to-day leadership and supervisory practices that support the policy.

Developing a Supportive Organizational Context

Research has shown the vital importance of the organizational context in developing a culture that prevents bullying and supports cooperative and productive behavior. An organizational context is described differently by various researchers, but typically refers to one or more of the multitude of factors, both internal and external, that influence organizations. For example, Cox (2001) identified and defined various internal factors that influence organizational success. Such concepts include aspects of positive leadership, providing employee education, developing plans to measure the level of success of organizational policies and progress towards goals, designing different policies and practices that are clear and align with stated goals, and conducting follow-up procedures regarding proposed initiatives.

Using the work of Cox (2001), Hurlic (2009) developed a streamlined description of organizational context and applied it to managing diversity in organizations. Hurlic's description can be applied to the design of an anti-bullying context in the organization and includes the aspects of leadership, alignment, and follow up as described by Cox (2001). The organization's effort to manage and influence the perceptions and behaviors of employees is found to be most successful when these factors are well managed and serve as the process by which the organization can develop an environment that is intolerant of bullying.

Leadership

The term leadership in this case casts a wide net and applies to many members of the organization holding responsibility for planning and implementing change. For example, researchers specifically identify leadership as impacting management's philosophy, organizational vision, or mission, and the overall communication strategy (Loden and Rosener, 1991; Northouse, 2010; Ulrich *et al.*, 1999). Granted, individual leadership is important with regards to initiating organizational change, but attributing all outcomes to one person's efforts is not realistic. A single person may be able to develop a broad level of awareness of the importance of an anti-bullying program, but moving beyond the awareness stage into the development and implementation of an anti-bullying program and policy takes the work of many (Randle *et al.*, 2007).

In essence, a collaborative effort is required among all organizational leaders, including supervisors, project managers, executives, and anyone else who may guard against bullying behavior. Loden and Rosener (1991) label the collaborative process of leadership as pluralistic leadership. Pluralistic leadership relies on the empowerment and involvement of employees and assumes that the organization's culture must view bullying as a true threat to the whole organization. This perspective of pluralistic leadership is vital to the process of creating the type of culture needed to combat workplace bullying.

One class of individuals in the prime position to demonstrate pluralistic leadership is the supervisor. The supervisor is in a particularly powerful role when it comes to enforcing bullying policy. The supervisor not only sets an example of acceptable behavior but also encourages specific behaviors either through active management or passively allowing behaviors to continue. Much of the behavior that occurs in the workplace can be attributed to supervisory style. First, the supervisor must make it very clear that he or she supports the bullying policy and intends to fully enforce the policy. Furthermore, the supervisor must commit to not using hazing, bullying, or uncivil behaviors themselves. Second, the supervisor must act quickly and decisively if an occurrence of bullying occurs. If a supervisor sees or knows of bullying behavior, or even the presence of antecedent behaviors, there must be quick action and investigation into the situation.

Sexual harassment policy and protocols give a great deal of background information regarding the best ways to address such a problem both through investigation and, depending upon the policy, the involvement of human resource representatives. Fast and decisive action will increase the likelihood that any unacceptable behaviors are stopped and will demonstrate to others in the organization that the policies will be enforced. This type of action by the supervisors will make it more acceptable for employees to report bullying and more difficult for individuals to think that bullying will be tolerated.

While supervisors play an integral role in preventing bullying, leaders beyond supervisory roles such as division managers, directors, vice presidents, and chief executives must also be supportive of an anti-bullying policy. This support from upper management will demonstrate that stopping bullying is important to all those in the organization and will set an important example for all other employees to follow. There will be very little importance placed upon policy that does not apply to all supervisors and other leaders in the organizations. Upper management will also want to support the direct supervisors because it is they who often have to take on the uncomfortable role of dealing with bullies, ensuring civility, calming feelings, and managing conflict.

Alignment

The idea that organizational attributes, decisions, and actions must be aligned with an organization's policies is a central focus of basic organizational theory (Daft, 2009). For example, Hickling (2006) identifies actions that organizations can implement to mitigate bullying, including creating a culture of tolerance, developing social support networks, and ensuring that organizational policies are enforced. By ensuring that these changes occur in the organizations, workers will see that company policies and actions align and they will feel safe to work to the best of their abilities. Additional areas that organizations need to make sure that policy aligns with practice include performance appraisal systems (Randle *et al.*, 2007), and employee training programs (Glendinning, 2001; Sheehan, 1999). For example, Randle *et al.* (2007) discuss the importance of defining clear roles and goals for work performance that reflect the true nature of each individual's work and accurately recognize individuals' contributions to the organization. This clarity and precision will help leaders to develop anti-bullying policies that are relevant to the organization and make policy implementation more successful.

Aligning the organization's practices with defined policy is important and necessary to make long-lasting change. There are many mechanisms within almost every organization that can be used to implement behaviors and encourage attitudes that support an anti-bullying policy. Three specific means by which organizational leaders can implement changes necessary to adhere to policy are explained and include socialization, training, and performance appraisals.

Socialization

During the first phase of employment, a new employee learns formally about the organization and more informally about accepted norms of behaviors. Choosing to use more formal, overt methods of communication is the more efficient and effective way to educate new employees about the organization rather than having them try to piece together opinions and ideas from multiple sources in the organization (Finkelstein *et al.*, 2003). During early socialization, employees will accept, to varying extents, the organizational culture and accepted norms of behavior. Employee orientation is the typical point at which new employees learn about formal organizational policies. This is a good starting point to explain the bullying policy and speak about its enforcement. As new employees may very well be the target of bullying behaviors, it is extremely important that newly hired staff members know what behaviors constitute bullying and with whom they can speak if they do begin to experience being bullied. However, if peers and supervisors already present in the organization do not model the appropriate behaviors and enforce company policies, then very little importance will be attached to what is learned in employee orientation. An effective means of continuing and supporting what is learned in employee orientation is ongoing training.

Training

Training on bullying policy is important for current employees and particularly important for all supervisory staff. Direct training on anti-bullying strategies, unacceptable behaviors, and protocols for action if a problem does occur is necessary to ensure that everyone knows how to enact the bullying policy. Supervisors in particular must know how to interpret and enact the policy and therefore supervisor training on bullying should be a focus of organizations. Above all, supervisor behavior must be beyond reproach when it comes to civility and professionalism in the workplace. A supervisor who bullies will undermine all policy and waste all the money spent on training, but supervisors who lack effective communication skills and a generally professional demeanor can just as easily dismantle efforts to create a civil, bully-free workplace. Therefore, it is also important to address supervisory skills independent of bullying training.

As discussed earlier, the leadership in the organization, including supervisors as the frontline of leadership, must have generally effective supervisory skills to ensure that the environment itself does not incite or encourage attitudes and feelings that may precede bullying. Supervisors, therefore, need specific training and effective supervision themselves to prevent creating an environment that may incite or encourage bullying behaviors. Further training on the specific anti-bullying policy and appropriate responses to reported incidents is also necessary. As with all training, one-off training will introduce the issue to staff, but ongoing, repeated training is more effective in changing behaviors over the long-run. Training may not need to be repeated at a specific time interval unless it becomes legally mandated, but certainly repeated opportunities to remind supervisors of their important role in enforcing bullying policy and engaging in effective supervision is necessary.

Performance Appraisals

Many performance appraisals used in organizations already include some aspect of communication effectiveness or getting along with others. If specific behaviors are extremely important, then the performance appraisal process is the mechanism by which organizations measure and reward those behaviors. If adhering to organizational policy is indeed a behavior that is deemed important, then one strategy is to include some aspect of measuring that behavior in the performance appraisal, particularly for supervisors. At the very least, bullying behaviors and working to prevent bullying in the workplace can be incorporated as a part of teamwork, leadership, or communication style measures.

Follow Up and Revision

The final aspect of organizational context is follow-up, or how management responds to incidents, questions, activities, and behaviors after implementation of the policy or program. Based on the research of Cowen (2011), organizational leaders must ensure that all communication, formal and informal, conveys the idea that anti-bullying measures are essential to the organization's success and will be acted upon. This means the establishment of channels that victims can use to lodge their complaints. Additionally, companies must educate employees about workplace policies regarding bullying to which individuals can refer and follow.

Finally, organizations must have in place a system that tracks the frequency of workplace bullying and develops a system to communicate those results openly and honestly. It is likely that employees are well aware of the climate in a department but by seeing that organizational leaders are aware of the workplace climate and are committed to upholding anti-bullying measures sends a powerful message that the company takes anti-bullying policy seriously and may build trust among employee groups (Loden, 1996). Accurate assessment of anti-bullying policy implementation also gives organizations valuable information to guide future strategy and improve specific programs.

Anti-bullying policies will need revision over time, as most policies do. Careful reporting and analysis of incidents and how supervisors and other organizational leaders dealt with them is a good start in formulating what revisions should be made. Careful monitoring of the legal climate for likely inclusion of more formal legal guidelines and regulation on bullying behavior in the workplace may also encourage policy revision. Those people deemed responsible for managing the policy should be attentive to all possible forms of feedback and initiate discussions among organizational leaders and general employees to see if revision is necessary. Several mechanisms, such as training feedback, employee surveys, exit interviews, and other more informal information sources are already in place in organizations and are potential sources of useful feedback to monitor the effectiveness of the anti-bullying policy and identify needed revisions.

After most organizational training, employees are given an opportunity to provide feedback on both the training content and the administration of the training. For all training, including anti-bullying education, employees can be surveyed about the value of the information. Both quantitative measures and qualitative responses can be obtained, and organizational leaders may find a great deal of valuable information through a brief survey or simple open-ended questions such as "What other topics should be included in this training?".

Beyond specific post-training survey questions, periodic employee surveys that are anonymously collected may identify not only potential areas for improvement in workplace climate but also perceptions of current anti-bullying policy. Suggested items to include in employee surveys include not only questions regarding whether or not an employee is aware of the anti-bullying policy, but also whether or not the employee perceives that bullying is currently occurring to either self or others. Also suggested are questions about whether or not organizational leaders support and enforce the current bullying policy.

Employees may withhold information on post-training surveys or anonymous employee surveys if there is any fear that they may be identified. However, surveys or interviews at the end of an employee's career may identify issues that the employee may not be willing to share otherwise (Bullivent and West, 2006). While there is no guarantee that information will be given, exit surveys via mail or in person after an employee gives notice may provide additional information on awareness of anti-bullying policy, bullying behaviors in the workplace, and perceived support and enforcement of anti-bullying policy by organizational leaders.

Formal methods of data collection, such as historical records based on incidents of alleged bullying, post-training surveys, anonymous employee surveys, and exit surveys may provide some useful information, but there are other, more informal methods that may also provide valuable information. Supervisors should have an awareness of the workplace climate, how employees treat each other, and how customers and employees interact. This, of course, is done best by someone present in the workplace environment and who has keen observation skills. Depending upon the climate created by organizational leaders, employees should be invited to speak openly about many topics through an open-door policy, town-hall meetings, or direct contact with a human resource representative.

Faking Follow Up

Often, organizational leaders will want to present an image of propriety; therefore, policies are written and training is delivered but then nothing is enforced. Sometimes, leaders have good intentions and want to enact change, but when negative feedback comes their way, it is dismissed. It is extremely important for organizational leaders to make an anti-bullying climate a priority and let all levels of employees know that bullying is not to be tolerated. Organizational leaders must be open to upward critical information, which is information that is not favorable to a leader but can be extremely useful in enacting real change (Tourish and Robson, 2006).

It is likely that bullying behavior will continue to receive more attention, not just from academic researchers but from governmental regulatory agencies, lawyers, and disgruntled employees. If not for reasons of health and productivity, organizational leaders should pay attention to workplace climate for the harmful and costly legal consequences that might result from a poorly managed situation of bullying.

CONCLUSION AND SUMMARY

Bullying in the workplace has gained more recognition as a hindrance to productivity and a cause of a dysfunctional organizational culture. Although there is little that organizational leaders can do about the personalities of individuals, there is a great deal leaders can do to develop a culture of acceptable and productive behaviors in their organization. Developing an effective policy on bullying in the workplace is a good starting point to develop a culture of civility, but requires a great deal of support from all leaders in the organization. Once developed, an effective bullying policy can be supported through many mechanisms within the organization, including socialization processes, training, performance appraisals, and leader enforcement. With more emphasis on bullying, a more productive and functional workplace environment may emerge.

REFERENCES

Adams, A. (1992). *Bullying at Work: How to Confront and Overcome it,* London: Virago Press.

Agervold, M., and Mikkelsen, E. G. (2004). Relationships between bullying, psychosocial work environment and individual stress reactions. *Work and Stress*, 18, 336–51.

Bullivent, D., and West, T. (2006). A case study approach. In J. Randle (ed.), *Workplace Bullying in the NHS* (pp. 47–61), Oxford: Radcliffe Publishing.

Cowen, R. L. (2011). "Yes, we have an anti-bullying policy, but ... ": HR professionals' understandings and experiences with workplace bullying policy. *Communication Studies,* 62, 307–27.

Cox, T. (2001). *Creating the Multicultural Organization: A Strategy for Capturing the Power of Diversity,* San Francisco, CA: Jossey-Bass.

Daft, R. L. (2009). *Organization Theory and Design* (10th edn), Mason, OH: South-Western Cengage Learning.

Escartín, J., Rodríguez-Carballeira, A., Zapf, D., Porrúa, C., and Martín-Peña, J. (2009). Perceived severity of various bullying behaviours at work and the relevance of exposure to bullying. *Work and Stress,* 23, 191–205.

Field, T. (1996). *Bully in Sight: How to Predict, Resist, Challenge and Combat Workplace Bullying,* Oxford: Success Unlimited.

Finkelstein, L. M., Kulas, J. T., and Dages, K. D. (2003). Age differences in proactive newcomer socialization strategies in two populations. *Journal of Business and Psychology,* 17, 473–502.

Glendinning, P. M. (2001). Workplace bullying: Curing the cancer of the American workplace. *Public Personnel Management,* 30, 269–86.

Harvey, M., Treadway, D. C., and Heames, J. T. (2007). The occurrence of bullying in global organizations: A model and issues associated with social/emotional contagion. *Journal of Applied Social Psychology,* 37, 2576–99.

Harvey, M., Treadway, D., Heames, J. T., and Duke, A. (2008). Bullying in the 21st century global organization: An ethical perspective. *Journal of Business Ethics,* 85, 27–40.

Hickling, K. (2006). Workplace bullying. In J. Randle (ed.), *Workplace Bullying in the NHS* (pp. 17–24), Oxford: Radcliffe Publishing.

Hume, C., Randle, J., and Stevenson, K. (2006). Student nurses' experience of workplace relationships. In J. Randle (ed.), *Workplace Bullying in the NHS* (pp. 7–24), Oxford: Radcliffe Publishing.

Hurlic, D., (2009). Diversity congruency within organizations: The relationship among emotional intelligence, personality structure, ethnic identity, organizational context and perceptions of organizational diversity, unpublished doctoral dissertation, Pepperdine University, Los Angeles, CA.

Loden, M. (1996). *Implementing Diversity,* Boston, MA: McGraw Hill.

Loden, M., and Rosener, J. B. (1991). *Workforce America! Managing Employee Diversity as a Vital Resource,* New York: McGraw Hill.

Lutgen-Sandvik, P., Tracy, S. J., and Alberts, J. K. (2007). Burned by bullying in the American workplace: Prevalence, perception, degree and impact. *Journal of Management Studies,* 44, 837–62.

Northouse, P. G. (2010). *Leadership: Theory and Practice* (5th edn), Thousand Oaks, CA: Sage.

Occupational Safety and Health Administration (2011). Violence in the workplace. *OSHA Field Safety and Health Manual* (pp. 10-1–10-6), Washington, DC: U.S. Department of Labor. Retrieved from http://op.bna.com/env.nsf/id/sbra-8hdrfp/$File/OSHA percent20manual.pdf.

Randle, J. (2003). Bullying in the nursing profession. *Journal of Advanced Nursing*, 43, 395–401.

Randle, J., Stevenson, K., and Grayling, I. (2007). Reducing workplace bullying in healthcare organisations. *Nursing Standard*, 21, 49–56.

Roscigno, V. J., Lopez, S. H., and Hodson, R. (2009). Supervisory bullying, status inequalities and organizational context. *Social Forces*, 87, 1561–89.

Salin, D. (2008). The prevention of workplace bullying as a question of human resource management: Measure adopted and underlying organizational factors. *Scandinavian Journal of Management*, 24, 221–31.

Sheehan, M. (1999). Workplace bullying: Responding with some emotional intelligence. *International Journal of Manpower*, 20, 57–69.

Tourish, D., and Robson, P. (2006). Sensemaking and the distortion of critical upward communication in organizations. *Journal of Management Studies*, 43, 711–30.

Ulrich, D., Zenger, J., and Smallwood, N. (1999). *Results-Based Leadership: How Leaders Build the Business and Improve the Bottom Line,* Boston, MA: Harvard Business School Press.

Willborn, S. L., Schwab, S. J., and Burton, J. F. (2007). *Employment Law: Cases and Materials,* Danvers, MA: Lexis-Nexis.

21

Legal Issues: The Role of Law in Addressing Bullying in the Workplace

Susan Harthill
Florida Coastal School of Law

INTRODUCTION

This chapter explores the role of law in addressing workplace bullying by summarizing existing labor and employment laws that potentially apply to claims of workplace bullying, and by examining various legal proposals aimed at deterring bullying behavior and providing legal redress for aggrieved individuals. In addition to exploring existing and proposed federal and state laws in the United States, selected comparative experiences of other countries are reviewed with the aim of drawing lessons for the role of law in the United States. This chapter will also briefly review the potential role for self-governance initiatives, such as internal company or union-initiated policies addressing workplace bullying.

The American workplace is regulated by hundreds of federal, state, and local labor and employment laws. There are, however, no federal or state laws expressly addressing workplace bullying, despite the growing body of national and international interdisciplinary work highlighting the prevalence, causes, and costs of this phenomenon (Cascio, 2000; Einarsen *et al.*, 2003).

Although several state legislatures have introduced anti-workplace bullying legislation, called the Healthy Workplace Bill, none has yet enacted the bill (Yamada, 2000).[1] Moreover, even when one or more states do enact the Healthy Workplace Bill, uniform nationwide remedies will remain elusive for many years to come in the absence of legislation at the federal level. In contrast, several countries have adopted varying legal approaches to combat the problem of workplace bullying. Some countries, such as France, have enacted specific workplace bullying legislation, while other countries have applied existing legislation to combat the problem (French Social Modernization Law, 2002; Höel and Einarsen, 2010). Courts in the United Kingdom have applied an anti-stalking law to workplace bullying cases, and some Australian and Canadian provinces, Sweden, Norway, and Finland have revised their existing occupational safety and health laws (Protection from Harassment Act, 1997; Occupational Health and Safety Act, 2007).[2] Thus, the United States lags behind several European countries, and a growing number of Australian and Canadian provinces, in terms of legal reform or use of existing regulatory frameworks and self-governance initiatives.

SIGNIFICANCE

In addition to providing post-harm remedial relief for targets, the prophylactic importance of legislation cannot be underestimated. Numerous overlapping and interlocking federal and state labor and employment laws have played a significant role in improving workplace conditions, safeguarding employee rights, and governing relationships between employer and employee, and between co-workers. Workplace laws effectuate change and ensure societally acceptable working conditions in several ways. First and perhaps most importantly, labor and employment laws incentivize employers to provide a safe and healthy working environment by providing civil, and sometimes criminal, penalties for noncompliance. Although some employment laws limit enforcement to government agencies, many laws provide concurrent private causes of action whereby an aggrieved employee can recover equitable or monetary relief for harm caused by a violation of the law.

The Occupational Safety and Health Act (OSHA) is an example of a federal law that provides for civil and criminal penalties enforced by the federal government, but does not provide any private cause of action

(OSHA, 2006). In contrast, the key anti-discrimination law, Title VII of the Civil Rights Act of 1964, provides for both government and private causes of action with compensatory and injunctive relief (Title VII, 2006). Workplace laws that provide a private cause of action obviously operate to compensate aggrieved individuals in addition to providing employer incentives to comply with the law.

Furthermore, although scholars debate whether norms influence laws, or laws influence norms, self-governance initiatives may be triggered as a response to legislation or pending legislation; and workplace laws do play an important role in setting workplace norms, which can aid in attaining the prophylactic goals of the applicable law (Ellickson, 1991; McAdams, 1997; Sunstein, 1996: Harthill, 2010). Interestingly, a majority of American workers believe that there *should* be a remedy under US law for bullying in the workplace (Employment Law Alliance, 2007).

Thus, it is to be expected that federal or state labor and employment laws may be a significant resource in preventing workplace bullying, changing workplace norms, and providing redress for aggrieved employees. Employers in the United States pay attention to potential legal claims that can be brought by or on behalf of aggrieved workers. Major advances in workers' rights are typically obtained in the United States through federal congressional intervention – Title VII of the Civil Rights Act of 1964 being a prime example. Yet, despite the significant role that legislation could play in the battle against workplace bullying, none of the innumerable laws that currently govern the workplace address the phenomenon.

Legislative responses to the problem in other countries may be instructive for law reform efforts in the United States. Comparative legal scholars have described developments in Sweden, Germany, France, Quebec, and the European Union, but have expressed doubt that the European model can be exported to the United States (Guerrero, 2004; Symposium, 2004; Yuen, 2005). These commentators do not regard the European model as exportable largely because they view European anti-bullying laws as based on a historical continental tradition of recognizing individual dignity, which is absent from the US model of workplace harassment law; the US model is based on equal treatment for historically disadvantaged minority groups (Guerrero, 2004; Symposium, 2004; Yuen, 2005). Nevertheless, not all anti-bullying laws are grounded in a dignitarian tradition; the United Kingdom's anti-stalking law and development of occupational safety and health laws in other countries may provide fruitful guidance (Harthill, 2008, 2011).

RELEVANT THEORY AND SALIENT FEATURES

Private and public sector American workers are protected by a complex system of overlapping and complementary federal and state employment laws. Professor David Yamada was the first US legal scholar to explore the legal landscape and identify the deficiencies in existing legal theories to combat workplace bullying, including Title VII of the Civil Rights Act of 1964, the National Labor Relations Act (NLRA), the Occupational Safety and Health Act (OSHA), and the Americans with Disabilities Act (ADA), as well as the common law doctrine of intentional infliction of emotional distress (Yamada, 2000). Professor Yamada (2004) adopted the definition of bullying from Drs Gary and Ruth Namie, co-founders of the Workplace Bullying and Trauma Institute, as the "repeated, malicious, health-endangering mistreatment of one employee . . . by one or more employees" (as cited in Namie and Namie, 2003: 3). Following Yamada's groundbreaking work, the Workplace Bullying Institute has worked with grassroots campaigners at the state level to introduce the Healthy Workplace Bill in numerous states, although no state has passed the bill to date.

Federal, state, and local laws prohibit harassment as a form of employment discrimination but these laws only prohibit harassment that is attributable to an employee's protected characteristic such as race, sex, religion, age, disability.[3] The law of sexual harassment under Title VII of the Civil Rights Act of 1964, for example, is well developed. Employers may be held vicariously liable for supervisor harassment of a subordinate if the harassment is because of sex and is "severe or pervasive" (Burlington Indus. v. Ellerth, 1998; Faragher v. City of Boca Raton, 1998). This same liability extends to harassment if the relevant statutory criteria are met, again provided the harassment is because of the target's protected characteristic of sex, race, religion, national origin, age, or disability. Furthermore, the Supreme Court's jurisprudence regarding defenses to employer liability encourages employers to implement workplace harassment policies and procedures, but since non-status-based harassment is not actionable under these laws, employers are not incentivized to include workplace bullying in their policies (Burlington Indus. v. Ellerth, 1998: Faragher v. City of Boca Raton, 1998).

Other statutory laws may also provide redress for aggrieved employees but under limited circumstances (Yamada, 2000). The federal labor law, the National Labor Relations Act (NLRA), 2006, protects workers' rights to collectively organize and collectively bargain (Yamada, 2000). Unfortunately, the NLRA is of limited utility because it excludes many workers from coverage, such as independent contractors and managerial workers, and the nature of most bullying activity does not lead to workers taking collective action solutions (Yamada, 2000). Nevertheless, unions can take and have taken a proactive role in developing anti-bullying policies, discussed below.

State common law causes of action may offer some hope in theory, but in practice no realistic recourse. The most promising common law theory for a bullying target to pursue is the tort of intentional infliction of emotional distress, which typically imposes liability in the following circumstances:

> One who by extreme and outrageous conduct intentionally or recklessly causes severe emotional distress to another is subject to liability for such emotional distress, and if bodily harm to the other results from it, for such bodily harm.
>
> (Restatement Second of Torts, 1965, Section 46)

In practice, however, the requisite threshold of "outrageous" conduct has been interpreted by courts to require an extreme and egregious level of conduct that most plaintiffs cannot demonstrate (Yamada, 2000). Yamada's analysis of cases demonstrated that this requirement has proven to be too high a hurdle for most workplace bullying claimants to overcome (Yamada, 2000). Yamada's case law review further evidenced that courts denied relief for workplace bullying targets on the grounds that "the employee did not suffer severe emotional distress" (Yamada 2000: 494). Another deficiency with this tort is that liability does not typically extend to the employer under either traditional *respondeat superior* or more recently developed negligent hire theories (Harthill, 2008). Additionally, liability premised on a speaking tort may infringe on the speaker's free speech rights, although this implication has not been fully developed by the courts (Coleman, 2006; Knechtle, 2006).

Because the likelihood of success is low, most potential causes of action are unattractive to plaintiffs' lawyers. In addition, the potential for large damages in workplace bullying cases awards is also probably quite low. Attorneys frequently rely on contingency fees, where the plaintiff pays them a percentage of any recovery, and since damages awards are uncertain and likely to be low even if the plaintiff is successful, attorneys who typically represent employees are less likely to take on such precarious representation.

Thus, despite the existence of workplace laws that superficially appear to apply to workplace bullying, there is a gap in the law. Legal scholars have suggested several solutions, starting with the campaign for a new federal or state status-blind law, modeled on the federal anti-discrimination laws (Yamada, 2000). Yamada drafted the Healthy Workplace Bill to fill the gap in existing legislation and the Workplace Bullying Institute has been a major instrumental force in introducing this bill at the state level – the bill has been introduced in almost half of the US states and will undoubtedly be enacted at some point.[4] Yamada identified four policy goals of any legislative response, and in addition to analyzing whether the existing laws discussed above fulfill these goals, he designed the Healthy Workplace Bill to meet each goal; the goals are: (1) encouraging employers to prevent workplace bullying; (2) protection and encouragement of workers who engage in self-help measures; (3) providing relief to targets; and (4) punishing bullies (Yamada, 2000: 492–3).

Rather than focusing on enacting new legislation, other legal scholars have explored whether the common law can develop to fill the gap and recognize a cause of action for workplace bullying (Austin, 1988; Chamallas, 2007; Corbett, 2003). Scholars in this camp tend to focus on the potential for developing the common law of intentional infliction of emotional distress (Chamallas, 2007) or the development of a "worker-centric" tort of outrage (Austin, 1988). Other scholars argue against the "tortification" of employment law generally because torts, as outlined above, are not particularly effective tools for vindicating workers' rights, particularly in cases of harassment (Duffy, 1994: 391).

Even if courts were to expand tort law to include status-blind harassment, tort law remedies may be excluded under some states' workers' compensation laws (Yamada, 2000). Workers' compensation statutes vary by state, but provide wage and medical benefits to workers injured as a result of their employment (Yamada, 2000). Many workers' compensation statutes provide, however, that workers' compensation is the exclusive remedy for intentional emotional distress injuries, thereby curtailing the availability of a tort cause of action for injuries caused by workplace bullying (Yamada, 2000). Alternative reliance on negligence torts might overcome the exclusivity problem, but applying negligence torts to workplace conduct is not looked upon favorably by the courts (Harthill, 2010). Yamada also explains why use of a workers' compensation remedy, even if it compensates targets, does not serve the other policy goals of addressing workplace bullying, primarily because it does not fully compensate victims, does not deter employers (because it is a no-fault system and the costs of paying into the state workers' compensation program are passed on to the consumer) and does not punish employers/coworkers (because punitive damages are not available; Yamada, 2000: 506–7).

The choice between new legislation and common law is not an either/or proposition – both can develop alongside each other. The experience of other countries may be illustrative of the potential for legal reform and may provide useful lessons for efforts to fill the current legal gap in the United States. Courts in the United Kingdom, for example, have addressed workplace bullying via an anti-stalking law, the Protection from Harassment Act of 1997 (PHA; Harthill, 2010). The PHA created both criminal and civil liability whereby a person "pursue[s] a course of conduct (a) which amounts to harassment of another, and (b) which he knows or ought to know amounts to harassment of another" (Harthill, 2010). Thus, because the PHA proscribes harassment in general terms, it covers harassment in the workplace. The British courts have allowed employees to use the PHA to hold employers vicariously liable for workplace bullying, most notably in the case of a Deutsche-Bank employee, Helen Green (Harthill, 2008; Majrowski v. Guy's and St. Thomas's NHS Trust, 2005). The court in that case upheld a verdict of £800,000 (US$1.6 million) against the employer and illustrates the power of utilizing existing laws to combat workplace bullying (Harthill, 2008).[5]

In an earlier article, I explored whether workplace bullying could similarly be actionable under existing US state or federal anti-stalking laws, but concluded that most state anti-stalking laws are a poor fit for victims of workplace bullying (Harthill, 2008). The most notable limitation is that all states have a criminal anti-stalking law but few states have a civil anti-stalking statute that could encompass workplace bullying (Harthill, 2008). Further, US anti-stalking laws typically require that the victim fear death or bodily injury, which may not be the case for many targets (Harthill, 2008). The PHA, in contrast, requires only that the harasser pursue a course calculated to harass another (Harthill, 2008). Nevertheless, some state laws have a lower threshold requirement; some statutes require only that the victim feel "terrorized, frightened, intimidated, or threatened,"[6] other statutes only require that the victim merely fears for his or her "safety,"[7] and some statutes use more generalized "harassment" language that could be interpreted to include some cases of workplace bullying.[8] The Michigan statute, for example, defines "stalking" as:

> [A] willful course of conduct involving repeated or continuing harassment of another individual that would cause a reasonable person to feel terrorized, frightened, intimidated, threatened, harassed, or molested and that actually causes the victim to feel terrorized, frightened, intimidated, threatened, harassed, or molested.
>
> (Michigan Comp. Laws, 2007)[9]

"Harassment" is further defined as:

> [C]onduct directed toward a victim that includes, *but is not limited to,* repeated or continuing unconsented contact that would cause a reasonable individual to suffer emotional distress and that actually causes the victim to suffer emotional distress.
>
> (Id. § 750.411h(1)(c): as cited in Harthill, 2008: 295, n. 255)

Thus, targets in states with generalized anti-stalking language could attempt to persuade a court that their claim falls within those laws, but would also need to apply the doctrine of vicarious liability to the statutory breach in order to hold the employer liable (Harthill, 2008). Alternatively, legislative reform efforts could include reformation of existing anti-stalking laws to better fit all forms of harassing conduct (Harthill, 2008).

Another untapped source of legal reform is OSHA (Harthill, 2010). Despite the Act's shortcomings identified by Yamada (2000) and others, it has the potential to be used or strengthened to cover workplace bullying; some European countries and Canadian provinces have used or revised their existing occupational safety and health laws for this purpose (Harthill, 2010).

Congress enacted OSHA in 1970 with a broad prophylactic goal "to assure safe and healthful working conditions for working men and women" (OSHA, §1, 84 Stat. at 1590). OSHA has a general duty clause that requires employers to maintain a safe workplace free of hazards that "are causing or are likely to cause *death or serious physical harm*" (OSHA, §5(a)(1), 29 U.S.C. §654(a)(1)). In a prior article, the author analyzed workplace bullying as an occupational safety and health concern covered by OSHA's general duty clause, thereby already obligating employers to take feasible measures to prevent and abate this problem (Harthill, 2010). Typically, workplace bullying results in emotional distress, and Yamada (2000: 521–2) has argued that it is therefore not a hazard that causes "death or serious physical injury." By explaining the link between workplace bullying and physical harm caused by stress, however, bullying can be brought within the definition of a workplace hazard (Harthill, 2010).

The advantage of utilizing OSHA is that it is a pre-existing, established statutory scheme and employers are fully familiar with OSHA's regulatory apparatus, in particular, the federal agency charged with enforcement and regulatory authority under the Act.[10] Another federal agency, NIOSH, provides research, education, and training in the field, and makes proposals for new safety and health standards.[11] These two federal agencies have already made some pronouncements on the topic of workplace bullying. The OSH Administration, for example, has estimated that approximately two million US workers annually are victimized by some type of workplace violence, although it has not released any data on the prevalence of workplace bullying as a subset of workplace violence (Harthill, 2010). NIOSH has also studied stress at work, with early findings evidencing that over 24 percent of companies surveyed reported that some degree of bullying had occurred there during the previous year (Harthill, 2010). Thus, small-scale forays into the topic have been undertaken under the auspices of OSHA, although much more would be needed to make any headway.

Interestingly, some states have already used existing state OSHA mechanisms to develop workplace bullying codes and policies in public sector employment (Harthill, 2010). In the US federal system, state efforts may provide broader workplace protection, particularly if the emphasis is not on *physical harm*. California's occupational safety and health statute, for example, does not limit the employer's general duty to provide a workplace free of hazards that are likely to cause death or serious physical harm; instead, it more broadly requires employers to "furnish employment and a place of employment that is safe and healthful for the employees therein."[12] California courts have held that the provisions of that statute "clearly make it an employer's legal responsibility to provide a safe place of employment for their employees .... Such responsibility appears to include the duty to adequately address potential workplace violence."[13] California's Occupational Safety and Health Administration has also issued guidelines stating that workplace violence is an occupational safety and health issue, which must be addressed in the employer's injury prevention program.[14]

Although not a state OSHA law, along the same lines, the New York legislature enacted a Workplace Violence Prevention Law in 2006.[15] The New York law[16] and the 2009 implementing regulations[17] require public (but not private) employers to develop and implement comprehensive workplace violence prevention programs that cover all employees at each of their worksites (Harthill, 2011). "Violence" under the New York law seems to include non-physical harassment, although the statute seems more concerned with physical threats and acts of violence.[18] Thus, OSHA laws at both the federal and state level have serious shortcomings and may not be a perfect fit for tackling workplace bullying, but nevertheless may be utilized to do so.

RECOMMENDATIONS, CONCLUSIONS, AND SUMMARY

The role of law in preventing workplace bullying and providing redress is paramount but can only be part of a multi-pronged approach, including self-help, employer self-regulation, and wider societal recognition of the problem (Harthill, 2010). Self-governance initiatives can obviously be spurred if legislative incentives are in place, but self-regulation can also be prompted by awareness through grassroots group campaign efforts and trade unions, among others (Harthill, 2010). Simply put, employers need to be educated about the costs of workplace bullying (Harthill, 2010). Studies in the US and UK estimate that the cost to an organization for every bullied worker who quits is approximately $50,000 (Cascio, 2000: 7–8; Einarsen *et al.*, 2003: 203–18). As Cascio (2000: 83–94) has illustrated, low employee morale and bad publicity caused by bullying are quantifiable organizational costs that can be avoided with good workplace practices (as cited in Harthill, 2010: 298).

In the United States, some unions have begun to push for employer recognition of the problem, and some have done so by viewing workplace bullying as a safety and health concern (Harthill, 2011). For example, the American Federation of Teachers has been proactive in this area, surveying union members about coworker violence, and producing training materials on workplace bullying[19] (Harthill, 2011). The union's survey found 34–60 percent of members reported at least one negative act in the prior six months, ranging from being humiliated or ridiculed, being intimidated or threatened, to being shouted or raged at.

The New York State Public Employees Federation has also been proactive and launched a Stop The Violence campaign in 2005,[20] which may have been instrumental in encouraging the New York legislature to enact the Workplace Violence Prevention Law, discussed above (Harthill, 2011). Other states, for example Oregon, have enacted laws requiring public *and private* employers to establish and administer safety committees to communicate and evaluate safety and health issues,[21] which could encompass workplace violence training initiatives (Harthill, 2011). Also at the local level, city governments appear to be more proactive (Harthill, 2008). The City and County of San Francisco recently adopted a resolution requesting the Department of Human Resources to recognize the detrimental impact of workplace bullying on creating a safe and productive workplace for all employees.[22]

In the United Kingdom, the Health and Safety Executive (HSE), the agency responsible for health and safety regulation, has relied upon a social partnership approach, issuing guidelines and tools for employers to use on a voluntary basis, such as the 2004 HSE Management Standards on Work-Related Stress (Harthill, 2008). Such initiatives, while government-backed, may potentially be useful in the United States. To date, however, employers are not incentivized to develop policies, training, or grievance procedures for instances of workplace bullying. Awareness campaigns such as the ones developed in New York can play a role in encouraging self-regulation, but to date, no studies seem to have been conducted on the efficacy of workplace policies or training.

A multi-pronged effort utilizing law reform and employer/employee-initiated awareness campaigns is likely to enjoy more success. Indeed, although workplace bullying laws have been in place for some years in countries like Sweden and France, there is a dearth of research regarding the effectiveness of these laws as a deterrent or remedial force (Höel and Einarsen, 2010: 30). Höel and Einarsen evaluated the effectiveness of Sweden's law and found that the law had several shortcomings (Höel and Einarsen 2010: 30). Their findings indicated that these shortcomings partially stemmed from weaknesses in the law itself and government enforcement of the law, but also included lack of support from employers and unions (Höel and Einarsen, 2010: 35–44). Not surprisingly, Höel and Einarsen recommended an integrated approach using legislation, self-regulation, and engaging the active support of employers, unions, and employees (Höel and Einarsen, 2010: 47–8). Drawing upon the lessons learned from existing legislation in countries such as Sweden, advocates for law reform in the United States might enjoy more success by combining the call for legal recognition of the problem with the approach outlined by Höel and Einarsen and others (Höel and Einarsen, 2010: 47–8; Harthill, 2008, 2010).

AUTHOR NOTE

Portions of the discussion in this chapter are adapted from the author's prior articles on workplace bullying: Susan Harthill, Bullying in the workplace: Lessons from the United Kingdom, 17 *Minnesota Journal of International Law* 247 (2008); The need for a revitalized regulatory scheme to address workplace bullying in the United States: Harnessing the federal Occupational Safety and Health Act, 78 *University of Cincinnati Law Review* 1250 (2010); A comparative analysis of workplace bullying as an occupational safety and health concern, 34 *Hastings International and Comparative Law Review* 253 (2011). Correspondence concerning this article should be addressed to Susan Harthill, Florida Coastal School of Law, 8787 Baypine Road, Jacksonville, Florida 32256. Email: sharthill@fcsl.edu.

NOTES

1 Workplace Bullying Institute: http://www.bullyinginstitute.org.
2 (Victoria, Australia); R.S.Q. ch. N-1.1 (1977) (Quebec, Canada); Occupational Health and Safety (Harassment Prevention) Amendment of 2007, S.S. 66 (2007) (Saskatchewan, Canada); Ordinance (AFS 1993:2) on Violence and Menaces in the Working Environment, 14 Jan. 1993; Ordinance (AFS 1993:17) on Targetization at Work, 21 Sept. 1993 (Sweden); Occupational Safety and Health Act, 738, ch. 5, sec. 28 (2002) (Norway); Organization for Economic Co-Operation and Development

(OECD), *The Inclusive Workplace Agreement: Past Effects and Future Directions*, at 4 (Nov. 2005) (Finland).

3 Title VII of the Civil Rights Act of 1964 prohibits discrimination on the basis of race, color, religion, sex and national origin. 42 U.S.C. §§2000e-2000e-17 (2006). The Age Discrimination in Employment Act prohibits discrimination on the basis of age. 29 U.S.C. §§621–34 (2006). The Americans with Disabilities Act prohibits discrimination of the basis of disability. 42 U.S.C. §§12101–213 (2006). All these federal statutes prohibit harassment as a form of discrimination.

4 Workplace Bullying Institute: http://www.bullyinginstitute.org/.

5 Green v. DB Group Services (UK) Ltd., [2006] EWHC 1898 (Q.B.).

6 Mich. Comp. Laws §750.411h (2005); Mich. Stat. Ann. §609.749 (West, 2005); Neb. Rev. Stat. §28-311.03 (2005); Nev. Rev. Stat. Ann. §200.575 (Michie, 2005); N.D. Cent. Code §12.1-17-07.1 (2005); Okla. Stat. Ann. tit. 21, §1173 (West, 2005); and Tenn. Code Ann. §39-17-315 (2005)) (as cited in Harthill, 2008: 294, n. 251).

7 Ariz. Rev. Stat. §13-2923 (2005); Cal. Penal Code §646.9 (Deering, 2005); Colo. Rev. Stat. §18-9-111 (2005); Conn. Gen. Stat. §53a-181d (2005); Fla. Stat. Ann. §784.048 (West, 2005) (in definition of "credible threat"); Ga. Code Ann. §16-5-90 (2005); Kan. Stat. Ann. §21-3438 (2005); Mo. Rev. Stat. §565.225 (2005) (in definition of "credible threat"); N.H. Rev. Stat. Ann. §633:3-a (2005); N.M. Stat. Ann. §30-3A-3 (Michie, 2005); N.C. Gen. Stat. §14-277.3 (2005); Or. Rev. Stat. §163.732 (2005); Vt. Stat. Ann. tit. 13, §1061 (2005)) (as cited in Harthill, 2008: 295, n. 252).

8 Kentucky e.g. makes it a Class B misdemeanor offense to, inter alia, use coarse or abusive language in a public place, or to engage "in a course of conduct or repeatedly commit acts which alarm or seriously annoy such other person and which serve no legitimate purpose." Intent to harass, annoy, or alarm is required. Ky. Rev. Stat. Ann. §525.070(1)(c), (e) (2006)(as cited in Harthill, 2008: 295, n. 253).

9 Mich. Comp. Laws §750.411h(1)(d) (2007). The offense is a misdemeanor punishable by imprisonment for not more than one year or a fine of not more than $1,000.00, or both. Id. at §750.411(2)(a). If the victim is a minor and the offender is more than five years older than the victim, the offense is a felony punishable by imprisonment for not more than five years or a fine of not more than $10,000.00, or both. Id. §750.411h(2)(b). The court can also order probation up to five years, including as a condition of probation, psychiatric counseling (as cited in Harthill, 2008: 295, n. 254).

10 OSHA §5(a)(2), 29 U.S.C. §654(a)(2) (2006)(as cited in Harthill, 2010: 1251, n.8).

11 OSHA §2(b)(3), 29 U.S.C. §651(b)(3) (authorizing Secretary of Department of Labor); OSHA §22, 29 U.S.C. §671 (creating NIOSH) (as cited in Harthill, 2010: 1252, n. 11).

12 Cal. Lab. Code §6400(a); see also id. §6401 ("Every employer shall furnish and use safety devices and safeguards, and shall adopt and use practices, means, methods, operations, and processes which are reasonably adequate to render such employment and place of employment safe and healthful. Every employer shall do every other thing reasonably necessary to protect the life, safety, and health of employees."); id. §6402 ("No employer shall require, or permit any employee to go or be in any employment or place of employment which is not safe and healthful."); id. §§6403, 6404. California Code of Regulations also requires employers to implement Injury and Illness Prevention Programs, but does not specifically mention workplace violence or bullying. 8 Cal. Code. Regs. tit. 8, §3203 (2009) (as cited in Harthill, 2010: 1266, n. 90).

13 Franklin v. Monadnock Co., 59 Cal. Rptr. 3d 692, 696-97 (Cal. Ct. App. 2007) (holding that employee stated a claim for wrongful discharge in violation of public policy, where employee was discharged for complaining internally and externally about coworker's threats of violence. Public policy stemmed from CalOSHA's requirement that employers maintain a safe and healthy workplace and policy of encouraging employees to report credible threats of violence in the workplace) (as cited in Harthill, 2010: 1267, n. 92).

14 See Cal. Dep't of Indus. Relations, Cal/OSHA Guidelines for Workplace Security (30 March 1995), http://www.dir.ca.gov/dosh/dosh_publications/worksecurity.html. The California Labor Code is supplemented by Code of Civil Procedure section 527.8, which allows employers to seek injunctive relief on behalf of employees to address "unlawful violence or a credible threat of violence" by an individual, including a coworker. Cal. Civ. Proc. Code §527.8(a) (West, 2009) (as cited in Harthill, 2010: 1267, n. 93).
15 N.Y. Lab. Law §27-b (McKinney, 2006).
16 N.Y. Lab. Law §27-b; N.Y. Comp. Codes R. and Regs. tit. 880.6.
17 N.Y. Comp. Codes R. and Regs. tit. 880.6 (2009).
18 N.Y. Comp. Codes R. and Regs. tit. 880.6(d)(7), (d)(11).
19 American Federation of Teachers, Health and Safety Program, *Work Shouldn't Hurt: Workplace Bullying Not To Be Tolerated*, AFT PSRP Conference, April 2010, http://www.aft.org/pdfs/psrp/conf10materials/PSRPConf10_58.pdf.
20 New York State Public Employees Federation, Stop Workplace Violence, http://www.pef.org/stopworkplaceviolence.
21 OR. Admin. R. 437-001-0765.
22 City and County of San Francisco Resolution on Anti-Bullying (24 Jan. 2007) (on file with author), available at http://www.bullyfreeworkplace.org/id18.html (accessed March 2008); see also City of Berkeley Proclamation Regarding Workplace Bullying (Jan. 2006) (on file with author), available at http://www.bullyfreeworkplace.org/id17.html (accessed March 2008).

REFERENCES

Austin, R. (1988). Employer abuse, worker resistance, and the tort of intentional infliction of emotional distress. *Stanford Law Review*, 41, 1–59.

Burlington Indus. v. Ellerth, 524 U.S. 742, 765 (1998).

Cascio, W. F. (2000). *Costing Human Resources: The Financial Impact of Behavior in Organizations,* Cincinnati, OH: South-Western College Pub.

Chamallas, M. (2007). Discrimination and outrage: The migration from civil rights to tort law. *William and Mary Law Review*, 48, 2115–87.

Coleman, B. (2006). Shame, rage, and freedom of speech: Should the United States adopt European "mobbing" laws? *Georgia Journal of International and Comparative Law*, 35, 53–99.

Corbett, W. R. (2003). The need for a revitalized common law of the workplace. *Brooklyn Law Review*, 69, 102–5.

Duffy, D. P. (1994). Intentional infliction of emotional distress and employment at will: The case against "tortification" of labor and employment law. *Boston University Law Review*, 74, 387–427.

Einarsen, S., Höel, H., Zapf, D., and Cooper, C. (2003). *Bullying and Emotional Abuse in the Workplace: International Perspectives in Research and Practice,* London: Taylor & Francis.

Ellickson, R. C. (1991). *Order without Law: How Neighbors Settle Disputes,* Cambridge, MA: Harvard University Press.

Employment Law Alliance (2007). Abusive Boss Poll. Retrieved June 2011, from http://www.workplacebullying.org/res/elacharts.pdf.

Faragher v. City of Boca Raton, 524 U.S. 775, 807 (1998).

French Social Modernization Law, C. TRAV. arts. L. 122-46 to L. 122-154 (2002). Retrieved from http://www.legifrance.gouv.fr.

Guerrero, M. I. S. (2004). The development of moral harassment (or mobbing) law in Sweden and France as a step towards EU legislation. *Boston College International and Comparative Law Review*, 27, 477–500.

Harthill, S. (2008). Bullying in the workplace: Lessons from the United Kingdom. *Minnesota Journal of International Law*, 17, 247–301.

Harthill, S. (2010). The need for a revitalized regulatory scheme to address workplace bullying in the United States: Harnessing the federal Occupational Safety and Health Act. *University of Cincinnati Law Review*, 78, 1250–1306.

Harthill, S. (2011). A comparative analysis of workplace bullying as an occupational safety and health concern. *Hastings Journal of International and Comparative Law*, 34, 253–301.

Höel, H., and Einarsen, S. (2010). Shortcomings of antibullying regulations: The case of Sweden. *European Journal of Work and Organizational Psychology*, 16, 101–18.

Knechtle, J. C. (2006). When to regulate hate speech. *Penn State Law Review*, 110, 539–78.

Majrowski v. Guy's and St. Thomas's NHS Trust, EWCA (Civ) 251 (Eng.) (2005).

McAdams, R. (1997). The origin, development, and regulation of norms. *Michigan Law Review*, 96, 338–433.

Michigan Comp. Laws § 750.411h(1)(d) (2007).

Namie, G., and Namie, R. (2003). *The Bully at Work: What you Can Do to Stop the Hurt and Reclaim your Dignity* (3rd edn), Naperville, IL: Sourcebooks.

National Labor Relations Act 29 U.S.C. §§151–69 (2006).

Occupational Health and Safety Act of 2004, VICT. REPR. STAT. § 21(1) (2007)

OSHA, 29 U.S.C. §§651–678 (2006).

Protection from Harassment Act, c. 40, §1 Eng. (1997).

Restatement (Second) of Torts §46(1) (1965).

Sunstein, C. (1996). Social norms and social roles. *Columbia Law Review*, 96, 903–68.

Symposium (2004). Symposium, Global Perspectives on Workplace Harassment Law: Proceedings of the 2004 Annual Meeting, Association of American Law Schools Section on Labor Relations and Employment Law. *Employee Rights and Employment Policy Journal*, 8, 151.

Title VII, 42 U.S.C. §§2000e-2000e-17 (2006).

Workplace Bullying Institute (n.d.). Healthy Workplace Bill FAQ. Retrieved May 2011, from http://www.healthyworkplacebill.org/faq.php.

Yamada, D. C. (2000). The phenomenon of "workplace bullying" and the need for a status-blind hostile work environment protection. *Georgetown Law Journal*, 88, 475–536.

Yamada, D. C. (2004). Crafting a legislative response to workplace bullying. *Employee Rights and Employment Policy Journal*, 8, 475–521.

Yuen, R. A. (2005). Note, beyond the schoolyard: Workplace bullying and moral harassment law in France and Quebec. *Cornell International Law Journal*, 38, 625–48.

Part V

Conclusion and Future Directions

22

Using Selection Techniques to Keep Bullies out of the Workplace

Scott Erker and Evan F. Sinar
Development Dimensions International, Pittsburgh, PA

Daniel S. Wells
Duquesne University

INTRODUCTION

Over the last 20 years, there has been a marked increase in the recognition that hiring the right people can have a dramatic impact on an organization's success. However, knowing which applicants will be successful in the organization has always been a difficult process for many organizations. In order to make the process more clear and data driven, companies have attempted to develop specific selection systems to use during their hiring process. Selection systems are fundamentally decision-making processes that are used to determine who will be hired as well as which workers already present in the organization should be promoted to a different level or functions within the organization.

These selection systems have been afforded significant investment, which has resulted in advances in the ability to predict new hire success, has made the process of hiring a new worker more efficient, and lessened the time it takes to fill an open position. Given the realization that identifying and then hiring the best and brightest employees is essential to improving the organization's bottom line, developing and utilizing effective selection systems is essential for sustained business success.

While selection systems have become fairly accurate at judging an individual's competence and necessary skills, techniques for determining an individual's propensity to engage in workplace bullying have not received adequate attention in terms of research or practice. The concept is worth exploring, however, due to the damage bullying can cause in the workplace. Such negative outcomes as lost productivity, workplace stress, and decreased morale can be all attributed to bullying in the workplace (Cortina *et al.*, 2001), which can threaten the retention of current talent and affect the attraction of new talent.

While it is difficult to accurately estimate the total cost of bullying at an organizational level since bullying often goes unreported and attributions of cost factors to bullying are imprecise, improving our ability to select for workplace bullying will not only serve as a humanitarian effort to make the workplace more enjoyable, but also it will yield advantages in a hypercompetitive environment. The purpose of this chapter is to discuss factors that should be considered when designing a selection system to target workplace bullying and to review the selection techniques that can be utilized in screening out those who will likely commit forms of peer aggression in the workplace.

SIGNIFICANCE AND RELEVANT THEORY

Bullying in the workplace has no shortage of definitions and conceptualizations. The Workplace Bullying Institute defines workplace bullying as:

> Repeated, health-harming mistreatment of one or more persons (the targets) by one or more perpetrators that takes one or more of the following forms: (1) verbal abuse, (2) offensive conduct/behaviors (including nonverbal) which are threatening, humiliating, or intimidating, or (3) work interference, or sabotage, which prevents work from getting done.
>
> (Workplace Bullying Institute, n.d.)

In the academic literature, it has been defined more generally as "a form of interpersonal aggression or hostile, anti-social behavior in the workplace" (LaVan and Martin, 2008). We recognize this latter definition as the basis for our exploration of the topic, although we reinforce the importance of considering workplace bullying as a multifaceted construct comprising a wide range of behaviors.

Bullying in the workplace can take a variety of forms, both in terms of the target and the aggressor. One key differentiator is which individuals are being targeted by the bullying. Peer-to-peer bullying is one form. Other forms include manager-to-subordinate or subordinate-to-manager bullying. In virtually all studies to have investigated the prevalence of different bullying targets, manager-to-subordinate bullying makes up the majority of occurrences (e.g. 81 percent of all workplace bullying cases; Namie, 2010). Individually focused bullying can range from intimidation and gossiping, to ostracizing and isolation, to actual physical violence. While each form of workplace bullying has unique attributes in a selection scenario, they would be addressed in a similar way – by attempting to identify those individuals likely to emerge as bullies within the organization. The selection system, then, would screen out those individuals, preventing them from negatively impacting the work environment regardless of the form of bullying – on peers or coworkers, subordinates, or on managers.

Given the wide range of perpetrators, targets, and behaviors used to bully others, it is important to narrow our scope of what types of bullying behavior are of chief concern. A particularly important distinction to draw is between workplace bullying (the focus of this chapter) and workplace violence. While workplace violence certainly is one extreme component of bullying, it is relatively uncommon compared to other forms of bullying, and has shown marked decreases during the past two decades (Harrell, 2011). Workplace bullying, however, appears to have remained more stable, with approximately 35 percent of adults experiencing some form of bullying in both 2007 and 2010 (Namie, 2010). Despite the fact that workplace bullying is more prevalent and consistent than workplace violence, workplace violence is often the subject of popular press or news articles. There is a risk, therefore, that the salience and impact of these stories can skew the perceptions of which behaviors constitute workplace bullying, how often these bullying behaviors actually occur, the characteristics of those who perpetrate such actions, and the full scope of how bullying is evidenced in the workplace.

While workplace violence is generally noticed in an organization due to its overt nature and extremely negative outcomes, predicting the more diffusely defined and covert behaviors of workplace bullying and precisely identifying which events or situations trigger bullying can present unique challenges. Workplace behaviors are determined by a complex interaction of people, job tasks and stress, and organizational culture. In addition, bullying can take many forms – from direct aggressive behaviors to passive-aggressive sabotage of other people's work efforts. Because there are so many different variables to consider, one of the fundamental concepts in the design of a selection system is that the system must be capable of identifying and screening people who will abstain from workplace bullying behaviors as well as be positively productive while on the job.

Whether workplace bullying is considered by an organization when screening potential employees or not, judging an individual's likelihood to be productive in the workplace is generally the most important consideration for a profit-orientated business. Various individuals may be desired by different organizations based upon the potential employee's interpersonal and working style that should match the culture already present in the organization. For example, some organizations may value employees taking initiative and having them take charge of deciding what is the best task to complete the job, while others may not value initiative but instead value compliance where employees take direction from managers who are responsible for deciding which tasks are most important for a greater number of employees. Neither approach has been shown to be unequivocally better or worse from a productivity viewpoint. The best approach, then, is determined by the specific needs and organizational style for each particular organization, and the selection techniques for each company should screen for employees that fit into their style.

Since workplace productivity is the ultimate goal for a selection system, the argument can be made that these selection systems should consider the potential employee's likelihood to commit workplace bullying behaviors due to the fact that most typical behaviors associated with bullying are counterproductive to the organization's ultimate goals. Therefore, one goal of an effective selection system is to identify characteristics in individuals that are predictive of eventual workplace bullying. One way this goal could be met is by trying to assess the individual's past behavior and aggressive tendencies that match the organization's definition of bullying.

An alternative strategy would be to identify characteristics that are likely to be the opposite of bullying behaviors, such as teamwork/collaboration, empathy, and interpersonal sensitivity. An effective selection strategy will employ both methods of design. The best methods of prediction will be multifaceted in nature, identifying clusters of constructs that are related to bullying (and anti-bullying) and measuring their presence (or absence) in job candidates. Through a multifaceted measurement approach and using multiple selection methods, organizations have the best chance for identifying bullies before they get into their workplace.

SALIENT FEATURES: SELECTION METHODS AND WORKPLACE BULLYING

Most selection methods fall into one of two types. One method employs the use of tools that provide "signs" as predictors. Measurement of motivations, attitudes, and personality are examples of signs of potential performance and are typically measured through the use of tests. The other method uses tools that measure "samples" of behavior to predict workplace performance. Job simulations are the best example of a selection tool that takes this approach. For measurement targets such as bullying, with a low occurrence rate and a large number of contributing factors, both "sign" and "sample" methods should be considered as part of the overall selection design.

Formal Assessment

In an employee screening system, tests are often used to gather quantitative data regarding an individual's preferences, working style, and personality. Some tests can be used to judge what types of working behaviors an individual enjoys or does not enjoy and how those behaviors relate to bullying. In this type of assessment, the examiner is looking for evidence that the job candidate enjoys building positive relationships, supporting coworkers and customers, and does not resort to an aggressive style toward others. Other tests can also be used to assess attitudes and on-the-job thinking style by asking test takers how they think, feel, or act during certain situations, using measurements known as "situational judgment tests".

Examiners can place the job candidate in hypothetical situations and ask the person to choose the best response among a number of alternatives. The test can be keyed (e.g. the right answer is given the most credit) to select for those that choose alternatives that are more supportive of a collaborative work environment, rather than those behaviors that are aggressive or hostile. The last type of test in this category examines the personality and intrinsic attitudes and beliefs of the individual. In these tests, constructs such as "Big Five" personality dimensions (agreeableness, neuroticism, emotional stability, openness to experience, and conscientiousness) are assessed, or candidates are asked to report their own past negative work behaviors to judge their level of integrity and ability to self-reflect. Job candidates who score high on these instruments tend to get along with others, work well under stress, and care about coworkers and their work environment more than those who score low. Tests can be an effective selection tool for giving human resource professionals predictive information about potential bullying behavior.

Although a full review of test-measured characteristics that can be linked to workplace bullying and aggression is beyond the scope of this chapter, several such characteristics are particularly notable based on past research. Personality constructs have been a primary focus of this work. Among the Big Five, conscientiousness has been the most consistent predictor of a range of counterproductive workplace behaviors, including aggression, with emotional stability and agreeableness also exhibiting low but consistent levels of prediction (Ones *et al.*, 1993).

Beyond the Big Five, two additional constructs showing consistent relationships with workplace aggression (a more narrowly defined outcome than workplace bullying) are trait anger, which is an individual's predisposition to react to situations by expressing hostility, and negative affectivity, which is defined as the likelihood that an individual will experience negative emotions more frequently and to a greater degree than those not possessing this disposition. A large-scale study summarizing the results of several studies regarding these two constructs found both of these to be strong predictors of workplace aggression across settings, with trait anger showing a slightly stronger relationship to workplace bullying than negative affectivity (Hershcovis *et al.*, 2007).

Two additional notable measurement approaches specifically focused on aggression are a technique called "conditional reasoning," which gauges an individual's likelihood of engaging in aggressive behaviors at work, and an overt integrity test, in which individuals are asked to directly report past negative behaviors such as workplace aggression. The conditional reasoning approach is based on the idea that individuals justify their behaviors in different ways, and these justifications will vary depending on someone's underlying tendencies.

In the context of aggression, individuals who are likely to act aggressively at work will respond in an aggressive manner toward an ambiguous situation, as compared to someone who does not have these aggressive tendencies. Large-scale reviews of this technique (e.g. Berry *et al.*, 2010) suggest cautious optimism about its potential for predicting on-the-job aggression. Overt integrity tests ask specifically about a range of past negative activities at or related to work, such as theft, drug abuse, and absenteeism. It is important to note that, although some overt integrity tests ask candidates to admit aggressive acts, it is only one of several topics covered by these tests. Overt integrity tests have generally been successful in predicting negative work behaviors (Ones *et al.*, 1993).

Job Simulation

Job simulations present the candidate with a challenge or task specific to the job for which the individual is applying and require the candidate to actually perform as he or she would if he or she held the job. It is difficult to create a job simulation that would elicit typical bullying behaviors because most job candidates will avoid showing negative behaviors in the hiring process. A more productive approach would be to administer simulations in which the candidate would be given the chance to display teamwork or supportive workplace behaviors. Job simulations in which a coworker is struggling with an aspect of his or her work or where a customer is upset are likely to elicit positive behaviors from some job candidates. Those who build relationships with coworkers, empathize with upset customers, or who acknowledge empathic feelings in the simulation are more likely to display these positive behaviors on the job and are therefore less likely to bully if given the chance.

Interview

The job interview is the most common selection method and, while it can be difficult to elicit accurate information regarding aggressive tendencies during an interview, the interview process can be designed to assess the likelihood of bullying behaviors. The most effective interviewing method is behavioral interviewing, in which interviewers probe the candidate's past work situations, behaviors used by the job candidate in these work situations, and the results he or she achieved. The method is built on the premise that past behavior predicts future behavior.

Bullying could be assessed directly using this method by asking questions such as, "Tell me about a time when you treated someone in a way that caused them to become angry with you. What was the situation? What did you do to try to remedy the situation? How did the situation resolve itself?" A related line of questioning could probe whether or not the candidate had observed bullying in the workplace. Follow-up questions would explore for sensitivity to bullying as negative behaviors and proactiveness in working against the bullying behavior.

Of course, the interviewer could ask more positive questions, looking for evidence that the candidate uses behaviors that are the antithesis of bullying. In this case, the interviewer would be looking for indicators that the candidate participated in teamwork, relationship building, and empathy, by asking questions such as, "Tell me about a time when you saw a coworker that was in need of help with a work assignment. What was the situation? How did you recognize that the coworker needed support? What was the result of your intervention?" Skilled interviewers will be able to identify potential bullies by probing for negative work behaviors from past work situations, and following up with the job candidate when details are vague or suspicious.

References

Job references (or background checks) are another common method used to identify workplace bullies. The hiring organization should ask the candidate for references from previous places of employment, volunteer organizations, or schools. The reference interviewer would ask the referring person questions about positive and negative work behaviors, probing for specific examples of work performance that would indicate bullying or, conversely, more supportive work behaviors. The limitation of the reference check, however, is that in most cases the job candidate selects the references who will comment on their past working performance. It is unlikely that the candidate would select someone who would speak negatively about them on their behalf. Legal considerations governing what previous employers can and cannot say about an individual's work performance, particularly for sensitive events such as bullying, may also limit the effectiveness of this method for screening out bullies (Woska, 2007). In addition to this common but limited source of reliable and accurate information about a candidate's past work experience, practitioners are advised to consider the use of more formal pre-employment screening processes if appropriate, given the nature of the job.

RECOMMENDATIONS

Important Considerations and Contextual Issues for Selection System Design

Selecting for attitudes, motivations, and behavior that typify bullying is not easy. When people apply for jobs and proceed through the hiring process, they put their best foot forward, generally trying to mask any negative thoughts or actions that could be assessed during tests and interviews. The relatively limited scope and duration of many selection procedures also gives individuals the opportunity to temporarily mask their bullying-related inclinations. Despite the intuitive appeal of a single "profile" gathered through one type of selection tool to predict bullying, this is likely not possible given the complexity of the associated issues (Barling *et al.*, 2009). A multi-method approach using a combination of selection tools is recommended to increase the likelihood that potential bullies will be identified before they are hired by an organization.

Assessing current incumbents for a new job affords the organization a definite advantage in identifying those likely to be bullies if they are promoted to a higher position within the organization, given the wide amount of personal experience and productivity data that are available regarding that individual. Job incumbents, those people who are currently employed by the organization and who post for a lateral move or a promotion to a higher level position, can be assessed by examining their current and past work performance, the type of information not available for external job candidates. Repetition is a key feature in distinguishing which individuals are guilty of bullying and which individuals may have simply perpetrated a single, isolated aggressive act (Lutgen-Sandvik *et al.*, 2009). Therefore, based on the individual's history of behavior, an organization can make a more informed prediction about the likelihood of future bullying behavior. However, in order to be able to make these accurate predictions, organizations need to ensure that managers recognize and document dysfunctional behavior. When internal people apply for a different job within the organization, those in charge of hiring need to have a clear picture of how the job candidate has performed and behaved in the past; especially when promoting an individual to a more managerial role, due to the increased risk of bullying occurring in the manager-to-subordinate relationship.

A key challenge in defining and understanding workplace bullying related to employee selection is that it results from the interaction of a multitude of factors – the aggressor, the target, the job context/situation, and perceptions of the incident from the target and observers. Factors that increase the chance for bullying – ongoing organizational changes (major restructuring), worker characteristics (age, gender, parental status), workplace relationships (inadequate information flow between levels, lack of employee participation in decisions), and work systems (lack of policies about behavior, staff shortages, role conflict) – can all be considered in part or as a whole when determining a strategy to mitigate the likelihood of workplace bullying.

For a practitioner charged with managing or preventing bullying behaviors, this is an important recognition, as it strongly suggests a multifaceted approach to addressing these activities. For example, sanctions – perceptions of consequences stemming from aggressive behaviors (e.g. reprimands) – appear to have a particularly salient effect on the links between individual characteristics and reported aggression, indicating that the strategies utilized to control the bullying behavior of employees can be met with a different amount of effectiveness from one employee to another (Inness *et al.*, 2008).

While selection techniques are one component of building a workforce that does not exhibit bullying behaviors, other contextual considerations such as workplace climate, leadership style, and cultural expectations are important as well. It is also strongly recommended that practitioners consider the widely ranging situational and individual factors impacting someone's likelihood to bully others at work when setting realistic expectations for what a selection tool can accomplish in establishing a bully-free environment if it is used in isolation from other organizational interventions. For example, a change to the selection process alone may not have the intended effect of controlling bullying behaviors in an organization when little is done to address the bullying behaviors that are already present among managers and lower-level employees.

Practical Considerations

Practitioners seeking to develop or purchase selection tools targeting workplace bullying must also consider other factors which, if not planned for, can limit the effectiveness of the tools or can produce unintended negative consequences for the organization. One example is how to target the behavior of bullying without creating problematic candidate perceptions about the selection system. Because selection processes must be universal and consistent across a particular job group, certain approaches to screening for workplace bullying may not be feasible or appropriate on a large scale. Targeting job groups may be a viable approach when the bullying is known from background research and past experience to cluster in a specific segment of the organization. Even in these situations, however, an HR manager should be cautious about selection approaches that could be viewed as invasive by applicants, or that may hinder recruitment efforts themselves, if inclusion of bullying-related content is viewed by candidates as a sign that this is a major component of the workplace, causing them to avoid pursuing employment in that particular organization.

Practitioners deploying tools focusing on workplace bullying must take particular caution that the information resulting from such tools (e.g. about an individual's likelihood of becoming a workplace bully) is closely monitored, kept confidential from other employees, and is appropriately linked to job effectiveness. Differences exist in state privacy laws that govern access to such information, but generally, the information should be restricted to the smallest possible group within an organization. Another important consideration is that some personality assessment tests, while useful in the prediction of aggressive tendencies, are designed to assess clinical or abnormal personality characteristics. Used in an employment selection situation, these tools can be seen as violating the Americans with Disabilities Act (1990) and are generally not advised. More broadly, it must be recognized that the use of any selection tool targeting bullying must still involve appropriate validation methods to link performance on the tool to performance on the job, based on the provisions of the Uniform Guidelines on Employee Selection Procedures (1978).

At its core, selection to avoid bullying, as with any other selection objective, is about risk reduction – and it is impossible to reduce this risk to zero. In fact, some methods which would be considered ideal from the level of information they provide (e.g. detailed knowledge of an individual's entire past job history) are simply not realistic. This leaves the practitioner in a position in which he or she must evaluate the range of available options, decide how these selection-oriented methods converge with practical considerations and with other steps being taken inside the organization (e.g. bullying seminars, sanctions), and assemble an approach balancing these goals that integrates the converging sources of evidence into an overall decision.

SUMMARY AND CONCLUSIONS

In general, there are a number of themes or practical recommendations that emerge from our examination of selection for workplace bullying and peer aggression. Organizations should set the bar high with regard to interpersonal skills and look for new hires that are capable of using empathy and developing positive relationships with coworkers and customers. Businesses and companies should try to avoid hiring abusive employees by asking the right interview questions, but not over-relying on the job interview. Multiple hiring methods that include tests and job simulations will increase the likelihood of identifying potentially poor performers. If an organization does decide to use pre-employment tests, that organization should focus on measures of agreeableness, emotional stability, and conscientiousness that are likely to predict a wide range of positive performance outcomes, and also consider measures that target the presence of more negative behaviors, such as overt integrity or conditional reasoning tests, or tests of trait anger and negative affectivity. Pre-employment background screening and/or reference-checking is an essential technique in avoiding hiring potential bullies. Organizations should use care in promotion practices as well so as not to promote a bully and therefore send the wrong message to employees that bullying behavior is tolerated, or even rewarded. A comprehensive, systematic approach to managing workplace bullying that includes improved selection methods will lead to a more productive and pleasant work environment for all current and future employees.

REFERENCES

Americans with Disabilities Act of 1990, Pub. L. No. 101-336, §2, 104 Stat. 328 (1991).

Barling, J., Dupré, K. E., and Kelloway, E. K. (2009). Predicting workplace aggression and violence. *Annual Review of Psychology*, 60, 671–92.

Berry, C. M., Sackett, P. R., and Tobares, V. (2010). A meta-analysis of conditional reasoning tests of aggression. *Personnel Psychology*, 63, 361–84.

Cortina, L. M., Magley, V. J., Williams, J. H., and Langhout, R. D. (2001). Incivility in the workplace: Incidence and impact. *Journal of Occupational Health Psychology*, 6, 64–80.

Harrell, E. (2011). *Workplace Violence, 1993–2009: National Crime Victimization Survey and the Census of Fatal Occupational Injuries,* Washington, DC: US Department of Justice.

Hershcovis, M. S., Turner, N., Barling, J., Arnold, K. A., Dupré, K. E., Inness, M., … Sivanthan, N. (2007). Predicting workplace aggression: A meta-analysis. *Journal of Applied Psychology*, 92, 228–38.

Inness, M., LeBlanc, M. M., and Barling, J. (2008). Psychosocial predictors of supervisor-, peer-, subordinate-, and service provider-targeted aggression. *Journal of Applied Psychology,* 93, 1401–11.

LaVan, H., and Martin, W. M. (2008). Bullying in the U.S. workplace: Normative and process-oriented ethical approaches. *Journal of Business Ethics*, 83, 147–65.

Lutgen-Sandvik, P., Namie, G., and Namie, R. (2009). Workplace bullying: Causes, consequences, and corrections. In P. Lutgen-Sandvik and B. D. Sypher (eds), *Destructive Organizational Communication* (pp. 41–88), New York: Routledge Press.

Namie, G. (2010). *The WBI U.S. Workplace Bullying Survey,* Washington, DC: Workplace Bullying Institute and Zogby International.

Ones, D. S., Viswesvaran, C., and Schmidt, F. L. (1993). Comprehensive meta-analysis of integrity test validities: Findings and implications for personnel selection and theories of job performance. *Journal of Applied Psychology*, 78, 679–703.

Uniform Guidelines on Employee Selection Procedures of 1978, §1607, 4 U.S.C. (2011).

Workplace Bullying Institute (n.d.). Definition of workplace bullying. Retrieved from http://www.workplacebullying.org/individuals/problem/definition.

Woska, W. J. (2007). Legal issues for HR professionals: Reference checking/background investigations. *Public Personnel Management*, 36, 79–89.

23

Designing Jobs to be Bully-Proofed

Michelle Barker and Sheryl Ramsay
Griffith Business School, Griffith University, Australia

INTRODUCTION

A primary and constant challenge facing managers, supervisors, and organizational behaviorists is how to organize work and the work environment so that workers are satisfied and productive. It is a multifaceted challenge that involves safeguarding individuals, teams, and the organization as a whole. One facet of the challenge, job design, refers to the structure, content, and configuration of a person's work tasks and roles (Parker and Ohly, 2008). The way that tasks are organized to achieve work outcomes is integrally related to job design. A relatively recent challenge in the workplace is the prevention of bullying to ensure that workers are safeguarded from stressful, negative, work environments that often result from environments characterized by peer victimization.

This chapter will consider the questions of whether and how job design can be used as a means of "bully-proofing" jobs. We will address this question by considering job design as a central human resource management task within organizations, and the relationship between job design and workplace bullying. To date, it is not an area that has been examined extensively in discussions about appropriate safeguards against workplace bullying (McCarthy and Mayhew, 2004). Further, we will provide recommendations about how organizations can help to insulate workers from the potential of being bullied in the workplace, and outline specific strategies to safeguard workers and the organization if and when bullying occurs. While total "bully-proofing" is likely not possible, there are numerous strategies that can be engaged to design jobs in such a way to prevent and redress bullying if and when it occurs at work.

SIGNIFICANCE

While workplace bullying is clearly an undesirable phenomenon from any perspective, especially given the significant impacts on individual and organizational health, safety, productivity, reputation, and market performance (Höel *et al.*, 2011; Hogh *et al.*, 2011; McCarthy, 2004), negative work behaviors are an increasingly recognized fact of organizational life (Penney and Spector, 2008), and it is essential to consider how organizations, and the people who work within them, may be protected from this phenomenon. Interestingly, in some of the earliest literature on bullying, pioneer researcher Heinz Leymann (1996) argued that anyone could become a target of bullying under specific circumstances. His emphasis on organizational antecedents of bullying, rather than on a specific "victim personality" (Salin and Höel, 2010) has sometimes been overlooked in subsequent research.

Job design is central to organizational functioning (Oldham and Hackman, 2010), and as such can provide a lens for an examination of the characteristics of jobs that link with valued personal and work outcomes, as well as points at which negative behaviors such as bullying may emerge. Within this framework, "bully-proofing" is a concept worthy of further exploration as a possible means for reducing the potential for bullying to emerge and develop. Designing jobs to be "bully-proofed" needs a part of a web of sustainable, human resource development safeguards in order to limit the likelihood, severity, and cost of bullying in organizations. The notion of safeguarding, according to McCarthy and Mayhew (2004: p. xii), connects "with feelings of threat and insecurity that pervade contemporary work and social life in ways that both echo and contribute risks of bullying and violence" and "raise temperatures in an age of fear and rage of global extent."

RELEVANT THEORY

While the definition of workplace bullying varies, it contains several largely agreed upon facets, which involve a pattern of identifiably negative and inappropriate behaviors that are persistently directed towards a target. In order for the label, bullying (or mobbing), to be applied to a particular activity, interaction, or process, it has to occur repeatedly and regularly (e.g. weekly) and over a period of time (e.g. about six months). Bullying is an escalating process in the course of which the person confronted ends up in an inferior position and finds self-defense difficult, which is a key aspect of the phenomenon (Branch *et al.*, 2007; Djurkovic *et al.*, 2008; Einarsen, 2000; Salin, 2008). While the behaviors involved could include harassing, offending, or negatively affecting someone's work tasks, the behaviors cannot be objectively listed (Rayner, 1997) as they are so varied, ranging from the overt (e.g. verbal abuse; McCarthy and Mayhew, 2004) to the more covert (e.g. malicious gossiping; Shallcross *et al.*, 2010), and are also subject to change (e.g. emergence of cyber-bullying; Kowalski *et al.*, 2008). Also, a person's "subjective perception of being bullied" can vary quite substantially across individuals (Agervold, 2007: 163). Without doubt, bullying is "a complex and multicausal phenomenon and can seldom be explained by one factor alone" (Salin and Höel, 2010: 228; Zapf, 1999).

Research indicates that the majority of workplace bullying emanates from those with more identifiable formal power and is directed towards others with less hierarchical power. People in positions of authority often have more latitude in their behaviors (Ramsay *et al.*, 2011) and are particularly exposed to pressures related to organizational goal achievement, which can spark the use of inappropriate behaviors, particularly where skills and associated training and development processes to deal with complex managerial tasks are inadequate (e.g. Margolis and Molinsky, 2008). Also, capitalistic societies emphasize traditional means of control, which may foster workplace bullying processes and create an element of acceptance (Beale and Höel, 2011). However, bullying also occurs horizontally between coworkers and upwards towards supervisors as power can be gained through informal means, such as alliances, and directed inappropriately towards a target (Branch *et al.*, 2007). Certainly, bullying appears to violate usually expected organizational norms, such as politeness and due process, which over time can make way for the emergence of new norms that allow and support such behaviors (Ramsay *et al.*, 2011). Thus, workplace bullying has been identified in both formally recognized teams (Ayoko *et al.*, 2003) and informal organizational networks whereby particular alliances can add to the power of individuals to produce their own desired outcomes (e.g. promotion for particular individuals; Hutchinson *et al.*, 2006).

A recent review of the literature focused on organizational antecedents of workplace bullying (Salin and Höel, 2010: 227). Specifically, the review examined the following work environment factors in relation to bullying: job design and work organization; organizational cultures and climate; leadership; reward systems; and organizational change. The authors concluded that, while further longitudinal and multilevel empirical studies need to be undertaken, there is support for the "work environment hypothesis," in which situational and individual factors interact to predict workplace bullying. Turning to job design in particular, the recent European research evidence indicates that role ambiguity and role conflict are "among the strongest predictors of workplace bullying" (Baillen and De Witte, 2009; Baillen *et al.*, 2008; Salin and Höel, 2010: 229). Similarly, Bowling and Beehr's (2006) meta-analysis of empirical research emphasized the predictive strength of role ambiguity and role conflict in relation to the occurrence of bullying at work.

Workplace bullying results in a range of well-established, undesirable outcomes for targets, including stress, ill-health, reduced job satisfaction, absenteeism, as well as negative impacts on others who may witness the events, resulting in reduced wellbeing, as well as lost organizational productivity (Höel *et al.*, 2011). Thus, bullying behaviors would appear to be incompatible with the orderly functioning of organizations, with negative implications for the sense of competence and confidence of individuals, as well as goal achievement and productivity across the organization. Given the high costs and consequences of workplace bullying, it is vital to investigate its antecedents so that it may be prevented.

Within this context, job design is an important lens. The way that tasks are organized to achieve work outcomes is integrally related to job design, which refers to the structure, content, and configuration of a person's work tasks and roles (Parker and Ohly, 2008). As such, job design represents a person's work environment, along with self-perceptions of success or otherwise, self-worth, and wellbeing (Erez, 2010). Importantly, job design is focused on tasks. Task conflict has been found to quite often precede relationship conflict (Gamero *et al.*, 2008), which is a feature of workplace bullying. As relationship conflict is difficult to restore, the prevention or at least positive management of initial task conflict is important, and can be considered from a job design perspective.

Early writings on job design focused on achieving efficiency through principles of simplification, standardization, and "scientific management" (Taylor, 1911). Later, Herzberg (1966; Herzberg and Zautra, 1976) introduced the opposing idea that jobs should be enriched, rather than simplified, to foster greater motivation (Oldham and Hackman, 2010). Herzberg (1966; Herzberg and Zautra, 1976) also proposed the importance of "hygiene" factors, such as working conditions and supervisory practices, in the design of work. Hackman and Oldham (1976) subsequently established the Job Characteristics Model of Work Motivation, which is seen as making a central contribution to job design theory (see Figure 23.1). Their model proposed the five core job characteristics of skill variety, task identity, task significance, autonomy, and feedback (which link to meaningfulness, sense of responsibility, and knowledge of results – which in turn link to motivation, performance, satisfaction, and low

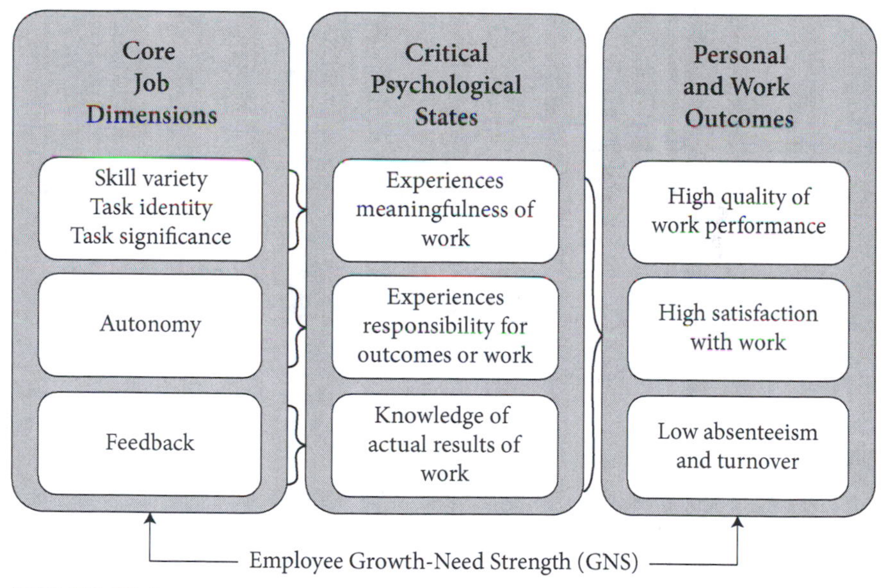

FIGURE 23.1
Job Characteristics Model. Adapted from J. R. Hackman and G. R. Oldham, Motivation through the design of work: Test of a theory. *Organizational Behavior and Human Performance*, 16 (1976), 250–79, by T. Hannagan, *Management: Concepts and Practices* (2nd edn), Harlow: Pearson Education, 2000.

absenteeism). The Job Characteristics Model has been shown to be quite robust, with experienced meaningfulness a particularly strong feature in rewarding jobs (Johns, 2010). However, Johns (2010) also suggests that balance is required in relation to all aspects of job design. For example, even rich and meaningful jobs can become compromised when there are excessive job demands on the person (Johns, 2010).

While the individual job has been the focus of job design, the social dimensions of work have been underplayed (Kilduff and Brass, 2010). More recent work has indicated the importance of social factors such as interdependence, feedback from others, social support, and interactions outside the organization for generating personal and work outcomes, including subjective performance, satisfaction, and reduced turnover intentions (see meta-analysis by Humphrey *et al.*, 2007). Indeed, Grant (2007) argues that it is the relational aspects of job design that can provide the most meaning and therefore the most motivation at work (e.g. interactions with customers and other team members in providing good service and reaching goals). By contrast, outcomes such as stress caused by emotional labour may also be linked to interactions with the public (Grandey and Diamond, 2010).

SALIENT FEATURES

Interestingly, with its focus on the various facets of the job and its context, as shown in the Job Characteristics Model, the job design literature has not directly addressed negative work behaviors. The phenomenon of workplace bullying has only gained prominence in the literature quite recently. Conversely, the seminal works on mutually supporting individual, organization, and governmental strategies to prevent bullying and violence in organizations (McCarthy and Mayhew, 2004) typically fail to address characteristics of job design.

A recent exception is Notelaers *et al.*'s (2010) proposition that specific job characteristics could inform research on the antecedents of workplace bullying. These authors used a somewhat broader conceptualization of job characteristics (based on Warr, 1987) and found role ambiguity (which involves unclear tasks and/or responsibilities), job insecurity, changes in the job, and the receipt of insufficient task-related feedback to be significant predictors of workplace bullying. In essence, bullying tends to thrive where employees perceive their jobs to be unclear and open to conflict and strain.

This lens of stress and strain has also been used to examine jobs in the literature, with Karasek's (1979) Job Demand Control Model being a widely used framework. It focuses on job demands and job autonomy, with implications for stress and health. As noted by Baillien *et al.* (2011: 191), despite the wide variety of health and wellbeing variables that have been studied using Karasek's model, "social behavioural outcomes that signal a stress response, such as workplace bullying" have been overlooked. Johns' (2010) research on the Job Characteristics Model and Karasek's model has largely operated in a parallel fashion, despite their propensity to each inform the other. Despite the mixed findings in relation to autonomy, there exists a common theme that jobs should be designed with a view to decreasing the propensity for stress and ill-health.

It is pertinent to ask what job design maximizes a person's sense of self-worth and wellbeing. The answer, inevitably, is that the optimum design is dependent on a myriad of factors which can vary from organization to organization, and from culture to culture (Erez, 2010). The importance of needs analysis cannot be overlooked because individual workers differ in their preferences about the jobs they undertake. Engagement and commitment to the job is enhanced if managers and supervisors encourage dialogue with individual workers to enable them to have a voice in the design and redesign cycle of their jobs.

Moreover, with much work in organizations now being team-based, the design of jobs can very often have explicit requirements for interdependence amongst members. As Johns (2010) indicates, job designs that are highly motivating for individuals may not necessarily translate into effective job designs in teams. For example, individual creativity can be stifled within a team in which it is expected that information should be acquired and shared in particular ways and where the rewards are team-based. While teams can provide social-emotional benefits for individuals, the relationships therein can actually be quite complex.

Williams *et al.* (2010) researched proactive team performance and found favorable interpersonal norms and transformational leadership to be important in gaining successful outcomes. Positive interpersonal norms are likely to reduce the likelihood of the emergence of bullying

(Ramsay *et al*., 2011), and such norms are likely to be influenced by leadership behaviors. Through role modeling and coaching, "team leaders can influence teams to behave in positive and constructive ways" (Williams *et al*., 2010: 317). Indeed, within the bullying literature, research indicates that both autocratic leaders and laissez-faire leaders can promote workplace bullying because attention to this level of detail and process is likely to be absent. Therefore, while successful team work design should involve interesting, meaningful, and truly interdependent tasks (Hackman, 1987) and may indeed contribute to positive interpersonal norms through the creation of shared meaning, the communication skills of the leader are very important.

According to Zapf (2001, as cited in McCarthy and Mayhew, 2004: 25), "Leadership problems and organizational problems cannot 'harass' an employee. Such behavior is only possible for human beings." Leaders, supervisors, and managers are such human beings with a myriad of responsibilities. The weight of these responsibilities is heavier in the current economic climate where there are severe economic pressures and stress in the external environment. The challenge is to avoid transmitting these pressures into unreasonable and excessive demands on employees (McCarthy and Mayhew, 2004).

As discussed above, while job design refers to specific roles, it is important to note that jobs are interrelated and cannot be considered in isolation. Figure 23.2 shows how each job is part of a broader social structure and organizational context, and that it is interrelated with immediate colleagues' roles, teams, and stakeholders such as customers. Jobs also have links with broader organizational groupings. Therefore, at the points of interaction between the individual and his or her immediate and more distant contacts, there is the necessity of competent and smooth communication (e.g. a manager may become an important intermediary in trying to attract resources). Therefore, when considering job design and the bully-proofing of jobs, it is important to consider the content of the job and the way that communications and interactions are managed for each job.

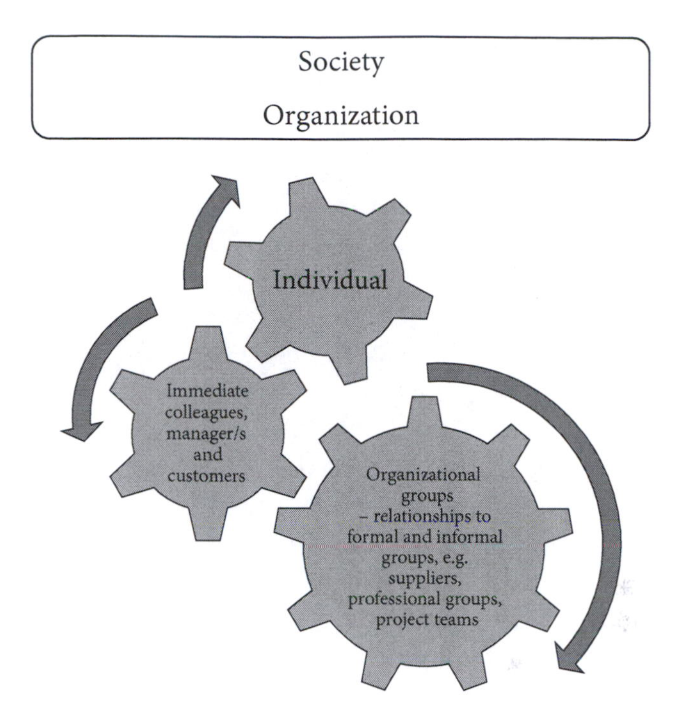

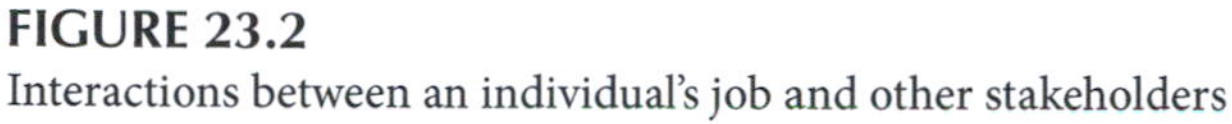
FIGURE 23.2
Interactions between an individual's job and other stakeholders

RECOMMENDATIONS

In terms of bully-proofing jobs, there are several perspectives to consider. These will be discussed in terms of the jobs and teams and the broader context of organizations.

Jobs and Teams

Based on the above discussion, which indicates the association between bullying and job design, it is recommended that roles be assessed in relation to the presence of ambiguity, conflict, and overload, which increase the risk of stress and strain associated with bullying processes (Notelaers *et al.*, 2010). However, it is unrealistic for jobs to be completely stress-free and indeed some optimal level of stress is conducive to goal achievement (de Janasz *et al.*, 2011). Moreover, the idea of meaningfulness is central to job design (Grant, 2007; Johns, 2010), and employees and managers can consider how such meaning can be derived and maintained within jobs (e.g. feedback from clients; knowledge of work outcomes; participation in important decisions).

Not only do jobs need to be well-designed, but also the initial selection processes need to ensure that there is clarity regarding role expectations so that potential employees and employers are well-informed with regard to their decisions. However, organizational tasks are inevitably subject to change and potentially increasing complexity (Davis, 2010), suggesting that renegotiation of tasks and roles will be required over time. Indeed, participative "job crafting" that allows for change is now recognized as a way to make jobs meaningful, and thus should be recognized within job design theory (Oldham and Hackman, 2010). This emphasizes the importance of communication and problem-solving skills, as well as needs analysis and associated training and development processes that allow individuals to grow in their capacities (de Janasz *et al.*, 2011) and ultimately avoid workplace bullying processes through initial and ongoing displays of competent communication.

Bully-proofing also requires competent leadership skills, as bullying is associated with both autocratic and laissez-faire leadership (Skogstad *et al.*, 2007), where it is indicated that such managers are not able to work in constructive or appropriately participative ways, which carries high levels of stress into the work environment. By contrast, competent leadership involves task-specific feedback that is additive to role clarity within the context of job design. While feedback can be derived from the task itself (Hackman and Oldham, 1976), it is often associated with interpersonal interactions with coworkers and managers.

An integral part of this communicative process should involve the provision of regular, constructive, task-specific feedback (de Janasz *et al.*, 2011) so that individuals can achieve role clarity and build their skills, making adjustments as needed so that conflict, role overload, and role ambiguity, with the associated risks of bullying, can be avoided. As such, each job is nested within a broader set of relationships. While this historically has not been emphasized by job design theory, more recent literature has been more focused on the communicative aspects of job design (Kilduff and Brass, 2010; Oldham and Hackman, 2010). Importantly, having clarity regarding the way in which tasks are carried out should help to prevent task conflict, which then reduces the chance of relationship conflicts being associated with workplace bullying (Gamero *et al.*, 2008).

As organizations are becoming more team-based (Oldham and Hackman, 2010), "bully-proofing" needs to specifically consider group dynamics (Ramsay *et al.*, 2011). Where there are positive social rules in place, with expectations of constructive approaches to goal-setting, problem-solving, as well as task and relationship management, workplace bullying is less likely to emerge (Ramsay *et al.*, 2011). Such an environment can reduce or prevent undue stress and strain and, accordingly, the risk of bullying.

By contrast, bullying is found in work environments that are particularly stressful (Skogstad *et al.*, 2007), the sources of which must be addressed. Therefore, job design theory and empirical research indicate important elements in the design of jobs that may be associated with "bully-proofing." Essentially, the recommendations have focused on job design elements that could prevent or possibly reduce bullying processes. As suggested above, jobs are part of a broader organizational context and "bully-proofing" must also be considered from this perspective.

ORGANIZATIONS

"Bully-proofing" organizations can be considered from a number of perspectives. Success would appear to depend on having formal policies that are supported by informal processes. However, this requires a commitment at all levels of the organization as well as society at large. As Beale and Höel (2011) note, workplace bullying may be linked to the actual structure of a capitalist society, which tends to consider that managers and employers may have to be quite forceful in achieving their goals. Consequently, "bully-proofing" jobs actually requires a commitment from managers and employers that bullying is not an acceptable way to approach the employment relationship. Such an approach reflects the move from authoritarian to more participative styles of leadership.

Where bullying exists, all organizational players can be potential witnesses, which may result in further victimization. A frequently overlooked domain of the study of organizational analysis in relation to the prevention of bullying is the role played by coworkers, supervisors, or other colleagues who witness bullying at work. Often referred to as "bystanders," these organizational members need to develop their awareness of bullying, as well as their coping and resilience capacities to address bullying behavior in their team or organization (Namie and Lutgen-Sandvik, 2010) in order to assist targets and also to intervene in the negative processes affecting their organization.

One such an approach seeks to tackle the problems by involving organizational members, through a skills development program, in taking effective actions should they witness the negative behavior. An example is the Mentors in Violence Program (MVP; Katz, 1995), which was initially designed to challenge preconceived views of violence directed at women, and has since been expanded to dealing with other types of violence, including bullying. The MVP program seeks to educate, engage, and increase the skills of bystanders in addressing negative behaviors that they witness (Katz, 1995).

A related approach from Canada is the Anti-discrimination Response Training (ART) program (Ishiyama, 2000), which employs an active witnessing model. The ART approach uses a cognitive and behavioral skills training format to empower otherwise passive and silent bystanders to become more active and vocal. While the program is currently used with Canadian teachers and youth workers, the ART model can be adapted for skills training related to preventing and responding to workplace bullying. Moreover, programs such as MVP and ART help to provide potential targets and bystanders with the knowledge and skills that will assist them in responding to, managing, and deescalating situations involving bullying. Furthermore, these programs offer strategies to those entrusted with the important role of supporting involved parties when they need it and developing preventive policies and practices to safeguard against bullying at work (McCarthy and Mayhew, 2004).

Such skills are useful additions to any role in organizations which, as noted above, increasingly require complex communication skills within teams and with stakeholders (Keashly and Neuman, 2009). As such, the training and development strategies discussed above are applicable to actual jobs and prevention of bullying on a broader scale. There is an emphasis here on the overall development of competencies that link to a specific job, the surrounding team and stakeholders, leadership qualities, and the overall enhancement of positive organizational norms, which ultimately provide safeguards against workplace bullying.

CONCLUSION AND SUMMARY

In overview, job design refers to the structure, content, and configuration of a person's work tasks and roles (Parker and Ohly, 2008) and is inter-related with self-perceptions of self-worth and wellbeing (Erez, 2010). As discussed, there are several reasons for job design to be considered in "bully-proofing" jobs. Importantly, from the perspective of actual jobs, workplace bullying has been found to have direct links to job design, stressing in particular the importance of achieving overall meaningfulness, lack of role conflict, ambiguity and overload, and a reasonable containment of stresses and strains both within jobs and the broader organizational environment (Baillien *et al.*, 2011).

Moreover, the communicative and relationship aspects of jobs have recently gained more prominence in the job design literature, and certainly job design must take into account the increase in teamwork within organizations and the importance of relating to stakeholder groups (which can make the job more meaningful as well as complex). Also, rapid environmental changes mean that job design cannot imply a static situation, with "job crafting" likely to achieve greater prominence. However, it is important to note research findings (Gamero *et al.*, 2008) that indicate that task conflict usually precedes relationship conflict, which is more difficult to overcome and more likely to lead to bullying, highlighting the importance of clarity regarding tasks and jobs.

Moreover, as every job is nested within a much broader set of processes and the phenomenon of workplace bullying is complex, it is important to consider both informal and formal policies and processes that, together, can provide a positive working environment. The role of competent leadership and the avoidance of laissez-faire and autocratic leadership approaches is also clearly indicated in "bully-proofing" organizations. Training and development processes are important for ongoing skill development in relation to competent work completion, development of positive norms, and prevention and intervention in relation to workplace bullying. In conclusion, job design theory has great applicability to the prevention and deterrence of workplace bullying. However, broader organizational facets need to be considered in the design of jobs and in the skill development of all organizational members. In particular, training programs that are focused on prevention of bullying and more general communication and leadership skill enhancement will be helpful in safeguarding organizations.

REFERENCES

Agervold, M. (2007). Bullying at work: A discussion of definitions and prevalence, based on an empirical study. *Scandinavian Journal of Psychology*, 48, 161–72.

Ayoko, O., Callan, V., and Hartel, C. (2003). Workplace conflict, bullying, and counterproductive behaviors. *International Journal of Organizational Analysis*, 11, 283–301.

Baillien, E., and De Witte, H. (2009). Why is organizational change related to workplace bullying? Role conflict and job insecurity as mediators. *Economic and Industrial Democracy*, 30, 348–71.

Baillien, E., De Cuyper, N., and De Witte, H. (2011). Job autonomy and workload as antecedents of workplace bullying: A two-wave test of Karasek's Job Demand Control Model for targets and perpetrators. *Journal of Occupational and Organizational Psychology*, 84, 191–208.

Baillien, E., Neyens, I., and De Witte, H. (2008). Organizational, team related and job related risk factors for workplace bullying, violence and sexual harassment in the workplace: A qualitative study. *International Journal of Organisational Behaviour*, 13, 132–46.

Banyard, V., Moynihan, M., and Plante, E. (2007). Sexual violence prevention through bystander education: An experimental evaluation. *Journal of Community Psychology*, 35, 463–81.

Banyard, V., Plante, E., and Moynihan, M. (2004). Bystander education: Bringing a broader community perspective to sexual violence prevention. *Journal of Community Psychology,* 32, 61–79.

Beale, D., and Höel, H. (2011). Workplace bullying and the employment relationship: Exploring questions of prevention, control and context. *Work, Employment and Society*, 25, 5–18.

Bowling, N. A., and Beehr, T. A. (2006). Workplace harassment from the victim's perspective: A theoretical model and meta-analysis. *Journal of Applied Psychology*, 91, 998–1012.

Branch, S., Murray, J., and Ramsay, S. (2012a). Workplace bullying: What can be done to prevent and manage it? In B. Benscoter (ed.), *HR Encyclopaedia*, vol. 3, *Topical Essays in Human Resource* (pp. 181–96), San Francisco, CA: Pfeiffer.

Branch, S., Ramsay, S., and Barker, M. (2012b). Workplace bullying, mobbing and harassment: A review. *International Journal of Management Reviews*. doi:10.1111/j.1468-2370.2012.00339.x.

Branch, S., Ramsay, S., and Barker, M. (2007). Managers in the firing line: Contributing factors to workplace bullying by staff – an interview study. *Journal of Management and Organization*, 13, 264–81.

Cortina, L. M., Magley, V. J., Williams, J. H., and Langhout, R. D. (2001). Incivility in the workplace: Incidence and impact. *Journal of Occupational Health Psychology*, 6, 64–80.

Davis, G. F. (2010). Job design meets organizational sociology. *Journal of Organizational Behavior*, 31, 302–8.

D'Cruz, P., and Noronha, F. (2010). Protecting my interests: HRM and targets' coping with workplace bullying. *Qualitative Report*, 15, 507–34.

De Janasz, S.C., Dowd, K. O., and Schneider, B. Z. (2012). *Interpersonal Skills in Organizations* (4th edn), New York: McGraw-Hill Irwin.

Djurkovic, N., McCormack, D., and Casimir, G. (2008). Workplace bullying and intention to leave: The moderating effect of perceived organisational support. *Human Resource Management Journal*, 18, 405–22.

Einarsen, S. (2000). Harassment and bullying at work: A review of the Scandinavian approach. *Aggression and Violent Behavior*, 5, 379–401.

Einarsen, S., Höel, H., Zapf, D., and Cooper, C. L. (2003). The concept of bullying at work: The European tradition. In S. Einarsen, H. Höel, D. Zapf, and C. L. Cooper (eds), *Bullying and Emotional Abuse in the Workplace: International Perspectives in Research and Practice* (pp. 3–30), London: Taylor & Francis.

Einarsen, S., Höel, H., Zapf, D., and Cooper, C. L. (2011). The concept of bullying and harassment at work: The European tradition. In S. Einarsen, H. Höel, D. Zapf, and C. L. Cooper (eds), *Bullying and Harassment in the Workplace: Developments in Theory, Research, and Practice* (2nd edn, pp. 3–40), London: Taylor & Francis.

Erez, M. (2010). Culture and job design. *Journal of Organizational Behavior*, 31, 389–400.

Gamero, N., Gonazalez-Roma, V., and Peiro, J. M. (2008). The influence of intra-team conflict on work teams' affective climate: A longitudinal study. *Journal of Occupational and Organizational Psychology*, 81, 47–69.

Grandey, A. A., and Diamond, J. A. (2010). Interactions with the public: Bridging job design and emotional labor perspectives. *Journal of Organizational Behavior*, 31, 338–50.

Grant, A. M. (2007). Relational job design and the motivation to make a prosocial difference. *Academy of Management Review*, 32, 393–417.

Hackman. J. R. (1987). The design of work teams. In J. W. Lorsch (ed.), *Handbook of Organizational Behavior* (pp. 315–42), Englewood Cliffs, NJ: Prentice Hall.

Hackman, J. R., and Oldham, G. R. (1976). Motivation through the design of work: Test of a theory. *Organizational Behavior and Human Performance*, 16, 250–79.

Hauge, L., Skogstad, A., and Einarsen, S. (2009). Individual and situational predictors of workplace bullying: Why do perpetrators engage in the bullying of others? *Work and Stress*, 23, 349–58.

Heames, J., and Harvey, M. (2006). Workplace bullying: A cross-level assessment. *Management Decision*, 44, 1214–30.

Herzberg, F., and Zautra, A. (1976). Orthodox job enrichment: Measuring true quality in job satisfaction. *Personnel* 53, 54–68.

Herzberg, F. I. (1966). *Work and the Nature of Man*, Oxford: World.

Höel, H., and Cooper, C. (2000). *Destructive Conflict and Bullying at Work*, Manchester: School of Management, UMIST.

Höel, H., Sheehan, M., Cooper, C., and Einarsen, S. (2011). Organisational effects of workplace bullying. In S. Einarsen, H. Höel, D. Zapf, and C. Cooper (eds), *Bullying and Harassment in the Workplace: Developments in Theory, Research, and Practice* (2nd edn, pp. 129–47), London: Taylor & Francis.

Hogh, A., Mikkelsen, E., and Hansen, A. (2011). Individual consequences of workplace bullying/mobbing. In S. Einarsen, H. Höel, D. Zapf, and C. Cooper (eds), *Bullying and*

Harassment in the Workplace: Developments in Theory, Research, and Practice (2nd edn, pp. 107–8), London: Taylor & Francis.

Humphrey, S. E., Nahrgang, J. D., and Morgeson, F. P. (2007). Integrating motivational, social, and contextual work design features: A meta-analytic summary and theoretical extension of the work design literature. *Journal of Applied Psychology*, 92, 1332–56.

Hutchinson, M., Vickers, M., Jackson, D., and Wilkes, L. (2006). "Like wolves in a pack": Stories of predatory alliances of bullies in nursing. *Journal of Management and Organisation*, 12, 235–51.

Ishiyama, F. I. (2000). Toward organizational maturation: Active witnessing for prejudice reduction, paper presented at Transcending Boundaries: Integrating, People, Processes and Systems Conference, Brisbane, Sept.

Johns, G. (2010). Some unintended consequences of job design. *Journal of Organizational Behavior*, 31, 361–9.

Karasek, R. A. (1979). Job demands, job decision latitude, and mental strain: Implications for job redesign. *Administrative Science Quarterly*, 24, 285–308.

Katz, J. (1995). Reconstructing masculinity in the locker room: The mentors in violence prevention project. *Harvard Educational Review*, 65, 163–74.

Keashly, L., and Neuman, J. H. (2009). Building a constructive communication climate: The Workplace Stress and Aggression Project. In P. Lutgen-Sandvik and B. Davenport Sypher (eds), *Destructive Organizational Communication: Processes, Consequences, and Constructive Ways of Organizing* (pp. 339–62), New York: Routledge/Taylor & Francis.

Kilduff, M., and Brass, D. J. (2010). Job design: A social network perspective. *Journal of Organizational Behavior*, 31, 309–18.

Kowalski, R. M., Limber, S. P., and Agatston, P. W. (2008). *Cyber Bullying: Bullying in the Digital Age*, Malden, MA: Blackwell.

Kramer, R., Bartram, T., De Cieri, H., and Noe, R. (2011). *Human Resource Management in Australia: Strategy People Performance* (4th edn), Sydney: McGraw-Hill.

Leymann, H. (1996). The content and development of mobbing at work. *European Journal of Work and Organizational Psychology*, 5, 165–84.

McCarthy, P. (2004). Costs of occupational violence and bullying. In P. McCarthy and C. Mayhew (eds), *Safeguarding the Organization Against Violence and Bullying: An International Perspective* (pp. 38–58), London: Palgrave.

McCarthy, P., and Barker, M. (2000). Workplace bullying risk audit. *Journal of Occupational Health and Safety Australia and New Zealand*, 16, 409–18.

McCarthy, P., and Mayhew, C. (2004). *Safeguarding the Organization Against Violence and Bullying*, New York: Palgrave Macmillan.

Margolis, J. D., and Molinsky, A. (2008). Navigating the bind of necessary evils: Psychological engagement and the production of interpersonally sensitive behavior. *Academy of Management Journal*, 51, 847–72.

Namie, G., and Lutgen-Sandvik, P. (2010). Active and passive accomplices: The communal character of workplace bullying. *International Journal of Communication*, 4, 343–73.

Notelaers, G., De Witte, H., and Einarsen, S. (2010). A job characteristics approach to explain workplace bullying. *European Journal of Work and Organizational Psychology*, 19, 487–504.

Oldham, G. R., and Hackman, J. R. (2010). Not what it was and not what it will be: The future of job design research. *Journal of Organizational Behavior*, 31, 463–79.

Parker, S. K., and Ohly, S. (2008). Designing motivating jobs: An expanded framework for linking work characteristics and motivation. In R. Kanfer, G. Chen, and R. D.

Pritchard (eds), *Work Motivation: Past, Present, and Future* (pp. 233–84), New York: Routledge/Taylor & Francis.

Penney, L. M., and Spector, E. (2008). Emotions and counterproductive work behavior. In N. M. Ashkanasy and C. L. Cooper (eds), *Research Companion to Emotion in Organizations* (pp. 183–96), Northampton, MA: Edward Elgar Publishing.

Ramsay, S., Troth, A., and Branch, S. (2011). Work-place bullying: A group processes framework. *Journal of Occupational and Organizational Psychology*, 84, 799–816.

Rayner, C. (1997). The incidence of workplace bullying. *Journal of Community and Applied Social Psychology*, 7, 199–208.

Rayner, C., and Lewis, D. (2011). Managing workplace bullying: The role of policies. In S. Einarsen, H. Höel, D. Zapf, and C. L. Cooper (eds), *Bullying and Harassment in the Workplace: Developments in Theory, Research, and Practice* (2nd edn, pp. 327–40), London: Taylor & Francis.

Salin, D. (2003). Ways of explaining workplace bullying: A review of enabling, motivating and precipitating structures and processes in the work environment. *Human Relations*, 56, 1213–32.

Salin, D., and Höel, H. (2010). Organisational causes of workplace bullying. In S. Einarsen, H. Höel, D. Zapf, and C. Cooper (eds), *Bullying and Harassment in the Workplace: Developments in Theory, Research, and Practice* (2nd edn, pp. 227–43), London: Taylor & Francis.

Shallcross, L., Ramsay, S., and Barker, M. (2010). A proactive response to the mobbing problem: A guide for HR managers. *New Zealand Journal of Human Resources Management*, 10, 27–37.

Shallcross, L., Ramsay, S., and Barker, M. (2012). Qualitative inquiry as tranformation and agency. The black sheep and workplace mobbing. In M. Vicars, T. McKenna, and J. White (eds), *Discourse, Power, and Resistance Down Under* (pp. 121–34), Rotterdam: Sense Publishers.

Shallcross, L., Ramsay, S., and Barker, M. (in press). The power of malicious gossip. *Australian Journal of Communication.*

Skogstad, A., Einarsen, S., Torsheim, T., Aasland, M. S., and Hetland, H. (2007). The destructiveness of laissez-faire leadership behavior. *Journal of Occupational Health Psychology*, 12, 80–92.

Taylor, F. (1911). *The Principles of Scientific Management,* New York: Harper & Brothers.

Warr, P. B. (1987). *Work, Unemployment, and Mental Health,* New York: Oxford University Press.

Williams, H. M., Parker, S. K., and Turner, N. (2010). Proactively performing teams: The role of work design, transformational leadership, and team composition. *Journal of Occupational and Organizational Psychology*, 83, 301–24.

Woods, P., Barker, M., and Hibbins, R. (2011). Tapping the benefits of multicultural groupwork: An exploratory study of postgraduate management students. *International Journal of Management Education*, 9, 59–71.

Zapf, D. (1999). Organisational, work group related and personal causes of mobbing/bullying at work. *International Journal of Manpower*, 20, 70–85.

Zapf, D., Escartin, J., Einarsen, S., Höel, H., and Vartia, M. (2011). Empirical findings on prevalence and risk groups of bullying in the workplace. In S. Einarsen, H. Höel, D. Zapf, and C. Cooper (eds), *Bullying and Harassment in the Workplace: Developments in Theory, Research, and Practice* (2nd edn, pp. 75–106), London: Taylor & Francis.

24

Future Challenges in Issues of Bullying in the Workplace

David D. Van Fleet and Ella W. Van Fleet
Arizona State University

INTRODUCTION

As discussed in other chapters, bullying in today's society has become a social problem that can be emotionally, financially, and legally expensive to both individuals and organizations. It is actually a form of workplace violence, albeit level 1 – the lowest form – of violence (for a discussion of the levels of workplace violence, see Baron, 1993; Van Fleet and Van Fleet, 2010). Most research, though, has focused on particular types of bullying, such as school-age bullying and "sexual harassment."

Experts and laymen have never established a firm agreement and definition as to what constitutes bullying versus what is aggressive behavior that may be acceptable or may be unacceptable (Carbo and Hughes, 2010). This is especially true in the workplace, where individuals in supervisory roles are given some amount of power as well as enforcement responsibility. So when we try to foresee future challenges of bullying in the workplace, we need to better distinguish among different types of behaviors: (i) bullying, (ii) unacceptable behavior that doesn't quite meet the definition of bullying, and (iii) aggressive but acceptable behavior that is merely a form of managing to accomplish organizational objectives.

This chapter will talk about (1) what we don't really know and still need to know about the characteristics that are common to bullies and targets that will help us screen out or terminate bullies; (2) the need for an operational and preferably legally viable definition of bullying that will help in training personnel, reassuring employees, and punishing bullies; and (3) what management needs to do to ensure that the organization and culture are not contributors to bullying behavior.

SIGNIFICANCE

Originally treated as a problem only with our youth and within schools in the United States, bullying is finally being recognized as an adult, workplace problem as well (Gurchiek, 2005; Shapiro and Jankowski, 2005). Workplace bullying is bad for both the organization and its people. It is costly in so many respects: litigation, lowered productivity, emotional wellbeing, morale, turnover, etc. (Needham, 2003). Researchers have suggested that each year about 10–20 percent of workers encounter bullying (Einarsen *et al.*, 2011; Rayner *et al.*, 2002), but that doesn't begin to reflect the damaging effects that linger for years. In extreme cases, not only the individual but also the whole organization can be threatened (Goldman, 2009, 2010; see also Lubit, 2004). As pointed out in previous chapters, the effects of bullying on the victims – and to a lesser extent the coworkers who observe it – do not necessarily end when the bullying ceases or the cause of the bullying is removed. Research has shown that it continues to take its toll emotionally if not physically (see e.g. Dombeck, 2007; Lewis, 2004; Vartia, 2001; Lutgen-Sandvik, 2008; McCarthy and Mayhew, 2004; Tracy *et al.*, 2006; Vaez *et al.*, 2004; Loh *et al.*, 2010).

In addition, the Occupational Safety and Health Act of 1970 clearly established the general obligation of organizations to establish and maintain safe work environments. It seems clear that obligation should encompass workplaces that are free from bullies. So regardless of whether there is anti-bullying legislation, companies already have sufficient reason to remove bullying and then "bully-proof" their workplaces. We cannot continue with our previous assumptions as to who are bullies and victims, and pretend that the organization has no responsibility for this behavior.

RELEVANT THEORY

In the past, bullying research has been primarily concerned with young, K-12 students in educational settings – classrooms, schoolyards, and the like (e.g. Bacchini *et al.*, 2009; Coloroso, 2003). In particular, the studies have attempted to identify traits and characteristics of bullies and victims. For example, Coyne *et al.* (2000: 335) cite a British study in which the ICES Personality Inventory (Bartram, 1994, 1998) strongly predicted that "Victims tended to be less independent and extroverted, less stable, and more conscientious than non-victims."

Other studies of workplace bullying have begun to consider the influence of external factors as well, such as status inequalities between bully and victim (see Cowie *et al.*, 2000, for an overview), and also how the organization itself may permit, reinforce, or mitigate the abuse of power in the form of bullying behavior (Leymann, 1990; Parzefall and Salin, 2010; Salin, 2003). For instance, in a study supported by the National Science Foundation, researchers Roscigno *et al.* (2009) examined top–down supervisory bullying for external influences such as status inequalities of the individuals, organizational structure, job control, leadership, and role conflict within the context of production when there are no capable guardians. In other words, it may well be that even those individuals who already seem to fit the profile of bullies and targets would not actually become such if they were in a different type of organizational climate.

Social theory tells us that relational powerlessness is a core determinant of victimization (Salin, 2003). Power relations affect both material livelihoods and personal dignity (Hodson, 2001). Could the relational power that epitomizes our workplaces make managers feel that in carrying out their responsibilities to fulfill their duties and their desire to protect their livelihoods, they are free to use whatever tactics they feel necessary to get the results for which they are accountable?

The environment inside some of our workplaces provides almost "the perfect storm" for bullying. We expect individually motivated employees from a variety of cultures with many interpersonal differences, including different beliefs, values, and attitudes to work together in highly competitive, high-stress, group-oriented environments. Add to this the lack of sufficient jobs and the resulting job insecurity that is prevalent in today's workplace, plus, in some cases, the presence of prejudice and jealousy, and you have the start of a good recipe for bullies and targets (Heames and Harvey, 2006).

Another aspect of the workplace that may contribute to or allow bullying to become prevalent is the structural organization of the company. The absence of formalized relations often leads to chaos in meeting goals, which in turn can cause individuals to turn to bullying in an effort to get the work done or to CYA (Cover Your "Assets"). Poor organization also tends to lead to disrespect and hence shouting, cursing, coercing, or other types of bullying.

Much of what is considered as bullying has been previously referred to as harassment. In our view this is just an example of singling out certain groups of individuals subject to unacceptable behavior that may or may not reach the level of bullying or even workplace violence. It may also be covered under the current laws regarding sexual harassment or discrimination on the basis of age, sex, race, religion, or ethnicity. No organization can be expected to change all social mores, but every organization can do some training and then enforce a policy of "not in our front or back yard." Research seems only now to be attacking the issue of differentiating between bullying and other unacceptable acts that have already been given a more restricted classification (Einarsen *et al.*, 2011).

In criminology, the "routine activities" model proposes that for deviant behavior like bullying to occur, motivated offenders must encounter suitable targets in the absence of guardians (Cohen and Felson, 1979). In other words, bullies need an environment in which to flourish. Again, the workplace is vulnerable because there are few if any guardians to protect the targets. Even the unions are said to be woefully lacking as guardians (Roscigno *et al.*, 2009; see Chapter 10). Without effective constraints that are enforced by management, the supervisors and even coworkers who might have a tendency to bully are implicitly given the freedom to do so by higher levels of management.

Job insecurity, although perhaps more the fault of the economy than the organization, may be one of the most important influences on bullying as it causes some individuals to act in a more powerful way in order to keep their jobs (Hearn and Parkin, 2001). At the same time, it may cause would-be targets to become less resistant to bullying behavior as they fear losing their jobs if they defend themselves (for advice on how to respond to this type of bullying, see Tracy *et al.*, 2007). Job insecurity may also result in targets who otherwise would not be subjected to this behavior on the basis of low status and power, such as professionals and even managers.

Finally, whether in the schoolyard, on the school bus, or in the workplace, society has not yet determined exactly how to define bullying behavior (McCarthy *et al.*, 1996). What some individuals may consider as bullying, others may consider as mere "child's play" or "boys will be boys." At what point does behavior cross that line to become bullying? This is even truer in the workplace where we have not established where top–down supervising is bullying and where it may be considered by others to be a legitimate managerial action ("aggressive management") that aims to manage performance. Many definitions have been suggested, but no single definition that will stand up in our legal system has been established. Until we can agree on what constitutes bullying behavior, we face limits in our ability to prevent or eradicate it by enforcing rules or laws against it.

In the meantime, however, nothing prevents organizations from researching the literature and writing their own definition along with examples of the more widely noted and agreed-upon behaviors that will be forbidden under that definition. Even if a company's definition does not stand up in court in cases where the organization has disciplined a bully or has ignored a would-be target, it should reduce the incidences and provide more security for non-bullies. In the absence of precise definitions, office managers can at least learn from the efforts of scholars to understand these concepts (Van Fleet, 2008).

SALIENT FEATURES

In the past, analytic interest in bullying has (1) concentrated largely on bullies and victims of a young age (primarily K-12 students), (2) emphasized "schoolyards" rather than "school workplaces," (3) focused on personal or psychological characteristics of bullies and victims, and/or (4) centered around a special type of bullying such as sexual harassment. There are several problems with these approaches.

First, bullying is not limited to young children and does not cease at a particular age. It does not stop at the playground or the schoolhouse door – it simply shifts to another workplace (see Chapter 5). Also, bullying apparently cannot be fully explained by internal influences, personal or psychological characteristics. All people with the same personal or psychological characteristics that we have assigned to bullies or targets do not necessarily become bullies or targets. This leads to the question of "Why?" Does the environment perhaps supply the external factors that facilitate or prevent bullying behavior (Van Fleet and Van Fleet, 2010)? Or is bullying the result of a combination of factors, including the psyche of the bully and the target, the social psychology of the workgroup, and the organization (Zapf and Einarsen, 2003)?

We need to know how and how much do society, culture, and the economic environment contribute to bullying behavior (Lutgen-Sandvik and McDermott, 2008). The organization, including the organizational structure and the organizational culture, is responsible for the immediate work environment. That includes whether the environment is chaotic, whether it gives workers enough autonomy and feedback regarding their own work, how the workers perceive management's perceptions of them, etc. Does the organization consist of too many Theory X (autocratic) managers? Does management's behavior or the company's use of electronic surveillance suggest that employees are not to be trusted; or does the absence of either of these suggest that management does not really care deeply about protecting the workers? What about the company's motivation methods? So what part may – or could – the organization play in facilitating or preventing bullying?

Earlier social science researchers have indicated that the more vulnerable targets of aggressive, bullying managers are what we would normally consider the "weaker" workers, such as minorities, women, lower-paid and lower status workers (Aneshensel, 1992; Clegg, 1990; Foucault, 1988). More recent research suggests that gender is not necessarily a factor except when combined with other identifiers such as minority or lower status (Zapf and Einarsen, 2003). In fact, if sexual harassment were removed from the equation, the percentage of bullied females and males is not too different.

Although people in general have previously regarded race, ethnicity, sex, religion, and low job security as the primary symbols of low status and power, there are markers other than these which we need to study more thoroughly. Roscigno *et al.* (2009: 1580) have suggested that "workers in highly paid settings can also suffer [because of the] intense competition and pressure cooker environments." So individuals whose high productivity and achievement threaten another's ego or vulnerability may also become innocent targets (Namie and Namie, 2009; Yamada, 2000; Vaez *et al.*, 2004).

RECOMMENDATIONS

Bullies and their targets could be anyone, and the only agreement is about the need to ban bullying in the workplace. It is a problem that must be tackled both inside and outside the organization (Kohut, 2008).

Internal to the Organization

Managers are legally responsible for providing safe workplaces and therefore must be held accountable for establishing respectful work environments. They must not only voluntarily comply with governmental regulations but also go beyond to demonstrate a genuine commitment to the members of the organization. Their thinking must expand beyond harassment, discrimination, and violence to include other forms of bullying as well, such as relational and social forms of bullying.

Thus, with or without new legislation, management can and must do its utmost to prevent workplace bullying. Such efforts will require the development of management commitment and action. We propose that the organization start by (1) developing and publicizing a strong anti-bullying policy, (2) defining bullying, and (3) then try to make some progress in identifying who are likely bullies and likely targets. Other commitments include providing effective orientation and training programs, walking the walk and talking the talk, changing the culture, modeling the desired behavior, establishing accountability, providing coaching, responding promptly to early warnings, and investigating problems thoroughly.

Establish Anti-Bullying Policy

As noted in previous chapters, policies are a must in any bullying prevention plan. While an organization might choose to have a general "anti-bad behavior" policy, it is probably preferable to have separate policies for bullying, sexual harassment, and workplace violence. Having separate policies tends to give additional emphasis to those key areas and may also then provide focal points for training. However, it is still advisable to have a "respectful workplace" policy. Such a policy would provide a positive statement by the organization that it expects professional, civil behavior from all members of the organization, management and non-management alike.

We think that at the moment the best way to proceed is to develop a policy centered on a definition, and clarifying examples primarily around some characteristics like attributed intent, repetition, duration, escalation, harm, power disparity, and distorted communication networks (cf. Lutgen-Sandvik *et al.*, 2009).

Define Bullying

As noted previously, a definitive definition needs to be established so that bullies, targets, and all others can know what behaviors will be considered as crossing that line between bullying and managing. Such a definition does not come easily, as bullying is more than a list of negative communication behaviors; it is a complex pattern of negative interactions exacerbated by distinctive features (Lutgen-Sandvik *et al.*, 2009).

The definition needs to establish the difference between bullying and legitimate management action. The State of Washington, for example, tells state employees that tough or demanding bosses are not bullies as long as they are respectful and fair and their primary motivation is to obtain the best performance by setting high yet reasonable expectations for workers (Washington, 2011).

Some researchers argue that the distinction lies in whether "the workplace bully treats his or her targets as incompetent, lazy, ineffective or weak, but *offers no legitimate manner for the employee to ever be viewed as a 'good' employee*" (Sepler, 2010: 5). The difference, according to Sepler, "*is that the bullied employee will not be coached, counseled or even fired, but belittled, badgered, blamed and ostracized*, usually ending in their resignation" (Sepler, 2010: 3). Others suggest more specific features for distinguishing workplace bullying, although all the same features may not be identified by individual researchers: for example, repetition, duration, escalation, harm, attributed intent, hostile work environment, power disparity, communication patterning, and distorted communication networks (Leymann, 1990; Leymann and Gustafson, 1996; Lutgen-Sandvik *et al.*, 2009; Rayner *et al.*, 2002). In our view, intent, harm, repetition, and duration are absolutely necessary components.

Try to Identify Potential Bullies

Logically, the hiring process is the first step in building, boosting, or avoiding a bullying environment (Slora *et al.*, 1991). As discussed in Chapter 22, organizations should strive to screen out potential bullies during the hiring process. To screen out bullies, we need to know what they "look like" or "act like." Yet, as mentioned so many times before, various individuals have different views and stereotypes as to what constitutes bullying.

Bullies often get away with their nonproductive or even counter-productive behavior because management and coworkers are not aware that bullies are often "smart, successful and worthy adversaries; their contributions and talents are unmistakable, and they have a way of creating an enduring impression that without them, the firm, company or clinic would fall to pieces" (Sepler, 2010: 2).

Also, as mentioned earlier in this chapter, bullies may even be the most skilled workers at ingratiating themselves with others, especially their superiors. Surprisingly to some, non-team professionals such as teachers, high-paid salespersons, physicians, lawyers, and advisors may be more prevalent bullies than most people think. In their non-team-based cultures, "individuals may become inured to conduct that would be considered unacceptable or abusive (elsewhere)" (Sepler, 2010: 3; Tepper *et al.*, 2011).

Previous research has shown that individuals who become early bullies tend to carry over that behavior to the workplace. If we could be sure of this, it could help in identifying and selecting young adult employees. In the absence of that information (because of privacy laws, among other reasons), we need to learn as much as we can from the more extensive research involving K-12 bullies. Some research has shown that two types of personalities tend to become older, workplace bullies: (1) those who feel insecure and use bullying as a defensive technique, and (2) those who feel superior in power or otherwise and therefore do not fear being held accountable for their actions. While most managers, workers, and researchers would probably agree that the higher organizational position, the lower the incidence of bullying (Hodson *et al.*, 2006), we also know that some bullies are successful when it comes to moving up the corporate ladder (Lutgen-Sandvik *et al.*, 2009).

Other research (Neuman and Baron, 1998; Randall, 2001) also suggests that anyone and everyone is a potential target, but three types of individuals seem to be more vulnerable: (1) individuals whom the bully considers to be physically weaker (smaller stature, younger, older, frail, female (some of what we previously considered sexual harassment may actually have been bullying); (2) individuals who have lesser status or seniority than the bully; and (3) individuals who make the bully feel insecure and therefore in need of "striking back."

Provide Effective Orientation and Training Programs

The best way to avoid bullying problems is to hire the right people from the start, but the organization is not always successful in doing that (Kelly and Nelson, 2011; Van Fleet and Van Fleet, 2007). When bullies already exist in an organization, selection and hiring are not perfect solutions. Then what? As indicated in previous chapters, proper orientation and training programs may be used to reduce the proclivity of individuals to engage in bullying behavior and to embolden would-be targets to take appropriate action before the situation escalates. Starting with orientation and continuing with ongoing training, all personnel should be trained in proper "civil" behavior as well as what constitutes bullying behavior (Futterman, 2004; Keashly and Neuman, 2005).

Training about bullying might be included in harassment training or done separately to give it greater emphasis. It should include modeling correct behavior as well as examples of incorrect behavior (Macintosh, 2006). The impact of bullying behavior should be covered first, and trainees should be asked for examples of employee conduct. Communication, conflict resolution, interpersonal relations, leadership, negotiation, stress management, and team-building are some of the skills that are most needed (Lutgen-Sandvik *et al.*, 2009; Tracy *et al.*, 2007; Zapf, 1999). Essential skills and training should also include interpersonal communication skills, including problem-solving skills, assertiveness training, giving and getting feedback, and listening skills (Sepler, 2010). That training should also inform personnel at all levels about what assistance is available to would-be targets and to their bullies. As with other forms of workplace violence, managers need to know how bullying progresses so as to deal with situations before they become critical (Rayner *et al.*, 2002; cf. Van Fleet and Van Fleet, 2010).

Walk the Walk, Talk the Talk

In other words, management at all levels must walk the walk and talk the talk. They must show that they are serious about bullying by continuing to emphasize that employees are expected to adhere to acceptable civil behavior in the workplace. That would include developing a strong policy statement and then backing it up with action, posting OSHA-type signs throughout the workplace, and reminding employees through standard communication channels such as newsletters.

It is of great importance, also, that managers model acceptable behavior in their day-to-day actions. Managerial behavior emanating from the top is one of the most powerful ways in which a bully-free culture is established and provides a clear guide to others in the organization about what is acceptable, proper behavior in the organization. If managers act professionally and respectfully, others will do so too. If upper management displays proper behavior and enforces anti-bullying policies – including the punishment of upper-level managers who are identified as bullies – the propensity for bullying behavior will be decreased:

> Leaders must be visible and vocal about a climate of respect or civility, acknowledge and address visible lapses in such policies, and promote the seeking and giving of feedback through implementation of 360 evaluation process, listening sessions and/or open door policies. Promotion of emotional intelligence, including self-awareness and empathy build the competencies which will have the effect of extinguishing disrespectful conduct before it escalates to bullying.
>
> (Sepler, 2010: 9)

Respond Promptly, Investigate, and Provide Assistance

Even when an organization tries to avoid hiring bullies, mistakes will be made; and follow-up training will not always transform the problem employee. The remaining alternative is to address remaining problems immediately. The best way to handle a problem is to have an early detection system so that it can be dealt with before it escalates. Management should be trained to watch for stress and displays of emotion that could lead to abusive behavior. Managers should always treat all employees with respect and dignity, especially when corrective or disciplinary action is warranted. It is also important to treat situations confidentially to protect the rights of all concerned (Van Fleet and Van Fleet, 2010).

Conducting a thorough investigation when a charge of bullying is made is also important. Such investigations involve due diligence on the part of the organization. This means that it is important to take enough time to obtain the truth in contentious situations while at the same time protecting the rights of everyone involved. It means that all reasonable steps are taken to demonstrate that all sides are heard and to assure that unbiased decisions or actions are made following the gathering of information. Since it is almost impossible to put aside personal differences, an unbiased person should be used and every effort to assure that due diligence is performed. Often this means that the company must go outside the organization unless they are able to find an "inside ombudsman" who is trusted by the majority of management and workers. Investigating bullying complaints should not be left to Human Resource Department employees as they are likely to side with management or to be perceived as doing so.

Coaching should be provided for those who need additional help in avoiding bullying behavior. Individuals who seem particularly prone to emotional outbursts should be identified as early as possible and referred to Employee Assistance Program for assistance. Coaching may also be necessary to assist targets of bullying in how to cope with their situations so that they can remain productive members of the organization.

Change the Culture

Finally, management must change the organizational culture, which, after all, determines in large measure how everyone acts, and how everyone acts in turn helps determine the culture. Organizational cultures that seem to foster bullying frequently are autocratic, highly political, and have substantial internal competition and low accountability (Sepler, 2010). The culture may also include one or more managers who model the wrong behavior – who fail to walk the walk and talk the talk. The potential for bullying increases if the organization is also undergoing change – restructuring, changed leadership, or increased competition – particularly if that change leads to workforce reductions or reallocation of scarce resources (Salin, 2003). As one might expect, chaotic, disorganized workplaces also provide fertile ground for bullies.

These types of cultures tend to persist for extended periods of time because the bullies obtain short-term results and so are either tolerated or outright rewarded. Indeed, "The bullying becomes 'invisible,' in that the pattern of conduct is so much a part of the fabric of the organization that it does not raise any concerns, and those who cannot 'handle it' are viewed as a poor 'fit,' rather than a target" (Sepler, 2010: 4). For a detailed list of organizational characteristics that increase the propensity for violence and, hence, bullying, see Van Fleet and Van Fleet, 2010: appendix C; Van Fleet and Van Fleet, 2007: part VI).

What can be done, then, to change the culture? Clearly, top management must first recognize that change is necessary. The organization must work to establish a positive, hostility-free workplace and, as mentioned above, that begins with strong anti-bullying, anti-harassment, anti-violence policies. Enforcement of those policies should be swift, applied to all levels within the organization, and made known to all personnel. Again, as noted earlier, everyone in the organization must be trained as to what is acceptable and unacceptable behavior. An early warning system with reporting mechanisms and contingency plans must be established to deal with behavior problems before they become more harmful.

External to the Organization

Clearly, managers and organizations have not been the only contributors to workplace bullying, and they alone cannot be expected to restore civility. Changes external to the organization will also be necessary to reduce the incidence of workplace bullying. What the organization must do is ensure that it does not contribute in some way to the development of bullies or the functioning of bullying.

Although we cannot legislate civility, state and/or national legislation would be one important source for change because of the message it sends. As discussed in previous chapters, legislation would be helpful, although the prospects for such legislation at the national level seem dim and only moderately better at state levels. Only 13 states have even proposed such legislation, and the Federal Government seems to think it has the bullying problem covered under its current legally protected categories such as sex, race, or ethnicity (Cohen, 2010; Martucci and Sinatra, 2009; Yamada,

2004, 2000). Nevertheless, continued efforts to try to bring about such legislation seem to be called for. The experience of other countries should serve to guide and support such legislative efforts (cf. Harthill, 2008; Höel and Einarsen, 2010; Yuen, 2005). However, we already know that there is only a limited amount of social or civil behavior that can be legislated, regardless of how harsh the punishment.

At the federal level, OSHA also could do more to explicitly deal with workplace bullying (Harthill, 2010). On the other hand, expecting an already overworked, underfunded bureaucratic government agency to do much may well be more wishful thinking than real assistance (Phillips, 1996). Nevertheless, a clear position by OSHA could serve as a strong signal to organizations that they need to develop anti-bullying policies and take seriously all claims of workplace bullying.

The single most important external change that is needed to reduce workplace bullying is to reduce bullying – indeed, the propensity for bullying – *outside* the work environment. School bullying, bullying in families, bullying by authority figures (e.g. church officials, law enforcement, teachers, administrators) must be reduced. If bullying does not occur in society in general, it is less likely to occur at the workplace. Anti-bullying efforts should be made by schools, clubs, churches, and other organizations to set the tone. That we leave to the non-business experts such as sociologists and psychologists.

CONCLUSION AND SUMMARY

Bullying is no longer just a public education problem but a widespread societal problem that must also be dealt with in the workplace and elsewhere. In the United States, most bullying research has concentrated on bullies and victims among students in K-12 educational institutions. That research has yielded some results that can be used by researchers who study organizational workplaces, but there is still much to be done. We still need (1) to know the characteristics that are common to bullies that will help us screen out or terminate bullies; (2) to develop an operational and preferably legally viable definition that will distinguish between bullying and other unacceptable behavior that may not quite reach the level of bullying; (3) to develop a better understanding of the targets of bullying so that we can avoid or remediate problems and develop more and better training programs; and (4) to encourage organizations to influence legislators, educators, and others to take up the bullying cause.

We have presented some ideas about what organizations can and should do internally to avoid causing or exacerbating the problem. Even without a precise "national" definition, organizations can (a) attempt to distinguish between bullying, aggressive management, and other less offensive behavior; (b) develop and rigorously enforce anti-bullying policies; (c) carefully examine hiring practices in an effort to screen out bullies and potential bullies; (d) train all personnel in proper behavior and how to deal with bullying should it occur; (e) model professional, civil behavior; (f) develop respectful, anti-bullying internal organizational cultures; and (g) support community efforts including legislative ones to prevent and deal with bullying in all units within society. Hopefully, more organizations will accept the challenge and accomplish these tasks so that our workplaces can be safer and even more productive.

REFERENCES

Adams, A., and Crawford, N. (1992). *Bullying at Work: How to Confront and Overcome it*, London: Virago Press.

Aneshensel, C. (1999). Social stress: Theory and research. *Annual Review of Sociology*, 1, 15–28.

Bacchini, D., Esposito, G., and Affuso, G. (2009). Social experience and school bullying. *Journal of Community and Applied Social Psychology*, 19, 17–32.

Baron, S. A. (1993). *Violence in the Workplace*, Ventura, CA: Pathfinder Publishing of California.

Bartram, D. (1993). Validation of the "ICES" personality inventory. *European Review of Applied Psychology/Revue Européenne de Psychologie Appliquée*, 43, 207–18.

Bartram, D. (1994). *PREVUE Assessment Technical Manual* (2nd ed.), Vancouver, BC: Prevue Assessments International.

Bartram, D. (1998). *PREVUE Assessment Technical Manual* (3rd ed.), Vancouver, BC: Prevue Assessments International.

Bartram, D., and Feltham, R. (1998). Comparison of the prevue ICES and BPI personality inventories: Trait- vs. function-oriented approaches. *International Journal of Selection and Assessment*, 6, 198–202.

Carbo, J., and Hughes, A. (2010). Workplace bullying: Developing a human rights definition from the perspective and experiences of targets. *Working USA*, 13, 387–403.

Clegg, S. (1990). *Modern Organizations,* Thousand Oaks, CA: Sage.

Cohen, A. (2010). New laws target workplace bullying. Retrieved April 2011 from http://www.time.com/time/nation/article/0,8599,2005358,00.html.

Cohen, L. E., and Felson, M. (1979). Social change and crime rate trends: A routine activities approach. *American Sociological Review*, 44, 588–608.

Coloroso, B. (2003). *The Bully, the Bullied and the Bystander: From Pre-School to High School,* New York: Harper Resource.

Cowie, H., Naylor, P., Rivers, I., Smith, P., and Pereira, B. (2000). Measuring workplace bullying. *Aggression and Violent Behavior*, 7, 33–51.

Coyne, I., Seigne, E., and Randall, P. (2000). Predicting workplace victim status from personality, *European Journal of Work and Organizational Psychology*, 9, 335–49.

Dombeck, M. (2007). The long term effects of bullying. Retrieved April 2011, from www.mentalhelp.net/poc/view_doc.php?type=doc&id=13057.

Einarsen, S., Höel, H., Zapf, D., and Cooper, C. L. (2011). *Bullying and Harassment in the Workplace: Development in Theory and Practice* (2nd edn), Boca Raton, FL: Taylor & Francis.

Foucault, M. (1988). *Politics, Philosophy, Culture: Interviews and Other Writings,* New York: Routledge, Chapman & Hall.

Futterman, S. (2004). *When you Work for a Bully,* Montvale, NJ: Croce Publishing Group.

Goldman, A. (2009). *Transforming Toxic Leaders,* Stanford, CA: Stanford University Press.

Goldman, A. (2010). *Destructive Leaders and Dysfunctional Organizations: A Therapeutic Perspective,* Cambridge: Cambridge University Press.

Gurchiek, K. (2005). Bullying: It's not just on the playground; Bosses report being targeted in the workplace. *HR Magazine*. Retrieved April 2011 from findarticles.com/p/articles/mi_m3495/is_6_50/ai_n13826260.

Harthill, S. (2008). Bullying in the workplace: Lessons from the United Kingdom. *Minnesota Journal of International Law*, 17, 247–302.

Harthill, S. (2010). The need for a revitalized regulatory scheme to address workplace bullying in the United States: Harnessing the Federal Occupational Safety and Health Act. *University of Cincinnati Law Review*, 78, 1250–1306.

Heames, J., and Harvey, M. (2006). Workplace bullying: A cross level assessment. *Management Decision*, 44, 1214–30.

Hearn, J., and Parkin, W. (2001). *Gender, Sexuality and Violence in Organizations,* London: Sage.

Hodson, R. (2001). *Dignity at Work,* Cambridge: Cambridge University Press.

Hodson, R., Roscigno, V. J., and Lopez, S. H. (2006). Chaos and the abuse of power. *Work and Occupations*, 33, 382–416.

Höel, H., and Einarsen, S. (2010). The effectiveness of anti-bullying regulations: The case of Sweden. *European Journal of Work and Organizational Psychology*, 19, 30–50.

Keashly, L., and Neuman, J. H. (2005). Bullying in the workplace: Its impact and management. *Employee Rights and Employment Policy Journal*, 8, 335–73.

Kelly, L., and Nelson, K. L. (2011). Workplace survival. In J. L. Pierce and J. W. Newstrom (eds), *The Manager's Bookshelf* (pp. 183–7), Upper Saddle River, NJ: Prentice-Hall.

Kohut, M. R. (2008). *Understanding, Controlling, and Stopping Bullies and Bullying at Work,* Ocala, FL: Atlantic Publishing Group.

Lewis, D. (2004). Bullying at work: The impact of shame among university and college lecturers. *British Journal of Guidance and Counseling*, 32, 281–99.

Leymann, H. (1990). Mobbing and psychological terror at workplaces. *Violence and Victims*, 5, 119–26.

Leymann, H., and Gustafson, A. (1996). Mobbing at work and the development of post-traumatic stress disorders. *European Journal of Work and Organizational Psychology*, 5, 251–75.

Loh, J., Restubog, S. L. D., and Zagenczyk, T. J. (2010). Consequences of workplace bullying on employee identification and satisfaction among Australian and Singaporeans. *Journal of Cross-Cultural Psychology*, 41, 236–52.

Lubit, R. H. (2004). *Coping with Toxic Managers, Subordinates, and Other Difficult People*, Upper Saddle River, NJ: Prentice Hall.

Lutgen-Sandvik, P. (2008). Intensive remedial identity work: Responses to workplace bullying trauma and stigmatization. *Organization*, 15, 97–119.

Lutgen-Sandvik, P., and McDermott, V. (2008). The constitution of employee abusive organizations: A communication flow theory. *Communication Theory*, 18, 304–33.

Lutgen-Sandvik, P., Namie, G., and Namie, R. (2009). Workplace bullying: Causes, consequences, and corrections. In P. Lutgen-Sandvik and B. D. Sypher (eds), *Destructive Organizational Communication* (pp. 41–88), New York: Routledge Press.

Lutgen-Sandvik, P., Tracy, S. J., and Alberts, J. K. (2007). Burned by bullying in the American workplace: Prevalence, perception, degree and impact. *Journal of Management Studies*, 44, 837–62.

Macintosh, J. (2006). Tackling workplace bullying. *Issues in Mental Health Nursing*, 27, 665–79.

Martucci, W. C., and Sinatra, K. R. (2009). Antibullying legislation: A growing national trend in the new workplace. Retrieved April 2011 from www.onlinelibrary.wiley.com/doi/10.1002/ert.20227/abstract.

McCarthy, P., and Mayhew, C. (2004). *Safeguarding the Organization Against Violence and Bullying*, New York: Palgrave Macmillan.

McCarthy, P., Sheehan, M., and Wilkie, W. (1996). *Bullying: From Backyard to Boardroom*, Alexandria, NSW: Millennium Books.

Namie, G., and Namie, R. (2009). *The Bully at Work: What you Can Do to Stop the Hurt and Reclaim your Dignity on the Job* (2nd edn), Naperville, IL: Sourcebooks.

Needham, A. W. (2003). *Workplace Bullying: The Costly Business Secret*, Auckland: Penguin Group Australia.

Neuman, J. H., and Baron, R. A. (1998). Workplace violence and workplace aggression: Evidence concerning specific forms, potential causes, and preferred targets. *Journal of Management*, 24, 391–419.

Parzefall, M., and Salin, D. (2010). Perceptions of and reactions to workplace bullying: A social exchange perspective. *Human Relations*, 63, 761–80.

Phillips, A. E. (1996). Violence in the workplace: Reevaluating the employer's role. *Buffalo Law Review*, 44, 139–44.

Randall, P. (2001). *Bullying in Adulthood: Assessing the Bullies and their Victims*, New York: Taylor & Francis.

Rayner, C., Höel, H., and Cooper, C. L. (2002). *Workplace Bullying: What we Know, Who is to Blame, and What Can we Do*?, London: Taylor & Francis.

Roscigno, V. J., Lopez, S. H., and Hodson, R. (2009). Supervisory bullying, status inequalities and organizational context. *Social Forces*, 87, 1561–89.

Salin, D. (2003). Ways of explaining workplace bullying: A review of enabling, motivating and precipitating structures and processes in the work environment. *Human Relations*, 56, 1213–32.

Sepler, F. (2010). Workplace bullying. Retrieved April 15 2012 from http://seplerblog.files.wordpress.com/2012/05/cle-handout-2010.pdf.

Shapiro, R., and Jankowski, M. (2005). *Bullies, Tyrants, and Impossible People,* New York: Three Rivers Press.

Slora, K. B., Joy, D. S., and Terris, W. (1991). Personnel selection to control employee violence. *Journal of Business and Psychology*, 5, 417–26.

Tepper, B. J., Moss, S. E., and Duffy, M. K. (2011). Predictors of abusive supervision: Supervisor perceptions of deep-level dissimilarity, relationship conflict, and subordinate performance. *Academy of Management Journal*, 54, 279–94.

Tracy, S. J., Alberts, J. K., and Rivera, K. D. (2007). How to bust the office bully: Eight tactics for explaining workplace abuse to decision-makers. Retrieved April 2011 from noworkplacebullies.com/yahoo_site_admin/assets/docs/HowtoBusttheOfficeBully.71152410.pdf.

Tracy, S. J., Lutgen-Sandvik, P., and Alberts, J. K. (2006). Nightmares, demons and slaves: Exploring the painful metaphors of workplace bullying. *Management Communication Quarterly*, 20, 148–85.

Vaez, M., Ekberg, K., and LaFlamme, L. (2004). Abusive events at work among young working adults. *Relations Industrielles/Industrial Relations*, 59, 569–84.

Van Fleet, D. D. (2008). Company on the couch: Filling a gap in understanding organizational dysfunctioning. *Journal of Management Inquiry*, 17, 241–2.

Van Fleet, D. D., and Van Fleet, E. W. (2010). *The Violence Volcano: Reducing the Threat of Workplace Violence,* Charlotte, NC: Information Age Publishing.

Van Fleet, E. W., and Van Fleet, D. D. (2007). *Workplace Survival: Dealing with Bad Bosses, Bad Workers, Bad Jobs,* Frederick, MD: PublishAmerica.

Vartia, M. (2001). Consequences of workplace bullying with respect to the well-being of its targets and the observers of bullying. *Scandinavian Journal of Work and Environmental Health*, 27, 63–9.

Washington State Department of Labor and Industries (2011). *Workplace Bullying and Disruptive Behavior: What Everyone Needs to Know*, Olympia, WA: Washington State Department of Labor and Industries. Retrieved April 2011 from www.lni.wa.gov/safety/research/files/bullying.pdf.

Yamada, D. C. (2000). The phenomenon of "workplace bullying" and the need for a status-blind hostile work environment protection. *Georgetown Law Journal*, 88, 475–536.

Yamada, D. C. (2004). Crafting a legislative response to workplace bullying. *Employee Rights and Employment Policy Journal*, 8, 475–521.

Yuen, R. A. (2005). Beyond the schoolyard: Workplace bullying and moral harassment law in France and Quebec. *Cornell International Law Journal*, 38, 625–48.

Zapf, D. (1999). Organizational, work group related and personal causes of mobbing/bullying at work. *International Journal of Manpower*, 20, 70–85.

Zapf, D., and Einarsen, S. (2003). Individual antecedents of bullying. In S. Einarsen, H. Höel, D. Zapf, and C. L. Cooper (eds), *Bullying and Emotional Abuse in the Workplace: International Perspectives* (pp. 165–84), London: Taylor & Francis.

Zapf, D., Einarsen, S., Höel, H., and Vartia, M. (2003). Empirical findings on bullying in the workplace. In S. Einarsen, H. Höel, D. Zapf, and C. L. Cooper (eds), *Bullying and Emotional Abuse in the Workplace: International Perspectives* (pp. 103–27), London: Taylor & Francis.

Author Index

C

D

E

F

G

H

L

M

N

O

P

Q

R

S

T

U

V

W

X

Y

Z

Subject Index

Note numbers are indicated by *n* following page numbers.

C

D

E

F

G

H

M

N

O

P

R

S

T

U

V

W